FamilyFun

VACATION GUIDE

California

& Hawaii

By Carol Terwilliger Meyers
and the experts
at FamilyFun Magazine

DISNEP

EDITIONS

New York

FamilyFun
California
&Hawaii

Editorial Director
Lois Spritzer

Design & Production
IMPRESS, INC.
Hans Teensma
Pam Glaven
Katie Craig
James McDonald
Katie Winger
Lisa Newman

Disney Editions and *FamilyFun*

Book Editors
Alexandra Kennedy
Wendy Lefkon
Lisa Stiepock

Research Editor
Beth Honeyman

Contributing Editors
Jon Adolph
Rani Arbo
Duryan Bhagat
Jodi Butler
Jaqueline Cappuccio
Deanna Cook
Tony Cuen
Ann Hallock
Jessica Hinds
Rich Mintzer
Jody Revenson

Copy Editors
Diane Hodges
Jenny Langsam
Monica Mayper
Jill Newman

Editorial Assistants
Laura Gomes
Jean Graham

Production
Janet Castiglione
Sue Cole

This book is dedicated to our *FamilyFun* readers, and contributors, and to traveling families everywhere.

Carol Terwilliger Meyers is the author of numerous books on traveling with children, including *Miles of Smiles: 101 Great Car Games & Activities* and *Weekend Adventures in Northern California.* She lives with her husband in Berkeley, California, and continues to travel *en famille* with her adult children.

Illustrations by **Kandy Littrell**

For information, address Disney Editions,
114 Fifth Avenue, New York, New York 10011-5690.

Printed in the United States of America

First Edition
1 3 5 7 9 8 6 4 2
Library of Congress Cataloging-in-Publication Data on File
ISBN: 0-7868-5303-4

Visit www.disneyeditions.com

CONTENTS

5   Dear Parents
6   How to Use this Guide
8   Introduction to
California and Hawaii
11   Ready, Set, Go!

CALIFORNIA
40   Introduction
43   San Francisco
89   Berkeley
103   Silicon Valley and
San Jose
115   Mendocino and
Fort Bragg
125   Gold Rush Country
139   Northern California's
National Parks
157   Highway 1 South:
Monterey Peninsula
and Beyond
181   Solvang

189   Santa Barbara
203   Santa Monica
217   Los Angeles
251   Anaheim
267   Southern California
Beach Towns
291   San Diego
315   The Desert: Palm
Springs and Environs

HAWAII
328   Introduction
331   Oahu
349   Maui
363   The Big Island (Hawaii)
379   Kauai

Dear Parents,

A FRIEND OF MINE—a dad—said something recently that rang true to me. "A great childhood," he said, thinking aloud, "is really made up of a thousand small good moments." His comment prompted me to step back and take stock of what those moments might be for my own two young sons. What will be their happiest memories? Topping the list in my mind are the simple but extraordinary pleasures we've had traveling together: the hermit crabs we discovered at a Maine beach, the afternoon spent playing catch on the Mall in Washington, the thrill of a first flight, a first train ride, a first hike to a mountaintop.

As parents, we all work incredibly hard to find the time and money to take our children on vacation. We want to show them the remarkably varied American landscape and introduce them to its many cultures and histories. We want to get away from jobs, homework, and household chores long enough to enjoy one another's company uninterrupted. And most of all, we want to have fun.

The editors at *FamilyFun* and I take great pride in this book and others in the series. They are a culmination of ten years worth of gathering for our readers' the best vacation advice out there. Traveling with children is an art—and our charge is to help with your decisions every step of the way so that you can make the most of every minute of your time away.

Alexandra Kennedy

Alexandra Kennedy
Editorial Director

How to Use This Guide

WELCOME TO THE world of *FamilyFun* magazine's new travel guide series. In our effort to present you with the finest in vacation options, we called on the best experts we know: our hardy group of writers. All are parents who travel with their kids, and all live and work in the area(s) about which they're writing. These are the people who can tell you where to find that teddy bear shop that isn't in the main mall, which restaurant has the best milk shakes, which museum will invite your toddler to roll up his sleeves and create art, and which theme park will give your preteen a good return on the price of admission. With all their recommendations comes the endorsement of their kids: our traveling children have been our best critics.

Since all of the guides in this series cover more than one state, we have divided them into easy-to-use sections. So here's a guide to the guide.

READY, SET, GO!—is a mini-encyclopedia of handy facts, practical advice, what to do/where to go/when to go/how to travel: in other words, all you need to know about planning a successful family vacation.

INTRODUCTION—will give you an overview of the states being covered in this guidebook. Read it—it will whet your appetite, and perhaps give you some new ideas for family activities.

CHAPTERS—States and chapters are presented in geographical order. Chapters represent the regions we think your family will enjoy most. We have omitted those places that we feel would not be family-friendly or are too expensive for what you get in return. We also make note of attractions that appeal only to a certain age range.

FamilyFun has given each entry a rating—stars (★) that range from one to four—to guide you to our favorites. Remember, however, that this guidebook contains nothing that we do not recommend—it's just that we liked some things better than others. We've also assigned a dollar sign rating (**$**)—in high season for a family of four, also ranging from one to four. Check the price range at the start of each chapter as the key changes. We hope that this will help you to decide whether a hotel, restaurant, or attraction will fit in with your budget.

Typically, we start each chapter with an introduction, followed by *FamilyFun*'s Must-See List of up to ten things to try to do while visiting. We've divided attractions into two categories: "Cultural Attractions" (museums, historic sites, and so on) and "Just for Fun" (water parks, zoos, aquariums, roller coasters, and the like). Wherever possible, we've included Web site information.

What more can we say? We hope that this guide helps you to fashion the best possible vacation for your family, one that is a pleasure in the planning, a delight in the doing, and one that will leave every member of your clan with memories that will last a lifetime—or at least until ninth grade.

Bon Voyage!

California and Hawaii

I T MIGHT SEEM UNWIELDY to combine California and Hawaii, two states that are a five-hour flight away from each other, in one guidebook—but we at *FamilyFun* think it makes perfect sense. First of all, the country's 31st state and its 50th state have more in common than many that share a common boundary. In both you'll find endless miles of sandy beaches, a sometime serene ocean for swimming and surfing, mountains, seaside towns, historic villages, outrageously popular tourist meccas and secret hideaways—and, best of all, unlimited sunshine in which to enjoy it all.

In its beginings, people traveled west to California with their dreams. Early settlers were rewarded with a gleaming gold rush, verdant valleys that would yield grapes and lush fields teeming with fruits and vegetables. A millionaire named Hearst built a castle here; a visionary named Disney made his mark with a mouse; Ghirardelli infused the air with the dizzying smell of chocolate; Getty brought priceless artworks.

And if you think all this will draw a yawn from youngsters, drive up (or down) the Pacific Coast Highway and get ready for the "wows." In this vast state, your kids can see where their favorite movie star lives (in Beverly Hills), enjoy the thrill of an amusement park (in Anaheim), visit a zoo (in San Diego), and ride a cable car (in San Francisco).

From Los Angeles to San Francisco—as Tony Bennett sang in "I Left My Heart in San Francisco"—California will surely win your family's hearts. And when you board one of those little cable cars "halfway to the stars" you'll know what he was talking about.

Long before it was a state, Hawaii was ruled by kings and queens, and was steeped in its own traditions and legends; it even has its own language. And although on August 21, 1959, the islands were granted statehood, happily for visitors, Hawaii has retained its unique character. Here, your family can walk on an active volcano, watch whales frolic in the ocean, stand high above the clouds, learn how to make a flowered lei, snorkel, and see fabulously colored fish.

Once you arrive (most flights from the mainland touch down on Oahu), getting from one island to another is easy—Hawaiian Airlines and Aloha each run frequent, 20-minute-long flights from one destination to the next—so you can choose one island as a base and take day trips to others. If time (and budget) allow, however, we recommend staying on a few islands and sampling their unique landscape and personality—each offers experiences that young (and older) travelers will never forget. Grand gardens galore, the bluest water anywhere, the tallest trees, the most spectacular sunsets. If it seems that this book speaks in superlatives, it does. If you think California and Hawaii are two of the top vacations on earth, they are. If you want to be sure that you don't miss a single attraction, that you will find the perfect hotel, enjoy the best meal, read on. Like the destinations outlined in this guide, we won't disappoint.

Let the fun begin!

Pack up and get going.
You're on vacation!

Ready, Set, Go!

Just ten years ago, *FamilyFun* was a fledgling magazine, and the family travel "industry"—now a booming, $100 billion annual trade—was as much a newcomer as we were. In a way, you could say we have grown up together.

FamilyFun was one of the first national magazines to actively research and publicize travel ideas for families with school-age children (a fun job, we must add). Over the last decade, as the numbers of traveling families increased, so did the business of family travel. These days, there are more resources, opportunities, and means for the vacationing family than ever before—which, in turn, gives *FamilyFun* the chance to be an even more valuable clearinghouse of ideas for you.

Through the years, we have been privileged to work with veteran travel writers and editors who have gone around the world with their kids. We've also taken time to listen to our readers—insightful, creative families from across the United States—and to note (and sometimes publish) their stories, recommendations, and tips on traveling as a family. A combination of those two wisdoms is what awaits you on the following pages.

Although it may not be readily apparent, a lot of trial and error underlies these pages. Each destination, before it reaches this book, undergoes a rigorous investigation, and not all make the grade.

We know that family vacations are a big investment, and we know that's why you're here. You're hoping to sidestep the pitfalls of experimentation and to locate destinations that will be a real hit with your family. Congratulations! You've come to the right place.

First Steps

At the outset, organizing a family vacation can seem as daunting as landing a probe on Mars. Better to stay home and watch the Discovery Channel, you think—maybe toast a few marshmallows in the fireplace.

The truth is that planning an adventurous vacation can be fun, especially if you prepare for it in advance and involve your kids. The onerous part is remembering all the things you have to think about.

That's where we come in. This introductory chapter covers family travel from A to Z, from deciding where to go, to getting there and making the most of your vacation. Some of this may seem like old news to you, but we want to make sure you don't forget a thing.

How much do we spend?

Chances are, you already know approximately what you have to spend on a vacation—and you've already got a modus operandi when it comes to money matters. Maybe you're a family that carefully figures a budget, then finds a vacation to fit it. Or maybe you're the type to set your heart on a once-in-a-lifetime trip, then scrimp and save until you can make it happen.

Determine the type of trip you will take. Before you even start your planning, take a moment to consider: what kind of trip are you taking? Are you splurging on a dream vacation, or conserving on a semi-annual getaway? What aspects of this trip are most important to you?

HAVE MODEM, WILL TRAVEL
For information on how to research and book travel plans on the Web, turn to page 31.

Budget carefully. Once you know what those broad parameters are, the next step is to think through your vacation budget in detail—if not at the outset of planning, then at an opportune point along the way. When you know what you have to spend, you'll make quicker and less stressful decisions en route and you'll be able to pay the bills without a grimace once you get home. You'll find lots of budget-saving tips in this introductory chapter.

When can we go?

Scheduling your vacation well can make a big difference in everyone's experience of the trip.

Consider each individual. Most likely, tight school and work schedules will decide when you travel — but if possible, aim for a time slot that allows everyone to relax. For instance, an action-packed road trip sounds exciting, but it might be just the wrong medicine for a parent who's squeezing it into a packed work schedule. End-of-summer trips may be tough for kids with back-to-school anxieties, and midyear trips that snatch kids from school sometimes cause more trouble than they're worth.

Where do we go?

In this book (and the others in this travel series), you'll find scores of winning family destinations. By all means, though, don't stop here. Doing your own research is half the fun, and these days, you have a wealth of resources at your disposal.

Make a list of destinations. What hot spots intrigue your clan? What adventures would you like to try? Draw up a big list, and don't worry about coming up with too many ideas—you can return to this list year after year. Here are a few trails you can follow: relatives, friends, and coworkers (who love to report on their own successful trips), a professional travel agent, local chambers of commerce and state tourism boards, and magazines, the Internet (see page 34 for some good family travel sites), and local hotels and outfitters in the geographic areas you're interested in.

Evaluate your family. A good vacation has to accommodate *everyone* in the family, no matter what their ages, limitations, or interests. While no destination will make everyone happy all the time, you should search vigilantly for those that offer a niche for each family member.

Involve your kids. The more involved your kids are in planning—especially during these early, brainstorming stages — the more likely they are to work to make the trip a success.

Experiment wisely. While experimentation can add spice to a trip, too much may overwhelm your kids (and you). If your child has her heart set on horseback riding, for example, make sure she tries it out at home before you put down a deposit on a dude ranch vacation.

Check the season. Be informed about travel conditions for the time of your trip and make sure you're not heading for trouble (hurricane season in Florida, for example, or black-fly season in the Adirondacks). This is especially important if you're cashing in on off-season deals.

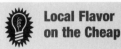

Local Flavor on the Cheap

Don't wait till you arrive at your destination to investigate opportunities for local fun—research a few in advance:

♦ Check out a regional festival or agricultural fair. For fairs in the western U.S., visit www.fairs net.org and for festivals nationwide, visit www.festivals.com

♦ Explore a college campus (which may offer green space, bike paths, museums, observatories, and more). To find a list, go to a general Internet search engine like www.yahoo.com, click on education, and search for colleges by state. Then, call the school's information office for a map and a roster of special events.

♦ Visit a farmers' market. For a list of markets around the U.S., log on to www.ams.usda.gov/farmersmarkets/

♦ Take in an air show (they're usually free at military bases). For a list of air shows by region, see www.airshows.org

♦ Find a local nature center or Audubon preserve.

Schedule appropriately. How much time do you need to give this particular destination its due? You don't want to feel like you're rushing through things—but neither do you want to run out of activities that will interest your kids.

Should we have an itinerary?

Drawing up a travel itinerary, whether it's rough or detailed, will ensure that you travel wisely, hit the hot spots, and give everyone in your group a say in what you'll see.

Include something for everyone. No doubt, each member of your family will have his or her own list of must-sees. If a unanimous vote on itinerary stops is out of the question, ask everyone to write down top choices, then create a schedule that guarantees each person at least one or two favorites. If your children span a wide age range, remind them that there will be some patient standing by while siblings (and Mom and Dad) have their moments in the sun.

Involve the kids (again). Once you've got the basic stops down, kids can help research destinations, plan driving routes, locate pit stops, and help plan rainy-day alternatives.

Make a plan, then break it. Don't let your preplanned schedule get in the way of spontaneous delights. What if your kids want to ride that water slide for an extra three hours? One fun moment in hand is usually worth at least two on the itinerary.

Beat the crowds. Remember to head for popular attractions first thing in the morning or in late afternoon and early evening. Save the middle of the day for poolside fun or activities that take you off the beaten path and away from crowds.

Travel in tune with your family's natural rhythms. Preschoolers tend to be at their best early in the day—a good time for structured activities. Many teens, on the other hand, are pictures of grogginess before noon. Adapt your itinerary to suit ingrained family habits—including your usual meal and nap times—and you'll have smoother sailing. When visiting very popular destinations, take the time to find out in advance when their slowest periods are.

Train-your-own tour guides

Guided tours at historic sites and museums are often a snooze (or too sophisticated) for young kids. Instead, create your own tour—have each family member study up on a different attraction by writing or calling for brochures, surfing the Web, and visiting the library. Then, when you arrive, you'll have an expert guide on board.

GETTING THERE

As we all know, the experience of taking kids from point A to point B runs the gamut from uneventful (read: bliss) to miserable. Knowing the ins and outs of your travel options will speed you toward a sane trip.

FamilyFun **READER'S TIP**

Hire Some Junior Travel Agents

When we were planning a summer trip to Louisiana, I overheard one of my kids tell another that they were going to have to do everything Mom and Dad wanted to do. That's when I decided that each family member would get to plan a full day of our trip. I purchased a regional travel guide and told everyone they had $200 for one day's activities, meals, and accommodations, so they would have to budget (a useful exercise for my 10- and 12-year olds). Every night, any money left over from that day was given to the next planner. I am proud to say that everything went well, and the kids proclaimed it the best vacation ever!

Cindy Long, Spring, Texas

By Plane

PROS: It's fast. And if you land a good deal, air travel can actually be affordable.

CONS: If you don't land a good deal, air travel can be prohibitively expensive, especially for a big family. Other pitfalls include flight delays, mounting claustrophobia on long trips, and strict baggage restrictions.

Look for deals. Traveling in off-peak season and taking off-peak flights (very early or very late in the day) may save you money; flying midweek and staying over Saturday night almost always will. You may also wish to research deals at different airports (for instance, T. F. Green Airport in Providence, Rhode Island, often offers cheaper fares than Boston's Logan Airport 45 minutes away). Also, remember that most sale tickets have a cutoff date—you'll have to book two, three, or four weeks ahead of your departure date to get the deal.

Consider using an agent. Booking your own airline reservations on the Web is a cinch these days (see pages 35 and 36), but there are still advantages to using a professional travel agent who knows your family's needs. First of all, for the $10 or $20 per-ticket surcharge you may pay, you'll save Web-surfing time, and you'll be spared the stress of babysitting the fickle airline market. Also,

an agent may be able to suggest a Plan B (such as using a smaller airport to get a better deal)—something the Web search engines can't do for you. Try to get a good agent recommendation through friends, coworkers, or relatives; if you need further help, the American Society of Travel Agents (703-739-2782, www.astanet.com) provides a list of members, as well as brochures on travel topics (including one on how to choose a travel agent).

By Car

PROS: Road trips are the cheapest way to get from here to there, and they can also be real adventures. In addition, the car is familiar territory for your kids, so they'll feel right at home (for better or worse) during the trip. And, of course, a road trip affords you priceless flexibility.

CONS: You're in for major advance planning, from making sure your car is in good condition to scheduling regular rest stops and having a dependable cache of road snacks, games, and other diversions. Even with those, the hours of close confinement may quickly erode your family's wanderlust.

Get a good map. If you belong to AAA, request a free "TripTik" map. Otherwise, you can map your route and download printed driving directions on Websites like www.map quest.com, www.freetrip.com, and www.mapsonus.com

WHEN YOU BOOK

♦ Try first for a nonstop flight. If that's not available, fly "direct," which means you'll stop at least once but won't switch planes.

♦ Book flights that depart early in the day, if possible. If your flight is delayed, you—and the airline—will have time to make other arrangements.

♦ Specify your ticketing preferences, whether paper or electronic.

♦ Check to see if a meal will be served in flight. If so, order meals your kids like. Many airlines offer kids' meals or a vegetarian choice that may be pasta. If not, plan accordingly.

♦ Ask for the seats you'd like, whether they're a window, an aisle, or the bulkhead for legroom.

PACKING TIPS

♦ Stuff your carry-on for every contingency. Pack all medications, extra clothes for little kids, diapers, baby food, formula, wet wipes, and snacks (they'll also help kids swallow to relieve ear pressure).

♦ Have each child carry a small backpack with travel toys, a light sweatshirt, and a pair of socks for the flight.

ON THE DAY OF YOUR TRIP

♦ Call ahead to check for delays.

♦ Have all photo IDs within easy reach (not necessary for kids under age 18 traveling with their parents on domestic flights; on most international flights, even infants will need a passport).

♦ If you have heavy bags, check your luggage first and then park.

♦ If you are early for the flight or run into long delays, don't go straight to the gate. Instead, meander through the airport's diversions: windows onto the runways, children's play areas (many major airports now have these), Web access computers, and, of course, stores where kids can find a treat to tide them over.

♦ Carry on extra bottled water. It's easy to get dehydrated on a plane, and the drink service may be slow in reaching you.

ON THE PLANE

♦ Ask if your child can view the cockpit (the best time may be after the flight is over).

♦ Secure pillows and blankets for family members who may want to nap.

♦ Take breaks from sitting; occasionally walk the aisles and switch seats.

FLYING FEARS

Most children are fearless fliers—and those who are afraid often can trace their concerns to adults who unintentionally transmit their own fears. If you need help answering your children's questions, you can ask them on-line at www.wic-kid.com

FamilyFun TIP

Bookworms

When you're on the road, there's nothing like a good story to pass the time. For night drives, audio books can be a lifesaver. Try borrowing or renting one from your local library, or visit www.storytapes.com, the Website for Village StoryTapes (800-238-8273). You can either rent or purchase from their excellent selection; three- to four-week tape rentals cost $6 to $17 (for *Harry Potter IV*); to buy, tapes cost $12 to $60.

Be prepared for emergencies, large and small. It goes without saying that your car should be in prime working order before you depart. You should have supplies for road emergencies on board, as well as a good first-aid kit (see page 33 for a list of what to include), and, if you have one, bring a cell phone.

Keep things orderly. We all know what happens to our cars within minutes of the time the kids buckle in; on long road trips, expect the chaos to rise by a factor of ten. In an effort to keep things in check, bring containers to hold trash and toys; pack the children's luggage so it's easiest to reach; divvy up the back-seat space so kids know where their boundaries are; and go over basic behavior rules before you leave.

Drive in time with your family's rhythm. Night driving offers less traffic and a chance that young kids will sleep (you can let them ride in their pj's). Alternatively, an early start may avoid late-afternoon, kid-cranky hours. When possible, go with your family's natural flow.

Help prevent motion sickness. Have frequent, small meals during your trip (symptoms are more likely to occur on an empty stomach). Over-the-counter medications such as Dramamine, as well as ginger ale, ginger tea, or ginger candy also can help, but once symptoms begin, it's usually too late for oral medications. Make sure the car is well ventilated, and have sickness-prone travelers take a window seat, which offers

WEATHER WATCHERS Before you leave, assign forecaster duties to one of your kids. Using the Internet, he or she can research and predict the type of weather you'll encounter (and advise everyone on what to pack). Try www.weather.com

fresh air and a view of the road. If a child feels nauseated, have him look straight in front of the car or focus attention on the horizon. If your child becomes carsick, stop the car to give him a break from the motion; having him lie down with his head perfectly still also may help.

By Train

PROS: First of all, trains are just plain cool, for kids and adults alike. Second, there's room to explore, and everyone can kick back and enjoy the view. And third, if you are headed to a major metropolitan area with a good public transit system, you'll avoid the expenses and hassles of city driving and parking.

CONS: There's only one national passenger rail service, Amtrak, and at press time its future was in question. Also, Amtrak's limited network may not be convenient to your destination (ask about connector trains and rental car agencies when you call). In some regions of the United States, Amtrak's city-to-city service rivals car, bus, and plane travel for efficiency; on cross-country hauls, this is not the case. If you're investing in a long train trip, you're in it more for the experience of train travel.

Inquire about special deals. Children ages 2 to 15 usually ride for half fare when accompanied by an adult who pays full fare. Each adult can bring two children at this discounted rate. Amtrak also offers

A Road Trip Survival Kit

A BAG OF TRICKS

- ◆ mini-puzzles with a backboard
- ◆ video games, cassette or CD player (with headphones)
- ◆ paper, pens, pencils, markers
- ◆ travel versions of board games
- ◆ stuffed animals
- ◆ Etch A Sketch
- ◆ colored pipe cleaners
- ◆ deck of cards
- ◆ cookie sheet (a good lap tray)
- ◆ word puzzles
- ◆ small action figures or dolls
- ◆ stickers
- ◆ Trivial Pursuit cards
- ◆ cotton string (for cat's cradle games)

A COOLER OF SNACKS

Bring lots of drinks and a cache of snacks like granola bars, trail mix, grapes, carrot sticks, roll-up sandwiches, fruit leather, and popcorn.

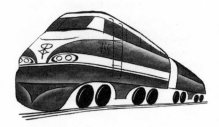

Keeping 'Em Busy: 60-Second Solutions

SQUABBLE SOLUTIONS
Give your kids 25 cents in pennies at the start of the trip. Each time they fight or whine, charge them a penny. Offer a reward, such as doubling or tripling their money, if they haven't lost a cent during the ride.

WAGER AND WIN
Kids are natural wagerers—they love to bet how much, how long, how far, how many. If you're in a bind for a moment's entertainment, ask them to guess the number of French fries on your plate or to estimate how many steps it will take to walk to your airport gate. The key here is to be able to verify the guesses—you'll need to wear a watch with a second hand and carry a calculator.

CREATIVE COMPETITION
Kids love challenges. Need to get rid of the trash in the car? See who can smash the trash into the smallest paper ball, then toss it in the wastepaper bag. Want quiet time? Hold a five-minute silence contest. Need to get through errands in a hurry? Challenge your kids to a race against time. You may feel that your motives are transparent, but your kids won't care.

special seasonal rates, other family deals, and Web-only deals.

How to find them. Amtrak's Website, www.amtrak.com, provides information on fares, schedules, reservations, routes and services, station locations, and special offers. You can also call Amtrak at 800-872-7245 for information and reservations. When you book, ask if there is a full-service dining car and ask whether you can reserve a block of seats for your family.

Consider a sleeper car. For overnight trips, sleep-in-your-seat fares are the cheapest, but first-class bedrooms are much more comfortable.

Arrive early. If your train seats are unassigned, get to the station early for the best chance of eveyone's sitting together. You can even have one parent run ahead to grab a group of seats while the other shepherds children and luggage to the platform.

By RV
PROS: It's a home away from home, which means you can eat, sleep, and use the indoor plumbing (as everyone will agree, one of the finest features of RV travel) whenever you want. In an RV, you are free to explore with independence, self-sufficiency, and freedom—three assets that can be priceless when you're traveling with kids.
CONS: It's a home away from home,

Patchwork Pillows

I am 10 years old, and every year my family goes camping. I collect patches from each place we visit, including the Grand Canyon, Yellowstone and Yosemite National Parks; San Francisco; Las Vegas; and, most recently, Santa Fe, New Mexico. I put all the patches I've collected during each year on separate pillows. I keep the pillows on my bed to remind me of our great trips.

Alex Smythe, Tucson, Arizona

which means you face dishes, cooking, and maintenance (generators, water pumps, waste tanks, and the engine, for starters). In addition, RV rentals are not cheap, although they can compare favorably to the cost of a week's lodging, food, and travel (especially for big families).

What they cost. Expect to pay rental fees between $500 and $1,500 per week, depending on location, model, and time of year you'll be traveling, and the luxury factor (RVs can get pretty posh). Gasoline costs will be high, but you'll save considerably on food and accommodations (campground fees average $20 to $40 per night).

How to find them. Rental information is available through auto clubs and through Go RVing (888-GO-RVING, ask for the free video and literature; www.gorving.com). Cruise America (800- 327-7799) offers 150 rental centers across the United States and Canada. The RV America Website (www.rvamerica.

com) has listings of dealers, clubs, and resources.

Be a savvy renter. Choose an RV that's big enough for your family, but know that many campgrounds only permit vehicles less than 30 feet long. Before you rent, ask how many people fit comfortably in the RV, what powers the appliances, how much insurance is required, and whether supplies such as linens and kitchen utensils are included in the rental price. Get a demonstration of how to work everything in the vehicle, read the manual, practice a little ahead of time, and you'll be ready to take the plunge.

By Bus

PROS: The major advantages of bus travel are that it's cheap, that it spares you the stress of driving, and that tickets usually can be purchased on the day of your trip, at the station. **CONS:** Unfortunately, traveling by bus often takes longer than by car. What's more, bus travel offers little opportunity for diversion for your

Thinking of Skipping School?

option. Both have Websites, www.greyhound.com and www.peter panbus.com, complete with fare and schedule information. To locate smaller local or regional bus lines, try the local Yellow Pages or the department of travel and tourism in the region you'll be visiting.

children. And since you're sitting close to other passengers, many lively family games are off-limits (some buses offer a TV movie; ask when you call).

How to find them: Greyhound Lines (800-229-9424) offers service across the United States. In the Northeast, between New Hampshire and Washington, D.C., Peter Pan Bus Lines (800-237-8747) is another

By Rental Car

PROS: This isn't exactly a pro, but if you've flown or trained into an area without a safe and dependable public transport system, you'll need a rental to get around. Plus, a rental car is cost-efficient for families (as opposed to solo travelers). Best of all, you won't be putting miles on your own car—and if you rent a minivan, you can have drink-cup slots and elbowroom for every single kid.

CONS: None, really, save the expense and a list of rental and insurance decisions that can be as daunting as a Starbucks menu.

How to find them: Your travel agent can book a car for you, but if you want to do it yourself, you'll find all the major agencies in the 800 directory.

Compare costs. Whether you shop on-line or over the phone, compare costs for as many companies as you can (no one company has the best deals in every city or state). In general, weeklong and weekend rentals are a better deal than per-day rentals. In your research, you may wish to inquire about companies' service records, especially if you're going with a local budget chain.

Ask about discounts. Membership in AAA or other associations, credit cards, entertainment book coupons, and package-deal reservations may net you bargains: ask about potential discounts when you make your reservation.

Ask about services and charges. Rental car companies put a lot of information in fine print. So, before you pay (and before you drive away), ask lots of questions. What are the mileage and one-way drop fees? Is there a fee for early or late car returns? Should you bring the car back with an empty gas tank or a full one to get the best refueling price? Does the company offer 24-hour breakdown service? Do the cars have air-conditioning, a jack, and a spare tire? Is there a fee for extra drivers (married couples are often exempt,

FamilyFun TIP

Compare Quotes

When you book a room at a major hotel chain, call both the hotel's local number as well as the toll-free reservation number; the rates you'll be quoted may differ.

but you should check). Are car seats available at no extra charge? (Even if the answer is yes, your own car seat may be cleaner, and, because it's familiar, more comfortable for your child.)

Pay only for the insurance you need. The car, and any damage to it, will be your responsibility for the duration of your trip. Before you purchase insurance from the rental agency, check to see whether your own auto or liability insurance provides adequate coverage. Some credit card agreements may also include rental protection; call the customer service

FamilyFun READER'S TIP

Tabletop Scrapbook

Here's a fun project my family has long enjoyed while traveling. After we have mapped out our vacation, my kids, and now grandchildren, use a laundry pen to draw our route on a cotton tablecloth. We pack up the cloth along with colored markers, and while on the road, family members take turns marking the name of towns and rivers and noting funny signs. When we stop for picnic lunches, we not only use the cloth but also continue adding drawings of sights we've seen and things we've done. After the trip is over, we have a memory-filled tablecloth to use for years to come.

Janet Askew, Adair, Iowa

number on the back of your card to inquire.

WHERE TO STAY

Where you tuck your kids in at night depends entirely on your family's traveling style and budget—and, of course, on what's available in the area to which you're traveling. There are so many options—hotels, motels, inns, cottages, cabins, condominiums, resorts, time-shares, campgrounds—it can be hard to know where to start.

Lists of local accommodations can be found through tourism boards, the Web, travel books, and the 800 numbers or published directories of major franchises. However, finding the places that really go the extra mile for families isn't easy. This book—and other family travel publications—will be your best bets, as will the time-tested recommendations of friends and acquaintances. Always, always ask your own questions as well: see our checklist on page 25 for some basics.

Hotels, Motels & Lodges

From generic chains, to mom-and-pop operations bursting with character, to ritzy palaces, this category really runs the gamut. If you don't have a dependable recommendation (from a friend, trusted travel agent, or guidebook like this one), you may wish to place your trust in the major chains (budget or no) where you at least know what you're getting.

How to find them: Most major chains can be found in the 800 directory (as well as on the Web) and can provide a list of property locations. Alternatively, you can contact regional travel bureaus or consult a national rating system, such as those in Mobil Travel Guides (available in bookstores or the on-line store at www.mobil.com) or the Automobile Association of America (call your local AAA office to order regional TourBook guides).

PICKY EATERS? If you have picky eaters in the family (or if you suspect a child may not enjoy the food at a certain restaurant), feed them ahead of time—and let them enjoy an appetizer or dessert during your meal.

Inns, B&Bs, and Farm Stays

These have traditionally been the domain of honeymooning couples and retirees. Increasingly, though, they are accommodating a growing family travel market. There are certainly gems out there for your discovery—but do your research rigorously (speak with the owner, if possible) to find out whether kids are *truly* welcome at the destination of your choice. The last thing you want to be doing on vacation is shushing your kids and shooing them away from pricey antiques. Look for inns and B&Bs attached to a working farm—these tend to be more kid-friendly, with animals to watch and feed and plenty of outdoor play space.

How to find them: Try travel magazines, regional chambers of commerce, and two excellent Websites, www.bedandbreakfeast.com and www.bbgetaways.com

Condos and Cottages

These are ideal if your group is staying put for the length of your vacation, since they offer room to spread out and cook your own meals. When you book, ask about amenities: does the condo come with linens, pots and pans, a television, phone, dishwasher, and washer/dryer? Are there extra tax and/or booking fees? If you rent directly from the owner, be even more rigorous in your questioning. Is there

WHAT TO ASK BEFORE YOU BOOK

1 **ACCOMMODATIONS:** What rooms (or condos or cabins) are available? How many beds are there and what size are they? Are the rooms nonsmoking? What amenities are included (laundry, phone, cable TV, refrigerator, balcony, coffee service, cots, cribs, minibar)? Are the rooms located in the main building? What specific views are available? Is there a charge for kids staying in the same room with parents? Are there family packages? Can guests upgrade rooms upon arrival?

2 **DINING:** Are there dining facilities on the property? If so, are there restrictions for kids? What are some menu items, and what does the average meal cost? Is there a kids' menu? Is there a complimentary breakfast offered? Are there snack and/or drink machines? If there are no dining facilities on-site, is there a family restaurant nearby?

3 **RECREATION:** What recreational facilities are available (game rooms, pool, tennis courts, equipment rental, and so on)? At what hours are they available? Are there additional charges for their use? Are there age or time restrictions for any recreation? What recreational options are available in the nearby community (movie theater, minigolf, bowling, and the like)?

a cancellation policy if the place is not up to your standards?

How to find them: The Internet has made it easy to connect potential renters with homeowners and rental brokers. Unfortunately, that means there are literally thousands of sites to sift through. Luckily, most sites offer very detailed information on properties, so you can actually make an informed decision on-line to pursue a place.

For starters, here are the Website addresses for a number of national and international vacation rental clearinghouses: www.eLeisure Link.com (888-801-8808); Barclay

International Group (800-845-6636; www.bar clayweb.com); and 10,000 Vacation Rentals, Inc. (888-369-7245; www. 10kvacationrentals.com).

To rent directly from a property owner, try Vacation Rentals by Owner at www.vrbo.com . You also can locate condos and cottages by inquiring at local tourism bureaus, local realtors (especially for seaside properties), and major resorts, which often keep lists of rentals on property or nearby.

Campgrounds

These range from the extremely rustic—grassy knolls with fabulous views to the luxurious—complexes with video games, sports areas, and fax and modem hookups.

Depending on where and how you prefer to camp, you'll have your pick of sites in state or national parks, national forests, or private campgrounds. (See "Happy Campers," page 38-39.)

When you book a site, inquire: What are the nightly fees? Does the campground accept reservations? If no, how early should you arrive in order to claim a site? Is there a pool or lake? Lifeguards? Equipment rentals? Laundry facilities, rest rooms, and hot showers? A grocery store nearby? Remember that campgrounds near major tourist attractions fill up early, so make reservations in advance (choice spots in some national parks, for example, fill up months ahead).

Family Hostels

A CHEAP SLEEP

If you think hostels are the exclusive domain of students and backpackers, think again: many of the neatest have private family rooms that can be reserved in advance. Some also offer special programs, such as historic walking tours, natural history programs, and sports activities. Hostels in the Hostelling International/American Youth Hostels system are as varied as their locations and include registered historic buildings, lighthouses, and a former dude ranch. For the latest edition of *Hostelling Experience North America*, call *202-783-6161* or visit www.hiayh.org

How to find them: In addition to the campgrounds recommended in this book, you can find lists of campgrounds on the Internet: check out About.com's camping section at www.camping.about.com, www.camping-usa.com, and the National Association of RV Parks & Campgrounds at www.gocamping america .com. For campgrounds in national parks, visit www.nps.gov and state. For a national directory of KOA campgrounds, visit www.koa kamp grounds.com

Resorts

A resort vacation is a big investment, and up-front research is essential to ensure you get your money's worth. When you are making inquiries, don't be shy about taking up the resort staff's time with questions. Be sure to grill them with the entire housing quiz on page 25. Ask, too, about programming for kids and families. If there is a children's pro-

FamilyFun TIP

Walk it through

When you're booking a room or condo over the phone, ask the reservation specialist to "walk" you through the place, virtually, from the front door to the balcony view (if there is one!). They may think you're going overboard — but you'll really know what you're getting.

gram, what days and times does it run? Is it canceled if not enough kids sign up? What is the ratio of counselors to children? What are the age divisions? What activities does the program offer? What are the facilities? What, if any, is the additional cost? Are there games, programs, or organized recreation especially for families? Baby-sitting services? Assistance for kids who get sick? What are the terms for these? If the resort is "all-inclusive," find out

FamilyFun READER'S TIP

Invent a Travel Kit

When our family flies, I make travel kits for my two sons, Noah, 8, and Paul, 4. I fill old wipes boxes with a variety of treats: chocolate kisses, fruit snacks, a sealed envelope with a love note inside, stickers, and a small wrapped package such as a pencil sharpener, pencils, and a blank book (I staple together scratch paper). I write the boys' names on the front with a permanent marker, and then, in flight, they decorate the boxes with stickers. The trick is not to give them the travel kits until we're on the plane. After they exhaust their supply of goodies inside, they can refill it with things they collect during the trip.

Kathy Detzer, White River Junction, Vermont

Travel Insurance

It's not for everyone, but some travelers like to invest in this just-in-case insurance. Cancellation policies cover losses if you can't make your trip due to illness or a death in the family (you may wish to consider this if you have to put down a hefty deposit or prepay for your vacation in full). Medical policies provide for some emergency procedures. You can buy travel insurance from a specialty broker (see below), from your travel agent, or directly from an insurance company. Do not buy insurance from the tour operator or cruise line you will be traveling with.

Travel Guard International
(800-826-1300; www.travel-guard.com)

CSA Travel Protection
(www.csatravelprotection.com)

Travel Assistance International (800-821-2828; www.travelassistance.com)

Access America (866-807-3982; www.accessamerica.com)

exactly what is covered. If you will be taking advantage of the services included in the price, it may mean a good deal for your family; if not, you might be better off elsewhere.

How to find them: Travel magazines, travel agents, and family travel Websites (see page 34) will all be able to offer recommendations on family resorts. Also, the Globe Pequot Press (www.globepequot. com) has two good resource books: *100 Best Family Resorts in North America* and *100 Best All-Inclusive Resorts of the World.*

SAVING MONEY

A great vacation balances moments of extravagance with activities that are as enjoyable as they are affordable. The key, then, is to find painless ways to cut costs so that you can feel good about indulging. Here's a host of secrets from budget-savvy travelers.

Stock up at home. Specialty items, such as sunscreen, film, batteries, over-the-counter medications, and first-aid supplies can be outrageously expensive in vacation spots. Buy them in bulk at home and bring them with you.

Travel off-peak. Whether it's a ski resort town in the summertime, or Yosemite National Park in the spring, or the Adirondacks in the winter, off-peak travel is one of the best ways to save, as long as you're primed to enjoy the unique flavor of an off-season trip. Rates for travel and lodging are often slashed considerably—and you can enjoy a different perspective (and fewer crowds) at the destination of your choice.

Don't delay. The sooner you begin planning and booking your vacation (six months to a year or more in advance is not too early), the more deals will be available to you.

Shop around. This is the cardinal rule of vacation planning. Take time to compare prices for every service that you'll be buying, from airfares, hotels, and rental cars to tickets for attractions.

Ask for discounts. Don't be shy about asking for discounts. Call ahead to the attractions that you plan to visit and ask where one finds discount coupons. When making

Guided Tours

WHEN DO YOU NEED ONE?

For certain types of specialty travel (technically challenging outdoor adventures, for example), an expert guide is a necessary aid for a safe and enjoyable trip. In addition, using a local guide for day trips (say, fishing or snowmobiling) can be a wonderful way to connect with local lore and culture in the region you're visiting. In general, however, guided tours (especially group tours that include full itineraries and meals) tend to be pricey, tightly scheduled, and lacking the freedom most families value highly.

hotel reservations, ask if discounts are available—if not on the room alone, then on a package that may include the room and tickets to a nearby attraction. Coupons are also available on-line: a good place to start is the coupon link at www.about.com

STRAP A SHOE BAG to the back of the front seat and stuff it with your small kid-entertainment supplies: crayons and coloring books; kids' magazines; craft supplies, such as pipe cleaners, markers, glue sticks, and construction paper; songbooks; paper doll kits; a deck of cards; and a cassette player with story tapes. And don't forget a Frisbee, jump rope, and chalk (to draw hopscotch grids) for rest stops.

- -

Make Your Own Postcards

While traveling by car or plane, my kids entertain themselves by creating their own postcards. Before the trip, I buy blank, prestamped postcards from the post office. Once we are under way, the kids draw pictures on the cards — usually of things they have done on vacation or are looking forward to doing. We address the cards to relatives and friends and drop them in the mail, making sure we send a few home for our own travel journal. This activity has been so successful, we now give friends travel kits of the prestamped cards and crayons as a bon voyage gift.

Lynette Smith, Lake Mills, Wisconsin

Look at package deals. At first blush, packages can seem outrageously expensive. But before you pass them up, compare them carefully to what you'd pay if you bought all the pieces of your vacation separately. Rates for airfare, lodging, and car rentals can be substantially lower when purchased together, especially for popular destinations. Contact your travel agent for information or research deals from travel clubs like AAA (call your local chapter or visit www.aaa.com), American Express Travel Services (800-346-3607; www.americanexpress.com), and from tour agencies affiliated with major airlines.

Use member benefits. Membership in an auto club, professional organization, or Entertainment book club may score you discounts on travel bills—ask before you book. Your credit card company, as well, may offer free services, such as collision-damage and travel-accident insurance, if you use the card to pay for travel expenses (call to request a copy of the company's travel benefits policy). If you travel regularly, the savings you'd garner from Web-saver clubs like www.bestfares.com can be well worth the $50 to $70 annual fee.

Tickets to attractions. Buying tickets to attractions in advance through an association or organization or at the hotel desk often will save you money. Equally important, you'll avoid the ticket line itself. On-line, try www.citypass.com for discount tickets in major metropolitan areas.

Keep your distance. Unless on-site housing offers necessary convenience for your family, consider lodging that's outside the major tourist area or city you're visiting. An extra 15 minutes of travel can considerably reduce lodging expenses, especially if you're staying more than a few days.

Check out kids' deals. Look for hotel deals where kids eat and/or stay free with their parents.

Consider cooking. Dining out is certainly part of the vacation experience, but three meals per person, per day add up quickly. Cooking your own meals can save you lots of money, even if you factor in the expense of a room with a kitchenette. In a regular hotel room, you can probably manage breakfast and/or lunch with a well-stocked cooler.

Pack your own minibar. Those high-priced hotel mini-bars are magnets for kids. Make a list of your kids' favorite treats, then purchase them in bulk as individually wrapped items. Pack a selection in a separate box or bag that can double as the designated minibar once you arrive at the hotel.

Let's do lunch. If you have a yen to try a particular fancy restaurant, head there during lunch. The atmosphere will be the same, and the menu will be similar, but smaller lunchtime portions will be accompanied by lower prices.

Revel in free fun. Remember the birthday when your child spent more time playing with the wrapping paper than with the actual toy? Vacations are filled with similar, low-cost but memorable moments, including hours at the beach, hiking trails, parks, and playgrounds. If you're in a new area, scan the local paper for listings, or call a local travel bureau or chamber of commerce for ideas.

Be savvy about souvenirs. Decide ahead of time how much you're willing to spend on souvenirs. Depending on the age of your kids, give each child his or her own spending money (they'll be stingier with their own funds than they are with yours). As an added incentive, let them keep a portion of any money they don't spend.

USING THE WEB

With the advent of the World Wide Web, individuals now have access to all the tools that travel agents use (and then some). The trick is to know how to use them well.

PROS: Researching travel ideas on the Web may draw in your kids more readily than a guidebook would.

Packing With—And For—Kids

Like so much of your family vacation, packing is a balancing act—in this case between including everything you need and making sure you can actually lift your bags. No matter where you're headed, this checklist should cover most of the essentials.

Give the kids a role. Every child has favorite outfits as well as clothing that he or she won't wear (and that you shouldn't bother packing). Young children can select the clothes they'd like to bring and set them aside for you. Older kids can do much of their own packing, especially if you help them write up a checklist of their own.

Don't worry about wrinkles. Like aging, this happens even with the best of precautions. Suggest some folding methods, but don't insist on your kids' finessing this. One surprisingly effective technique for kids is simply to roll everything up.

Make each child responsible for his or her own luggage. A backpack and a soft-sided suitcase for each child will do the trick. Let your kids decorate their bags with stencils and stickers — and remember to attach a name tag.

Separate toiletries in sealed, waterproof bags. Lids on toiletries often pop off or open during travel.

Take precautions in case of lost luggage. If you're flying to your vacation destination, pack at least one complete outfit for each family member in each suitcase. That way, if a piece of luggage is lost, everyone still has a change of clothes. Also, pack medications, eyeglasses, and contact lens solution in carry-ons.

Clothing

Include an outfit for each day of the week, plus extra shirts or blouses in case of spills. If your children are younger, encourage them to choose brightly colored outfits that will make them easier to spot in the crowd.

- Comfortable shoes or sneakers
- Socks and undergarments
- Sleepwear
- Light jackets, sweaters,or sweat-shirts for cool weather
- Bathing suits
- Sandals or slip-on shoes for the pool
- Hats or sun visors
- Rain gear, including umbrellas

Toiletries

- Toothbrushes, toothpaste, dental floss, and mouthwash
- Deodorant
- Combs, brushes, hair accessories, blow-dryer
- Soap
- Shampoo and conditioner
- Shaving gear
- Feminine-hygiene items

- Lotions
- Cosmetics
- Nail care kit
- Tweezers
- Cotton balls and/or swabs
- Antibacterial gel for hand washing
- Sunscreens and lip balm
- Insect repellent

Miscellaneous "must-haves"

- Essential papers: identification for adults, health insurance cards, tickets, traveler's checks
- Wallet and/or purse, including cash and credit cards
- Car and house keys (with duplicate set packed in a different bag)
- Eyeglasses and/or contact lenses, plus lens cleaner
- Medications
- Watch
- Camera and film (pack film in your carry-on bag)
- Tote bag or book bag for day use
- Books and magazines for kids and adults
- Toys, playing cards, small games
- Flashlight
- Extra batteries
- Large plastic bags for laundry
- Small plastic bags
- Disposable wipes
- First-aid kit
- Travel alarm
- Sewing kit

Keep Your First-Aid Kit Handy

There's no such thing as a vacation from minor injuries and ailments, so a well-stocked first-aid kit is essential to have on hand. You can buy a prepackaged kit or make your own by packing the following items in an old lunch box:

- Adhesive bandages in various sizes, adhesive tape, and gauze pads
- Antacid
- Antibacterial gel for washing hands without water
- Antibacterial ointment
- Antidiarrheal medicine
- Antihistamine or allergy medicine
- Antiseptic
- Antiseptic soap
- Pain relief medicine—for children and adults
- Cotton balls and/or swabs
- Cough medicine and/or throat lozenges
- Motion sickness medicine
- Fingernail clippers
- First-aid book or manual
- Ipecac
- Moleskin for blisters
- Ointment for insect bites and sunburn
- Premoistened towelettes
- Thermometer
- Tissues
- Tweezers and needle

FamilyFun TIP

The Internet Travel Bible

If you're serious about researching (and especially booking) travel plans yourself, consult *Online Travel* by Ed Perkins (Microsoft Press, $19.95). This paperback tome is an invaluable resource on getting the best deals available and navigating the benefits and pitfalls of today's travel market, both on- and off-line.

Plus, when it comes time to book reservations, the Web can be a treasure trove of bargains—if you know how to hunt for them (see "The Internet Travel Bible" above). Why is that so? In essence, the Internet allows travel service providers to change their bargain pricing structures and unload unsold seats and rooms at a moment's notice. Of course, agents are still out to make as much money as they can—but you often can reap the benefits of their last-minute sales. In fact, many of these sales are available only on-line.

CONS: Keeping tabs on the travel market on-line can be extremely time-consuming if you are determined to find the best deal possible. In addition, since Web search engines can't read your mind and ask you questions, they can't ferret out all your options—just the ones that fall within the parameters you specify. So if you aren't a savvy searcher, you might miss the best deals (or the best destinations) even after hours of research.

Family travel Websites. It's a challenge to locate truly family-friendly sites among the hundreds available. For researching travel ideas and gathering travel tips, here are some of the best sites. Try our own website too—www.familyfun.com—it too has a lot of travel ideas.

♦ www.vacationtogether.com is a searchable database of family vacation ideas, reprinted from various publications (including *FamilyFun* magazine). You'll also find packing checklists and links to reservation sites here.

♦ www.travelwithkids.about.com is a terrific clearinghouse for family vacation ideas, package deals, current bargains, lists of accommodations, packing checklists, travel tips and games, downloadable maps, and more.

♦ www.thefamilytravelfiles.com is a well-organized family travel Website that showcases a range of trip ideas and offers a free travel e-zine.

♦ www.familytravelforum.com is a monthly on-line newsletter specializing in well-screened links to family-friendly accommodations, airfare deals, seasonal events, and more.

General travel sites. In addition to family-specific sites such as the ones listed above, there are literally thousands of useful Websites that can help you plan and book your vacation. They are too numerous to list here! We have included many of our favorites throughout this chapter; in addition to those, here are a few you may find useful.

♦ www.officialtravelinfo.com lists contacts for travel and tourism bureaus worldwide (you can search the United States by state).

♦ www.fodors.com, www.frommers.com, and www.nationalgeographic.com are sites related to travel magazines. Often, they'll post selections from current issues, as well as other travel-related articles.

♦ www.travel-library.com (a wide range of travel topics, travelogues, and destination information) and www.about.com (a general site with good travel links) are sites that can lead you to travel information that you may (or may not!) be looking for.

Book your own airline reservations. Using the same databases as travel agents use, the leading travel sites have made booking your own flight as simple as typing in when you'd like to leave, when you'd like to return, your origin and destination, and airline choice. They kick back a list of flights that most closely match

Broker a Hotel Deal

Great deals at major hotels usually turn up off-season or at the last minute, but here's another tactic families can try: work with a hotel consolidator (also called a hotel broker or discounter).

Consolidators work by securing blocks of hotel rooms at wholesale prices, then reselling them at rates that are—in theory, at least—lower than the published "rack" rate. Some consolidators will only reserve your room; you pay the hotel directly. Others require a prepaid voucher that you present to the hotel upon arrival. Many consolidators claim savings of 10 to 50 percent (some even more), but as with any bargain, it pays to know what you're getting into.

SOME TIPS:

- Ask about service charges. Is there a user fee for the consolidator?
- Are there financial penalties for trip cancellation or rescheduling?
- Compare rates. The consolidator may not beat a hotel's special offers.

With those caveats, try:

Quikbook: Good selection and easy to use, with hotels in 33 cities. Call 800-789-9887 or see www.quikbook.com

Central Reservation Service: Lists hotel deals in ten major cities. Call 800-555-7555 or visit www.roomconnection.com

Gumshoe Games

The detectives in your group will just love these tests of their sleuthing ability.

Secret highway messages: Pass out the pencils and paper, and keep your eyes peeled for official road signs. Each time you spot one, write down the first letter. When you've passed five to seven signs—and have five to seven letters—you're ready to crack the code. Here's how: each letter stands for a word. So the letters D, S, C, S, and A could stand for the secret message "Drive slowly, construction starts ahead." Of course, others in your family may interpret it as "Dad, stop, candy store ahead."

Two truths and one lie: The first person makes three statements about himself or herself. Two are true; the other is a lie. For example, you could say, "I had a dog named Puddles. My sister cut off my hair once when I was asleep. I won the school spelling bee when I was in third grade." Everybody then holds up one, two, or three fingers to show which statement they think is the lie. Reveal the answer and let the next person fib away.

your specifications and then let you choose the flights you want. After confirming your choices, you pay with a credit card, print your itinerary, and either receive your paper tickets in the mail or, more likely, pick up your tickets when you check in at the airport. **NOTE:** Some people prefer paper tickets because if a flight is missed or cancelled an e-ticket may not be exchangable at a different airline's counter.

Our favorite flight sites are Expedia (www.expedia.com), Travelocity (www.travelocity.com), and Trip.com (www.trip.com). Don't assume that all offer the same flights or the same prices; the important thing is to shop around, even among these sites.

Before you pay for your tickets, you should double-check with two other sources. First, look at your chosen airline's home site to see if they offer extra miles for booking flights on-line, or special, unadvertised Web deals. And call your travel agent, tell her the flight you're interested in, and see if she can beat the price. Lastly, be sure you're aware of the taxes, airport surcharges, and possible site use fees that may be added to your ticket price.

For more information about airlines, airports, and online reservations, go to www.iecc.com/airline/. Also, check out Ed Perkins' *Online Travel* (Microsoft Press, $19.95). To find out more about frequent flier mile programs, visit www.frequent flier.com

Book hotel and rental car reservations. In general, hotel and rental car reservations work the same way that airfare reservations do. The Web is an excellent source of hotel deals (especially for vacation packages, if you're a savvy shopper); rental car companies, on the other hand, generally offer little in the way of discounts above what you can get at the desk.

FREE ATLAS

Best Western offers free road atlases with Best Western sites: call 800-528-1234.

Sign up for e-mail newsletters. If you find a good travel Website that offers a free newsletter, it doesn't hurt to sign up—you may receive timely notice of travel deals that you otherwise would miss. Just be sure that you save any information on how to cancel the subscription in case you want to opt out.

Are Internet travel arrangements foolproof? No, unfortunately. The Internet is prime territory for scams, although you can guard against most of them with a few protective strategies. First, deal with major sites (like the ones listed in this book) or directly with brand-name company sites (like Avis or Holiday Inn) whenever possible. When you're transmitting your credit card information, make sure your connection is secure (your browser should tell you when one has been established). Also, you should double-check to see that the service provider's Website has a secure server. (Look for a locked padlock in the corner of your browser's window or "https"—the "s" stands for "secure"—in the URL.) If a site doesn't seem completely aboveboard, it may not be. Finally, when in doubt, back out. As long as you don't give a company your credit card number, they can't charge you anything.

FamilyFun READER'S TIP

A Colorful Road Game

This homemade road game is a big hit with my 4-year-old son, Tommy. I clip cards out of colored construction paper and print a different letter of the alphabet on each. During a car ride, each of us picks a card and searches for an object or a structure that matches the color and begins with the letter on our card. For example, a player with a *B* on a yellow card might spot a school bus. Since we began playing this game, my son tends to remember many more details about our travels. Instead of hearing, "Are we there yet?" we hear, "Oh no, I haven't found mine yet!"

Susan Robins, Cottage Grove, Oregon

If your family's idea of a vacation involves nightly campfires, sleeping bags, and potential wildlife sightings near (or in!) your living space, check out these great resources for tent and RV camping.

The Trailer Life Directory provides travelers with a list of several thousand campgrounds and RV parks throughout the United States and Canada. Each location is rated on a three-step scale that assesses the park's facilities, cleanliness, and overall appeal; ratings are updated on an annual basis. You can register at www.tldirectory.com to search the directory for free or order your own copy for the road online or at bookstores.

Woodall's campground directories also rate a large number of parks—more than 14,000 locations throughout the United States and Canada are scored on their facilities and recreation. You can purchase a directory which covers the entire area, or shorter versions of the guide are available for the western and eastern regions. Woodall's also publishes a directory exclusively for tent campers. Again, you can register to access campground listings for free at www.woodalls.com, but the online directory does not include Woodall's convenient rating system. The complete directories can be purchased at Woodall's Website or bookstores.

There's no centralized reservation system for every campsite within the **National Park system**, so your best bet is to contact each individual park. Campground reservations here usually must be made several months in advance since the sites are so popular, so don't count on finding a space unless you've planned ahead. Contact information for the National Parks can be found at their Website, www.nps.gov. Policies for state parks also vary from place to place, so you'll have to contact individual campgrounds for camping information.

Veteran car campers recognize **KOA Kampgrounds** by their familiar yellow, red, and black signs. KOAs allow your family to rough it while enjoying many of the amenities of home. Novice campers will be thrilled to have access to hot showers, flush toilets, laundry facilities, and convenience stores. All KOA locations have both tent and RV sites, and some even have cabins that your family can rent. If you plan to stay multiple nights at one or more KOA Kampgrounds, consider purchasing a Value Kard. You'll get a 10 percent discount on your registration fees and a free copy of the KOA directory (you'll still pay for shipping). You can also research KOA locations for free at www.koakampgrounds.com or purchase your own directory on-line or by calling 406-248-7444.

If you're looking for camp-grounds where your family can pitch a tent in peace and quiet, check out *The Best in Tent Camping* series (published by Menasha Ridge Press). The books detail the best in scenic, tent-only sites without all of the bells and whistles.

One key to a great camping trip is remembering all of your supplies. If your family is RV or car camping, you can usually purchase any forgotten items on the road. However, if you're traveling far off the beaten path, you'll need to be careful to double-check your belongings.

Here's a checklist of supplies to make your camping experience go smoothly. If you're renting an RV, be aware that you may be able to rent your bedding and cooking supplies for an additional fee and save the trouble of bringing your own.

- Tent(s) and tent stakes
- Plastic ground cloth/tarp
- Sleeping bags (or bedding, for an RV)
- Sleeping pads
- Camp stove (with extra fuel)
- Pots, plastic dishes, mugs, and utensils
- Water bottle or canteen
- Lantern and/or candles
- Bottle and/or can openers
- Sharp knife (parents should hold on to this)
- Plethora of plastic/trash bags

- Dish soap (preferably biodegradable)
- Stocked coolers
- Water (or a portable filter or purifying tablets)
- Waterproof matches or lighter(s)
- Flashlights (and extra batteries)
- Bandanna (for use as a head covering, pot holder, and napkin)
- Trowel
- Folding saw
- First-aid kit, medications
- Sunscreen
- Insect repellent
- Toilet paper
- Day packs
- Child carriers (for little ones)
- Compass and area map
- Clothing (make sure to pack many layers)
- Two pairs of shoes (in case one gets wet)
- A hat
- Sunglasses
- Toiletries (try to take only necessary items)
- Camera
- Binoculars
- Kid supplies (toys, books, favorite stuffed animal)

California

IF YOUR FAMILY is California dreamin', why not plan your next vacation here? Just don't get Southern California mixed up with Northern California. They are two very different places.

If you're after sunshine, sand, and surf, head to Southern California. If you're after striking scenery or ski slopes, you'll want to head for Northern California.

From south to north, the state has a very long and gorgeous ocean shoreline. Southern California boasts the best water temperature for swimming and the best air temperature for sunbathing. The north coast tends to

be wilder (and colder) and have a far more dangerous surf.

One thing California isn't, is small. So especially with kids in tow, you'll enjoy your visit more if you try to see less. Perhaps plan to explore one of the major cities plus a side trip—and come back another time to see more.

Fortunately, you have lots of choices in accommodations— California offers everything from full-service luxury resorts to inexpensive hostels and campsites on the beach. (See "Hosteling for Families" on page 215.)

California is a state of contrasts. That's why most people manage to find what they came looking for. If you're in search of a fabulous family vacation, success is a sure thing.

ATTRACTIONS

$	under $5
$$	$5 - $10
$$$	$10 - $20
$$$$	$20 +

HOTELS/MOTELS/CAMPGROUNDS

$	under $100
$$	$100 - $200
$$$	$200 - $300
$$$$	$300 +

RESTAURANTS

$	under $10
$$	$10 - $15
$$$	$15 - $25
$$$$	$25 +

***FAMILYFUN* RATED**

★	Fine
★★	Good
★★★	Very Good
★★★★	*FamilyFun* Recommended

San Francisco's Chinatown is home to 80,000 people and is the largest Chinese community outside of Asia.

San Francisco

A FTER DYLAN Thomas visited San Francisco in the 1950s, he wrote, "And all the people are open and friendly." Before him, Rudyard Kipling said, "San Francisco has only one drawback. 'Tis hard to leave." The city still lives up to those sentiments, welcoming visitors young and old—and after a visit here, all of you will agree, 'tis indeed hard to leave.

Whatever your kids' ages, San Francisco offers something for everyone. You can look forward to crossing the longest suspension bridge in the world, the Golden Gate Bridge; entering a *real* prison cell on Alcatraz Island; watching fortune cookies being made by hand in Chinatown; riding a cable car "halfway to the stars"; and boarding an authentic World War II submarine—and that's only the beginning.

THE FamilyFun LIST

Alcatraz Island (page 45)

Cable Car Museum (page 45)

California Academy of Sciences (page 46)

Crookedest Street in the World (page 53)

Exploratorium (page 47)

Ghirardelli Chocolate Manufactory (page 76)

Golden Gate Bridge (page 58)

Golden Gate Park (page 58)

Metreon (page 59)

San Francisco Maritime National Historical Park Maritime Museum (page 50)

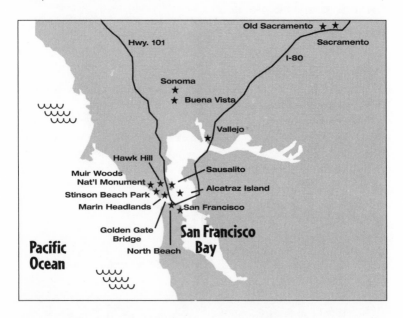

Even if you wanted to, you wouldn't be able to see everything and do everything in this fabulous city during a typical vacation of a week or less. So, you'll need to pick and choose. Perhaps each member of the family can add his or her top spot or spots to the vacation itinerary. It's a good idea to focus on one or two particular areas each day, minimizing the need for crosstown transportation. For example, spend one day touring North Beach, another around Union Square, another in Golden Gate Park. A guided specialty tour that explains the mysteries of Chinatown or that takes you across the Golden Gate Bridge on a fire truck can also be fun and will give you the lay of the land.

In this city known for its morning and evening fog in summer, it's wise to dress in layers. As you go about your sight-seeing, the fog will burn off and, most likely, return again in the evening. No matter what the weather looks like when you start out, and no matter how fiercely your kids insist they don't need one, always bring sweaters or jackets. This isn't a beach town—don't be caught in shorts here. Heed the words of Mark Twain, who declared, "The coldest winter I ever spent was a summer in San Francisco." Year-round temperatures fall in the general range of 45° F to 75° F.

Despite the temperature, San Francisco will warm your heart and leave everyone—from toddlers to preteens—with glowing memories of this magical city by the bay.

CULTURAL ADVENTURES

Alcatraz Island
MUST-SEE FamilyFun ★★★★/$-$$
MUST-SEE

This is one of those places that actually does have something for every member of the family. And everything—the boat ride, the tour, and the 360-degree bay view—is as good as it's cracked up to be. Alcatraz was a fort in the 19th century, a federal penitentiary from 1934 to 1963, and it was occupied by Native Americans from 1969 to 1971. When it was a maximum-security prison, it held some of the country's most hardened criminals, including Al Capone, George "Machine Gun" Kelly, and Robert "Birdman of Alcatraz" Stroud. Opened to the public in 1973, it is now part of the Golden Gate National Recreation Area—the largest urban park in the world. Everyone, even locals, enjoy the short, scenic ride to this infamous island—but little kids get a particular kick out of it. Once here, you can explore at your own pace, following a self-guided tour. A top-notch audio tour of the cell block, narrated by former inmates and guards, is optional but highly recommended. Kids (especially 7- to 12-year-olds) and adults alike enjoy entering the cells and hearing the intriguing stories of escape. A 214-foot-tall, still-operating lighthouse here dates from 1854, when it was the first on the West Coast. You can check out the exterior—the interior is closed to the public. No food service is available, so bring along some snacks, but note that no picnicking is permitted. Wear comfortable shoes, dress warmly, and expect cool, windy weather—even in summer. Reservations are essential. *Alcatraz Island; Ferry service; (415) 773-1188 or (415) 705-5555; www.nps.gov/alcatraz/*

Cable Car Museum
MUST-SEE FamilyFun ★★★★/Free
MUST-SEE

If riding the cable cars seems to be the highlight of your kids' visit to San Francisco, they'll enjoy this informative museum. Located two blocks from the heart of Chinatown, it is set inside the lovely brick cable car barn and powerhouse dating from the 1880s. You can view the huge, noisy flywheels controlling the underground cables that move the cable cars along at 9½ miles per hour. But cover your

FamilyFun GAME

Guessmaster

Name a guessmaster— the person who poses a guessing challenge. He or she could ask passengers to guess the color of the next passing car, or how long before you get to the next town. Or, with three clues, what it is that someone else sees.

ears; they're noisy—very noisy. Cross the street to catch a cable car downtown or to Fisherman's Wharf. For more information, see "Cable Cars—History on Track" on page 53. *1201 Mason St., San Francisco; (415) 474-1887;* www.cablecarmuseum.com

MUST-SEE FamilyFun MUST-SEE California Academy of Sciences ★★★★/$

If you want to experience the excitement, but not the danger, of the area's famous temblors—and knock the socks off your kids in the process—plan on a visit to the oldest scientific institution in the West (founded in 1853) and one of the ten largest natural history museums in the world. The Earthquake exhibit here re-creates the infamous quake of 1906 using a shake table that simulates the ground motion of an earthquake. But never fear, the simulated quake only reaches 5.6 on the Richter scale, and almost everyone exits giggling.

Young geologists will be wowed by the 1,350-pound quartz cluster in the impressive Gem and Mineral Hall; cartoonists-in-the-making will want to check out the permanent Far Side of Science Gallery displaying original *Far Side* cartoons by Gary Larson; and dinosaur lovers (what kid of a certain age isn't?) will want to see the Life Through Time exhibit, which takes visitors on a dinosaur-

DAY TRIP
Marin County: Redwoods and Beaches

10 A.M. Drive over the **Golden Gate Bridge**. Pull over onto the turnoff just before you start across and pose for family photos with this magnificent big orange structure in the background.

10:30 A.M. Take the Alexander Avenue exit off Highway 101 in Sausalito for a visit to the wildly beautiful **Marin Headlands**. For an introduction to this 12,000-acre park, stop at the visitors' center located inside Fort Barry's old chapel. As you leave, follow *McCullough Road east to Conzelman Road*, which leads past some of the old bunkers and gun batteries from the area's military past. Stop for some bird-watching at **Hawk Hill** at *Battery 129*. More than 25,000 hawks and other raptors migrate over this area each year. Farther on, several twists in the road offer magnificent views of the Golden Gate Bridge, and behind it, San Francisco. A photo taken here makes the subjects look as if they are standing on the edge of the earth.

11:30 A.M. Follow scenic Highway 1 to **Muir Woods National Monument**. The paved half-mile loop Main Trail through this magnifi-

studded 3.5 billion-year journey through life on Earth.

The Steinhart Aquarium is bound to be a hit with all ages. In addition to hundreds of fish tanks, the aquarium features a popular black-footed penguin environment, a tropical shark habitat, and "The Swamp," home to alligators, turtles, and snakes. Kids can touch and hold live sea animals such as sea stars and urchins at the California tide pool exhibit, and the doughnut-shaped 100,000-gallon Fish Roundabout tank gives everyone the amusing experience of being on the inside while the fish are on the outside.

Older kids will appreciate the show *What's Up*, at noon on Saturdays and Sundays (additional $1.25 for kids, $2.50 for adults) at the Morrison Planetarium. Tickets for planetarium shows can be purchased in advance and at the academy's front entrance a half hour before show time (cash only). *In Golden Gate Park, San Francisco; (415) 750-7145; Planetarium (415) 750-7141; www.calacademy.org*

MUST-SEE FamilyFun MUST-SEE Exploratorium ★★★★/$

Described as "a mad scientist's penny arcade, a scientific fun house, and an experimental laboratory all rolled into one," this museum explains scientific and natural phenomena through a large

---

cent virgin redwood forest is easy for everyone and has interpretive exhibits. Seven other unpaved, more challenging, trails lead away from the crowds. At the visitors' center you can borrow Junior Ranger Discovery packs full of tools that will assist you in teaching your children about the park. Remember to bring along warm jackets, as this dense forest is usually damp, foggy, and cold. Picnicking is not permitted, but inexpensive food service is available. Have a quick lunch here.

1:30 P.M. Continue on winding Highway 1 to **Stinson Beach Park**. This magnificent sandy stretch offers a little taste of the Southern California beach scene. Conditions often permit swimming here, though the water is cold and usually lifeguards are on duty only in summer. If the day is cool, take a long walk along the beach. The tiny town of Stinson Beach has several shops that are fun to browse in.

4:30 P.M. Backtrack along Highway 1, stopping in the artsy-craftsy town of **Sausalito**. Look around town for a while, and then have dinner at Margaritaville, where Mom and Dad can indulge in fruit margaritas and burritos and kids can eat tacos.

7 P.M. Head back across the Golden Gate Bridge to San Francisco.

collection of fun hands-on exhibits. Located inside the cavernous Palace of Fine Arts, which dates back to 1915 and is said to be the world's largest artificial ruin, the very modern Exploratorium was described by *Scientific American* as the best science museum in the world when it opened in 1969. Kids 5 and up have the most fun here. They can take a dizzying ride on a Momentum Machine, step through a miniature tornado, and encase themselves in bubbles. Teenage "Explainers," who love to do just that, wander the premises ready to help with answers when parents get stuck. Reservations are required for the Tactile Dome, a set of 13 sensory chambers that you make your way through in complete darkness, with only your sense of touch for guidance. (Older kids love it, but skip it if you have anyone under 7.) Plan ahead for a picnic outside by the picturesque reflecting pond populated with ducks and swans. *3601 Lyon St., in the Marina, San Francisco; (415) 561-0360; www. exploratorium.edu*

Roughly **two billion vehicles** have crossed the Golden Gate Bridge since it opened in 1937.

Fort Point National Historic Site
★★/Free

Some kids love forts, and this is the only Civil War–era one on the West Coast. Located directly under the south anchorage of the Golden Gate Bridge, it was built between 1853 and 1861 to guard San Francisco from sea attack. School-age history buffs will enjoy the museum, which houses Civil War guns, swords, uniforms, and photographs. A demonstration of cannon loading and firing is held daily at noon. Tours and videos about both the bridges and the fort are also offered. The big booms are exhilarating for some kids, scary for others. *Take Lincoln Blvd. to Long Ave. and turn left; at the bottom follow the road along the water to the fort, San Francisco; (415) 556-1693; www.nps.gov.fopo/*

Historic Houses
★★/$

As you drive around San Francisco, keep your eyes peeled for the many beautiful turn-of-the-century Victorian houses. In the area around Alamo Square at Hayes and Steiner streets, you can see many "painted ladies"—as the more colorful ones are called. The 700 block of Steiner, nicknamed "postcard row," is packed with Queen Anne Victorians. Another good viewing area is along the Golden Gate Park Panhandle, particularly on the Fell Street side. Fans of the movie *Mrs. Doubtfire* can check out the house used in exterior scenes. It's in the Pacific Heights neighborhood at 2640 Steiner Street. Interior scenes were filmed in a studio, so don't peek in the windows!

If you'd like to actually tour one of these beauties, visit the Haas-Lilienthal House. This mansion survived the infamous 1906 earthquake and fire relatively unscathed. Most of the furnishings are original to the house. The kids will be especially fascinated by the dollhouse in the second-floor nursery. *2007 Franklin St., Pacific Heights, San Francisco; (415) 441-3004.*

Randall Museum
★★/Free
Located below Buena Vista Heights, this small, admission-free children's museum offers few bells and whistles but lots of smile-getters for kids from 3 to 12. An indoor Animal Room is inhabited by uncaged but tethered hawks and owls and other small, accessible animals. Kids can get up close and personal with the

creatures, most of which are recovering from injuries inflicted in the wild. A highlight is the Touching Pen, where children can pat and hold domesticated animals such as rabbits, chickens, and ducks. Among the few exhibits is an earthquake display with a replica of a 1906 refugee shack and an operating seismograph. Nature walks and children's science and arts-and-crafts classes are scheduled regularly. *199 Museum Way, San Francisco; (415) 554-9600;* www.randallmuseum.org

Rooftop at Yerba Buena Gardens
★★★/Free-$
The kids will really love this one. All of the attractions in this new entertainment complex situated atop the Moscone Convention Center are designed for young people to learn and have fun. Expansive lawns, fountains, a maze, and play circle invite investigation. At the interactive Zeum, a hands-on center designed for children ages 8 through 18, your kids can learn how to create videos and see filmed performances in a state-of-the-art theater. They'll also learn about animation as art. More rooftop offerings include an ice-skating center, a 12-lane bowling center, and a beautifully restored, historic 1906 Looff carousel with 62 hand-carved animals twirling inside a glass enclosure (fees). *Fourth St. and Howard St., South of Market, San Francisco; (415) 777-2800;* www.zeum.org

FLOATING MUSEUMS

THE COLLECTION of historic ships berthed along the San Francisco waterfront is the largest (by weight) in the world. Exploring these vessels is sure to spark the imaginations of kids ages 4 and up.

Hyde Street Pier ★★★★/$

Of the historic vessels moored here, some can be boarded and toured. The *Balclutha*, a 301-foot steel-hulled Victorian merchant ship that carried coal as well as whiskey, wool, and rice around Cape Horn to San Francisco, is the last of the Cape Horn fleet. The *Eureka*, a double-ended, wooden-hulled ferry, was built in nearby Tiburon in 1890 to carry railroad cars and passengers across the bay. Later she became the world's largest commuter ferry, holding 2,300 people plus 120 automobiles. Her four-story "walking beam" steam engine is the only such engine still afloat in the United States. A model demonstrates how it operates, and a ranger-guided tour through the engine room is sometimes available. The *C. A. Thayer*, a three-masted lumber schooner, was once part of a fleet of 900 ships that carried lumber from the north coast forests to California ports. She was the very last commercial sailing ship in use on the West Coast. Kids love climbing into her clammy wooden hold to see the crew's bunk room and the captain's lushly furnished cabin with its gilded canary cage. Fun chantey "sings" designed especially for children are held in her cozy hold on the second Saturday of every month from 3 to 3:45 P.M. On the first Saturday of every month are Chantey Sings for the whole family at 8 P.M. Reservations are required for the family sings. More ships are moored at the pier but are not open for boarding. *2905 Hyde St., Fisherman's Wharf, San Francisco; (415) 561-7100; chantey sings: (415) 556-6435;* www.nps.gov/fafr

San Francisco Maritime National Historical Park Maritime Museum
★★★/Free

Appropriately resembling a ship, this "merry time" museum displays parts of old ships and elaborately carved and painted figureheads. Kids and adults alike will be awed by the exquisitely detailed ship models. *At*

the foot of Polk St., across from Ghirardelli Square, Fisherman's Wharf, San Francisco; (415) 561-7100; www.maritime.org

S.S. Jeremiah O'Brien
★★★★/$

Not far away from Hyde Street Pier, this massive 441-foot gem is the last unaltered Liberty Ship from World War II that is still in operating condition. It's now a National Monument. Visitors have access to almost the entire ship, including sleeping quarters, captain's quarters, wheel house, and guns, as well as the catwalks in the eerie three-story engine room. Her triple expansion steam engine is operated on select weekends. *Berthed at Pier 45, Fisherman's Wharf, San Francisco; (415) 544-0100;* www.ssjeremiahobrien.com

USS Pampanito ★★★★/$

Just next door to the *O'Brien*, this 312-foot-long World War II submarine is credited with sinking six Japanese ships and rescuing a group of British and Australian POWs. As you walk through the cramped belly of the sub, an audio narrative helps you imagine what it must have been like for men to be cooped up in this small space for days at a time. Family members with claustrophobia will want to skip this one. *Berthed at Pier 45, Fisherman's Wharf, San Francisco; (415) 775-1943;* www.maritime.org

San Francisco Museum of Modern Art ★★/$

Children, even very young ones, seem to have a natural affinity for modern art. Unencumbered by conventional expectations, they respond to the colors, shapes, and images with open curiosity and delight. If possible, plan your visit to coincide with the Family Sundays program, held on the third Sunday of each month from noon to 3. The program features activities such as drawing, painting, collage, and printmaking—that are included in the price of admission. Don't miss the museum gift shop; the casual Caffe Museo serves tasty light meals and really yummy chocolate chunk cookies. *151 Third St., South of Market, San Francisco; (415) 357-4000;* www.sfmoma.org

Young Performers Theatre
★★★★/$

A combination of professional adult performers and young actors-in-training, this company employs imaginative stage settings and costumes. The weekend matinee performances are fast-moving and usually short as well, making them a good introduction to theater for children ages 4 through 10. Past productions have included *Charlie and the Chocolate Factory, Wind in the Willows,* and *The Secret Garden. Corner of Buchanan and Marina Blvd., Fort Mason Center/Bldg. C, San Francisco; (415) 346-5550.*

JUST FOR FUN

Angel Island State Park
★★/Free

The largest of the islands in the bay is a good place to do some walking or hiking and let the kids run around unrestrained, all the while enjoying the natural beauty of San Francisco Bay. After a scenic, kid-pleasing ferry ride over to the island, you'll disembark at Ayala Cove where there are picnic tables and a pleasant little beach for sunbathing. (There's no swimming here, as the water is sometimes dirty.) Pack along a picnic lunch or buy a snack at the island's small cafe. Once a holding camp for quarantined immigrants, this has also been a prisoner-of-war processing facility and a missile defense base. Except for Park Service vehicles, cars are not permitted on the island, but you can bring bikes over on the ferry or rent them onsite. Marked hiking and biking trails completely circle the mostly flat perimeter of the island. One 3.2-mile loop trail leads from the cove to the top of 781-foot-high Mount Livermore, offering a 360-degree view. Kids ages 6 and older can probably manage the hike on their own, but if you don't bring a stroller you'd better plan on toting younger children at least part of the way. If your kids are at least 6, consider a kayak tour. It's a great way to get up close and personal with the bay waters and some of their occupants. Arrange tours through Sea Trek Ocean Kayaking Center *(415/488-1000)*. A sight-seeing tram often runs as well, circling the island via the five-mile-long perimeter road. For a real back-to-nature experience, camping in primitive campsites can be arranged. Fee for ferry and tram. *Departures from Pier 41, Fisherman's Wharf, San Francisco; Ferry Service: (415) 773-1188; Park information: (415) 435-1915;* www.angelisland.com

Bay Boat Tours ★★/$-$$

Young fans of the *Guinness Book of World Records* will love this relaxing narrated cruise, which goes under the world's most beautiful bridge—the Golden Gate—and the world's longest bridge—the 8¼-mile-long San Francisco/Oakland Bay Bridge. The boat also passes close to Alcatraz Island. *Departures from Pier 39, Fisherman's Wharf, San Francisco; (415) 773-1188; reservations, (415) 705-5555;* www.blueandgoldfleet.com/bcruises.htm

Beaches: Aquatic Park and Baker Beach ★★★/Free

Though by now you know that San Francisco is not the place to come to go to the beach (Los Angeles is *that* California), the city does have a few good spots for soaking up rays. But make sure everyone understands ahead of time that the ocean surf is too cold and too dangerous for swimming—you don't want disappointed water babies. Across from Ghirardelli Square, Aquatic Park has great views of the bay and is a good spot for children to wade. Out by the Presidio, off Lincoln Boulevard near 25th Avenue, Baker Beach is prime for sunning and strolling and offers spectacular views of the Golden Gate Bridge.

Coit Tower ★/$

Sitting atop fashionable Telegraph Hill, this 210-foot-tall tower (that's almost 18 stories) offers a magnificent 360-degree view (unless you're afraid of heights and have to keep your eyes closed the entire time). You'll see the landmark Golden Gate Bridge as well as the Bay Bridge leading to Oakland and Berkeley; on a really clear day, perhaps even a few more local spans. Colorful murals on the ground floor depict area activities during the Depression. The entrance fee includes a ride to the top on an old-fashioned, attendant-operated elevator. (Some kids find this more interesting than the views.) **NOTE:** Parking is extremely limited in this area. *At top of Lombard St., in North Beach, San Francisco; (415) 362-0808.*

 ### Crookedest Street in the World
★★★★/Free

Going one way downhill, this famous curvy, bumpy street has eight tight turns and is a little like a

Cable Cars– History on Track

Designated the country's first moving National Historic Landmark in 1964, San Francisco's cable cars have carried people up the city's steep hills since 1873. Before this now-beloved mode of transportation was developed by Andrew Hallidie, horses had to pull carts up these daunting hills. Sadly, many died in the process. Now 26 cable cars operate on the two Powell Street routes and 11 operate on the California Street run.

For the most scenic and thrilling ride, catch a **Powell-Hyde cable car** at the turnaround located at the base of Powell Street and ride it up and over the hills all the way to Aquatic Park at Fisherman's Wharf. This line goes up and down the steepest hills and affords the most breathtaking views; it ends at Bay Street, a few blocks from Fisherman's Wharf.

The less used **California Street line** begins at Market Street and runs along California Street, passing Chinatown and then climbing over Nob Hill, ending at Van Ness Avenue.

Ticket machines are provided at turnarounds, but you can also board at designated stops along the routes and pay the conductor. Though riders enjoy hanging off the edge of the cable cars, this is dangerous and ill-advised. The safest place for small kids is inside the cab with the gripman. *For cable car schedule and information, call (415) 673-6864.*

brick-paved roller coaster. Kids love the thrill of it, as do most adults. If you're driving, try not to be distracted by the magnificent view. Get here by driving up the steep incline on the west side of Lombard Street, or, for an easier time of it, drive up from the south side of Hyde Street. *Lombard St. between Hyde and Leavenworth Sts., San Francisco.*

If you still need more excitement, try descending and ascending some of the city's other steep streets: Filbert Street between Hyde and Leavenworth streets (with a 31.5 percent grade), *22nd Street between Church and Vicksburg* streets (with a 31.5 percent grade), and *Jones Street between Union and Filbert streets* (with a 29 percent grade). About halfway down, be sure to shout, "Oh, no! My brakes aren't working!"—it's guaranteed to elicit squeals from the backseat.

The Explorers' Club ★/$-$$$

This company offers fun-filled custom-designed tours designed especially for children and families. The tours are geared to your family's interests and available time (most last five to seven hours). They give you a chance to relax with the kids while the tour guide takes care of the planning and parking. One preset itinerary includes Muir Woods and Sausalito, another focuses on the tide pools at Fitzgerald Marine Reserve down Highway 1. You can also let the kids go on an adventure of their own, sans parents, while you take in some sights that would bore them silly. Each trip is led by Susan Edwards, an educator for 25 years. The minimum age for the kids-only excursions is generally 6, although 4- or 5-year-olds are sometimes allowed to tag along with older siblings. *(415) 566-7014;* www.eckidsclub.com

Fleet Week ★★★★/Free

It's worth some effort to arrange to be in town for this annual birthday party for the Navy, usually held in mid-October. In the past, the festivities have included demonstrations of high-speed-boat maneuvering, parachute drops, and a flyby of World War II vintage aircraft. Most kids

---

Foil Boredom

This one is so simple you won't believe it. Just buy a roll of aluminum foil (make sure to remove the saw on the box), and toss it into the backseat. Although foil is hardly a traditional sculpture material, it works. In the hands of your kids, aluminum foil can be turned into snakes, crowns, masks, and more. (You might need to switch activities when it turns into a bat and balls.)

Angela de la Rocha, Sterling, Virginia

WINE COUNTRY WITHOUT WHINING

I T'S HARD TO IMAGINE A VISIT to Northern California without a jaunt into the quiet, low-key Sonoma Wine Country, an easy hour's drive north of San Francisco. But you need to approach such an excursion thoughtfully if you have young children in tow. Most wineries don't have much to offer young visitors, and while older kids might be interested in the wine-making process, little ones may get restless during winery tours. (Note, too, that strollers are not usually allowed.)

If you do decide to take your tots on a wine tour, you'll want to bring snacks, toys, books, or other distractions. A better plan might be for parents to take turns. At one winery, one parent can explore the grounds or have a picnic with the children while the other goes on a tour. Mom and Dad then switch places at the next winery. Another option is to visit a winery that offers a self-guided tour so you can go at your own (or your child's) pace. Or just skip the tours altogether—most wineries don't require them before tastings.

To make tastings more fun for your future oenophiles, bring along some plastic wineglasses and a bottle of grape juice so they can "taste," too. Many wineries have picnic areas; for an enjoyable excursion for young and old, stock up on picnic supplies (see page 57); tour a winery and attend a tasting, then purchase a bottle of wine to drink with your alfresco lunch. Afterward, check out some of these other family-friendly spots in Sonoma.

Buena Vista Winery
★★★★/Free
Founded in 1857, this is California's oldest winery. Park among the grapevines and enjoy the short, pleasant walk to the winery, where you can take a self-guided tour. After tasting wines in the welcoming old Press House (don't miss the nutty cream sherry, available only here), select a bottle for your picnic. Eat your lunch at one of the outside tables, all shaded by stately old eucalyptus trees growing on the banks of a tiny brook. Your kids might not remember the winery itself, but they'll remember the picnic. *18000 Old Winery Rd., Sonoma; (707) 938-1266; (800) 926-1266; www.bue navista winery.com*

General Vallejo's Home
★★★/$
About a half mile west of Sonoma Plaza, this house was the residence
continued on the next page

of the founder of Sonoma. A classic two-story Victorian Gothic with the original furnishings, it stands at the end of a long, tree-shaded lane. Docent-led tours are offered on Friday, Saturday, and Sunday at 2 P.M.; at other times you can look around on your own. Even if your young children aren't interested in old houses, they'll like the old-fashioned toys, including a dollhouse and dolls, and the pre-TV modes of entertainment including a chess set and musical instruments. The grounds feature shaded picnic tables and a giant prickly-pear cactus garden. *W. Third St. and W. Spain St., Sonoma; (707) 938-9559;* http://www. parks.sonoma.net/sonoma.html

Sonoma Plaza
★★★★/Free

The largest town square in the state was designed by General Mariano Guadalupe Vallejo in 1834 for troop maneuvers. Now it's basically an old-fashioned park with a playground, a tiny duck pond, and picnic tables. http://www.parks.sonoma. net/sonoma.html

Sonoma State
Historic Park ★★★★/Free

Here's another stop for history buffs young and old. This extensive park preserves structures dating from the early 1800s, when General Vallejo was Mexico's administrator of Northern California. The two-story,

whitewashed adobe barracks, which once housed Vallejo's soldiers, now contains historical exhibits. Also in the park is the re-created Mission San Francisco Solano, founded in 1823 and the most northerly and last in the chain of California missions. *Off the plaza along Spain St., Sonoma; (707) 938-1519;* www.parks.ca.gov

Sonoma Traintown Railroad
★★★★/$

Your kids will barely be able to contain their excitement as they board the miniature steam train here (a diesel engine is used on weekdays). During the 20-minute ride, the train winds across ten acres, passing through forests and tunnels and crossing both a 70-foot double truss bridge and a 50-foot steel girder bridge. During a ten-minute stop at a miniature 1800s mining town, where the train takes on water, you can take the kids for a quick visit to the petting zoo inhabited by sheep, goats, ducks, and llamas. Back at the station, there's an antique merry-go-round, full-size Ferris wheel, snack bar, and picnic area. A stop here can serve as a reward for good winery behavior; make it your final Sonoma destination. It's open daily in summer, Friday through Sunday the rest of the year. *20264 Broadway, Sonoma; (707) 938-3912;* www.train town.com

Viansa Winery
★★★/$

Another winery that is quite family-friendly (they even hand out balloons), this one is built on top of a hill commanding magnificent views of the area. Guided tours are given every day. Noteworthy wines produced here include the Barbera Blanc, a light blush wine perfect for picnics and sold only at the winery, and the Cabernet Sauvignons. The state-of-the-art tasting room features a magnificent "wall of wines" behind the two tasting bars.

This is a one-stop winery: you can taste and buy wine, do your picnic shopping, and enjoy your purchases right here. A magnificent Italian Marketplace food hall, designed after the mercato in Lucca, Italy, offers extraordinary food selections. The kitchen staff prepares wonderful things for picnics. The older members of the family will appreciate the country pâté, torta rustica, panini (Italian sandwiches), and tiramisu; little ones will love the focaccia and triple-chocolate chunk cookies. The Tuscan Grill has a kids menu featuring hot dogs and hamburgers. On nice days, you can picnic at one of a bevy of tables on a knoll with a panoramic view of the Sonoma and Napa valleys. On cooler days, sit at the tables inside. If you're here January through March, you can view a large variety of southward migrating birds on the expansive Viansa wetlands. *25200 Arnold Dr./Hwy. 121, five miles south of Sonoma center; (800) 995-4740; (707) 935-4700;* www.viansa.com

Where to Buy Picnic Provisions

Cucina Viansa ★★★/$

Located on the town square, this simple self-service deli operated by the Viansa Winery dispenses sumptuous sandwiches and salads for takeout or to eat on the premises. Desserts include a tasty and good-for-you (don't tell your kids) housemade fig bar. Call ahead for a ready-to-go boxed lunch. Free wine tasting is available with purchase, otherwise it's $1. *400 First St. E., Sonoma; (707) 935-5656;* www.viansa.com

Sonoma Cheese Factory
★★★★/$

Also on the plaza, this crowded shop stocks hundreds of cheeses (including their famous varieties of Sonoma Jack, made from old family recipes). There are also cold cuts, salads, and marvelous marinated artichoke hearts. Sandwiches are made to order, so everyone can have their favorite, and cheese samples are yours for the asking. A few tables are available inside, with more outside on a shaded patio. Kids love to watch the cheese factory in action through large windows in the back.

and adults find it hard to stay seated when the Blue Angels, the Navy's precision flight demonstration team, perform the screaming, breathtaking culmination of their show, which serves as the festivities' finale. As part of the celebration, all Navy ships moored at the piers are usually opened for public visits. It's hard to believe, but this fabulous party is free. *Held along the waterfront, the Marina, San Francisco; (805) 684-0155;* www.airshownetwork.com

Golden Gate Bridge
FamilyFun ★★★★/$

You should probably tell the kids ahead of time: the bridge is not a shiny metallic gold but a dull red-orange known officially as International Orange, which makes it visible in dense fog. But that doesn't mean it's not spectacular. One of San Francisco's most famous sights, this "bridge that couldn't be built" is the longest suspension bridge in the world and its 746-foot-high towers are the tallest ever built.

FamilyFun SNACK

Good for You

Make some rocket fuel for your kids with a mix of dried apples, pineapples, cranberries, mangoes, and cherries, as well as banana chips and raisins. (1 cup of this will fulfill 2 of the recommended 5 minimum daily servings of fruits and vegetables.)

Crossing it by car, foot, or bicycle is a must; views are breathtaking. (Remember the sweaters—it's breezy up there!) The round-trip is about two miles and it's not impossible to fall over the side, so an auto tour is probably the best choice if you're traveling with small children. Here's something that will impress the troops: bungee-jumping is said to have originated here in 1979. *Rte. 1/I-101, San Francisco.*

Golden Gate Park
FamilyFun ★★★★/Free

Once no more than sand dunes, this is now one of the world's great metropolitan parks, as well as the largest man-made park in the world. Encompassing 1,017 acres, it is nearly 200 acres larger than Manhattan's Central Park, after which is was patterned. The Children's Playground, constructed in 1887, was the very first playground in a U.S. public park. Now equipped with creative modern play structures, it still delights kids. Adjacent to the playground, an antique carousel makes its rounds within a protective hippodrome enclosure. Built in 1914 by Herschel Spillman, it has 62 beautifully painted, hand-carved animals, and its original Gebruder band organ still grinds out lively tunes. On Sundays, the main road through the park is closed to automobiles, and car traffic is replaced with heavy bike, skate, and pedestrian traffic.

You can join the crowd by renting skates or bikes at shops on Stanyan Street. And there's more: you can also ride a horse here, rent a paddleboat, and sip tea in the Japanese Tea Garden, where the fortune cookie was introduced to America in 1914. And don't miss the park's unsung small herd of honest-to-goodness buffalo. *Bounded by Fulton St., Stanyan St., Lincoln Way, and the Great Hwy., San Francisco; (415) 831-2700.*

MUST-SEE Metreon
FamilyFun ★★★★/Free-$$

MUST-SEE Fun is the focus at this new $85-million entertainment complex. The little ones will shriek as Maurice Sendak's *Where the Wild Things Are* comes to life in a fantasy play space. The Wild Things store sells enticing items drawn from the pages of this and other Sendak books, and family fare is available at In The Night Kitchen, a whimsical restaurant based on the Sendak story of the same title. Action Theater is a new Japanese animation theater featuring animated cartoons in Japanese (fun to watch, and with cartoons, language isn't such a great barrier). Alongside the theater is a shop full of comic books and action figures. Preteens will love the fast-paced action of the Portal One, which features interactive games. There's a 15-screen movie complex, including an IMAX screen, Microsoft's PlayStation store, and

eight restaurants and a Starbucks. **NOTE:** You may want to give your kids a spending limit before you arrive. *101 Fourth St., South of Market, Yerba Buena, San Francisco; (415) 369-6000;* www.metreon.com

Pier 39 ★★★★/Free-$$

Just behind Walt Disney World and Disneyland in terms of the number of visitors it attracts each year, this popular spot offers myriad diversions, in addition to more than 110 stores and 11 restaurants.

There's no doubt that kids from toddler to teen will be entertained. Street performers go through their routines daily. Bumper cars and a vast video games arcade are inside an entertainment center at the pier entrance, as is The *Great San Francisco Adventure*—an enjoyable 30-minute motion picture that shows off some of the city's best locations. At the far end of the pier is a contemporary two-tiered San Francisco Carousel and the decidedly less genteel Turbo Ride—a simulated thrill ride that synchronizes hydraulically powered seats to the action on a giant movie screen. Sea lions have taken up permanent residence on the west side of the pier and can be seen there basking, barking, and belching on their floating docks. The newest attraction here is Aquarium of the Bay, which uses moving sidewalks to transport visitors through transparent acrylic tunnels for a diver's-eye view of the

59

The Skinny on Seals

California sea lions and harbor seals are just two animals that inhabit San Francisco Bay. How can you tell them apart? Harbor seals tend to be gray with dark blotches, while California sea lions are brown or tan in color. If you're having trouble determining the animal's coloring, try to watch it move on land. Sea lions are much more agile and can support themselves on their front flippers. The harbor seal cannot push itself up, so it drags itself on its belly.

fish, sharks, and other sea life residing there. Among the pier's shops are one that specializes in puppets, another in chocolate, and another in kites. Yet others specialize in hats and cat-related items. *Beach St., Fisherman's Wharf, San Francisco; (415) 705-5500;* www.pier39.com

San Francisco Fire Engine Tours & Adventures
★★★/$-$$

A jolly husband-and-wife team operates this happy business driving sightseers over the Golden Gate Bridge in their awesome, bright red 1955 Mack fire engine. This exhilarating 75-minute adventure can be chilly in the open-air truck, but authentic firefighter jackets are available for kids to bundle up in. An added bonus is the fact that children are taught a bit about fire safety during the tour through original sing-along songs. Afterward, the tour guides go back to their home, which was originally a vintage firehouse. *Beach St., at The Cannery, Fisherman's Wharf, San Francisco; (415) 333-7077.*

San Francisco Zoo ★★★★/$

A ride on the Safari Tram gives a quick 20-minute introduction to the layout of this scenic zoo. Of special note are the half-acre Gorilla World, which is one of the world's largest gorilla habitats, and the Primate Discovery Center, with its 15 species of monkeys and gorillas. Another highlight is the unusual nocturnal exhibit, where you'll get to see animals that are usually active only when it is dark. The zoo's collection of extremely endangered snow leopards is one of the most successful captive breeding groups in the world, and the lions and tigers are particularly interesting to visit when they are fed each afternoon from 2 to 3 (except on Monday, when they fast). Your kids will love the separate Children's Zoo. The ones who think the petting area, with its gentle sheep and goats, is for babies will love the Insect Zoo, populated with the likes of six- to eight-inch-long walking sticks and giant Madagascar hissing cockroaches. Just outside the Children's Zoo is a large playground and an antique carousel built in 1921 by the William Dentzel Carving Company. *1 Zoo Rd., at 45th Ave., in the Sunset, San Francisco; (415) 753-7080;* www.sfzoo.org

BUNKING DOWN

The American Property Exchange ★★★★/$$-$$$

If your family would like to have plenty of space to spread out, consider renting an actual apartment or home. You can live like a native in an interesting residential area, maybe in a cottage with a garden and a view of the Golden Gate Bridge, or in a penthouse with the cityscape spread out below you. You can request a property with specific amenities such as a pool, hot tub, sauna, fitness center, or tennis courts. Some places even have free parking. According to this office, "We have it all. Just call." *San Francisco; (800) 747-7784; (415) 447-2000;* www.amsires.com

Best Western Tuscan Inn at Fisherman's Wharf ★★★★/$$-$$$$

This comfortable, pleasantly appointed 221-room hotel is said to be popular with filmmakers. Children under 18 stay free in their parents' room, and pets are welcome. The appealing hotel restaurant, Cafe Pescatore, has windows that open to the sidewalk in warm weather and a menu of fresh fish, pastas, and pizza baked in a wood-burning oven. It is equipped with high chairs and booster seats and has a children's menu. *425 North Point St., Fisherman's Wharf, San Francisco; (800) 648-4626; (415) 561-1100;* www.tuscaninn.com

Dockside Boat & Bed ★★★★/$$$-$$$$

Imagine yourself a pirate or a sea captain or a wealthy Internet mogul when you spend the night on a luxury yacht anchored near Fisherman's Wharf. There are about a dozen vessels, all with separate staterooms; some have several and are particularly comfortable for families. Each is also equipped with a VCR and galley, and a continental breakfast is included in the rate. These accommodations are not recommended for families with small children (who wants to worry about their falling overboard?). *Pier 39, Fisherman's Wharf, San Francisco; (800) 436-2574; (415) 392-5526;* www.boatandbed.com

Fairmont Hotel ★★★★/$$$$

Kids and adults alike are impressed by this elegant, and expensive, land-

mark hotel sitting atop one of San Francisco's highest hills. You'll feel positively tiny in the gargantuan lobby filled with marble columns and a valuable art collection. Accommodations in this 596-room hotel are spacious, and the cable cars, which stop in front of the hotel, can be heard from some. Be sure to stop in at the Tonga Room and Hurricane Bar for an exotic drink (or Shirley Temple). Adding to the tiki-hut atmosphere is a simulated tropical rainstorm that occurs every 40 minutes. (Watch the kids' eyes grow wide as the indoor storm begins.) Even if you don't dine in the upscale Crown Room, you'll want to ride the famous glass elevators up to see the breathtaking views. (Some family members will want to ride up and down all night!) *950 Mason St., Nob Hill, San Francisco; (800) 527-4727; (415) 772-5000;* www.Fairmont.com

Fisherman's Wharf Hostel
★★★/$

Though the location isn't convenient, this hostel offers inexpensive accommodations in an exceptional setting. Inside Fort Mason, a goodly walk from the Fisherman's Wharf action, it is in a former Civil War barracks situated on a peaceful knoll with a magnificent view of the bay. The largest (150 beds) and busiest hostel in the country, it has private rooms that are large enough for families; reservations are advised. For more on hostels, see "Hosteling for Families" on page 215. *Bay St., Bldg. 240, San Francisco; (415) 771-7277; (800) 909-4776;* www.norcalhos tels.org

Holiday Inn Fisherman's Wharf
★★★/$$-$$$

Families who stay in this 580-room hotel appreciate the central loca-

---

Seals, Seals, Everywhere

10 A.M. Cross the Golden Gate Bridge and take the Alexander Avenue exit *off Highway 101 in Sausalito.* Drive through the Marin Headlands to the **Marine Mammal Center** *(415/289-SEAL),* one of the largest wild animal hospitals in the world. Injured, sick, and orphaned seals, dolphins, porpoises, and whales are brought here to be nursed back to health by volunteers. When recov-

ered, they are released back into their natural habitat. Docent-led tours are available on weekends, self-guided tours during the week.

11:30 A.M. Drive back across the Golden Gate Bridge to Pier 39 in San Francisco. Sea lions have taken up permanent residence on the west side of the pier and can be seen there basking, barking, and belching on their floating docks. Have lunch in the casual **Bay View Cafe,** where you can get a simple meal of soup, salad,

tion, the heated pool, and the fact that children under 19 stay free in their parents' room. There are two restaurants on the premises, including a family-friendly Denny's, and—another plus—a coin-operated laundry. *1300 Columbus Ave., Fisherman's Wharf, San Francisco; (800) HOLIDAY; (415) 771-9000; www.hiwharf.com*

Hotel Diva
★★★/$$$-$$$$

Built in 1913, this 111-room hotel features cutting-edge contemporary design that tickles the fancy of guests young and old. The room decor calls to mind a 1920s ocean liner, with beds featuring sculptured steel headboards and sumptuous linens, buffed steel and maple wood furniture, cobalt blue carpeting, and black granite bathrooms. Children under 12 stay free in their parents' room;

the reasonably priced two-room suites are especially comfortable for families and have a wall bed in the living area that kids just love. The entertainment here begins with the exterior window in the lobby, designed to resemble a layer of ice. Movies and music videos are screened continuously on four TVs above the reception desk. A fitness center is available, complimentary continental breakfast is included in the rate, and the hotel restaurant is an airy, pleasant, extremely family-friendly California Pizza Kitchen. *440 Geary St., near Union Square, San Francisco; (800) 553-1900; (415) 885-0200; www.hoteldiva.com*

Hotel Triton
★★★/$$-$$$$

Across the street from the dragon-gate entrance to Chinatown in the heart of San Francisco's French

---

a sandwich, or fresh seafood, also with a great view of the sea lions.

1:30 P.M. Head to **Golden Gate Park** and the **California Academy of Sciences** (see page 46). Among the many exhibits is the notable Wild California hall featuring life-size elephant seal models and a 14,000-gallon aquarium. Also here in the Steinhart Aquarium is a tank populated with harbor seals. Spend some time viewing the many other exhibits in this exciting complex.

4:30 P.M. Drive through the western part of Golden Gate Park to the edge of the Pacific Ocean and the **Cliff House**. Barking sea lions and brown pelicans out on Seal Rocks can usually be seen with just the naked eye or through one of the coin-operated antique telescopes in the viewing area here. After exploring the area, have an early dinner at **Upstairs at the Cliff House** or one of the other restaurants in this historic complex (see page 73).

A Travel Scrapbook

This suitcase-style scrapbook is just right for your child to pack with mementos of his vacation adventures—and it's a cinch to make.

Start with two cardboard report covers. Use one for the suitcase itself and one to cut out two U-shaped handles and two 1$\frac{1}{2}$- by 18-inch straps.

Attach one handle to the front of the suitcase by gluing the ends to the inside of the upper edge. Match up the second handle with the first one and glue it to the back side. Now close the suitcase and glue on the straps. Position the strap tops on the front of the suitcase 1 inch down from the upper edge, then wrap the straps around the back of the suitcase. Finally, fold down the strap ends so that they overlap the tops and attach stick-on Velcro-type fasteners.

For a handy photo pocket, glue a large open envelope to the inner cover, as shown. Then, fill the suitcase with manila folders for storing ticket stubs, brochures, and other souvenirs.

Quarter, this playfully decorated 140-room hotel is sophisticated, casual, amusing, and chic all at the same time. Theme suites are a highlight here: Suites honor Carlos Santana, Jerry Garcia, marine-life artist Wyland (the kids will like this one), and other notables. One suite that is particular fun for families has an in-room hot tub. The less-expensive standard guest rooms are on the small side, but children stay free in their parents' room and the location is prime, just three blocks from Union Square. And if you've forgotten your bath toys, purchase a must-have souvenir rubber ducky inscribed with the hotel logo from the room minibar. In the morning, take breakfast at casual Cafe de la Presse, adjacent to the hotel. *342 Grant Ave., San Francisco; (800) 433-6611; (415) 394-0500;* www.hoteltriton.com

Hyatt Regency San Francisco
★★★/$$$-$$$$

This elegant 17-story, 805-room hotel resembles a pyramid, and every room has a view of either the city or the bay. Young guests love riding the glass elevators that run the height of the hotel's magnificent atrium interior. Kids under 18 stay for free in their parents' room. There are also Family Plans. One end of the California Street line is just outside the front door, so you can usually jump on an empty cable car without even waiting in line. *5 Embarcadero Center, Financial District, San*

Francisco; (800) 233-1234; (415) 788-1234; www.hyatt.com

Hyatt at Fisherman's Wharf
★★★★/$$$-$$$$

Built on the site of a historic marble-works building, this attractive 317-room hotel offers a superior location, a heated pool, a hot tub, a sauna, a fitness center, and (especially handy) washers and dryers on each floor. The recently renovated rooms are slightly oversized, and kids under 18 stay free in their parents' room. A children's room-service and restaurant menu are available, and the restaurant has a games section with a pool table and shuffleboard. *555 North Point St., Fisherman's Wharf, San Francisco; (800) 233-1234; (415) 563-1234;* www.hyatt.com

The Laurel Inn ★★★★/$$-$$$

You'll need a car if you want to stay at this bargain-priced 49-room motel far from the usual tourist haunts in a nice residential area, near Sacramento Street shopping. Rooms are spacious, stylish, and comfortable for families, and many have good city views. Some kitchens are available, and a complimentary continental breakfast is included. Also, you can park your car for *free*—a fabulous perk in this car-crowded city. *444 Presidio Ave., Pacific Heights, San Francisco; (800) 552-8735; (415) 567-8467;* www.thelaurelinn.com

Motel Row

A plethora of moderately priced lodging places line the 20-block corridor *stretching along Lombard Street from Van Ness Avenue to the Presidio. San Francisco. For more information, contact the Convention and Visitors' Bureau at (415) 391-2000.*

Ocean Park Motel ★★/$

Conveniently located near the ocean and just a block from the zoo, this 24-room property dates from the 1930s and was San Francisco's first motel. It still has its original nautical Art Deco–style decor, with some windows shaped like portholes. (The kids can pretend they're aboard a ship.) Rooms are attractive and homey, and several spacious family suites with kitchens are available. Also nice for families are the playground and barbecue area; there are gardens and a hot tub as well. Parking is free, another plus. *2690 46th Ave., the Sunset, San Francisco; (415) 566-7020; fax: (415) 665-8959;* www.oceanparkmotel.citysearch.com

Palace Hotel ★★★★/$$$$

This place, a few blocks from Union Square, will make children feel like real princes and princesses—and their moms and dads feel like kings and queens. Facilities include an indoor pool and hot tub (which most kids adore), plus a sauna and a fitness room. Among the restaurants is the Garden Court, which features Prince and Princess Teas

Sacramento–A Capital Excursion

7:30 A.M. Have breakfast and begin your drive early. Sacramento, the capital of California, is approximately 90 miles northeast of San Francisco via Highway I-80. Allow two hours for the drive.

9:30 A.M. Tour the **California State Capitol Museum** *(10th and L Sts., 916/324-0333)*. Restored to its turn-of-the-century decor, it is quite a showcase and will probably impress school-age kids. When you arrive, ask for a free *Kids' Guide to the California State Capitol,* which children and their parents can read together. Free tickets can be picked up in the basement a half hour before each one-hour general tour, which often takes kids to see the "birthday cake" ceiling in the Archives Room. Alternatively, you can take a self-guided tour, or just view the proceedings in the Senate and Assembly chambers without taking the tour. If the timing is right, in summer you can take the 10:30 guided tour of the surrounding park, which is the largest arboretum west of the Mississippi and home to more than 300 varieties of trees and flowers from all over the world. Otherwise, spend some time walking through the park on your own. The circular California Vietnam Veteran's Memorial is located by the

rose garden at the park's east end. It is similar to the memorial in Washington, D.C., with names (far too many) etched in the shiny black granite panels. A visit is sobering but can also be meaningful and memorable for older children, particularly if someone they know served in Vietnam.

11 A.M. Established in 1940, the **California State Indian Museum** *(2618 K St. at 26th St.; 916/324-0971)* has especially interesting samples of bark clothing and a permanent basket collection featuring colorful Pomo feather baskets. Nearby, **Sutter's Fort State Historic Park** *(2701 L St./27th St.; 916/445-4422)* is a reconstruction of the settlement founded here in 1839 by Captain John A. Sutter. Kids interested in the olden days will be intrigued by the 19th-century carpenter, cooper, and blacksmith shops as well as the prison and living quarters. A self-guided audio tour is included in the admission fee.

12:30 P.M. Drive to **Old Sacramento**, famous as the western terminus for both the Pony Express and the country's first long-distance telegraph. It was also where the country's first transcontinental railroad started. It is now a 28-acre living history museum of the Old West, said to be the largest historic preservation project in the West. The vintage buildings, wooden walkways, and cobblestone streets recall the period from 1850 to 1880. For a quick lunch, family-friendly choices include **Buffalo Bob's Ice Cream Saloon** *(110 K St.; 916/442-1105),* and funky **Fanny Ann's Saloon** *(1023 2nd St.; 916/441-0505),* which serves hamburgers, varieties of nine-inch hot dogs, and curly French fries.

1:30 P.M. Walk over to the **California State Railroad Museum** *(111 I St. at 2nd St.; 916/445-6645),* the largest interpretive railroad museum in North America. You'll see 21 beautifully restored, full-size railroad locomotives and cars dating from the 1860s through the 1960s. There are train rides offered, and also a large collection of toy trains. www.esrmf.org

2:30 P.M. Continue on to the **Central Pacific Passenger Depot** *(930 Front St.)* about a block away, where nine more locomotives and cars are displayed. The entrance fee for the California State Railroad Museum includes admission here.

3 P.M. Drive to the **Governor's Mansion State Historic Park** *(1526 H St. at 16th St.; 916/323-3047)* for one of the last tours of the day (they stop at 4). This 1877, 30-room Victorian mansion was home to 13

governors and their families and remains just as it was when vacated by Governor Ronald Reagan, its last tenant. Kids 4 and older will love seeing the claw-footed tub's painted toenails, done by Kathleen Brown when her father, Pat, was governor. They'll also be amused to learn that kids who lived in the mansion got to slide down the banisters and roller-skate in the basement. The whole family will enjoy conjuring up the image of Governor Pat Brown running across the street in his bathrobe to use the pool at the Clarion Hotel (it was the Mansion Inn then); www.governorsmansion @infostations.com

4:30 P.M. For dinner, head down to the river to **Chevy's** *(1369 Garden Hwy., at Riverside Marina, north of Old Sacramento; 916/649-0390)* for Tex-Mex food at waterside tables. Call for directions—it's easy to get lost, but well worth finding. Or check out one of the other popular restaurants in this area.

6 P.M. This is a good time to head back to San Francisco and your hotel for a restful evening.

Wednesday through Sunday afternoons (each youngster receives a crown or scepter). For dinner, try Maxfield's, with its high-back booths and children's menu. As you pass by the Pied Piper Bar on the way to the restaurant, make sure to point out the celebrated Maxfield Parrish mural depicting the fairy-tale Pied Piper of Hamelin leading a band of 27 children. To really pull out all the stops here, order up a bedtime treat of cookies and milk for the kids and chocolate-covered strawberries and champagne for you. Children under 18 stay free in parents' room. *2 New Montgomery St., South of Market, San Francisco; (415) 512-1111;* www.sfpalace.com

Park Hyatt San Francisco
★★/$$$$

Conveniently located across the street via an elevated walkway from the upscale Embarcadero Center shopping complex, this luxurious 24-story property has 360 rooms, each with a bay or city view. Children under 17 stay free in their parents' room. Rooms with two double beds are spacious enough for a family,

and a few extralarge rooms are also available. By request, the minibar in your room can be emptied before your arrival so that you can use it a refrigerator, or you can request an additional refrigerator. If you want to go sightseeing in style, a Cadillac DeVille is available at no charge to shuttle guests around town (within a three-mile radius). *333 Battery St., Financial District, San Francisco; (800) 233-1234; (415) 392-1234;* www.park hyatt.com

Radisson Miyako Hotel
★★★/$$$$

A stay here offers you the chance to introduce Japanese culture to your children, especially if you include a visit to the adjacent Japantown Center for a bowl of traditional noodles and some window-shopping. The exotic 220-room hotel has two traditional Japanese-style suites, with futon feather beds on tatami mats, as well as Western-style rooms with Asian touches. Most of the serene rooms here have deep Japanese furo bathing tubs, and some suites have a private redwood sauna. Rooms with two double beds are available

IN THE NINETEENTH CENTURY, ships were often outfitted with figureheads. The decorative bow conveyed prosperity. Figureheads were created in a wide range of subjects, including the ship owner, members of his family, mythological figures, and celebrities.

and comfortable for families, and in-room refrigerators are available upon request (there's a small fee). Children under 18 stay free in their parents' room. The hotel has a library of children's books and games, and video games that can be borrowed if you rent a VCR. The tasteful lobby overlooks a Japanese garden where you can enjoy a short family stroll. *1625 Post St., Japantown, San Francisco; (800) 333-3333; (415) 922-3200;* www. radisson.com

Cable cars have not one, not two, but three sets of brakes!

The Ritz-Carlton ★★★★/$$$$

Despite its elegant setting within a restored 1909 neoclassical landmark building, this 336-room branch of the classy chain does not overlook its young guests. About halfway up Nob Hill, just off the California Street cable car line, the hotel offers an indoor heated pool and twice-daily maid service. Families with children under 5 receive a free bag of safety items, including outlet plugs, night-lights and bathtub spout covers. Children stay free in their parents' room. And for a price, you can request special treats for your children to be delivered to your room: perhaps cookies and milk at bedtime, or sodas and popcorn to go with a family movie. *600 Stockton St., Nob Hill, San Francisco; (800) 241-3333; (415) 296-7465;* www.ritz-carlton.com

Royal Pacific Motor Inn
★★/$$

Situated on the Chinatown–North Beach border, this five-story, 74-room bargain motel is right in the thick of things. The central location and reasonable rates make it a good choice for families on tight budgets and make it worth squeezing everyone into a smallish room with two double beds (children under 8 stay free). It has a sauna, and parking is free. *661 Broadway, Chinatown, San Francisco; (800) 545-5574; (415) 781-6661;* www.royalpacific.citysearch.com

San Francisco Marriott Fisherman's Wharf
★★/$$$-$$$$

Comfortable public spaces—including a lobby with fireplaces and TVs and a large fitness room where children are welcome when accompanied by an adult—enhance the appeal of this posh, contemporary 285-room hotel. It has all the family features associated with a Marriott: the restaurant and room service menus have special children's items, and there's no charge for children under 18 staying in their parents' room. Rooms equipped with two double beds are roomy enough to accommodate small families. *1250 Columbus Ave., Fisherman's Wharf, San Francisco; (800) 228-9290; (415) 775-7555;* www.marriotthotels.com/ sfofw

Sheraton at Fisherman's Wharf
★★★/$$-$$$$

This huge, 524-room contemporary hotel features spacious rooms and that rarest of San Francisco amenities—a heated outdoor swimming pool. Children under 17 stay free in their parents' room. *2500 Mason St., Fisherman's Wharf, San Francisco; (800) 325-3535; (415) 362-5500; www.sheraton.com*

Union Square Hostel ★★/$

Ninety-two private family-size rooms are available at this large, 258-bed hostel, which—as its name promises—is on Union Square. Make reservations as far in advance as possible, especially for a summer stay. For additional details, see "Hosteling for Families" on page 215. *312 Mason St., San Francisco; (415) 788-5604.*

The Westin St. Francis
★★★★/$$$$

Right on Union Square, this landmark 1904 hotel is classy, but family friendly. Upon check-in, children 12 and under get a free Westin Kids Club packet filled with an assortment of age-appropriate goodies. Strollers, cribs, high chairs, bottle warmers, potty seats, and step stools are available at no additional charge, and children under 18 stay free in their parents' room. Many of the 1,192 rooms are spacious enough for a family of four. Kids love the outside glass elevator that goes nonstop from the lobby to the 32nd floor in less than 30 seconds. Be sure to tell your kids that this is now the only hotel in the world that still washes its money—a custom that originated in the 1930s to keep women's white gloves from being soiled by dirty coins. *335 Powell St., Union Square, San Francisco; (800) WESTIN-1; (415) 397-7000; www. westin.com*

GOOD EATS

San Franciscans are definitely food-obsessed, so it is actually difficult to get a bad meal here. Though many of the more famous restaurants can be budget-busters and not particularly welcoming of children, there are plenty of moderately priced establishments with both great food and a children's menu. Ethnic restaurants are generally good bets with kids; try a taqueria for fast-food Mexican-style or head for Chinatown (see "It's Dim Sum—Try Some" and "Chinatown" on pages 74 and 85). If all else fails, the usual (and beloved) fast-food places abound. When you're looking for a snack, keep your eyes open for locally made treats such as Double Rainbow ice cream, Ghirardelli chocolate, and Tom's cookies. To wash it all down, there's Calistoga water—flavored and unflavored, still and sparkling.

Alioto's
★★/$$$

The view here—fishing boats, the bay, the bridge—lets you know that you really are in San Francisco. The family will be comfortable in an oversized booth in this popular upstairs restaurant. Lunch is the best time for families, as the menu then is less expensive (though less extensive), and there is a Little Fisherman's Menu. At dinner you can order seafood, Sicilian regional specialties, and pasta dishes, including potato gnocchi with creamy tomato sauce. Split portions can be prepared for children. If you want a more casual meal, try the downstairs Cafe 8, a sort of fast-seafood deli that also serves up sandwiches and pizzas. Whatever you do, don't miss seeing David Mizer at the crab stand out front. Sometimes referred to as "the Mozart of crab-crackers," he puts on quite a show tossing his plastic hammer in the air like a baton as he cracks shells. *8 Fisherman's Wharf, at the bottom of Taylor St., San Francisco; (415) 673-0183.*

Bill's Place
★★★★/$

Definitely not part of a chain, this bustling neighborhood restaurant has been around seemingly forever. A large variety of tasty hamburgers named after local celebrities stars on the menu here along with other kid favorites like hot dogs, giant French fries (made from fresh potatoes), and milk shakes (made with Dreyer's ice cream and served in old-fashioned metal canisters). There are also sandwiches and made-from-scratch soups. Seating is at an assortment of tables or at a long counter with swivel stools (more fun!). In mild weather, eat at a table on the pleasant outdoor patio landscaped with a Japanese garden complete with waterfall and orchids. *2315 Clement St., the Richmond, San Francisco; (415) 221-5262;* www.bills place.citysearch.com

His Beak Can Hold More Than His Belly Can

The brown pelican was put on the endangered species list in 1970 when it was considered in danger of becoming extinct. The Environmental Protection Agency placed serious restrictions on the use of pesticides, and the East Coast brown pelican population is no longer endangered. Unfortunately, the Pacific Coast brown pelicans are still struggling: The Southern California population is currently estimated at 4,500 to 5,000 breeding pairs.

Bubba Gump Shrimp Co.
★★★★/$$

This theme chain restaurant, based on the shrimping scenes in the movie *Forrest Gump*, resembles a seafood shack at the end of the pier and is wildly popular with families.

BACKSEAT GAMES

In the privacy of your own car, you can laugh as loud as you want or shout out the answers to questions. So don't hold back when you play these games— laugh, yell, or sing your hearts out. The ideas are well suited to driving as they don't involve writing.

THE HOUSE ON THE HILL

Invent stories about people in the houses you are driving by. What do you think they do for work? What's their favorite food? Where do you go on vacation? Get into lots of details, such as whether they snore loudly or are afraid of spiders. Give them names, hobbies, pets, and so on.

BUZZ

This is a team effort to try to reach 100 without making a mistake. Take turns counting, beginning with one. Every time you get to a number that's divisible by seven (7, 14, 21, . . .) or has a seven in it (17), say "Buzz" instead of the number. If one person forgets to say "Buzz," everyone has to start over. If this is too hard, say "Buzz" for every number divisible by 5. If you want a real challenge, try Fuzz Buzz. Say "Fuzz" for every number with a three in it or that's divisible by three, and "Buzz" for every number with a seven in it or that's divisible by seven.

Not surprisingly, the menu has many shrimp selections, most of them deep-fried, as well as fresh fish entrées and baby back ribs. There's a kids' menu with the usual favorites, too. The bar serves up fun drinks, including some nonalcoholic, good-for-you ones like the peanutty-chocolate Alabama Sweet Smoothie and the frothy pink Run Forrest Run. Mom and Dad may want to try one or two of the several kinds of margaritas (the Delta Sunset is particularly tasty). Dessert should, of course, be a box of chocolates, and that is one option. As a bonus, most tables have magnificent views of the bay. An adjacent shop sells everything Gump. (Winston Groom lived in San Francisco when he wrote the book *Forrest Gump*. In fact, he named the main character after this city's famous department store.) *Pier 39, Fisherman's Wharf, San Francisco; (888) 561-GUMP; (415) 781-GUMP;* www.bubbagump.com

Buca di Beppo
★★★★/$$

The party begins upon entering the door at this festive, happy, old-time southern Italian spot, whose name translates as Joe's Basement. Choose from a warren of small subterranean rooms, or pick one of the comfortable booths in the boisterous upstairs bar where kids can wiggle and squirm to their heart's content. Study the menu posted on the wall while being entertained by favorite tunes from the '50s. Portions are huge and meant to be shared. Don't dare arrive without a *big* appetite, and don't say we didn't warn you about ordering a "large" of anything here. Kid-pleasing choices include a tall bowl of spaghetti with one base-ball-sized meatball, and an oblong, thin-crusted pepperoni pizza that is nothing short of great. Kids have been known to grow saucer-eyed when they find out soft drink orders include *two* refills. *855 Howard St., South of Market, San Francisco; (415) 543-POPE;* www.bucadibeppo.com

Capp's Corner
★★/$$$

There's lots of fun on the other side of this eatery's saloon-style swinging doors. Reputed to be the liveliest and noisiest of the North Beach family-style Italian restaurants, this popular spot is usually crowded. Your family will be stuffed after downing the bountiful three-course dinner of minestrone soup, salad, and entrée (steak, roast duck, chicken breast piccata, osso buco, lasagna, seafood cannelloni, and the like). Children's portions are available. *1600 Powell St., North Beach, San Francisco; (415) 989-2589;* www.capscorner.com

The Cheesecake Factory
★★★★/$$

This popular restaurant offers an extensive, eclectic menu and, as might be expected from the name,

a large selection of cheesecakes. Also see Good Eats in Beverly Hills and Century City/Los Angeles. *In Macy's, Eighth floor, Union Square, San Francisco; (415) 391-4444;* www.thecheesecakefactory.com

Chevy's
★★★★/$$

When you're hankering for some reliably tasty Tex-Mex, try this pro-lific chain, which, happily, seems to be everywhere. Everyone's favorites are on the menu—tacos, enchiladas, burritos, tamales—and their acclaimed fajitas are fun for the whole family to share. Waiting for the food to arrive is almost pain-less, thanks to frosty margaritas (virgin versions are available), superb house salsa with thin, crisp corn chips, and crayons and color-ing menus for your kids. Children also get a kick out of watching El Machino—the restaurant's intrigu-ing tortilla-making machine. *Corner of 3rd St. & Howard St., San Francisco; (415) 543-8060;* www.chevys.com

The Cliff House
★★★★/$$$-$$$$

Perched solidly on bedrock at the edge of the Pacific, offering spec-tacular views of the ocean and the critters on Seal Rocks, this historic treasure is the only oceanfront restaurant in San Francisco. There has been a restaurant on this site since 1863, and this 1909 structure is now part of the National Park

IT'S DIM SUM—TRY SOME

THERE IS NO BETTER PLACE to try dim sum than San Francisco, where there are said to be more dim sum parlors than in any other city in the United States. Basically a meal of appetizers, dim sum makes for an interesting change of pace for breakfast or lunch—if your children are open to eating new things and can tolerate a wait to be seated. (Remember that you can always order something off the menu if you get too many "yucks" from what comes around on the carts.) Dim sum houses are appropriate for kids of all ages: the restaurants are usually loud and bustling, most have high chairs for the littlest diners, kids find a meal at a dim sum parlor to be quite an adventure—even if they eat nothing at all.

The seemingly endless variety of dim sum treats were originally served for breakfast during China's Tang dynasty (A.D. 618 to 907). A typical dim sum meal includes steamed buns, fried dumplings, and turnovers (all of which children tend to enjoy), as well as delicacies such as steamed duck beaks and feet (from which kids tend to recoil—although a child who refuses to touch a carrot may jump at the chance to try duck feet). The entire family will enjoy selecting items brought to tables Hong Kong-style on carts or trays that circulate nonstop. Just flag down the servers as they pass. Most teahouses charge about $2 to $4.50 per plate, and tips are usually divided by the entire staff.

Gold Mountain
★★★★/$

Dim sum is served on floors two and three of this gigantic, bustling restaurant, which is so big that the waiters use walkie-talkies to communicate. Though floor two alone seats 280 people, there still is usually a wait. Once seated, if carts don't arrive fast enough, flag down someone who looks in charge and order directly from the kitchen. Crisp deep-fried taro balls and roasted duck are particularly good here. *644 Broadway, in Chinatown, San Francisco; (415) 296-7733.*

Harbor Village
★★★★/$$

It is well worth the wait generally required to dine on the upscale dim sum served at this Hong Kong-style spot. Request a seat in the back room, where large windows offer views past the treetops to the Vaillancourt Fountain and Ferry Building. Items are made with impeccably fresh ingredients, and a tasty complexity characterizes many of the refined renditions, often satisfying even the pickiest little palate. The staff is great with kids. *Four*

Embarcadero Center, lobby level, in Financial District, San Francisco; (415) 781-8833.

Meriwa Restaurant
★★★★/$

Able to seat 1,000 people, this popular spot roars during dim sum. The little dishes here are among the very best and most varied currently available. *728 Pacific Ave., in Chinatown, San Francisco; (415) 989-8818 or (415) 989-8868.*

New Asia
★★★★/$

Even with 1,000 seats, this busy spot usually requires a wait for seating in its popular ground level dining room. However, immediate seating is often available upstairs. Head servers here use walkie-talkies to communicate across the vast, noisy interior. Delicate shrimp dumplings, deep-fried taro balls filled with sweet poi, and cloudlike pork bows are all especially good. A dim sum-to-go counter operates by the waiting area. *772 Pacific Ave., in Chinatown, San Francisco; (415) 391-6666.*

Ton Kiang
★★★★/$

Operating on two floors, this attractive spot specializes in Hakka-style cuisine. Exemplary dim sum items—which many consider to be the very best in San Francisco—include deep-fried taro croquettes, ethereal chive-shrimp dumplings, exquisite steamed pea shoots, puffy deep-fried stuffed crab claws, miniature egg-custard tarts, and crisp walnut cookies filled deliciously with lotus paste. *5821 Geary Blvd., in the Richmond district; (415) 387-8273.*

Yank Sing
★★★★/$$

Opened in 1957, this was the first dim sum parlor in the city to serve the cuisine as it is known in Hong Kong. Two compelling reasons to forsake tradition and visit this upscale parlor outside of Chinatown are that they take reservations and that the parking is easier. Also, servers are friendly and can usually answer questions. Top items include cloud-soft rice noodles stuffed with a variety of meats, succulent stuffed black mushroom caps, and deep-fried crab claws. Children usually like the sweet deep-fried taro balls and wedges of orange peel filled with shimmering orange Jell-O. *101 Spear St., in Rincon Center, San Francisco; (415) 957-9300.*

WHY IS THE GOLDEN GATE BRIDGE orange instead of gold? The bridge is actually named for the Golden Gate Strait, which is the entryway to San Francisco Bay from the Pacific Ocean.

Service's Golden Gate National Recreation Area. (The park is a great place to build up an appetite or work off those newly ingested calories.) There are three dining rooms and two bars—all welcome children. The main dining room, the Seafood & Beverage Company, is the most formal of the three; it serves steaks and fresh seafood and is the choice spot for Sunday brunch. On the main level, the Phineas T. Barnacle Bar and Deli serves a casual menu of soups, salads, and sandwiches, as well as snacks and mixed drinks. Upstairs at the Cliff House has an informal atmosphere and a lunch menu featuring 30 omelettes, hot and cold sandwiches, salads, chili, and hamburgers. At dinner, the upstairs menu adds pasta and seafood entrées and becomes more pricey. *1090 Point Lobos Ave., Outer Richmond, San Francisco; (415) 386-3330;* www.cliffhouse.com

Franciscan Restaurant
★★★★/$$$

For kids, waiting for meals to arrive is the most difficult part about dining out. Here, a drink menu starts things off with some playful con-

coctions, including several nonalcoholic versions that appeal to children—and that famous San Francisco sourdough bread keeps hunger at bay. The special kids' coloring menu—another diversion—includes grilled prawns as well as the more traditional hamburger and spaghetti. For grown-ups there's clam chowder, oysters on the half shell, Dungeness crab Louie, and more. *At the foot of Powell St., Pier 43½, Fisherman's Wharf, San Francisco; (415) 362-7733;* www.fran ciscanrestaurant.com

 **Ghirardelli Chocolate Manufactory**
★★★★/$

Operating within a real chocolate factory built in 1900, this yummy spot dishes up the best sundaes in San Francisco. If your growing offspring have extra-large appetites, you might consider splitting "The Earthquake," composed of eight scoops of ice cream and eight different toppings, not to mention bananas, whipped cream, chopped almonds, and whole cherries. The table usually looks like an earthquake has struck when people finish this one! Less daunting shakes, sodas, and cones are also available. Ghirardelli chocolates are sold in the small adjoining shop. Allow time to stroll through this beautiful brick complex, which is now a National Historic Landmark and home to a slew of shops and restaurants. Street performers often entertain on the courtyard stage, to the delight of young onlookers. *900 North Point St., in Ghirardelli Square, San Francisco; (415) 771-4903;* www.ghirardelli.com

Hard Rock Cafe
★★★/$$

Young music lovers and kids who can't wait to be teenagers like this extra-cool branch of the hip restaurant chain. Rock 'n' roll blasted at earsplitting levels easily covers up the noise of even the most rambunctious group of young diners. The bill of fare features classic

American-style food such as hamburgers, fries, malts, and devil's food cake. Preteens won't want to leave without the de rigueur T-shirt or other souvenir logo items. Children's portions can be arranged with your server. *1699 Van Ness Ave., Pier 39, Building Q, San Francisco; (415) 885-1699;* www.hardrockcafe.com

Hornblower Cruises
★★★★/$$$$

The boat ride is *the* thing as far as kids are concerned. For adults, a brunch cruise is a relaxing way to enjoy both a family meal and magnificent San Francisco bay views. As you embark you will be seated, and then in orderly fashion be shown to the groaning board of tasty brunch items. Children are provided with crayons and coloring books, and adults are soothed by live music. Touring the vessel is part of the fun. **NOTE:** High chairs and booster seats are not available, but strollers with wheel locks are permitted on board and may be used for seating toddlers. Reservations are required. *Pier 33, The Embarcadero, San Francisco; (415) 394-8900;* www.hornblower.com

Just Desserts
★★★/$

Your kids' eyes will light up when they see the goodies-filled bakery cases here. Croissants, cupcakes, cookies, muffins, cheesecakes, and pies. And then there are the cakes:

77

carrot cake with cream-cheese frosting, chocolate fudge cake with a rich fudge frosting, lemon cake topped with a choice of lemon or bittersweet chocolate glaze, and the sublime Mocha Cream Cake—just to name a few. *248 Church St., Upper Market; (415) 626-5774. Branches are all over town: Three Embarcadero Center, (415) 421-1609; 3735 Buchanan St., the Marina, (415) 922-8675;* www.justdesserts.com

La Taqueria
★★★/$

Experience fast food Mexican-style at this atmospheric spot, where a colorful folk mural decorates the wall and a jukebox plays Mexican tunes. After placing your order, you can watch busy cooks in the open kitchen preparing your meal. The simple menu satisfies most family

members. Tacos made with two steamed corn tortillas and burritos made with chewy flour tortillas come with your choice of filling: pork, beef, sausage, chicken, or vegetarian. Save room for dessert, which you can pick up next door at Dianda's Italian-American Pastry, where everything is made from scratch and the cannolis are particularly good. **NOTE:** No credit cards are accepted. *2889 Mission St., the Mission, San Francisco; (415) 285-7117.*

Leon's Bar-B-Q
★★★/$$

Keep this tiny, extremely casual spot in mind when you visit the zoo; it's located just across the street. Everything can be prepared to go, and the picnic area in the zoo or the nearby beach are both good places to eat it. Known for delicious, messy

DAY TRIP
A Six Flags Fun Day

9 or 10 A.M. The ferry to Vallejo departs twice daily from Pier 39 in San Francisco (operates only on summer weekends); in Vallejo, you'll board a bus for the park. For current details, call the **Blue & Gold Fleet** at *(415) 705-5555.* The entire trip will take about an hour and 15 minutes.

10:30 or 11:30 A.M. Enjoy Six Flags Marine World *(707/643-ORCA).*

Just a few years ago this theme park completely reinvented itself, adding rides to its world-famous collection of wildlife shows. It is now the nation's only combination wildlife park, oceanarium, and theme park. The exciting animal shows feature dolphins, sea lions, elephants, tigers, and exotic birds, and daredevil humans put on a spectacular Ski Extreme water ski-boat show. You and your family can walk through animal habitat areas to see African animals and ride on the back of an Asian elephant. Another favorite is

pork ribs slathered with a tangy sweet sauce, Leon's also serves up good beef ribs, hot links, and barbecued chicken. Meals come with a corn muffin and choice of baked beans, spaghetti, potato salad, or coleslaw. The menu is rounded out with a half-pound hamburger, housemade chili, and tiny pecan or sweet-potato pies. Jefferson Starship (depending on your age, you may remember him as part of Jefferson Airplane, not Starship) member Paul Kantner, who is a local resident, has been spotted here with his children. *2800 Sloat Blvd., the Sunset, San Francisco; (415) 681-3071;* www. leansbarbq.com

Max's Diner
★★★★/$$

The extensive menu at this glossy yet comfortable spot offers fare to please any stage, or age, of hunger. Dinner entrées include hamburgers, fresh fish, and steaks, and there are huge New York–style deli sandwiches. Kids can order scrambled eggs at lunch and dinner, and a special children's menu offers up hot dogs, fried chicken, and half-sandwiches. But the items that get most kids and parents excited are the gargantuan desserts, including a delicious seven-layer cookie topped with hot fudge and ice cream. *311 Third St., South of Market; (415) 546-MAXS.* Across town, at **Max's Opera Cafe** you get similar fare but with the added bonus of talented servers who take turns singing at the mike between 7 and 11 P.M. *601 Van Ness Ave., San Francisco; (415) 771-7300. Also Max's Diamond Grill by PacBell ball park, 128 King St., San Francisco; (415) 896-6297;* www.maxworld.com

the Looney Tunes play area, where they can meet some of their favorite cartoon characters and enjoy the Acme Foam Factory, with slides and climbing structures and orange foam balls for tossing and shooting from air cannons. There are 10 rides designed especially for kids under 54 inches tall. Butterfly Habitat is the first walk-through free-flight butterfly enclosure in the western United States—have the camera handy in case a butterfly lands on your 6-year-old's head! The whole family will go nuts in the walk-in Lorikeet Aviary, where you can feed these birds out of your hands. Now adding thrills to the mix are five monster roller coasters, the world's first 3-D motion simulator ride, and an assortment of other wild rides. If you have a 3- or 4-year-old in tow, rent one of the dolphin-shaped strollers; www.sixflags.com

4:30 or 7 P.M. Depart Marine World for return via bus and ferry.

6 or 8:30 P.M. Arrive back in San Francisco.

McCormick & Kuleto's Seafood Restaurant
★★★/$$$-$$$$

If your children like the grown-up feeling of getting dressed up and dining in a nice restaurant, this splendidly appointed seafood restaurant is a good choice. Adult and kid menus change daily and are designed to please every appetite. Families with young children may want to opt for the restaurant's more casual Crab Cake Lounge—the same incredible view with a less expensive, less extensive menu. *900 North Point, in Ghirardelli Square, Fisherman's Wharf, San Francisco; (415) 929-1730;* www.mccormick andkuletos.com

Mel's Drive-In ★★★★/$$

This once was a real drive-in where carhops hopped out to the cars with trays so that you could actually eat in your car. Today, black-and-white photos of 1950s scenes decorate the walls; updated, computerized mini jukeboxes are within reach of most seats, allowing you to select an oldie-but-goodie for a quarter (did you know that jukeboxes were invented

in San Francisco in 1888?); and items on the kids' menu are served in boxes designed to resemble fifties cars. Finicky youngsters can even order scrambled eggs or waffles at dinnertime, since Mel's serves breakfast all day long. Specialties of the house include the "Famous Melburger" and flavored colas (cherry, chocolate, vanilla, and lemon). *2165 Lombard St., the Marina, San Francisco; (415) 921-2867. Also at 3355 Geary Blvd., San Francisco; (415) 387-2244; two other locations: 801 Mission St., San Francisco; (415) 227-4477; and 1050 Van Ness Ave., San Francisco; (415) 292-6357.*

Mifune Restaurant ★★★/$

Kids who love noodles and are willing to try something new are the perfect candidates for a meal at this local branch of a well-established chain in Japan. Meals are based on one of two types of easily digested and low-calorie homemade noodles: udon (fat, white-flour noodles) and soba (thin, brown buckwheat noodles) are the specialty. Topping choices for either noodle type include chicken, beef, and shrimp tempura as well as more exotic raw egg, sweet herring, and seaweed. Before walking through the noren (slit curtain), take a look at the realistic plastic food displays in the exterior windows. Some kids will love the child's Bullet Train plate, served in a ceramic replica of the famous Japanese train and consisting of cold noodles with shrimp and vegetable tempura. Others won't. *In Japan Center, in Kintetsu Mall, San Francisco; (415) 922-0337.*

North Beach Pizza ★★★★/$

This restaurant serves an unfussy kind of pizza in a relaxed, authentic atmosphere. An outstanding cannelloni is among the pasta choices, and a submarine sandwich is also on the menu. *1499 Grant Ave., in North Beach; (415) 433-2444. A branch is one block up the street at 1310 Grant Ave., San Francisco; (415) 433-2444.*

Palomino Euro Bistro ★★★/$$$$

Offering a great view of the Bay Bridge, this bustling spot has a raised seating area and interior palm trees that echo those lining the street outside. Kids (who are amused by the indoor trees) might enjoy a pasta dish or the pizza with cracker-thin crust prepared in an apple wood-fired oven. They get a color-in place mat to occupy them while the adults contemplate a more sophisticated menu. All dinners start with a loaf of rosemary ciabatta bread and a delicious crushed tomato-feta-kalamata spread, which are terribly easy to fill up on. The crisp hearts of romaine salad deliciously tossed with a creamy herb vinaigrette, toasted pine nuts, and gorgonzola makes a choice appetizer before an entrée of either fish or a spit-roasted meat. Sixteen beers are on tap,

Teaching Your Kids How to Pack

Encourage your kids to think of mix-and-match outfits for various activities, just as they do when dressing paper dolls. (You even can have them practice by packing a doll wardrobe — trying out the different outfits — while they pack for themselves.) For example, ask a preschooler, "We're going hiking. Which of your comfortable pants do you want to wear?" After he lays these out, ask him to match them with two T-shirts (for two outfits), a sweatshirt in case it is cold, and appropriate shoes. Then, consider another vacation activity. Ask him to find two bathing suits, for instance, with a sun cover-up and a hat. Next, ask him to think about nighttime, laying out toothbrush and toothpaste, pajamas, a beloved but small stuffed animal, bathrobe, and slippers.

and a large selection of wine varietals are available by the glass. *345 Spear St., in Hills Plaza, The Embarcadero, San Francisco; (415) 512-7400; www.palominosf.com*

Polly Ann Ice Cream
★★★★/$

There may be quite a wait while your children mull over the selection of ice-cream flavors here. Fifty-two flavors are available every day, and there are more than 425 varieties in all. Some of the flavors are seasonal, and some—like Batman (black vanilla with lemon swirls) and Star Wars (blue-colored vanilla with rainbow marshmallows)—are trendy. Among the many unusual flavors are Bumpy Freeway (basically Rocky Road with more of those colored marshmallows), sunflower seed, chocolate peanut butter, and American Beauty (made with real rose petals). There are also vegetable ice creams, including carrot cake and corn—they're one way to get your kids to eat some veggies! Polly Ann claims to be the only ice-cream store in the world where babies and dogs always get a free ice-cream cone. *3142 Noriega St., Outer Sunset, San Francisco; (415) 664-2472; www.pollyann.com*

Tommaso's ★★★★/$$

Expect a wait to get in, as this place is very popular, and they don't take reservations, but if your school-age kids can handle the delay, Tommaso's is well worth it. Almost 20 kinds of pizza, made with a thin, crisp-yet-chewy crust, are top choices. Calzones are also available, as are pastas, seafood, veal, and chicken entrées. The dessert selection includes cannoli, spumoni ice cream, and homemade tiramisu. Families are usually seated at tables in semiprivate compartments separated by wooden partitions. **NOTE:** Movie director Francis Ford Coppola has been known to dash in from his nearby office to whip up his own creations in the kitchen. *1042 Kearny St., North Beach, San Francisco; (415) 398-9696; www. tommasos.com*

World Wrapps ★★★/$

It's good for visiting families to know about this local fast-food chain,

IN ITS 29-YEAR history as a federal prison, 36 men attempted to escape from Alcatraz Island. According to official records, none of them ever succeeded. However, there are still five inmates who are listed as "missing and presumed drowned."

which offers tasty, wholesome, made-to-order meals. The children's menu offers a popular pizza fold (a wrapper filled with marinara sauce and melted Monterey Jack cheese) as well as a bean-and-cheese wrap. For Mom and Dad, and more adventurous kids, an international array of stuffed tortillas are the big draw here; signature mixtures include salmon and asparagus, portobello mushroom and goat cheese, and Thai chicken. There are "unwrapped" rice bowls and soups, too, and assorted smoothies. The decor is colorful and the mood casual, so kids feel right at home. The counter stools offer great people-watcing, but if you'd rather picnic, everything can be nicely packed to take to the park. *2257 Chestnut St., at Pierce St., San Francisco; (415) 563-9727.*

Zao ★★★/$$

Offering quick and inexpensive meals with oodles of flavorful and kid-friendly noodles, this local chain has a high-energy, casual atmosphere. The delicious, healthful cuisines of Thailand, Vietnam, China, and Japan are featured. Menu standouts include Middle Kingdom chicken cups (a tasty appetizer consisting of a minced mixture of chicken, shiitake mushrooms, and water chestnuts eaten taco-style in lettuce wrappers), a low-fat chicken salad, and the "surf 'n' turf" (a big bowl of fresh handmade fat noodles topped with a sautéed mixture

of chicken, prawns, and vegetables flavored with ginger, garlic, and chilies). It's not the best place for fussy eaters, but kids might be satisfied with a simple chicken dish, a bowl of plain noodles, or a cup of rice. For dessert, try the popular deep-fried banana spring roll with chocolate sauce, or the mango, green tea, and Kona coffee ice-cream balls served in individual rice wrappers. *2406 California St., Upper Fillmore, San Francisco; (415) 345-8088. Also at 2031 Chestnut St., the Marina, San Francisco; (415) 928-3088; www.zao.com*

SOUVENIR HUNTING

Anna's Danish Cookie Co.

Sold nowhere but at this store, Anna's Danish butter cookies have been made here since 1933. You can buy just a few, or a box or tin filled to the brim. *3560 18th St., the Mission, San Francisco; (415) 863-3882;* www.annascookies.com

Basic Brown Bear Factory

Bears of all kinds—from your basic brown to your quite elaborate cream-colored Beary Godmother with pink satin wings and a magic wand—are available in this tiny shop. The close-to-wholesale prices range from $2 for a mouse to $145 for a 4-foot-tall, fully-jointed bear with leather paws, and there are lots of options in between. If you call ahead for an

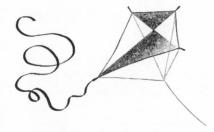

appointment, your children can stuff their own specialty bears. *444 DeHaro St., San Francisco; (415) 626-0781. Also at 2801 Leavenworth on The Cannery, Fisherman's Wharf, San Francisco; (415) 931-6670; (800) 554-1910;* www.basicbrownbear.com

The Disney Store

Everything Disney is here: Simba and Tarzan, Belle and Ariel, and Snow White and Dumbo and Pluto and the whole gang, emblazoned on everything from sweatshirts and sheets to towels and tote bags. Oh, yes, there are toys, too. If you can't decide what to buy, pick up a free Disney Catalog and mull it over at home. *400 Post St., on Union Square, San Francisco; (415) 391-6866;* www.disney.com

Esprit Outlet

Esprit's popular line of clothing for girls and female teens originated in San Francisco. Your preteen won't want to miss this factory outlet store, a great spot to pick up a stylish souvenir T-shirt or sweatshirt and more at bargain prices. *499 Illinois St., San Francisco; (415) 957-2550.*

FAO Schwarz

The city's largest toy store, this three-story wonderland is filled with elaborate displays and exclusive, unusual, and trendsetting merchandise. Shoppers are greeted at the door by a live toy solider, and just steps from the entrance a whimsical two-story mechanical clock tower emits charming music. A good selection of San Francisco-themed books and games is available. *48 Stockton St., Union Square, San Francisco; (415) 394-8700;* www.fao.com

Metreon

See JUST FOR FUN on page 59.

Old Navy

This new downtown flagship store is spacious in an industrial sort of way, and its exterior is lit colorfully with bright neon at night. Kids love the whimsically decorated third floor that is dedicated to their sizes, from babies to teens. If your taste runs to jeans and sweatshirts, it's possible for your whole family to walk out in matching outfits. Should you get hungry, stop in for some fast food at the old-time military hut housing Torpedo Joe's in the back of the store. You can get a kids' lunch for $2—if your kids are happy with grilled cheese and milk. *801 Market St., South of Market, San Francisco; (415) 344-0375.*

Pier 39

See JUST FOR FUN on page 59.

CHINATOWN

COVERING 24 SQUARE blocks and home to approximately 80,000 residents, San Francisco's **Chinatown** is the largest Chinese community outside of Asia. It is bounded by Broadway and Bush, Kearny, and Powell streets. The most memorable way for you and your family to enter Chinatown is on foot through the ornate dragon-crested archway on Grant Avenue and Bush Street. Take time to examine and admire it. Designed according to the Taoist principles of feng shui, the gate features Foo dogs to scare away evil spirits, dragons for fertility and power, and fish for prosperity. After passing through the gate, stroll pedestrian-crowded Grant Avenue, San Francisco's oldest street. For good souvenir hunting, stop in one of the many shops. Favorite items with children include golden dragon-decorated velvet slippers, silk coin purses, and rice candy in edible wrappers.

To introduce your children to the fine arts of China, plan a short visit to the **Chinese Culture Center** *(750 Kearny St., near Washington St., on the third floor of the Holiday Inn; 415/986-1822).* It mounts rotating exhibits of historical and contemporary Chinese art by both native Chinese and Chinese-Americans; www.c-c-c.org

Another good way to teach the kids about Chinese culture is to take a guided walking tour. Cultural and culinary tours of Chinatown, sponsored by the **Chinese Culture Foundation**, are scheduled year-round. All welcome children (they are most fun for kids ages 8 and older), and all require reservations; *call (415) 986-1822.* The Culinary Walk includes stops at markets, a fortune cookie factory, an herb shop, and a tea shop; it concludes with a dim sum lunch. The Heritage Walk stresses the history and cultural achievements of the area; stops might include a Chinese temple and the Chinese Historical Society, where kids can learn about the lives of Chinese children past and present. Chinese New Year Walks are given only during that time of year (in January, February, or March, depending on the lunar calendar). A history of the holiday is presented, and all participants sample special Chinese sweets from a "Tray of Togetherness."

Kids and adults both enjoy walking through this area's narrow streets and alleys in search of a fortune cookie factory. Though workers aren't often pleased to see tourists, it is usually possible to get at least a glimpse of the action by peeking in through a door or window.

continued on the next page

Proprietors are ordinarily glad to sell cookies, and bags of broken "misfortune" cookies can be picked up at bargain prices. Look for the **Golden Gate Fortune Cookie Company** *(56 Ross Alley, near Washington St.)*, which is tucked in a picturesque alley in the heart of Chinatown and also sells delicious mini-almond cookies. Or venture to the border of Chinatown and North Beach, where **Mee Mee Bakery** *(1328 Stockton St., near Broadway)* has been baking fortune cookies longer than anyone else in town.

The Chinese calendar is largely based on lunar cycles, so **Chinese New Year** is on a different day each year.

Though there are many temples in Chinatown, only one seems to welcome visitors: **Tin How Taoist Temple** *(125-129 Waverly Pl., near Washington St.)*, located in the heart of Chinatown on a lane known for its ornate, colorfully painted balconies. Follow the scent of incense leading up narrow wooden stairs to the fourth floor. Built in 1852, this is the oldest Chinese Taoist temple in the United States. Though there is no charge to visit, donations are appreciated and appropriately reverent behavior is expected. This stop is appropriate only for older children who understand that the temple is still used for worship.

If you're in San Francisco for Chinese New Year, usually in January, February or March, you're in for a real treat. The city's famous Golden Dragon Parade was first held in 1851 and has taken place here every Chinese New Year since. One of the few illuminated night parades in the country, it is particularly colorful and exciting, with the spectacular block-long golden dragon the prime attraction. At this time of year it's particularly fun to stroll through Chinatown. An outdoor carnival sets up shop here for a while, and you'll probably hear firecrackers and maybe see a smaller "dragon" blessing one of the local shops, as is the tradition. For further information, call (415) 391-9680.

When in Chinatown, it's fun to eat as the natives do. Most (though by no means all) kids can find something they like on a Chinese menu. Bland Cantonese-style dishes are a better bet than spicier Hunan- and Szechuan-style ones, and it's hard to go wrong with a simple noodle or fried-rice dish. Many young diners like potsticker dumplings, too. If your kids are adventurous eaters, encourage each to order an item and then share it with the family, also trying everyone else's dish.

Kids will enjoy learning that turning over the lid on the teapot signals a server that you want more tea, and that crossed chopsticks are usually an omen of bad luck (except in dim sum houses, where they signal the server that you have finished).

Here are some winners for a good Chinese meal.

Far East Café ★★★★/$$

This intriguing restaurant has 30 private wooden booths with curtain "doors." Kids love it. The enclosures can be especially nice for hiding away with cranky kids who are tired of sight-seeing. An extensive à la carte menu includes sizzling rice soup, fried wontons, and a variety of chow mein and chop suey dishes. Any of the family-style Cantonese dinners, which include items like bland winter melon soup, barbecued pork chow mein, and crispy deep-fried prawns, are good choices, too. *631 Grant Ave., San Francisco; (415) 982-3245;* www.fareastcafe.com

Lichee Garden ★★★★/$

Located on the North Beach side of Broadway, this restaurant attracts throngs of local families and is known for its exceptional soups, Hong Kong-style crispy noodles, and crisp Peking-style spareribs. Seating is at large round tables, portions are generous, and sodas are served in their original large plastic bottles, making it easy to provide refills to thirsty tykes. *1416 Powell St., San Francisco; (415) 397-2290.*

The Pot Sticker ★★★★/$

Situated in a picturesque alley famous for its historic buildings with ornate painted balconies, this spot is known for its lightly spiced Mandarin-style cuisine and hand-made noodles and dumplings— items children adore. Dishes tend to be lightly sauced with lots of vegetables. Good choices include hot-and-sour soup, Mongolian beef, Princess chicken, and, for adults, a dramatic Hunan crispy whole fish (which most kids will think is yucky). *150 Waverly Pl., San Francisco; (415) 397-9985.*

Sam Wo ★★/$

The main reason to come here is for the fresh homemade noodles and the unusual layout of the tiny dining rooms. You enter through the kitchen and climb narrow stairs to the second and third floors. The house specialty, noodle soup, is available in a dozen varieties. Wonton soups and chow fun dishes are on the menu, and the cold roasted-pork rice-noodle roll is especially good. Alas, no fortune cookies arrive with the amazingly inexpensive check. Don't attempt this one with children under age 7. *813 Washington St., San Francisco; (415) 982-0596.*

Berkeley's on a roll with outdoor adventures, campus events, and diverse cuisine.

Berkeley

THERE'S NO PLACE quite like Berkeley. Thanks to the city's interesting history and unique character, a visit here with kids can be both fun and educational.

The little ones won't much care about the historical stuff, but don't fail to acquaint preteens (who may have rediscovered the beauty of tie-dye T-shirts and bell-bottoms—now known as flares) with Berkeley's role in the political and social upheavals of the 1960s and 1970s. Politically aware grade-schoolers may also be intrigued by the current ultraliberal political climate of this in-your-face city. Berkeley has been a pioneer on many frontiers: it was the first city in the nation with a public health department, the first to have a lie-detector machine, the first to create curb cuts for wheelchairs, the first to ban Styrofoam, the first to rename Columbus Day the more politically correct Indigenous Peoples Day (see for yourself—it's listed that way under "Holidays" on parking meters), and most recently, the first to offer all-organic school lunches.

THE FamilyFun LIST

MUST-SEE · MUST-SEE

Adventure Playground (page 92)

Lawrence Hall of Science
(page 91)

Tilden Regional Park (page 93)

University of California, Berkeley
(page 91)

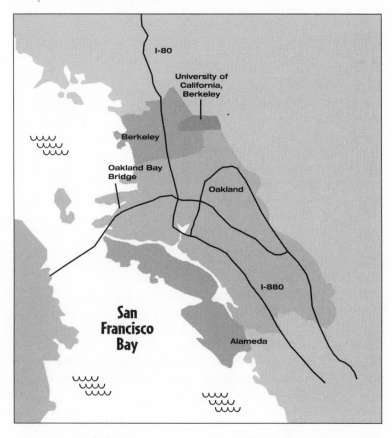

This is also the home to the University of California, Berkeley, one of the state's most prestigious public universities. Take the kids to the campus to give them a feel for the exciting atmosphere of an institution of higher learning. Who knows? It might even motivate less-than-stellar students to aim for college. But more likely, the kids will only be interested in the dinosaur bones at the university's Museum of Paleontology. Berkeley is also home to the extremely kid-friendly Lawrence Hall of Science as well as several great parks. Your youngest kids will love the country's first Adventure Playground, and you'll want to picnic at Tilden Park, where you can take a spin on the carousel and a trip on the miniature railroad.

You can dress casually in this most informal of towns, and your kids will fit in just about anywhere—even in many of the city's acclaimed restaurants.

CULTURAL ADVENTURES

The Magnes Museum
★/Free-$

The first Jewish museum established in the western United States, this institution exhibits Jewish ceremonial and fine arts from communities around the world. It is housed in a converted 1908 mansion, the gardens for which were landscaped by John McLaren, designer of San Francisco's Golden Gate Park. Older kids (8 to 12), particularly those who want to know more about their cultural heritage, will probably get the most out of a visit here. Donation requested. *2911 Russell St., Berkeley; 121 Stuart St., San Francisco; (415) 591-8800 for both; www.magnesmuseum.org*

 **Lawrence Hall of Science**
★★★★/$

A button-pusher's paradise, this hands-on museum is high in the hills behind the University of California, of which it is part. Kids love the games (they usually don't realize they're educational), and the whole family will enjoy checking out the Earthquake Information Center, seismic recorder, and mini planetarium. Permanent exhibits include Forces That Shape The Bay, an interactive exhibit on the evolution of the bay, Within the Human Brain, which explains how our brains function, and The Idea Lab, which lets kids imagine what it's like to be a scientist. On weekends, kids can experiment with mazes and learn about a variety of small animals in the Biology Lab. There's a stargazing program at dusk on Saturday (weather permitting). Be sure to have a snack in the Bay View Cafe, where the spectacular panoramic view of the bay and San Francisco is thrown in for free. Before leaving, check out the fabulous gift shop, filled with intriguing educational games and toys and books. *Centennial Dr., below Grizzly Peak Blvd., Berkeley; (510) 642-5132; www.lawrencehallofscience.org*

University of California, Berkeley
★★★/Free

Known for academic excellence, this distinguished university has a visitor-friendly campus with many noteworthy facilities that are open to the public. You can take a guided tour of the sprawling campus *(call 510/642-5215 for information)* or do the self-guided tour described in a free brochure, available from the University Visitors Center (*101 University Hall*). But most families with younger-than-high-school-age kids will probably just want to hit the campus's top attractions, the Campanile and the Museum of Paleontology. In the

FamilyFun ACTIVITY

Q & A

Laminate a map of your route, then create question-and-answer cards keyed to highlights along the way. Play with them like flash cards.

center of the campus, the 307-foot-tall Campanile tower has an observation platform (accessible by elevator; admission fee) that offers a breathtaking 360-degree view of the area. Modeled after the slightly taller campanile in St. Marks Square in Venice, this campus landmark has a 61-bell carillon that plays mini concerts several times each day. The Museum of Paleontology, in the Valley Life Sciences Building, has dinosaur bones. Enough said. No self-respecting young lover of extinct lizards will want to miss the fossil collection, one of the largest and oldest in North America. It includes a complete Tyrannosaurus rex skeleton, the largest triceratops skull ever found, a frozen mammoth, ancient bacteria, and the skeleton of a saber-toothed tiger—California's state fossil. *Telegraph Ave./Bancroft Way, Berkeley; (510) 642-6000;* www.berkeley.edu

Zellerbach Hall
★/$$$-$$$$

Check to see what's going on at this university theater while you're in town. Many performances here are

fine for kids. One of the best—the International Taiko Festival—is held each November. Dating back 2,000 years, taiko drums were once used in Japan to stimulate rain and to lead armies into battle. At the festival, one muscle-bound taiko drummer after another beats out an exhilarating primal rhythm. San Francisco's internationally acclaimed Taiko Dojo group usually performs on a one-ton, 12-foot-high drum, the largest in the Western Hemisphere. Kids love it, as do most adults. There's also a Family Fare series of matinee performances, with half-price tickets for kids 16 and under. *On the UC Berkeley campus, Berkeley; (510) 642-9988.*

JUST FOR FUN

Adventure Playground
FamilyFun ★★★★/Free

Designed like popular post–World War II playgrounds in Europe, this unusual play place provides kids with nails, hammers, saws, and scrap wood for building whatever they like. They can add to structures left by other young carpenters, or tear everything down and start over. The playground also has a tire swing, a climbing net, and a fast-moving trolley hanging from a pulley. Kids too little to wield real tools (younger than 6) can play in a large grassy area with more traditional toddlers' play equipment. Just across the street, the Shorebird Nature Center has a 100-gallon aquarium, where they often hold special family programs. *160 University Ave., Berkeley; (510) 644-8623; www.ci.berkeley.ca.us/marina/ marinaexp*

Berkeley Iceland ★★/$

With a rink measuring 100 feet by 200 feet, this ranks as one of the largest indoor ice-skating surfaces in the country. Though a relic from the past, the old-fashioned rink is busy and popular nonetheless. Don't let the crowds stop you and your kids from enjoying a whirl around the rink. You can rent skates. Nonskaters can watch from the warm observation room with vending machines that dispense hot soup and cocoa. *2727 Milvia St., Berkeley; (510) 843-8800; www.berkeleyice land.com*

Berkeley Rose Garden ★★/Free

Planted at the turn of the century, this garden has gorgeous views of the bay and San Francisco. Kids love sniffing the fragrant blooms and skipping along the pleasant paths. Tennis courts adjoin, and across the street is Codornices Park, with a playground and basketball court. (But do watch the little ones on the playground's long slide—it's slippery and superfast, which makes it treacherous as well as fun.) *Euclid Ave., Berkeley; (510) 981-5150.*

Tilden Regional Park

FamilyFun ★★★★/Free-$$

Just the place for an afternoon of outdoor fun, this beautiful park has 35 miles of hiking trails and plenty of picnic spots. Your older kids will particularly enjoy the Environmental Education Center, where interactive exhibits stress local natural history (fee). Educational programs and naturalist-guided walks, many designed especially for families and children, are scheduled regularly. Take the little ones next door, where they're sure to love the brightly painted, well-maintained Little Farm that's home to an assortment of friendly barnyard animals. Just a short walk away, kids can ride

A GOOD EGG Hard-boiled eggs are a perfect road food if you peel them first, wrap them in plastic, and chill them. Here's a foolproof recipe: place eggs in a saucepan and cover with water. Bring to a boil, reduce heat, and simmer 15 minutes (add 2 minutes if eggs are straight from the fridge). Plunge eggs into cold water. Keep in the cooler or eat within two hours.

ponies and horses (fee). Tots ages 2 to 4 are strapped securely into a saddle with a back support and given an exciting ride at the pony wheel. Children 5 and older can ride real horses in a larger ring. All ages will enjoy a ride on the carousel in the park's center (fee). An antique gem built in 1911 by the Herschel Spillman firm in New York and restored in 1978, it is one of only four classic four-row carousels remaining in Northern California. Among its colorful animals are a stork, a dragon, and a frog, as well as a herd of horses. Its large band organ operates like a player piano. In summer, when lifeguards are on duty, you can swim in Lake Anza, and kids get special rates at a scenic, well-priced 18-hole golf course (fee). Whew! That should take care of an entire day, but do leave time for a ride on the 15-inch gauge, 5-inch

scale narrow gauge Redwood Valley Railway steam train (fee). It chugs along a scenic one and one-quarter-mile route, through one tunnel and over two trestles. *The park stretches for about five miles off Grizzly Peak, below Wildcat Canyon Rd., Berkeley; (510) 525-2233;* www.ebayparks.org/parks/tilden.htm

BUNKING DOWN

Claremont Resort & Spa
★★★★/$$$$
Families looking to enjoy a little resort life during their visit to Berkeley can retreat to this property's extensive facilities after a day of sight-seeing. The 267-room Victorian hotel, built in 1915, was once described by architect Frank Lloyd Wright as "one of the few hotels in the world with warmth,

DAY TRIP
Berkeley with the Locals

9:30 A.M. Begin your day in Berkeley the way the locals do, with breakfast at **Fat Apple's**. (See Good Eats)

10:30 A.M. Head across the street to the **Mr. Mopps** toy store *(1405 Martin Luther King; 510/525-9633)*. You'll love the old-fashioned feel of this stuffed-to-the-gills shop, and your kids will have no trouble

spending their trip allowance here. Pick up some bubbles and balls to take along with you to Tilden Park.

11 A.M. Buy picnic supplies at **Andronico's Market** *(1550 Shattuck Ave.; 510/841-7942)*. This upscale supermarket is located within what was once the consumer-owned Co-op, a supermarket that operated here from 1938 to 1988 and was the country's largest urban cooperative. Andronico's carries delicious take-out fare and locally made gourmet

character, and charm." The kids will especially appreciate the two pools and hot tub surrounded by several long rows of chaise lounges—looking more like something you'd expect to find in sunny Southern California or Hawaii. There are also four saunas, two steam rooms, a fitness room, ten tennis courts, and a full-service health spa. The Claremont Kids Club operates daily year-round on a drop-in basis for an hourly fee. Open to all ages but appealing mostly to kids under 12, the program has four rooms dedicated to age-appropriate activities. Try to arrange your stay to include a Sunday, when you can indulge in the dining room's expansive brunch. Your kids' eyes are sure to open wide when they see the magnificent dessert spread. *41 Tunnel Rd., Berkeley; (800) 551-7266; (510) 843-3000;* www.claremontresort.com

Hotel Durant
★★/$$

Families are welcome at this 140-room hotel that's one block from the university. Some of the attractively appointed rooms have views of the campanile. Children under 12 stay free. The hotel restaurant has a comfortable pub atmosphere and kid-friendly food, including a very good hamburger, fresh fish items, and a variety of inexpensive sandwiches and salads. *2600 Durant Ave., Berkeley; (800) 2-DURANT; (510) 845-8981.*

Radisson Hotel Berkeley Marina
★★★/$$

In a tranquil setting on the bay, this comfortable 375-room property offer easy and free parking (a rarity in these parts) and rooms with marina views. The kids will like the

treats. Boxed lunches are available (order them 24 hours in advance). Each person in your family can select what appeals to them. Don't forget some carrots for the rabbits you'll visit later at the Little Farm.

11:30 A.M. Drive up Marin Avenue, Berkeley's steepest street, to Grizzly Peak and on into **Tilden Regional Park**. Depending on when you get hungry, stop at any of the many picnic areas. Before and after lunch, tour this magnificent park, stopping

to visit the animals at the **Little Farm** and ride the antique carousel, miniature train, and ponies. Allow some time for the kids to romp on the expansive lawns.

3 P.M. Discover the wonders of the **Lawrence Hall of Science**.

6 P.M. Since you'll probably be real tired about now, stop at **LaVal's** for a quick, cheap pizza, then head back to your room to relax for the evening.

95

indoor pool and hot tub where they can frolic even on cold winter days; there's a fitness center, too. Rates are discounted on Friday and Saturday night, and packages are sometimes available. The restaurant has bay views and a kids' menu. *200 Marina Blvd., Berkeley; (800) 333-3333; (510) 548-7920;* www.radisson.com

Rose Garden Inn
★★/$$

Situated seven blocks from the university, this charming 40-room lodging complex includes two landmark Tudor-style mansions, a carriage house, and a garden house with attractively decorated, comfortable guest rooms, some with views of San Francisco. Nicely decorated but without the fragile antiques and other breakables that give parents gray hair, the inn buildings open onto a central garden filled with fountains, patios, and hundreds of rosebushes. Families are accommo-

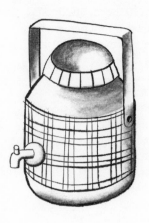

dated comfortably in the larger junior suites, which have refrigerators. Many rooms have fireplaces and one has a fully stocked kitchen. Kids and parents both will appreciate the free full breakfast and the always full cookie jar for snackers. *2740 Telegraph Ave., Berkeley; (800) 992-9005; (510) 549-2145;* www.rose gardeninn.com

GOOD EATS

Blakes
★★★/$$

A campus hangout since 1940, this restaurant serves family-friendly food, including a variety of hamburgers, sandwiches, and snacks. The best seats are upstairs on the main floor next to the windows, which offer excellent views of the sidewalk parade outside. Kids might also enjoy dining downstairs in the funky rathskeller, with its sawdust-covered floor and old wooden booths. *2367 Telegraph Ave., Berkeley; (510) 848-0886;* www.blakesontelegraph.com

Cactus Taqueria
★★★/$

Mexican fast food at its best is served cafeteria-style in this popular taqueria. Kids can decide on their own made-to-order burritos, with a choice of several kinds of tortillas (chili, tomato, spinach, plain), black or pinto beans, and a variety of well-seasoned fillings. Young diners can

THE MASCOT of the University of California at Berkeley is the golden bear. The grizzly bear is the official state animal and the gold color represents California's gold rush history.

also try smaller tacos (a good choice for children under 10) and tamales. Tortillas are lard-free, meats are the best quality, and tortilla chips are fried in safflower oil. Kids especially like the housemade beverages, including several *aguas frescas* (fresh fruit drinks) and *horchata* (a sweet rice drink). Adults appreciate the addictive salsas on each table—a tangy green tomatillo and a smoky mole. Everyone enjoys sitting at colorfully stained wooden tables and listening to the soothing sound of the indoor water fountain. *1881 Solano Ave., Berkeley; (510) 528-1881.*

Cha-Am ★★/$

Though Thai restaurants don't leap to mind when dining with children in tow, this gem is too good to miss. It's the perfect place to introduce your kids to this exotic cuisine (assuming they've moved beyond the nothing-but-peanut-butter-and-jelly phase). The chef produces complex flavors and interesting combinations. Among the spicy winners on the exciting menu are *laap-gai* (a chopped chicken salad tossed with fresh mint and coriander), *pad-makua-yao* (chicken sautéed with basil, chile, and eggplant), and *pad-ped-gung* (prawns sautéed with sweet

curry sauce, fresh Thai herbs, and green beans). Better for kids who don't like spicy food are the chicken satay with peanut sauce and the plain barbecued chicken. For dessert, there's kid-pleasing coconut or mango ice cream. *1543 Shattuck Ave., Berkeley; (510) 848-9664.*

Chez Panisse
★★/$$$

Opened in 1971 by UC graduate Alice Waters as a hangout for her friends, this fabulously famous restaurant features the definitive California cuisine—simply prepared food made with the freshest ingredients. A different fixed-price menu is served each night in the legendary, expensive downstairs dining room, which is not really appropriate for children. A better choice for families is the less expensive upstairs café. (Call for reservations the same day, after 9 A.M.) Its seasonal menu features simple items such as baked goat-cheese salad, Spanish-style grilled chicken with lentils, and strawberry shortcake. Pizza and pasta are available for kids. Meals in both venues are almost always a perfect "10." **NOTE:** A 15-percent service charge is automatically added to the bill and is divided among the entire staff. *1517 Shattuck Ave., Berkeley. Cafe: (510) 548-5049; Restaurant: (510) 548-5525; www.chezpanisse.com*

Fat Apple's
★★★★/$

This popular restaurant is always overflowing with families and sometimes even attracts celebrities such as Robin Williams. Everyone comes for the good food, made from scratch with basic ingredients. The lean beef used for the hamburgers is ground on the premises; the soup is fresh; the blue cheese salad dressing is made with the real stuff; and robust Peet's coffee is freshly ground and served with heavy whipping cream. Everyone, including kids, seems to love the famous hamburger, served on a toasted housemade wheat or white bun, and the just-right milk shakes served in the metal mixer canister. For dessert, it's impossible to go wrong with a slice of the puffy apple pie the restaurant is named for, but the chocolate velvet and lemon meringue pies are also winners. Breakfast features fresh-squeezed orange juice, crisp waffles served with pure Vermont maple syrup, omelettes, buckwheat or whole-wheat pancakes, and freshly baked pastries. Yum! *1346 Martin Luther King, Jr. Way, Berkeley; (510) 526-2260.*

> The bells of the **Campanile** are played 18 times per week when UC Berkeley is in session. The music is heard throughout the city.

Ginger Island ★★/$$$

Famous for being the spot where celebrity chef Mark Miller first dished out his Southwestern cuisine (he's since moved on to the Coyote Cafe in Santa Fe and Red Sage in Washington, D.C.), this restaurant now serves up American fare with an Asian flair in its inviting (also casual and kid-friendly) contemporary space. Among the best items on the menu are the sensuously soft appetizer wontons that explode with flavor (kids generally like these), the sweet-sauced tender baby back ribs, and the memorable gingery ginger cake. Ask your server about the available kids' items, which usually include a hamburger, grilled chicken strips, a grilled white cheese on sourdough sandwich, and a pasta dish. Drinks include a potent Singapore sling served in a tall glass (a grown-ups-only treat!), iced lychee tea, and housemade ginger ale. *1820 Fourth St., Berkeley; (510) 644-0444; www.gingerisland.com*

La Note ★★/$$

Très casual and touching just the right culinary notes, this charming restaurant delivers the French Provençale dining experience without the negatives of small dogs and smoking in its cheery dining room. On a warm, sunny day you can sit on an outside patio and sip a café au lait from a big bowl while *les enfants* enjoy hot chocolate made with real milk. Winning items on the breakfast menu include lemon-gingerbread pancakes with poached pears, fluffy scrambled eggs, and perfectly fried rosemary potatoes. French-style lunches and dinners are also served. It's time the kids learned the meaning of *"Bon appetit!"* *2377 Shattuck Ave., Berkeley; (510) 843-1535;* www.lanote.citysearch.com

La Val's
★★★★/$

Located on the quieter north side of the UC campus, this long popular student hangout is also a good choice for families. It has good pizza, pastas, and (for Mom and Dad) brews. The interior is casual, with overhead TVs that broadcast sporting events. On warm days, try the courtyard beer garden with picnic tables. Your older children can pass their waiting time playing video games. There's a cover charge for the downstairs Subterranean, which offers live music and plays. You can order food there, and children are welcome, although this may be a better bet for the older kids who can sit still during the performances. *1834 Euclid Ave., Berkeley; (510) 843-5617.*

Pyramid Brewery & Alehouse ★★★★/$

The one gargantuan room that makes up this massive, very noisy

Oakland: What's There There

The most famous comment about this much-maligned city is Gertrude Stein's often quoted, "There is no there there." But while Oakland usually loses in the struggle with San Francisco and Berkeley for media attention, families will find at least a few things here to amuse them.

First, some fun facts about Oakland: "The Wave"—sports fans' synchronized movement in stadiums—was "invented" here; it is the most ethnically diverse city in the United States; and Mother's Cake & Cookie Company, the largest cookie producer in the United States, has been here since 1914.

For pre- and grade-schoolers, the biggest attraction in Oakland is Children's Fairyland, *699 Bellevue Ave., located on Grand Avenue by Lake Merritt (510/452-2259).* Designed especially for children ages 8 and under, this was the country's first educational storybook theme park when it opened in 1950. Mother Goose rhymes and fairy tales come to life in more than 30 colorful fantasy sets, some inhabited by live animals. Among the attractions is an Alice in Wonderland–themed maze, a variety of slides, a mini carousel, and a small Ferris wheel. Your kids can also sit in and steer their own motorboats and giggle at the popular award-winning puppet shows staged daily at 11, 2, and 4. N O T E : When buying your admission tickets, do also purchase one of the magic keys that unlocks story boxes found throughout the park.

To Dye For

Help your kids to get into the spirit of the '60s by making tie-dye socks!

MATERIALS

♦ Plastic bowl or pan
♦ Nontoxic fabric dye
♦ White socks
♦ Rubber bands
♦ Rubber gloves
♦ Plastic spoon

STEP 1: Begin by covering the work area with newspaper. In a plastic bowl or pan, dissolve a packet of nontoxic fabric dye in hot water, according to the package directions. Add more hot water until there is enough to cover a couple of pairs of socks.

STEP 2: Dampen the white socks with clear warm water, then bundle them up in rubber bands.

STEP 3: Wearing rubber gloves, submerge the bound socks in the warm dye and stir occasionally with a plastic spoon.

STEP 4: After 20 minutes or so (the color will lighten after the fabric is rinsed and dried), run them under cool water, squeezing until the water runs clear.

STEP 5: Remove the bands, smooth out the socks, and rest them flat on newspaper. Let them dry overnight.

TIPS: Wash the socks separately from the rest of the laundry the first few times to prevent damage from bleeding dye.

operation can feel cozy if you get one of the comfy private booths. The expansive, eclectic menu offers enough choices to satisfy the various cravings of an entire family: snacks, soups, pizzas, sandwiches, burgers, and salads, as well as heftier entrées of fish-and-chips, baby back ribs, and assorted steaks. Fifteen beers are on tap, all brewed on the premises in huge brewery vats visible from the dining room. A children's coloring menu offers kid-size portions of fish-and-chips as well as cheeseburgers, hot dogs, and cheese pizza. For dessert, order root-beer floats for the kids and Espresso Stout floats for the grownups. Children are welcome on the brewery tours offered Monday through Friday at 2 and 4 P.M., and Saturday and Sunday at 1, 2, and 4 P.M. On summer evenings, take the kids to see the classic movies that are screened outdoors in the parking lot. *901 Gilman St., Berkeley; (510) 528-9880;* www.pyramidbrew.com

Telegraph Avenue Food Stalls
★★★★/$

Kids love food courts, and this is one—Berkeley-style. Each weekday from approximately 11 A.M. to 3 P.M., informal stands dispense simple fast foods such as doughnuts, soft pretzels, fresh juices and smoothies, falafels (Middle Eastern vegetarian sandwiches), and other ethnic dishes. Use the nearby benches, steps, and grassy areas as impromptu picnic spots, and the kids will have plenty of space to wiggle. This famous intersection attracts all kinds of entertainers—jugglers, musicians, revivalists, you name it—so you get an amazing free floor show with your lunch. *At the campus entrance, Bancroft Way/Telegraph Ave., Berkeley.*

Top Dog
★★/$

Hot dogs are the extent of the menu at these two atmospheric holes-in-the-wall. The kids can choose from among 12 different kinds of franks and (surprising for this town) not a veggie version is among them. The one topped with sauerkraut and mustard is one of the best hot dogs on the West Coast. Grab one of the few counter stools, sit on the bench outside, or just stomp and chomp. *2503 Hearst Ave.; (510) 843-1241. Also at 2534 Durant Ave., Berkeley; (510) 843-5967.*

SOUVENIR HUNTING

Telegraph Avenue
Running four blocks between Bancroft Way and Dwight Way, south of the UC campus, this street is probably best known as the gathering spot and point of confrontation during the 1960s Free Speech Movement. Today, a daily street bazaar of crafts stalls sells souvenirs with major kid appeal, including colorful tie-dyed clothing and handmade toys. A vast selection of trendy items makes this a preteen heaven. You can also feast on a delicious assortment of junk food sold in shops along the avenue—everything from Blondie's counterculture pizza to Mrs. Fields' corporate cookies. In the 2400 block, Cody's legendary bookstore *(2454 Telegraph Ave., Berkeley 510/845-7852)* stocks obscure new tomes along with the latest best-sellers and also has an extensive children's collection.

The hands-on experiences at the Children's Discovery Museum of San Jose include a tower maze, a life-size fire engine, and the Bernoulli blower *(pictured)*.

Silicon Valley and San Jose

YOUR KIDS were probably weaned on this valley's most important commodity—the computer. In fact, they probably already know as much or more about things technological as Mom or Dad. So your kings and queens of the keyboard will feel right at home in Silicon Valley, where the computer revolution began. An estimated 12,000 high-tech companies are located in the area, and those that are headquartered elsewhere maintain a significant presence here. For computer whiz kids, the biggest attractions in Silicon Valley are the glitzy Tech Museum and the computer museum at the Intel Corporation headquarters. But there are also plenty of places in the region for more low-tech family fun, including an old-fashioned farm, three amusement parks, a real-life

THE FamilyFun LIST

Children's Discovery Museum of San Jose (page 105)

Intel Museum (page 106)

Kelley Park (page 108)

Paramount's Great America (page 109)

Rosicrucian Egyptian Museum (page 106)

The Tech Museum of Innovation (page 107)

Winchester Mystery House (page 110)

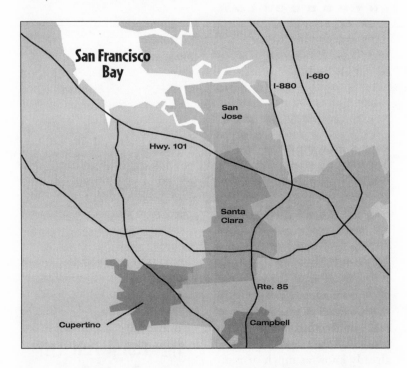

fun house, and several interesting museums. Among these are a children's museum and one focused on ancient Egypt, a civilization of enduring interest to kids.

There is much debate about where Silicon Valley exactly is. The entire area known as The Peninsula qualifies, but San Jose, 50 miles south of San Francisco, currently touts itself as the capital of Silicon Valley. In addition to its high-tech image, it's also home to many of the region's most family-oriented attractions. Founded as a Spanish pueblo in 1777, San Jose was California's first civilian settlement. It was the state capital from 1849 to 1851 and is now the third-largest city in California and the 11th largest in the country. Despite its interesting history and its reliably mild climate, San Jose's attractions have received relatively little attention compared to those in San Francisco. But that seems to be changing. In recent years the city has revitalized its downtown area, allowing visitors to enjoy its many cultural offerings as well as its great weather.

San Jose will most likely be your family's base of operations during your Silicon Valley visit. But some of the region's must-see sites are in neighboring towns such as Santa Clara and Campbell.

CULTURAL ADVENTURES

Children's Discovery Museum of San Jose
★★★★/$

Children ages 1 through 10, for whom it was designed, are sure to be entertained at the largest children's museum in the West. Located in Guadalupe River Park, the striking purple-colored building includes plenty of places for adults to sit and watch while their kids have a great time doing everything from making corn husk dolls to blowing gigantic bubbles to climbing on a full-size fire engine. Featured are 150 hands-on exhibits, including a Water Works exhibit and Magic Beans Creative People, which celebrate how things grow. Steve Wozniak, of Apple Computer fame, sponsored the Jesse's Clubhouse, where happy kids clamber through a multilevel tower maze. The exhibit is named in honor of Wozniak's son. (And who do you suppose Woz Way, the street the museum is located on, is named for?) A snack bar serves inexpensive things that children like to eat: hot dogs, hamburgers, peanut-butter-and-jelly sandwiches. *180 Woz Way, San Jose; (408) 298-5437; www.cdm.org*

The Gaslighter Theater
★★★★/$$

After being greeted in the street and at the door by the exuberant cast, the whole family has a blast hissing the villain and cheering the hero at this old-fashioned melodrama theater. An endless supply of complimentary popcorn to munch on, and throw, adds to the fun. Each two-part production includes a melodrama (such as *Ignorance Isn't Bliss* or *No Mother to Guide Her*) and a vaudeville performance featuring dancing, singing, and comedy. The shows are not at all subtle, making them great for children. Tickets can be purchased at the door, but call ahead to avoid

---

FamilyFun READER'S TIP

Reward Good Backseat Behavior

Backseat squabbles were a big problem for the Niehues family of Red Wing, Minnesota, on long car trips. "Four kids can find a lot to fight about!" says mom Mary. Now, though, Mom and Dad give each of the kids a roll of quarters at the beginning of the trip. Every time they have to correct a child's behavior, the culprit forfeits a quarter. But any quarters still remaining at the trip's end are the child's to keep. "My husband and I came out even the first time," Mary says, "but we never have again!"

Mary Niehues, Red Wing, Minnesota

disappointment. *400 E. Campbell Ave., Campbell; (408) 866-1408;* www.thegaslighter.com

Intel Museum
FamilyFun ★★★/Free

Everything you and your budding computer geeks/wanna-be billionaires want to know about how computer chips are made and how they are used in everyday life is explained here. Intel is the world's largest semiconductor company and the inventor of the Pentium processor, so it is fitting that this technology museum is located in the main lobby of Intel Corporation's headquarters in Santa Clara. Children of all ages are welcome, but school-age kids will get more out of a visit here. (Age 6 is the recommended minimum age for the guided tour, available by reservation.) Visitors learn the history of computer chips, the differences between the various types,

and how they are constructed. Hands-on educational exhibits that appeal to both children and adults change regularly. There's even a live video feed from the company's chip-fabrication facility, which lets you see computer-chip construction direct from the "clean room," which operates around the clock. FYI: it's nothing like those old Intel commercials with the dancing guys in silver space suits. But you might see employees wearing "bunny" suits to keep lint, hair, and skin flakes from contaminating wafers. *2200 Mission College Blvd., Santa Clara; (408) 765-0503;* www.intel.com/go/museum

Rosicrucian
FamilyFun Egyptian Museum
★★★★/$

For kids, the mummies are without a doubt the highlight of this museum, which houses the largest exhibit of Egyptian, Babylonian, and Assyrian artifacts in the Western United States. Among the six human mummies is one that has a nine-inch metal pin in his knee—the first known attempt at knee surgery. Children find the animal mummies especially interesting; there are several cats, some fish, a baboon, and the head of an ox. There's also fine jewelry and a full-size reproduction of a 4,000-year-old rock tomb. **NOTE:** Strollers are not permitted in the museum. After visiting the mummies, take some time to walk through the surrounding seven-and-a-half-acre

The Core of the Apple

In 1975, Steve Wozniak and Steve Jobs designed and built one of the first home computers in Jobs' Cupertino, California, home and garage. Although there was little public interest in the computer at the time, the men formally founded Apple Computer in 1976 and today, the company is a multimillion-dollar corporation.

park. It's adorned with beautiful and exotic trees and flowers and unusual Egyptian statuary, and picnicking is permitted. *1342 Naglee Ave., San Jose; (408) 947-3636;*www.rosicrucianegyptianmuseum.org

The Tech Museum of Innovation
★★★★/$

School-age keyboard kings and queens will meet Vanna the spelling robot, design a bike on a computer, and learn how silicon chips are produced at this shrine to the high-tech world. Most of the exhibits, which focus on current projects at local technology companies, are child-friendly. Guided tours of each gallery are scheduled, and volunteers are on hand to answer questions. Operating within the museum but with a separate admission fee (a combination ticket is available, and purchasing tickets in advance is advised), the IMAX Dome Theater is a must-see. You'll find yourself almost completely surrounded by a film projected onto an 82-foot-diameter screen—the only one in Northern California. As you leave the vibrant mango and purple build-ing, don't miss the whimsical audio-kinetic sculpture by George Rhoads, located just outside the exit. The whole family will find it mesmerizing. *201 S. Market St., San Jose; (408) 294-TECH;* www.thetech.org

JUST FOR FUN

Alum Rock Park
★★★/Free

Careful! In some spots hot mineral water bubbles up from sulphur springs at California's first park. The springs made this a nationally known health spa in the early 1900s, but kids will be more interested in the science behind that naturally hot water than its medicinal benefits. Young visitors also love seeing the live birds of prey, including hawks and owls, and other native animals at the park's Youth Science Institute. It also has a large taxidermy collection and offers hands-on activities for children. Other features of this 730-acre park, located in the foothills of the Diablo Range northeast of town, include picnic tables, barbecue pits, and a children's playground. Families enjoy hiking and bicycling here. (But bring your own wheels—there are no bike rentals.) *End of Alum Rock Ave., east of Hwy. 101, San Jose; (408) 259-5477.*

Emma Prusch Farm and Park
★★★/Free

Not all apples are computers. This is just one of the things your family will learn when you visit this old-fashioned farm. The 47-acre dairy farm gives folks the opportunity to step back in time to San Jose's rural past. The original 19th-century white farmhouse is now the information center. The barn is home to an assortment of domesticated farm animals that thrive in spite of their proximity to the freeway. Kids will love getting close to the cows, sheep, and pigs. They can feed the poultry if you pack along fruits and vegetables. Don't miss a romp through the orchard, where more than 100 kinds of rare fruits grow, among them limequat, pawpaw, gumi, and sapote as well as exotic varieties of cherries, guavas, persimmons, grapefruit and other citruses—and, yes, apples. *647 S. King Rd., at Hwys. 680 and 280, San Jose; (408) 926-5555.*

Kelley Park
FamilyFun ★★★★/Free

Loads of fun awaits your family in this expansive park. Start at the Happy Hollow Park and Zoo, which offers amusement park rides as well as lots of critters. After you've said good-bye to the animals, board the miniature Kelley Park Express Train just outside the zoo and ride it to the Japanese Friendship Garden. Later, reboard the train to visit the San Jose Historical Museum. (See below for details on all three.) Parking fee. *Located three miles southeast of downtown, 1300 Senter Rd., San Jose.*

Happy Hollow Park and Zoo
★★★★/$

Children ages 10 and younger love this place, which claims to be the only combination mini amusement park and zoo in the United States. Spacious and shady, it offers a satisfying combination of kiddie rides and more than 150 animals. The zoo features a bird enclosure, and an area where for small change children can hand-feed domestic and exotic animals. The admission fee covers five rides, daily puppet shows, the zoo, and use of a concrete maze and playground equipment. The two-story Crooked House is a particular favorite; it takes a different slant on the typical playhouse. A corkscrew slide carries kids from the top level to the ground floor, where they come shooting out the front door onto the porch. The park has picnic tables, so this is a good spot to stop for lunch. Free for mothers on Mother's Day and fathers on Father's Day. *1300 Senter Rd., in Kelley Park, San Jose; (408) 277-3000;* www.happyhollow parkandzoo.org

Japanese Friendship Garden
★★★★/Free

Patterned after the Korakuen Garden in San Jose's sister city of Okayama, this 6.5-acre garden has four heart-shaped ponds populated with rare koi. Children are sure to be delighted with these super-size goldfish. Don't forget to walk over the Moon Bridge for good luck and cross the Zigzag Bridge to get rid of evil spirits. *Kelley Park, San Jose.*

San Jose Historical Museum
★★★★/$

Are your kids always peppering you with questions about how people lived in "the olden days"? Bring the young historians here. The ever-growing 25-acre museum is the site of more than 28 relocated and replicated historic homes and business buildings that illustrate the culture and history of San Jose and the Santa Clara Valley. There are structures from turn-of-the-century San Jose and other periods, including a Chinese temple dating from the mid-1800s and a gas station from the 1920s. Docent-led museum tours begin at the Pacific Hotel. Or stop at the hotel to pick up a brochure outlining a self-guided tour (a good option when you have small folk who might not be up for the entire guided tour). When everyone has had enough history for the day, stop for refreshments at O'Brien's Ice Cream and Candy Store *(1650 Senter Rd.; 408/287-2290)*, the first place west of Detroit to serve ice cream and sodas. *Kelley Park, San Jose;* www.ci.sanjose.ca.us/cac/parks/kp/sjhm.html

 ## Paramount's Great America
★★★★/$$$$

There's no question about it. The thrill rides at Northern California's most elaborate theme park are spectacular, and the roller coasters are great, shocking fun. Kids ages 10 and older just might want to ride them nonstop. The Vortex is the West's first stand-up roller coaster; the Demon features two 360-degree loops and a double helix; and the Grizzly is a classic wooden coaster based on the late, lamented Coney Island Wildcat. The Drop Zone Stunt Tower free-fall ride is Santa Clara's tallest structure, and the circa 1976 double-decker Carousel Columbia is the world's tallest merry-go-round. Don't miss Stealth, the world's first flying coaster. But

---

FamilyFun TIP

Cool It

Whether you use a cooler, an insulated bag or box, or Tupperware, here's how to keep snacks cool without messy, melting ice: Add frozen juice boxes; make sandwiches on frozen bread; pack some frozen grapes; include a smoothie frozen in a tightly sealed container; use sealed ice packs.

IN-THE-CAR SCAVENGER HUNT

Hand your kids a pack of index cards and ask them to write or draw pictures of 50 things they might see on a trip. Keep the cards for scavenger hunts when players vie to match what they see with the cards.

the pint-size members of the family aren't forgotten. The new Kidzville has colorful rides and attractions especially for children ages 12 and under. They feature Hanna-Barbera characters such as Yogi Bear, Fred Flintstone, and Scooby-Doo. Several live shows daily put the icing on this great big cake. *On Great America Parkway, off Hwys. 101 and 237, Santa Clara; (408) 988-1776; www.pgathrills.com*

Raging Waters ★★★★/$$

Slide and splash the day away at this water-oriented amusement park located in San Jose's Lake Cunningham Regional Park. It's the Bay Area's largest such facility, and it also claims to have the fastest water slides this side of the Rockies: sliders can reach speeds up to 25 miles per hour. Another slide sends kids zooming down six stories into a catch pool below. An inner-tube ride, a sled ride, and a rope swing are among the myriad other water activ-

ities. Parents will be pleased to know that an army of 40 lifeguards watch over frolickers, making it easier for you to relax and enjoy. Facilities include free changing rooms and showers plus inexpensive lockers. Food and beverages may not be brought into the park, but there's a public picnic area just outside the main gate and fast food is sold inside. *2333 S. White Rd., San Jose; (408) 238-9900; www.rwsplash.com*

MUST-SEE FamilyFun MUST-SEE Winchester Mystery House ★★★★/$$

Kids get a kick out of the story, which goes like this: Sarah Winchester, heir to the $20-million Winchester rifle fortune, believed that, to make amends for a past wrongdoing, she had to continuously build additions to her circa 1884 Victorian mansion. Her eccentric ideas resulted in some unusual features. Everyone is surprised by the asymmetrical rooms and the doors that open into empty shafts, and kids can get positively giddy maneuvering the narrow passageways and zigzag stairwells. The guided tour of this city landmark takes in 110 of the 160 rooms, climbs more than 200 steps, and covers almost a mile. (All the walking and climbing may be too much for young children—and strollers are not permitted. Though many visitors bring toddlers, you'll enjoy your visit most with school-age children.) After exploring the house, head for the six-acre Victorian garden, sprinkled liberally with fountains and statues and a good place for the kids to romp. There's a snack bar, and picnic tables are available. Spooky Halloween tours are offered in October. *525 S. Winchester Blvd., San Jose; (408) 247-2101;* www. winchestermysteryhouse.com

BUNKING DOWN

Crowne Plaza ★★★/$$-$$$$

A good location, large rooms, and a pool—what more could a traveling family ask for? Centrally located in downtown San Jose, this nine-story, 239-room hotel is within easy walking distance of all the downtown attractions. Accommodations are spacious, and children under 17 stay free in their parents' room. In addition to the pool, there's a fitness center that's open around the clock. Tennis courts, racquetball courts, and jogging paths are nearby. *282 Almaden Blvd., San Jose; (800) 2-CROWNE; (408) 998-0400;* www.gc.com

Embassy Suites Hotel
★★★★/$$-$$$$

Just minutes from Paramount's Great America theme park, this 257-room hotel offers packages that include theme park admission tickets. Perfect for families, the spacious two-room suites consist of a bedroom plus a separate living room with a sofa bed. Each unit is equipped with two TVs (for fewer squabbles over the remote) and a kitchenette with a coffeemaker and a refrigerator. On-site facilities include an indoor heated pool (hurray!), a hot tub, a sauna, and a fitness center. The room rate includes a cooked-to-order breakfast and—for Mom and Dad—evening cocktails. *2885 Lakeside Dr., Santa Clara; (800) EMBASSY; (408) 496-6400;* embassysuites.com

Fairmont Hotel
★★★★/$$-$$$$

Built on the site of what was California's capitol building from 1849 to 1851, this 20-story, 541-room luxury high-rise hotel is within walking distance of all downtown attractions. Children under 18 stay free in their parents' room, and there are some larger family rooms available (located, appropriately, off the nicely landscaped swimming pool). There's also a fitness room and sauna (a plus for the grown-ups). An on-site restaurant offers casual dining and old-fashioned soda fountain treats. *170 S. Market St., San Jose; (800) 527-4727; (408) 998-1900;* www.fairmont.com

Hayes Mansion Conference Center ★★★/$$-$$$$

With all the resort amenities (volleyball courts, tennis courts, a swimming pool, a fitness room, and a jogging/walking trail running through a scenic park) and plenty of space to run around, this place is like one big playground. Once the largest private home in Northern California, the fabulous mansion is now a 135-guest conference center. **NOTE:** It's only open to other visitors (read: families) on the weekends. Kids find it a delightful challenge to find the "hidden" subterranean billiards room bar. The hotel dining room puts on an expansive weekend brunch buffet that shouldn't be missed—there's something to please even the pickiest eater. *200 Edenvale Ave., San Jose; (800) 420-3200; (408) 226-3200; www.hayesmansion.com*

Hotel De Anza ★★★★/$$$

Known as the Grand Lady of San Jose, this cozy 101-room hotel dates from 1931; renovations have restored its original Art Deco grandeur. The guest rooms are spacious and attractively appointed. Kids will get a kick out of the telephone and TV in the well-designed tile bathrooms (okay, you probably will, too). The best perk is the complimentary "Raid Our Pantry" nighttime snack buffet in the special guests' pantry. You can perch on the kitchen counter in your bathrobe while gobbling up goodies such as chocolate-chip cookies and salami cracker sandwiches. An extensive breakfast buffet is available for a small fee. *233 W. Santa Clara St., San Jose; (800) 843-3700; (408) 286-1000; www.hoteldeanza.com*

GOOD EATS

Buca di Beppo
★★★★/$$

Huge portions of Southern Italian fare are served at this lively restaurant. Also see Good Eats in San Francisco. *1875 S. Basom Ave., Campbell; (408) 377-7722.*

Crocodile Cafe
★★★★/$-$$

This casual spot serves L.A.–style fare, including salads, sandwiches, pizza, calzones, pasta, and grilled meat. Also see Good Eats in Santa Monica. *2855 Stevens Creek Blvd., San Jose; (408) 260-1100.*

The Old Spaghetti Factory
★★★★/$$

There will be a lot of slurping at the table as the kids make their way through plates piled with oodles of noodles. Spaghetti connoisseurs can dine on their favorite pasta with regular marinara sauce, with mushroom sauce, with white clam sauce, or with meat sauce. There's even spaghetti with a sampler of sauces, great for kids who can't make up their minds. Meatballs, spinach tortellini, and baked chicken are also available. Complete dinners come with bread, soup or salad, a beverage (coffee, tea, or milk), and spumoni ice cream. The restaurant is housed in what was once the warehouse for the *San Jose Mercury News* and offers a variety of interesting seating options, including a restored streetcar and a brass bed converted into a booth. The fun decor and the availability of familiar fare make this a hit with young diners. *51 N. San Pedro St., San Jose; (408) 288-7488;* www.osf.com

World Wrapps
★★★/$

This local fast-food chain serves up tasty, wholesome, made-to-order meals. Stuffed tortillas are the specialty of the house. Also see Good Eats in San Francisco. *3125 Mission College Blvd., Santa Clara; (408) 486-9727;* www.worldwrapps.com

SOUVENIR HUNTING

San Jose Flea Market

Most everything can be found here (including plenty of outgrown toys) and at bargain prices. Said to be the largest in the world—bigger even than the famous Paris market that started the whole thing—this out-

door flea market features more than 2,700 vendors spread out over 120 acres; there are more than 35 restaurants and snack stands. Most kids like poking around the stuff in search of small treasures. When their quarters are spent, they can play Skee-Ball, visit one of three playgrounds, or ride the merry-go-round or a real live pony. There's also a variety of free entertainment. Thursday and Friday are least crowded; weekends and Wednesday are usually quite busy. *1590 Berryessa Rd., between Hwys. 680 and 101, San Jose; (408) 453-1110;* www.sjfm.com

Take a scenic trip between Fort Bragg and Willits on the Skunk Train. You'll chug over bridges, into tunnels, and through a forest of redwoods.

Mendocino and Fort Bragg

NOTHING QUITE MATCHES the thrill of seeing a huge creature propel itself out of the sea, fly through the air amidst foam and spray, and then land seconds later with a resounding splash. Your kids won't be the only ones shrieking with delight. Which is why the best time to visit Mendocino and Fort Bragg, towns about 150 miles up the coast from San Francisco, is during the annual whale migration period, from December through April.

In December, whales start passing through this area on their way down from Alaska's Bering Sea to Baja California, in Mexico, for breeding in the warm waters of Cabo's Sea of Cortez. They come by this way again in large numbers in March and April as they head back to the Bering Sea for summer feeding. The behemoths can sometimes be seen from town headlands and the shoreline—and even from some inns—as they "breach" (jump out of the water) and swim by. Both Mendocino and Fort Bragg hold whale festivals each March; Mendocino on the first weekend of the month and Fort

MUST-SEE

THE **FamilyFun** LIST

MUST-SEE

Mendocino Coast Botanical Gardens (page 118)

Skunk Train/California Western Railroad (page 119)

Van Damme State Park (page 119)

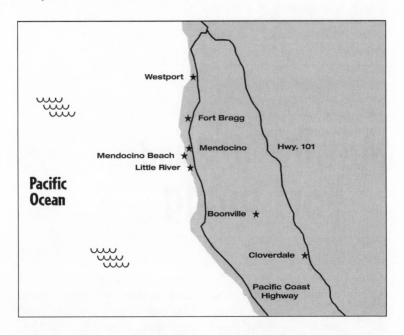

Westport ★

Fort Bragg ★

Mendocino Beach ★ ★ Mendocino   Hwy. 101

Little River ★

Pacific
Ocean

Boonville ★

Cloverdale ★

Pacific Coast
Highway

Bragg on the third weekend. Whale-watching cruises are scheduled during those times; ask around town for more information. You can also take the kids to interpretive programs about whales at the Ford House Museum and Visitor Center (see page 117) and nearby Mendocino Headlands State Park during migration season.

But even when they aren't providing front-row seats to a parade of migrating whales, remote Mendocino and Fort Bragg give you a perfect escape from the hectic pace of city life—or a break from the rat race anywhere. A historical district in itself, Mendocino lets you and your family step back in time. Known in the late 19th century as

"The Town of the Water Towers," it still has numerous water-collection tanks perched high above the town roofs. Today some of these picturesque towers have been converted into intriguing lodging places and restaurants that are sure to tweak the kids' imagination. Your grade-schoolers and up will be interested in the town's logging history as documented in the Kelly House and Ford House Museums. It's also fun to stroll along the town's main streets, where charming shops are plentiful—including a nifty toy store. If you stay in town, you can leave your car parked (no charge) for the duration of your visit, and easily walk anywhere. Mendocino also offers lots of ways to enjoy the great outdoors, with many state parks, a botanical garden, a lovely beach, and places where you can canoe, bicycle, and go horseback riding (rentals are available). If you're lucky, you might be in town for one of the quarterly Sunday morning pancake breakfasts put on by the town's volunteer fire department. (But be advised that Mendocino's fire alarm, which sounds like an air-raid siren, sometimes goes off in the middle of the night and can be quite startling, especially to children.)

Fort Bragg is 10 miles north of Mendocino. It is more low-key, generally less expensive, and famous for its Skunk Train historic railroad. Fort Bragg also has some great inexpensive fish restaurants in Noyo Harbor, where kids can watch the fishing boats come in with their daily catch.

The nightlife in these towns is of the early-to-bed, early-to-rise variety, which suits most families just fine. Make lodging reservations as far in advance as possible; the best places fill up fast.

Driving to this area from San Francisco takes about four hours nonstop. If you opt for scenic Highway 1, a longer route, plan to stop at Fort Ross State Historic Park to stretch your legs and enjoy a picnic. If you decide to drive on faster Highway 101 and cut over at Cloverdale to Highway 128, stop in at the Buckhorn Saloon in Boonville for a casual lunch in a family-friendly pub.

CULTURAL ADVENTURES

Ford House Museum and Visitor Center
★★★/By donation
Take the kids to this historic 1854 house to learn about the cultural and natural history of the area. During whale-watching season, in March and April, check out the short film about whale migration. In good weather, the backyard here is a great place for a family picnic—the tables offer a spectacular ocean view. An important family-friendly note: one of the few public bathrooms in town is located here. *735 Main St., Mendocino; (707) 937-5397.*

JUST FOR FUN

Catch A Canoe & Bicycles, Too
★★★★/$-$$$$
For total relaxation, rent a canoe here and spend the day drifting down Mendocino's calm Big River. Pack a picnic lunch and bring your swimsuits, because you'll find many secluded swimming holes. Canoe rentals include life jackets (but no lessons are offered). You can rent bicycles, too. *On Comptche-Ukiah Rd., Mendocino; (707) 937-0273; http://www.mcn.org/a/stanford inn/canoes.html*

117

Glass Beach ★★★★/Free

A great place to look for buried treasures, this Fort Bragg beach is (appropriately enough) a little hard to find. It's best to ask for precise directions when in town. Park in the dirt lot and then jump, skip, and walk down the path to the shore. Many years ago this was a dump, but now it is the source of great joy for kids and adults who scoop up bits of pottery and glass that have been smoothed by the sand and water into jewels. Local artists make jewelry from their finds. Your kids can put them in a clear glass of water when they return home for a fabulous free souvenir. *On the north end of town, across from Noyo Bowl at 900 N. Main St., Fort Bragg.*

Mendocino Beach
★★★/Free

A little path behind Mendocino's landmark 1868 Presbyterian Church on Main Street leads down to the town's beach. Once on the sand, impress your kids by making a kelp horn. Just cut the bulb off the end of a long, thin piece of fresh bull kelp. Rinse out the tube in the ocean so that it is hollow. Then wrap it over one shoulder and blow through the small end. The longer the tube, the greater the resonance.

 **Mendocino Coast Botanical Gardens**
★★★★/$

These 47 acres of flowering plants are a beautiful place to wander. Young gardeners and naturalists will appreciate the lovely growing things (and the bugs that live on and around them), while other kids will just like all the space to scamper around. There are picnic facilities, too. Known for its rhododendrons, fuchsias, and heathers, the garden also has a major collection of succulents, camellias, and old heritage roses. For gardening families: an impressive collection of unusual perennials is sold in the gift shop. For a living reminder of your trip, let your children select plants to tend themselves at home. *18220 N. Hwy. 1, two miles south of Fort Bragg; (707) 964-4352;* www.gardenbythesea.org

---

FamilyFun **READER'S TIP**

Time in a Bottle

Our kids (Kiersten, 12, Nicolai, 10, Jarin, 4, and Micah, 1) love to collect rocks, so whenever we go someplace special, we choose one to mark the trip. We write on them—where we went, the date, the initials of those who were there, and other notes, if there is room—and save them in glass jars. Memories of Sunday drives, camping trips, fairs, birthday parties, and family vacations are all recorded and "bottled."

Ron and Marci Clawson, Sandy, Utah

Ricochet Ridge Ranch
★★★/$$$

Even if you don't have a pony-crazy preadolescent, riding horses on the beach or through majestic redwood forests is a wonderful way to spend an afternoon. (If you *are* traveling with young horse lovers, they may consider this the highlight of their life thus far.) The ranch offers guided riding excursions at an hourly rate. Children must be age 6 or older, but riding experience is not required. Riding lessons are also available, as are weeklong horseback-riding trips with nightly stops at inns; catered trips; camping expeditions; and private tours. *24201 Hwy. 1, across from MacKerricher State Park, Fort Bragg; (888) TREK-RRR; (707) 964-7669; www.horse-vacation.com*

Skunk Train/California Western Railroad
FamilyFun ★★★★/$$$

The kids will want to know, so here's the story behind the funny name: The original logging trains on this railroad discharged bad odors from their gas engines—loggers used to say they "could smell 'em before they could see 'em." Today most of the trains are pulled by less-offensive-smelling diesel engines. Sure to charm the choo-choo lovers in your group, this popular excursion train travels into dense redwood forest, through deep mountain tunnels, and over many bridges and trestles on the run between Fort Bragg and Willits, where there is a stopover for lunch. The train also stops along the way to deliver mail. If you're traveling with the young and the restless, the half-day trip (just over three hours) is probably a better choice than the full-day excursions (seven to eight hours, with an hour for lunch). Children under 3 ride free if they don't occupy a seat. *Foot of Laurel St., Fort Bragg; (800) 77-SKUNK; (707) 964-6371; www.skunktrain.com*

Van Damme State Park
FamilyFun ★★★★/$

Children tend to be fascinated by things that are particularly large or especially small, which is why an unusual Pygmy Forest, where stunted trees grow in leached soil, is one of the highlights of this 2,069-acre park. Kids love the miniature forest, and the short boardwalk trail is stroller and wheelchair accessible; stop at the trailhead and pick up a copy of the brochure describing the various types of trees. In late summer have everyone look for tiny, purple wild huckleberries; they're delicious! Other things to check out: a canyon wall covered with ferns, and the one-third-mile-long Bog Trail, which leads to a large area of skunk cabbage. Picnic facilities and campsites are available. To reach the forest, follow Little River Airport Road approximately 3 miles inland. *8125 Hwy. 1, Little River; (707) 937-5804; www.parks.ca.gov*

BUNKING DOWN

DeHaven Valley Farm
★★★★/$$-$$$

Perhaps the greatest endorsement for this inn set on a 20-acre farm is this: one adolescent who stayed was actually heard to utter, "Mom, you did right. This place is great!" With kids in tow, one of the two cottages (which accommodate three to four people) is perfect. Kids are welcome to play with the many resident cats and to walk the goats. The whole family will like the hilltop hot tub with views of the valley and ocean. Westport Union Landing Beach, just across the highway, has tide pools for little ones to explore (but there are no lifeguards, and swimming is not recommended). For the evening's entertainment, select a family favorite from the large video library to watch in the parlor. A full breakfast is included in the rate, and delicious four-course dinners are available by reservation. *39247 N. Hwy. 1, Westport, ten miles north of Fort Bragg; (877) DEHAVEN; (707) 961-1660; www.dehaven-valley-farm.com/*

The Grey Whale Inn
★★★/$$-$$$

A relaxing stay here can be just what the doctor ordered. Originally a hospital, this stately redwood building is now an especially spacious 14-room inn. Some rooms some have kitchens (handy for families) and fireplaces, some have private decks, and some have ocean views that let you watch whales from your room during migration season. The whole family can hang out in a large communal area equipped with a TV, fireplace, pool table, and plenty of board games. An elaborate breakfast buffet is included in the rate. *615 N. Main St., Fort Bragg; (800) 382-7244; (707) 964-0640; www.greywhaleinn.com*

Hi Sea Inn ★★/$-$$

This traditional motel at the north end of town offers bargain-basement rates and a surprising amenity—an ocean view from each of its 14 rooms. Children stay free in their parents' room. *1201 N. Main St., Fort Bragg; (800) 990-SEAS; (707) 964-5929.*

MacCallum House Inn
★★★★/$$-$$$

Built in 1882 by William H. Kelley for his newlywed daughter, Daisy MacCallum, this converted Victorian home was one of the area's first inns. Families with one child can be accommodated in some of the six rooms in the main house, which are furnished with antiques. (Children of all ages are welcome, but these rooms may not be the best choice for the toddlers and other kids who are especially rough on the furniture.) Much more interesting and fun for young travelers is a stay in the property's water tower, which sleeps four. There's a bed on the first floor, a bathroom with ocean view on the second, and another bed with ocean view on the third. The novel setting is sure to tickle your child's fancy. But plan ahead—the tower books up well in advance. There are no TVs on the premises, so you might actually be able to get in some of that elusive quality family time here. The property also has an upscale restaurant (not really appropriate for little ones) and an informal bar that serves light dinners and snacks. *45020 Albion St., Mendocino; (800) 609-0492; (707) 937-0289;* http://www.maccallumhouse.com

Mendocino Coast Reservations
★★★★/$$-$$$$

Traveling families are usually most comfortable staying in homelike places. This vacation-home rental service can book you into privately owned local studio apartments, cabins, cottages, and houses. The service offers oceanfront properties, places with ocean views, and accommodations with fireplaces and/or private hot tubs. There's a two-night minimum stay; during July and August it becomes a four-night minimum. *1000 Main St., Mendocino; (800) 262-7801; (707) 937-5033;* www.mendocinovacations.com

Mendocino Hotel & Garden Suites
★★★★/$$-$$$$

Built in 1878, this authentic Victorian hotel dates back to when the town was a booming port for the

logging trade. There are 26 rooms in the old hotel building, but families generally stay in one of the 25 contemporary rooms located in cottages behind the hotel amidst almost an acre of well-tended gardens. You and the kids will be more comfortable in these roomier accommodations, especially if you stay in one of the two luxurious suites with canopied beds and marble bathrooms. A casual café with ocean views serves both breakfast (the eggs Benedict and potato cake wedges are both superb) and lunch. Dinner is available in a more formal restaurant where (the kids will love this!) a Victorian lady ghost is said to haunt tables number six and eight. Everyone will gobble up the house specialty dessert—deep-dish ollalieberry pie topped with homemade ice cream. *45080 Main St., Mendocino; (800) 548-0513; (707) 937-0511;* www.mendocinohotel.com

Stanford Inn by the Sea
★★★/$$$$

Located a tenth of a mile from downtown, this luxurious yet cozy contemporary inn has lots of fam-

A Perfect Day in Mendocino and Fort Bragg

8:30 A.M. Have breakfast at Egghead's.

About 10 A.M. Board the **Skunk Train** for a half-day excursion. (The schedule varies, so call ahead.)

3 P.M. Search for souvenirs at **Glass Beach**.

4 P.M. Stroll Mendocino's main streets, taking time to shop in the **Spunky Skunk** toy store and (depending on the shopping tolerance of offspring and spouses) the town's unique boutiques.

5 P.M. Relax at your lodging place for a while.

6:30 P.M. Dine in a water tower at the **Bay View Café.**

8 P.M. Back to the room for some family time. Read a nice bedtime story, perhaps from a new book purchased at the town bookstore, and get to sleep early.

ily-friendly qualities. Perched above a scenic llama farm and a duck pond with black swans, it has an organic garden, nursery, and working farm spread over 10 acres. You'll feel as if you're in a tropical retreat when you're swimming in the greenhouse-enclosed pool and basking in the hot tub, and you can borrow mountain bikes for free. Each of the 33 rooms has either a four-poster or sleigh bed plus a wood-burning fireplace, and many have views overlooking the gardens to the ocean beyond. Most are spacious enough to accommodate a family. Afternoon tea, an evening snack, and a full breakfast are included in the rate. The Ravens, the gorgeous restaurant here, is open for dinner only and is totally vegetarian. It offers an exciting, refined cuisine using only the freshest ingredients. Adults can choose from complex dishes such as wild mushroom galette and blackened tofu creole. Not to worry: for the kids there's pizza and polenta. *On Comptche-Ukiah Rd., Mendocino; (800) 331-8884; (707) 937-5615; http://www.stanfordinn.com/*

GOOD EATS

Bay View Café
★★★★/$-$$
If you aren't lucky enough to stay in one of this town's old water towers, you can at least dine in one. The flight of stairs leading up to the din-

ing room here winds right through a water tower, reaching a dining room with fabulous ocean views. The setting and the scenery will distract the kids while they're waiting for the food to arrive. The fare is simple and low-priced, with special items for young diners such as a grilled cheese sandwich and noodles with Parmesan. Hours vary with the demands of the season; call ahead. *45040 Main St., Mendocino; (707) 937-4197.*

Egghead's Restaurant
★★★★/$

Do plan to have at least one breakfast in this cheerful, tiny diner, decorated with *Wizard of Oz* movie photos and film-related knick-knacks. (Someone at the table is sure to break into a chorus of "We're Off to See the Wizard.") Choose from more than 40 varieties of crepes and omelettes, plus traditional breakfast items and an assortment of sandwiches. Parents will appreciate the privacy of the enclosed booths—what 4-year-old has perfect table manners? *326 N. Main St., Fort Bragg; (707) 964-5005.*

Mendocino Bakery
★★★★/$

This exceptional bakery dispenses tasty homemade soup and thick-crusted, kid-pleasing pizza warm from the oven. For dessert, choose a hunk of fragrant, moist ginger-bread, or chewy cinnamon twists, or chocolate chip-oatmeal "cowboy" cookies. Better yet, get them *all* and share. Stop in next door at the Mendocino Chocolate Company for delicious handmade candies—free samples are always available. *10485 Lansing St., Mendocino; Bakery: (707) 937-0836. Candy shop: (800) 722-1107; (707) 937-1107.*

Mendo Burgers
★★/$

Behind the bakery, this tiny eatery dishes up the obvious, plus all the other kid staples—hot dogs, fresh fish-and-chips, homemade soups, salads, and fresh-cut fries. Roomy picnic tables offer prime outside seating on a sunny day. *On Lansing St., Mendocino; (707) 937-1111.*

SOUVENIR HUNTING

Village Toy Store and Spunky Skunk

Kids love these stores, in Mendocino and Fort Bragg respectively, because they're both well supplied with cool stuff. They're also both on main streets, so parents of older kids can amuse themselves in a nearby coffeehouse or browse a boutique while their offspring study the goods. *Village Toy Store: 10450 Lansing St., Mendocino; (707) 937-4633. Spunky Skunk: 350 N. Main St., Fort Bragg; (707) 961-5443.*

Your family can rough it like the old prospectors
by camping under the stars in Gold Rush Country.

Gold Rush Country

NATURAL TREASURE hunters, kids are sure to love a trip to California Gold Rush Country. For grade-schoolers the area brings to life a particularly exciting time in California history; they are sure to enjoy a tour of one of the region's gold mines. Your younger kids will enjoy panning for gold and riding a historic train.

First, a little geographical and historical background (so you can answer some of the questions posed by the young historians and geologists in the backseat).

Veins of gold run underground from Northern California to South America, surfacing in the region of California between Jamestown and Auburn, and again in Nevada City. The Mother Lode, as this area is sometimes referred to, stretches along the entire length of Highway

THE **FamilyFun** LIST

Calaveras Big Trees State Park (page 130)

Columbia State Historic Park (page 128)

Indian Grinding Rock State Historic Park (page 129)

Railtown 1897, State Historic Park (page 133)

Sutter Gold Mine (page 133)

Sutter's Mill at Marshall Gold Discovery State Historic Park (page 133)

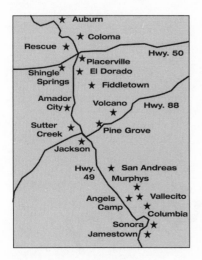

49 (once called the Golden Highway) from near Yosemite at its southern end to Nevada City in the north.

The gold rush began when gold was discovered at Sutter's Mill in Coloma in 1848. At the time, 4,000 people lived in El Dorado County. A year later, 200,000 people called the county home, and more than a dozen new towns had sprouted up. More than $2 billion worth of gold was removed from the area, mostly by hydraulic mining that eventually washed away the hills and ruined the landscape. But more than 80 percent of the gold is still here, waiting to be found, and professional miners continue to go for the gold.

Your family could spend weeks exploring this region thoroughly, but a few days are enough to cover some interesting territory. All the main gold rush towns are along Highway 49—but don't even think about try-

ing to drive all of Highway 49 in a just few days, especially with kids in the car. The following route covers Jamestown north to Coloma; probably the most interesting spots, if you have to choose, are Columbia State Historic Park (a doable day trip from San Francisco) and Coloma.

Also try to take time to explore some of the scenic side roads leading to tiny hamlets with intriguing names such as Fiddletown and Rescue. The picturesque countryside, with its rustic ruins and wide open spaces, is not yet heavily promoted and packaged. It provides many low-key and inexpensive joys for your hype-weary travelers.

Unfortunately, many of the area's charming bed-and-breakfast inns do not welcome families. Some of the interesting historic hotels in the region are family-friendly, however—and you'll find numerous soda fountains for afternoon treats (see "There's Ice Cream in Them Thar Hills!" on page 130).

Two classic books—*The Celebrated Jumping Frog of Calaveras County* by Samuel L. Clemens (aka Mark Twain) and *The Luck of Roaring Camp* by Bret Harte—will give your kids a great introduction to this history-steeped area. Consider reading them aloud together before or during your gold rush country trip (check to see if they're available in audio format).

Once a boomtown, **Jamestown** is now filled with antiques shops in architecturally interesting old buildings. The kids probably won't care if you skip the shops and head straight to a gold-prospecting expedition and a ride on a historic steam train.

Once the richest and wildest town in the southern Mother Lode, **Sonora** is now a busy crossroads to other places. A cabin that was the home of Mark Twain and a museum housed in a former jail are worthwhile short stops for your school-age kids.

In its prime, when more than 6,000 people lived here, **Columbia** was one of the largest mining towns in the southern Mother Lode. The state historic park is a must-see.

Long ago, the sleepy town of **Murphys** had gold strike after gold strike, making the founding Murphy brothers very rich. It is now best known as a home to rare giant sequoias—jaw-dropping natural wonders that elicit "wows" from kids and grown-ups alike.

Taking its name from George Angel, who founded it as a trading post in 1848, **Angels Camp** is a bustling little burg that is thought to be the town Bret Harte wrote of in *The Luck of Roaring Camp*. Today it is best known as the home of the annual Jumping Frog Jubilee and Calaveras County Fair.

Progress has stripped **San Andreas** of most of its historic character, but the historical museum is interesting.

Two important gold-bearing quartz mines are near the busy town of **Jackson**. One will resume mining

operations soon; you can take fascinating tours of both.

Make the drive to **Volcano** during the daylight, so the kids can enjoy the

----

CRIME RHYME

Black Bart was a famous stagecoach robber during the late 1800s. He robbed more than 20 Wells Fargo stagecoaches, but Black Bart was also well known for leaving poems at his crime scenes. Here's a verse that he left for pursuing lawmen:

Here I lay me down to sleep
To wait the coming morrow,
Perhaps success, perhaps defeat
And everlasting sorrow.
Yet come what will, I'll try it once,
My conditions can't be worse,
And if there's money in that box,
'Tis money in my purse.

scenery. Take a good map, too; it's worth its weight in gold. Sleepy and quiet now, during the gold rush Volcano was a boomtown filled with boisterous dance halls and saloons. Today kids can learn about the area's earlier Native American inhabitants at a nearby historic park. There's also a botanical garden with resident animals to scamper after, and a family-friendly community theater.

Named for a cool spring that surfaced near a shingle mill here in 1849, rural **Shingle Springs** is now, just as it was then, the perfect spot to set up camp.

The only thing of interest in **El Dorado** nowadays is one popular restaurant set in a former stagecoach stop.

Once known as Hangtown because hangings here were so common (you may not want to mention that to the younger kids), historic **Placerville** is where meat-packer Philip Armour and automobile-maker John Studebaker got their financial starts. Today you can tour

the gold mine and countryside dotted with apple farms.

Coloma is where James Marshall, a sawmill foreman who worked for Captain John Sutter, discovered gold in 1848. The entire town is now a National Historic Landmark. Don't miss it.

CULTURAL ADVENTURES

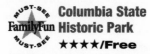

Columbia State Historic Park
FamilyFun ★★★★/Free

A living museum, this reconstructed gold rush town is closed to all but foot traffic and the occasional stagecoach. Your kids will get a kick out of watching a blacksmith practice his craft in a ramshackle shed and sample yummy old-time candies made with fascinating antique equipment from century-old recipes. The whole family can tour a still-operating gold mine, ride in an authentic stage-

---

FamilyFun READER'S TIP

It's in the Cards

My family loves to travel, and I have found a wonderful way to preserve our vacation memories. First, we buy postcards at all the different locations we visit. On the backs, I jot down the highlights of the trip or funny things that happened while we were there. After we have returned home, I laminate the postcards, punch holes in the top left corners, and put them all on a ring clip. It's exciting to see all of the places we have been, and the cards are inexpensive souvenirs of our travels.

Stefanie Wirths, Camdenton, Missouri

coach, and learn how to pan for gold in a salted sluice. For the perfect souvenir, head for the photography studio, where you can all don gold rush–era clothing for a charming family portrait taken with vintage camera equipment, but developed with quick modern processes. When the kids' whistles needs wetting, stop in the town saloon for an old-fashioned root-beerlike sarsaparilla; Mom and Dad can have a cold mug of beer. Columbia might look familiar: *High Noon* and episodes of *Little House on the Prairie* were filmed here. *Main St., Columbia; (209) 532-0150;* www.sierra.parks.state.ca.us/coconten.htm

 Indian Grinding Rock State Historic Park
★★★★/$

Kids accustomed to food processors will be interested to learn that Native Americans used pestles to grind their acorns and other seeds. The largest grinding rock is a huge flat bedrock limestone, 175 by 82 feet; it has more than 1,185 mortar holes and approximately 363 petroglyphs. Kids will be fascinated by the rock carvings and by the reconstructed Miwok Village, which has a ceremonial roundhouse, a covered hand-game area, several cedar bark houses, and an Indian game field. Stop at the regional museum for an orientation video and interpretive displays. The park also has a self-guided nature trail, picnic facilities, and campsites. A

Miwok celebration is held here each September. *14881 Pine Grove-Volcano Rd., Pine Grove, southwest of Volcano; (209) 296-7488;* www.sierra.parks.state.ca.us/

Mark Twain's Cabin
★/Free

Samuel L. Clemens (aka Twain) lived here on Jackass Hill in 1864–65, when he wrote *The Celebrated Jumping Frog of Calaveras County* and *Roughing It.* This replica of his cabin is constructed around the original chimney, and you can view it from the outside only. *Off Hwy. 49, midway between Sonora and Angels Camp.*

Tuolumne County Museum and History Center
★★/Free

Inside what was a jail, built in 1866, this museum displays gold rush–era relics such as pioneer firearms and gold samples. The jail-guns-and-gold combination makes this a hit with some 12-year-olds. Make reservations to have lunch at one of the picnic tables. *158 W. Bradford Ave., Sonora; (209) 532-1317;* www.tchistory.org

Just for Fun

Apple Hill ★★★/Free
Drive the historic path originally blazed in 1857 by Pony Express riders. Request a free driving-tour map

from the El Dorado County Chamber of Commerce, or pick one up at their office (*542 Main St.; 800/457-6279*). Apple Hill is especially fun to visit in the fall, when the 40-plus apple orchards along the route sell more than 20 varieties of tree-fresh apples at bargain prices. A few farms let you pick your own. You can picnic at many of the farms; some have snack bars, and a few also have pony and train rides, hiking trails, fishing ponds, and live jazz. In addition to apples, the farms sell an impressive selection of homemade apple goodies: fresh-pressed apple cider, hard cider, apple wine, spicy apple butter, caramel apples, apple jelly, dried apples, apple cake, apple sundaes, apple syrup, and, of course, apple pie. The apple season generally runs from September through December, but there are activities at other times of the year as well.

Nine Christmas tree farms open the day after Thanksgiving, and cherry season begins on Father's Day weekend. *Off Hwy. 50, Placerville; (530) 644-7692.*

Calaveras Big Trees State Park ★★★★/$

MUST-SEE FamilyFun

Big trees indeed! In this ancient forest grow the mammoth, and now rare, giant sequoia variety of redwood, which can reach the height of 300 feet. If you have young children, try the easy one-mile Big Trees Nature Trail for a trek. There are also other trails, as well as campsites and picnic and barbecue facilities. This is a year-round attraction: in warm weather, your kids can get wet at the Beaver Creek Picnic Area's wading spot. In winter, the family can cross-country ski. Stop in town for picnic provisions or eat at one of the in-town restaurants. *1170 E. Hwy.*

There's Ice Cream in Them Thar Hills!

Most of the gold is long gone, but California gold rush country still has its riches. The region offers a wealth of old-fashioned ice-cream parlors serving exceptional treats. All of the following are in towns along Highway 49.

Buffalo Chips Emporium
★★★/$

Buy a simple cone here and then sit outside on one of the weathered benches and leisurely watch the busy world drive by. Or sit inside what was once the town's Wells Fargo Bank and indulge in a fancy fountain item. Either way, your kids will be pleased. (Don't tell them what buffalo chips are until *after* you've finished your treats.) *14179 Hwy. 49, Amador City; (209) 267-0570.*

The Fallon Ice Cream Parlor
★★★★/$

Operating on the ground floor of the Fallon Hotel in Columbia State Historic

4, Arnold, 15 miles east of Murphys; (209) 795-2334; www.sierra.parks. state.ca.us/cbt/cbt.htm

Daffodil Hill
★★★/By donation

Your little ones will be charmed by the peacocks, chickens, and sheep that wander the grounds of this spectacular garden, and even kids with no interest in gardening enjoy running along the brightly colored flower beds. Originally planted in the 1850s by a Dutch settler, and maintained and expanded by direct descendants, the six acres here boast more than 300 varieties of bulbs that bloom from mid-March through April. The thousands of daffodils also have a few tulips and hyacinths mixed in. The family plants new bulbs every year, and now more than 400,000 bloom each spring, making for a spectacular dis-

play. Bring a lunch to eat in the picnic area. Donations are requested. *18310 Rams Horn Grade, off Shake Ridge Rd., three miles north of Volcano; (209) 296-7048.*

Gold Bug Mine
★★★/$

If the cute-as-a-bug name doesn't win you over, the facilities should. You and your kids can take a self-guided tour through a chilly quarter-mile-long lighted mine shaft; see a working model of a stamp mill (once used to crush granite to get out the gold) inside an authentic stamp mill building; picnic at creekside tables; and hike in rugged 62-acre Gold Bug Park. Closed weekdays September through March. *Off Bedford Ave., one mile north of Placerville; 2635 Gold Bug Lane; (530) 642-5232;* www.goldbugpark.org

Park, this old-fashioned ice-cream parlor offers comfortable seating at sturdy tables. *Washington St., Columbia; (209) 532-5341.*

The Peppermint Stick
★★★★/$

When it was built in 1893, this building was the town icehouse. Now it is a cheerful ice-cream parlor serving up old-fashioned sodas and cleverly named sundaes. What kid wouldn't wolf down a "Murphys Turtle," made with vanilla ice cream, hot fudge and caramel sauces, and topped

with a cute little chocolate turtle candy? Sandwiches, soups, and candies are also available, and everything can be packed to go. *454 Main St., Murphys; (209) 728-3570.*

Sutter Creek Ice Cream
★★★/$

This old-fashioned ice-cream and soda fountain dispenses ice-cream specialties and more than ten kinds of homemade fudge. Sandwiches, tamales, and kid-pleasing corn dogs are also on the menu. *51 Main St., Sutter Creek; (209) 267-0543.*

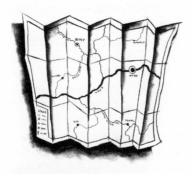

Gold Prospecting Expeditions ★★★/$$

This is a good bet for kids 7 and up. The company supplies all the equipment, but be prepared to get down and dirty in a stream (kids love that part), where you'll be taught the basics. The company claims that gold has been found on every trip lasting two hours or more—and the rule is "finders, keepers." Trips by river raft or helicopter can also be arranged. Children can pan for free in a trough in front of the gift shop that the company operates in the old livery stable—it's a good alternative to the full-fledged expedition if your kids are small. *18170 Main St., Jamestown; (209) 984-GOLD; (800) 596-0009; www.goldprospecting.com*

Jumping Frog Jubilee/ Calaveras County Fair ★★★★/$

If you're in the area on the third weekend in May, stop here. First, read the kids *The Celebrated Frog of Calaveras County* by Samuel L. Clemens, also known as Mark Twain. You can bring your own frog to enter in the historic contest, held here annually since 1937, but rental frogs are also available on site. A rental frog has never won, but maybe yours will be the first. Prize money is usually won by "frog jockeys" who are serious about the sport and enter 50 to 60 frogs in the contest. In 1986, Rosie the Ribiter set the current world's record by landing, after three leaps, 21 feet 5 $^3/_4$ inches from the starting pad. She earned her jockey $1,500. The frog-jumping contest is held daily during the fair, which features carnival rides, livestock exhibits, a rodeo, a demolition derby, headliner entertainers, and fireworks. *2465 Gun Club Rd./Hwy. 49, two miles south of Angels Camp; (209) 736-2561; www.frogtown.org*

Kennedy Gold Mine ★★★★/$

Once one of the richest gold mines in the world, it produced more than $34.2 million worth of gold from 1880 to 1942. At 5,912 feet deep, it also was once the deepest mine in North America. Kids of all ages will want to try their hands at panning for gold in one of the troughs. The older kids will also want to check out the historic mining buildings, the display of mining equipment, and the aboveground, roller-coasterlike 125-foot-high metal head frame, once used to haul up unwanted mining materials. Everyone should take a look down the mine shaft, although the mine itself is now full of water. Tours operate weekends March through October only. *Jackson; (209) 223-9542.*

 **Marshall Gold Discovery State Historic Park ★★★★/$**

Encompassing 70 percent of the town, this lovely 265-acre park contains a reconstruction of the original Sutter's Mill, where the Gold Rush began in 1848. Your grade-schoolers will like the history-made-real elements here. The park features gold rush–era buildings and artifacts, including an exact replica of the piece of gold found by James Marshall (the original is at the Smithsonian Institution in Washington, D.C.). Marshall's grave is on a hill overlooking the town; a statue there depicts him pointing to the spot where he discovered gold. Younger kids will enjoy the nature trails and the abundance of space to run around. Try the picnic facilities for an outdoor family feast. *On Hwy. 49, Coloma; (530) 622-3470.*

Railtown 1897 State Historic Park ★★★★/$

Board *The Mother Lode Cannonball*, a historic steam train, for a 40-minute, six-mile round-trip. Almost as exciting as the ride itself is the hubbub in the depot as the train is prepared for departure—the huge steam trains roll in and out, sounding their whistles and belching a mix of fire, smoke, and steam. If you have train buffs in the family, tour the old six-stall roundhouse turntable and machine shop, where the trains are still serviced. If it all looks familiar, that could be because many TV shows and movies have been filmed here, including *Bonanza, Little House on the Prairie, The Virginian, High Noon*, and *Pale Rider*. The train operates May through September only, but the roundhouse is open daily year-round. *Fifth Ave., Jamestown; (209) 984-3953;* www.csrmf.org/railtown

 **Sutter Gold Mine ★★★★/$-$$**

Made up of 16 historic mines that have produced more than 1.3 million ounces of gold, this is about to become the first active gold mining operation in the area since the Central Eureka Mine closed in the late 1940s. You and the kids can see both active and restored underground workings, pan for gold, and see gold bars being poured. The gold bars are real kid pleasers, but even more exciting is the underground tour. After everyone dons hard hats, a "boss buggy" (a jeeplike safari car shuttle) takes passengers down, 1280 feet into the earth, inside an actual gold vein. Picnic facilities are available. **NOTE:** Children must be at least 4 for the underground tours. *Hwy. 49, between Amador City and Sutter Creek; (888) 818-7462;* www.suttergold.com

Whitewater Connection ★★★/$$$$

They'll be talking about this for months to come! Rushing down a river on a raft while the water splashes and foams all around you is a laugh-out-loud thrill. This white-water rafting outfit offers half- and full-day trips daily from mid-April through September. Some family-oriented trips offer discounts for children (kids must be at least 6). If you're taking a river trip, you can camp at the outfitter's riverside facility adjacent to the state park. Longer trips are also available. *Office: 7237 Hwy. 49, Coloma; (800) 336-7238; (530) 622-6446;* www.white waterconnection.com

BUNKING DOWN

City Hotel ★★★★/$$

This 10-room 1856 hotel will give your kids a feel for the town's history. The restored rooms are furnished with Victorian antiques from the collection of the California State Parks Department, and eager-to-please students from the Hospitality Management Program at Columbia College dress in period clothing,

---

FamilyFun SNACK

Cranberry-Nut Snack Mix

Measure 2 cups raw sunflower seeds, 1 cup pine nuts, 1 cup raw pumpkin seeds, 1 cup sweetened, dried cranberries, and 1 cup raisins into a mixing bowl and stir with a wooden spoon until well combined.

---

supplementing the full-time staff by performing such esoteric duties as fluffing pillows and de-crumbing tables in the beautifully appointed restaurant downstairs. Since there are no TVs, guests congregate in the parlor in the evening for conversation and games. To make the trek down the hall to the bathrooms more civilized, guest rooms are equipped with a wicker basket packed with a shower cap, slippers, robe, soap, and shampoo. The hotel restaurant prepares elegant regional cuisine and fixed-price, seasonal four-course dinners. Special children's portions of simple dishes such as fresh pasta with tomato sauce are always available. Continental breakfast is included. *Main St., Columbia; (800) 532-1479; (209) 532-1479;* www.cityhotel.com

Fallon Hotel
★★★★/$$

Part of Columbia State Historic Park, this historic 14-room hotel dates from 1857 and has been beautifully restored to its Victorian grandeur. The several large rooms with balconies are perfect for families. Rooms have no TVs, so you might actually enjoy some of the quality family time you've been longing for. The kids will want to stop in the ice-cream parlor on the main floor, where you also stop for your complimentary continental breakfast. The adjacent Fallon House Theatre stages live productions, many of which are family-friendly. Be sure to have the hotel make dinner reservations for you at their sister property, City Hotel (above), a block away. Hotel-dinner-theater packages are available. *Washington St., Columbia; (209) 532-1470.*

Murphys Hotel and Historic Lodge
★★★★/$$

Built in 1856 and a historical landmark since 1948, this nine-room hotel provided lodging for such Gold Rush–era luminaries as Ulysses S. Grant, J.P. Morgan, Mark Twain, Horatio Alger, and Black Bart, each of whom actually stayed in the room now named after him. Adjacent to the hotel are modern motel rooms. Though the vintage hotel rooms are immeasurably more interesting, they have one big drawback: the noisy hotel bar, reputed to be the best in the Mother Lode, stays lively until the wee hours. Families who want to sleep should browse the hotel rooms for their historic interest, but sleep in the newer—and infinitely quieter—motel rooms. The very kid-friendly hotel restaurant serves hearty, made-from-scratch American country and continental fare, and portions tend to be large. There's a children's menu, too. *457 Main St., Murphys; (800) 532-7684; (209) 728-3444; www.murphyshotel.com*

Pyrite, a natural mineral, is also called **fool's gold** because its color can trick people into thinking they have found gold.

National Hotel ★★/$

The decor is modest, but so are the prices, making this a good choice for traveling families. Opened in 1862, the 30-room hotel claims to be the oldest in continuous operation in California. Prior guests have included every California governor since 1862, two U.S. presidents (Garfield and Hoover), and John Wayne. You can dine in the on-site restaurant. *2 Water St., Jackson; (209) 223-0500.*

Roaring Camp Mining Co.
★★★★/$$

Staying at this former mining camp is like taking a step back in time. You leave your car behind and make the one-hour trip into the remote canyon via truck. The kids will get a kick out of the accommodations—rustic prospector cabins without electricity—provided they're not total TV addicts. You bring all your own gear and food, but there's a saloon, short-order restaurant, and general store for when you get tired of roughing it. Activities are low-key, nonelectric, and family-friendly: swimming, fishing, and panning for gold in the Mokelumne River, as well as hiking and perhaps collecting some rocks. Weekly stays run Sunday to Sunday. For stays of less than a week, call the Monday before the anticipated date of arrival. Shorter four-hour day tours are also available. On Saturday evenings, a group of diners is trucked in

135

for a riverside steak cookout; weekly guests can join this event at no charge. *Pine Grove; (209) 296-4100;* www.volcano.net/pineacre

St. George Hotel
★★★/$$

For safety reasons (the hotel is creaky and cluttered), families with children under 12 must stay in this 1862 hotel's newer and charmless annex. But the modern rooms are comfortable and have private bathrooms—a big plus. Annex-dwellers are welcome to relax in the main hotel's cozy, memorabilia-crammed bar and parlor area, complete with a fireplace and games. Start the day with a deluxe continental breakfast included in the rate. *16104 Main St., Volcano; (209) 296-4458;* www.stgeorgehotel.com

KOA Kampground ★/$

In addition to Kamping Kabins, facilities here include a swimming pool and hot tub, miniature golf,

- -

NAME OF THE GAME

San Francisco's football team received its name from the California gold rush. A huge number of gold miners moved to San Francisco in 1849, thus creating the "49ers" nickname.

a playground, and more. See "KOA Kamping in Kalifornia" on page 306. *4655 Rock Barn Rd., Volcano; (800) KOA-4197; (530) 676-2267;* www.koa.com

GOOD EATS

Smoke Café ★★★★/$

Within a modern Santa Fe–style stucco building with lots of tile, this popular, casual spot specializes in delicious Mexican cuisine. A kid-pleasing hamburger is on the menu, or if your kids like Mexican food, they can try chicken with mole and other dishes. *18191 Main St., Jamestown; (209) 984-3733.*

Poor Red's ★★★★/$

Your school-age kids will get a charge out of eating in a former Wells Fargo stagecoach stop—even if the exterior today looks more like an unsavory bar. The whole family will appreciate the down-home food— ham, ribs, chicken, and steak, all cooked over an open oak-wood pit. **NOTE:** Because the restaurant is so popular and so small, on weekends the wait at dinnertime can run over an hour. If you're traveling with restless little ones, aim for lunch or an early dinner, or order takeout for a picnic. Show your young historians the mural behind the bar, which depicts the town as it appeared in the late 1800s. *6221 Pleasant Valley Rd., El Dorado; (530) 622-2901.*

A Look Around Underground:
GOLD RUSH COUNTRY CAVERNS

ANY KID WHO HAS EVER tried to dig a hole all the way to China will jump at the chance to do some exploring under the earth's surface. As luck would have it, gold rush country is the site of a number of underground caverns, many of which were originally discovered and explored by gold miners, who abandoned them when they didn't find the treasure they sought. Now you and your kids can go see what's underground.

California Caverns
★★★★/$

This cavern was first opened to the public in 1850. On the Trail of Lights tour, experienced guides lead you through subterranean "rooms," including the recently discovered Jungle Room, named for the array of crystalline "vines," many several feet long, covering the ceiling. Children relish the fanciful names given the rooms and formations— and the spookiness of the dimly lighted passages. The tour takes an hour to 80 minutes, the terrain is level, and the walk is not strenuous. If your 3- and 4-year-olds don't mind walking for an hour straight— no strollers allowed—they can manage here. *9565 Cave City Rd., off Mountain Ranch Rd., ten miles east of San Andreas; (209) 736-2708; www.caverntours.com*

Mercer Caverns ★★★★/$
Discovered in 1885, this is said to be the longest continually operating commercial cavern in the state. The tour of the well-lighted, cool (55°) limestone cavern takes an hour and includes 10 underground "rooms." Best for kids 6 and up, it involves descending stairs to a depth of 161 feet. Tours begin every 20 minutes. *1665 Sheepranch Rd., off Hwy. 4, one mile north of Murphys; (209) 728-2101; www.mercercaverns.com*

Moaning Cavern
★★★★/$$

The 45-minute tour descends a 235-foot spiral staircase into the largest public cavern chamber in California, said to be big enough to hold the Statue of Liberty. Native Americans discovered the cavern, and many are thought to have fallen to their deaths here. In fact, prehistoric human remains were found in the cavern. Because of the long staircase, the cavern is not recommended for children under 5. You can camp at the site. *5350 Moaning Cave Rd., Vallecito, five miles west of Murphys; (209) 736-2708; www.caverntours.com*

YOSEMITE

NATIONAL PARK SERVICE

Department of the Interior

NATIONAL PARK

In addition to beautiful mountains and waterfalls, Yosemite National Park is also home to nearly 300 animal species and 1,500 types of plants.

Northern California's National Parks

NATIONAL PARKS are always great places to go with kids. The wide-open spaces invite running, jumping, and exploring; the flora, fauna, and assorted natural wonders delight and intrigue young naturalists; and the beautiful scenery can be appreciated by the entire family. Northern California is home to five national parks: Yosemite National Park, in the central part of the state; Sequoia and Kings Canyon National Parks, just south of Yosemite; Redwood National Park, on Highway 101 way up north near the Oregon border; and Lassen Volcanic National Park, off Highway 5 in the northeastern part of the state.

Many national parks, including Yosemite, Lassen, Sequoia/Kings Canyon, and Redwood, operate Junior Ranger Programs in summer. Usually designed for kids ages 8 through 12 (but sometimes including children who are younger and older), the programs vary from park to park but generally feature nature

THE **FamilyFun** LIST
MUST-SEE · MUST-SEE

The Ahwahnee (page 145)

Bumpass Hell (page 154)

Generals Highway (page 148)

Giant Forest (page 149)

Mariposa Grove of Giant Sequoias
  (page 143)

Redwood National Park (page 152)

Rockefeller Forest (page 153)

Tunnel View (page 144)

walks and other educational activities. Participants pledge "to do what I can to protect and preserve the plants, animals, and history of our national parks." Why, some Junior Rangers have even been known to grow up and become *real* Park Service rangers! During summer evenings, most parks also schedule scenic movies and slide shows about park wildlife, history, and sights at area campgrounds and hotel amphitheaters. Check upon arrival for times and locations.

Yosemite National Park

Spectacularly beautiful Yosemite was designated a national park in 1890. Most families visit this grand national park in the summer, when it is at its busiest, with congested roads and accommodations filled to capacity. The summer crowds make it harder to focus on what was the original draw here—the scenic, natural beauty of the High Sierra.

FamilyFun TIP

Pass It On

If you're planning on visiting multiple national parks on your vacation, consider purchasing a National Parks Pass. For $50, the pass will admit either you and the other passengers in your vehicle or you, your spouse, parents, and children to any of the national parks for a full year (it depends whether the park admits visitors on a "per vehicle" or "per person" basis). For information, call 1-888-GO-PARKS or go to the National Park Service's Website at www.nps.gov

But summer is also the best time for families with school-age children to travel, so, on the plus side, you'll be assured of plenty of other kids for yours to make friends with, plus a variety of special activities designed just for them. However, do try to return in the off-season: the colorful foliage change is spectacular in fall; snow blankets the valley floor in winter; and in spring the famous waterfalls are at their fullest.

Don't miss the amazing natural attractions here: El Capitan, the largest piece of exposed granite in the world, and Yosemite Falls, the highest waterfall in North America. Also be sure to hike one of the many self-guided trails. The Mist Trail to Vernal Fall is the most popular trail in the park. A moderate three-mile round-trip hike, it features breathtaking vistas and a close-up view of the 317-foot-tall waterfall. An easier half-mile round-trip trail (and a better choice for younger children) leads to Bridalveil Falls. Family Discovery Walks, guided by park

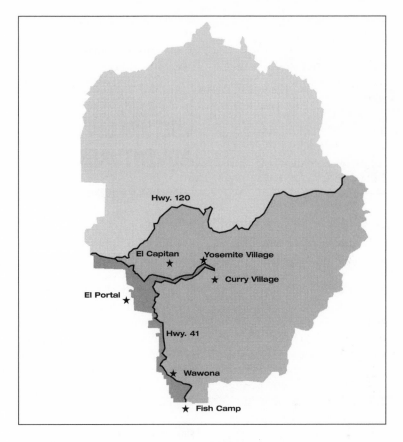

rangers, are also available. (Bear in mind that falls and rivers can be dangerous as well as beautiful. Be especially careful when hiking with young children.) If your children are 7 or older (and unafraid of large animals), the whole family can saddle up and ride horses or mules on a wrangler-led trail ride, perhaps the most fun way of all to see Yosemite.

The park offers many special children's programs in the summer. They include story-telling sessions,

sing-alongs, nature walks, and a photography workshop for junior shutterbugs ages 7 to 12.

The park has two entrances; one is most convenient for those coming in from the Bay Area, the other closest to the Fresno area. When you pay your entrance fee you'll be given a newsletter containing a map and listing what is happening in the park that week.

Located on the floor of Yosemite Valley, Yosemite Village is the

A Day at Yosemite

8 A.M. or sunrise Breakfast in the magnificent **Ahwahnee** dining room.

9 A.M. Drive the circular route through the valley, or take the free shuttle bus, stopping at **Bridalveil Fall** for a short hike and a view of El Capitan.

10:30 A.M. Continue on to Yosemite Village and the visitors' center for orientation. Visit the Indian Cultural Museum, also located here.

Noon Stop at **Yosemite Falls** for the short walk to its base. Select a scenic spot for a picnic lunch (any park hotel will pack one for you if you put in a request the night before—or pick one up at Degnan's Deli in the village).

1:30 P.M. Rent a bike and spend a few hours enjoying the valley up close. The trail through the valley from Yosemite Lodge to the Yosemite Chapel, on to Curry Village, and then back to the lodge, is particularly pleasant.

4 P.M. Spend some time **at the pool** or napping before dinner at your hotel. All that fresh air means an early bedtime for everyone.

center of activities in the park. Most of the area's hotels, campgrounds, restaurants, and shops are here. The main park visitors' center also is in the village, as is the Indian Cultural Museum *(see below)*.

CULTURAL ADVENTURES

Indian Cultural Museum
★★★★/Free
The whole family can learn more about the Yosemite Valley's original settlers—the Awaneechee Indians—through artifacts, cultural demonstrations, and recorded chants. A reconstructed village located behind the museum features a self-guided trail pointing out plants that the Native Americans used for food, clothing, and shelter. *Yosemite Village, Yosemite National Park;* (209) 372-0200; www.nps.gov/yose

Pioneer Yosemite History Center ★★/Free
Your kids can walk across an authentic covered bridge to reach this village of restored historic pioneer buildings, dating from the late 1800s. Originally scattered around the park, the various structures were moved here in the 1950s and 1960s. In summer, you can bring the kids to watch demonstrations of soap-making, yarn-spinning, rail-splitting, and other pioneer crafts that give them a sense of just how different

things were way back then. Horse-drawn carriage rides are sometimes available. *Hwy. 41, Wawona; (209) 372-0200.*

JUST FOR FUN

Bicycling ★★★★/$-$$

Bicyclists can rent bikes daily from April through October at Yosemite Lodge and Curry Village lodge. All rental bikes are of the old-fashioned, one-speed variety. A map to the eight miles of bike paths is provided and helmets are available at no charge, and child carriers (trailors) are not available. *Yosemite Lodge, Curry Village, Yosemite National Park; Yosemite: (209) 372-1208; Curry Village: (209) 372-8319.*

Curry Village Ice-Skating Rink ★★/$

This outdoor rink, open in winter only, is situated so that skaters can view the landmark chunk of granite known as Half Dome. *At the Curry Village lodge, Yosemite National Park; (209) 372-8341.*

Mariposa Grove of Giant Sequoias ★★★★/$

About 35 miles from the valley, this 250-acre grove holds approximately 500 giant sequoias. Some measure 15 to 25 feet in diameter, and some are more than 2,000 years old. Kids love having their pictures taken next to these giants, and everyone enjoys traipsing through the fragrant, pine-needle-padded forest. May through October, the Big Trees Tram Tour takes passengers on a scenic loop in open-air trams. In winter, this is a choice spot for cross-country skiing. Admission fee for the tram only. *Hwy. 41, 35 miles from Yosemite Valley; (209) 372-1240.*

Merced River Float Trip ★★★/$$

Your older kids who know how to swim will love rafting along the scenic and calm area of the Merced River between Pines Campground and Sentinel Bridge. Rafts, life jackets, and paddles are available for rent in June and July at Curry Village; *(209) 372-8341.*

A Sweet Stop

If you're driving to Yosemite National Park from San Francisco, the Hershey's Visitors Center makes for a sweet rest stop. It's just off Highway 120, in Oakdale *(120 S. Sierra Ave.; 209/848-8126),* about 100 miles from San Francisco.

If you're looking to eat something a bit more substantial (though not necessarily more nutritious) than chocolate, note that Oakdale is something of a fast-food heaven. In addition, there are numerous cafés and produce stands located along Highway 120.

★ Tunnel View
FamilyFun ★★★★/Free

If you're in the east end of the valley, on Highway 41, you get your first glimpse of this spectacular view as soon as you exit the Wawona tunnel. The Tunnel View turnout provides you with a magnificent photo opportunity. Take advantage of it by asking a fellow traveler to take a photo of your whole family in front of this panoramic view of the Yosemite Valley.

Yosemite Mountain Sugar Pine Railroad
★★★★/$-$$

Almost every family has at least one railroad buff. This narrow-gauge steam train is sure to please the locomotive lover in yours. Located four miles south of the park's southern entrance, about an hour's drive from the valley, the train takes passengers on an hourlong, scenic excursion through the Sierra National Forest. Passengers sit in open-air touring cars made of logs that have been carved out to form long benches and hear a live narration on the area's history. If you like, you can get off at the midway point to picnic or hike—just catch another train for the return trip. Moonlight rides are scheduled on Saturday night in summer and include a steak barbecue and campfire program. Smaller Jenny rail cars, provide a shorter half-hour ride along the same route. There's a picnic area and a snack shop. *56001 Hwy. 41, Fish Camp; (559) 683-7273;* www.ymsprr.com

BUNKING DOWN

Some of the nicest, and most conveniently located lodging places near Yosemite are those operated by the national park itself. The park runs four hotels, ranging in style from luxurious to rustic; there are park-run campgrounds as well. Reservations are essential—and the earlier, the better, especially for summer, when it is recommended that you make them the permitted 364 days in advance. Call (559) 252-4848 or go to www.yosemitepark .com for information or to make reservations at any park lodging facility. If you are unable to find accommodations in the national park, there are some lodging places in the nearby town of El Portal.

All of the national park restaurants are open daily and equipped with high chairs and booster seats. Box lunches can be reserved from hotel kitchens the evening before they are needed, and supplies can also be picked up at Degnan's Deli in the Village.

The Ahwahnee
FamilyFun ★★★/$$$$

Built in 1927 of granite blocks and concrete beams, this sedate luxury hotel is a National Historic Landmark. It is decorated with priceless Native American baskets and Oriental rugs, and interesting historic photos and artwork hang on the walls. The grand Great Lounge, with a walk-in fireplace at either end, is a delightful place for afternoon tea.

The 123 rooms have refrigerators and TV sets. Some cottages are available, and (yes, kids) there is an outdoor pool. The best time to dine in the rustic splendor of the magnificent Ahwahnee Dining Room is during the day, when you can fully enjoy the spectacular views of the valley offered by 50-foot-tall, floor-to-trestle beamed-ceiling leaded-glass windows.

Breakfast and lunch are the best times to bring children here anyway, as dinner is expensive and formal (men are expected to wear a sport or suit jacket and women to dress appropriately).

Guests of the hotel get first choice at dinner reservations, so if you are staying elsewhere, be prepared for either an early or late seating; *(559) 252-4848.*

> Oddly enough, most **black bears** are not entirely black. In fact, they are found in a variety of colors including **black**, **brown**, **blond**, and **cinnamon**. Yosemite National Park is home to 300 to 500 American black bears.

Campgrounds
★★★★/$

Most of the Yosemite camping areas are open April through October only, but several are open year-round. Most permit both tents and RVs, though there are no RV hookups. One tent-only, walk-in campground is also available. Don't have a tent or RV? A new 266-unit Housekeeping Camp permits you to experience camping beside the Merced River without the bother of setting up a tent. Units, which accommodate up to six people, consist of three concrete walls, a concrete floor, a canvas roof, and a canvas curtain closure. Basic furniture is provided and there's an outdoor-pit grill for cooking. *For reservations, call (800) 436-7275 or go to* www.nps.gov

Curry Village
★★★★/$-$$

Accommodations include 103 cabins without bath, 80 with bath, and 427 inexpensive tent-cabins near the Merced River that sleep up to six people. The tent-cabins are a particularly fun choice for children during the summer, but they can be too chilly at other times. There's an unheated outdoor pool, a casual cafeteria-style restaurant, and an ice cream shop; *(559) 252-4848.*

Stories of Yosemite

Many good children's books star Yosemite National Park. Here are two to look for while you're here. They're fun to read on the spot and make great souvenirs.

EASY DAY HIKES IN YOSEMITE, by Deborah J. Durkee (Yosemite Association, $4.50), guides you to the best hiking trails for children and details 20 easy hikes, mentioning distance, suggested time allowance, level of difficulty, and points of interest along the way.

LEGENDS OF THE YOSEMITE MIWOK, compiled by Frank LaPena, Craig D. Bates, and Steven P. Medley (Yosemite Association, $11.95), details 18 Native American myths and legends that translate into personal terms—abstract concepts such as life and death. They are illustrated with beautiful pencil drawings resembling woodcuts.

Wawona Hotel
★★★/$$

Built in 1879, this charming 104-room Victorian hotel is 30 miles from the valley and six miles from the national park's southern entrance, near the Mariposa Grove of Big Trees. A National Historic Landmark, it is said to be the oldest resort hotel in the state. Though most rooms accommodate only two people, a few in the annex (added in 1918) accommodate three. For a larger family, you'll need to book several rooms. Facilities include an unheated "swimming tank" built in 1917, a tennis court, and a nine-hole golf course. The restaurant's vintage dining room, where huge multi-paned windows provide views of the surrounding pines, serves simple, satisfying fare. The inexpensive Sunday brunch is highly recommended for families; Jell-O and pudding and other things kids especially like are available. Breakfast and lunch during the rest of the week are also pleasant. Open April through November, for Christmas vacation, and weekends January through Easter; *(559) 252-4848.*

Yosemite Lodge
★★★★/$$

The 245 hotel rooms here are modern and comfortable. Amenities include an unheated outdoor pool and two restaurants, including a casual food court and the Mountain Room Restaurant; *(559) 252-4848.*

Outside the Park

Tenaya Lodge at Yosemite
★★★★/$$-$$$$

Unaffiliated with Yosemite National Park, this plush resort property is two miles outside the park's south entrance. It is a cross between the Yosemite Lodge and the Ahwahnee hotel, with a majestic public reception area featuring three-story-tall beamed ceilings, two restaurants, and 244 comfortable guest rooms with forest views. Kid-pleasing facilities include both indoor and outdoor heated pools; Moms and Dads will like the hot tub, two saunas, two steam rooms, and fitness room. Guided nature walks are scheduled most mornings, weather permitting. Campfire programs and wagon rides are also on tap and mountain bikes are available for rent. The Camp Tenaya children's program, especially for kids ages 5 to 12, operates from 6 to 10 P.M. each evening in summer, on weekends and holidays fall through spring; there's a fee. *1122 Highway 41, Fish Camp; (800) 635-5807; (559) 683-6555;* www.tenayalodge.com

Sequoia and Kings Canyon National Parks

Although only a three-hour drive south of Yosemite National Park, vacationing families often overlook these two scenic national parks. That's a shame because they, too, offer spectacular scenery, but are much less crowded than Yosemite.

Sequoia National Park, established in 1890, was California's first national park and is the country's second oldest (Yellowstone is the oldest national park). Kings Canyon National Park was established in 1940. The main attractions at both parks are the enormous cinnamon-colored sequoia trees, which grow as high as 275 feet. There are also caves to explore, more than 900 miles of hiking trails, plenty of places to fish, and stables that offer horseback-riding excursions.

Geographically and administratively, Sequoia and Kings Canyon are actually one park, covering 860,000 acres. Located in the southern Sierra Nevada, east of Visalia and Fresno off Highway 99, Sequoia National Park is reached via Highway 198 east. Kings Canyon National Park is just north of Sequoia and is accessible via Highway 180 east.

Visitors' centers are conveniently located at Lodgepole, Grant Grove Village, and Foothills. Stop in at one

147

of the centers to find out about scheduled nature walks, evening campfire programs, and the parks' great Junior Ranger program for kids ages 5 through 12. Participants earn a patch while learning about the parks' resources and how to protect them. The centers also offer exhibits of the area's wildlife as well as displays on Native Americans and the sequoias.

There's a per-vehicle admission charge. *For general information on the parks, call (559) 565-4212 or visit* www.nps.gov/seki

JUST FOR FUN

Boyden Cavern ★★★/$
Located in spectacular 8,000-foot-deep Kings River Canyon—the deepest canyon in the United States—this cavern can be seen on a 45-minute guided tour. *In Sequoia National Forest, just outside Kings Canyon National Park; (559) 736-2708;* www.caverntours.com

Giant Forest Museum ★★★/$
There's an opportunity to go to a theater built inside a replica of a giant sequoia. Inside, kids can watch a video about the survival of these majestic trees. The museum, located within Sequoia National Park, also offers exhibits about ecology. Kids will want to check out the exhibit that compares and measures the

height of famous monuments against the mighty trees. Ranger programs—which include hikes, nature walks, and campfires—are also offered. The large Pinewood picnic area is a pleasant place to settle down for lunch. *From the foothills entrance to the park, travel about one hour along General's Highway to the Giant Forest Grove; (559) 565-3341;* www.nps.gov/seki

Crystal Cave ★★★/$
You reach this 48° F cavern via a steep quarter-mile trail. **NOTE:** Temperatures are around 50°, so sweaters are recommended. Strollers and backpacks are not permitted, there are no rest rooms for quite a stretch, and once you start out there's no way to turn back. Best for children 6 and older—with strong bladders! The guided tour takes about an hour. *In Sequoia National Park; (559) 565-3759;* www.sequoiahistory.org

MUST-SEE Generals Highway
FamilyFun ★★★★/Free
MUST-SEE This 46-mile highway, which connects the two national parks, offers memorable encounters with some pretty spectacular trees. For a great "What I Did on My Summer Vacation" photo, drive your car onto the Auto Log and snap a shot. The kids will also get a kick out of driving through the Tunnel Log, a tree that fell across the road in 1937. Also here are the Senate Group and the House Group of sequoias,

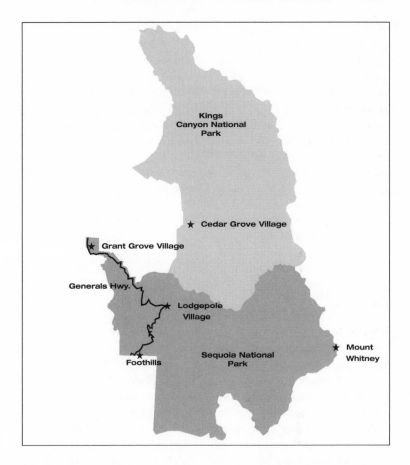

among the most symmetrically formed and nearly perfect specimens of the giant trees. *Between Sequoia and Kings Canyon National Parks.*

★ Giant Forest
FamilyFun ★★★★/Free
MUST-SEE
The main attractions here are the enormous sequoia trees. The 275-foot-high General Sherman Tree in Sequoia National Park is the largest of the trees in the two parks.

You can see more big trees in Kings Canyon's Grant Grove Village.

Mount Whitney ★★★★/Free
This is the highest point in the United States (outside of Alaska). You won't be able to see it without hiking a great distance—it's a one- to three-day trek to the top. Still, it is exciting to know you are so close to this 14,494-foot-tall peak. *In Sequoia National Park.*

BUNKING DOWN

Choices are few here. There are four lodges offering options between deluxe hotel rooms or rustic cabins. Reservations are accepted five months in advance—and that's not too soon for a summer visit. *Call (559) 335-5500 for lodging information and to make reservations.*

Most of the parks have campsites available on a first-come, first-served basis. In the summer, however, some accept reservations and are highly recommended; *(800) 365-2267; www.reservations.nps.gov*

Bearpaw High Sierra Camp
★★★/$

Backpack 11 miles (no little ones on this trek!) into this established camp in Sequoia National Park. Accommodations are in tent-cabins with canvas sides and wooden floors. You'll live like a lion king, with hot showers, linens, cots, and meals provided. It makes a great bonding getaway with older kids. Reservations are necessary. *(800) 365-2267.*

Wuksachi Lodge
★★★★/$$-$$$

Sequoia National Park's new 102-room hotel offers deluxe rooms in three price categories. In the evening, ranger programs are scheduled several times weekly on the premises, and guests can also attend nightly ranger programs at Lodgepole campground. There's a restaurant on site; *64740 Wuksachi Way, Sequoia National Park; (888) 252-5757; www.visitsequoia.com*

Outside the Parks

Montecito-Sequoia Lodge
★★★★/$$$

Family vacations take a lot of planning. That's the appeal of this all-inclusive mountain resort—all the planning is done for you rather than by you. When lodging, meals, and activities are all included in one price, you can focus your attention on relaxing. Tucked in the Sequoia National Forest between Kings Canyon and Sequoia National Parks, the property has 36 spacious rooms with queen- and king-size beds for you and bunk beds for your kids, as well as 13 cabins with nearby bathhouses. Light snacks (fruit, peanut-butter-and-jelly sandwiches) are always available, and the down-home style buffet meals satisfy even the hardest-to-please young 'uns. They'll even pack you a picnic lunch if you ask. This place is lots of fun in the summer: lake activities include swimming, sailing, and canoeing, and land activities include mountain biking, horseback riding, and archery. But the low-key lodge is perhaps even more enjoyable in the winter. There are a variety of cross-country ski trails groomed for all ability levels, and lessons (including special classes for children 5 through 11) and guided ski tours are scheduled daily. You can also rent "pulkas" to pull little ones along as you ski. (Child care is also available for children ages 4 and older.) Other cold-weather activities include ice-skating, snow tubing, snowshoe walks, and building snowmen outside the lodge. Evenings are best spent in front of the gigantic fireplaces getting cozy, making new friends, and playing board games. Because of the high altitude (7,500 feet), the resort offers skiing until midspring; *8000 General's Hwy., Kings Canyon National Park; (800) 227-9900; (650) 967-8612;* www. mslodge.com

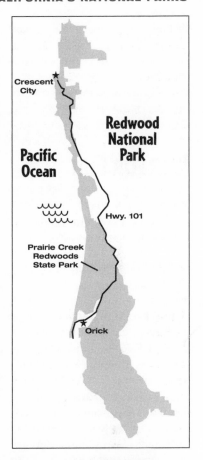

Redwood National Park and Redwood Country

If you want to see California's most spectacular redwood groves, you need to take an approximately four-hour car journey from San Francisco up Highway 101 to Phillipsville, where the incredibly scenic drive through the Avenue of the Giants begins. Paralleling the freeway and the Eel River, this breathtaking route winds for 32 miles through grove after grove of huge redwoods, ending near Pepperwood. It is estimated

151

that most of the remaining ancient virgin, or old-growth, redwoods (meaning they've never been cut) are preserved by the state park system here and by Redwood National Park located further north, above Eureka.

JUST FOR FUN

NOTE: The following attractions are listed geographically, heading north from San Francisco.

Humboldt Redwoods State Park
★★★★/$

Approximately half of the area's huge old trees are found in this park in the town of Weott (70 miles south of Redwoods National Park). Its main attractions are Rockefeller Forest and the Children's Forest *(see below)*. The park also offers camping facilities and a visitors' center, located two miles south of Weott, next to Burlington Campground; *(707) 946-2409;* http://www.humboldtredwoods.org

Children's Forest
★★★/$

Dedicated to the nation's children in 1941, this 1,120-acre forest has a 2.4-mile round-trip trail that leads through a dark redwood forest and by a hillside Douglas fir forest. The trail takes about two hours to walk and is moderately difficult, with a few short, steep slopes. It's good for

all ages; you can turn back partway in if the little ones start griping. *Off Williams Grove, three miles south of the visitors' center, Humboldt Redwoods State Park.*

MUST-SEE FamilyFun Rockefeller Forest ★★★★/$
MUST-SEE This 10,000-acre forest is the world's largest grove of old-growth redwoods. Trails here lead to the Flatiron Tree, so called because it is shaped like an iron (the kind great-grandma used to press her clothes); the Giant Tree, which, based on its combination of height, circumference, and crown size, is considered the champion redwood by the American Forestry Association; and the (aptly named) 356-foot Tall Tree. Campsites are available. *Accessed from Mattole Rd., Humboldt Redwoods State Park.*

MUST-SEE FamilyFun Redwood National Park ★★★★/$
MUST-SEE North of Eureka, this magnificent 105,000-acre park contains the Tall Trees Grove, home to the tallest tree in the world (367.8 feet) as well as the world's second-, third-, and fifth-tallest trees. (Young fans of the *Guinness Book of World Records* are gonna love this!) In summer, you can do one of the ranger-led interpretive programs that are scheduled daily. There are visitors' centers in Orick, Crescent City, and Hiouchi; *(707) 464-6101;* http://www. redwood.national-park.com/

Prairie Creek Redwoods State Park ★★★/$

Keep your eyes open for wildlife here, as this park is a refuge for one of the few remaining herds of native Roosevelt elk. An unpaved gravel road leads to Gold Bluffs Beach (where it's not safe to swim) and to Fern Canyon, where there's a short and easy hiking trail. For safe water fun, head to nearby Freshwater, Big, and Stone lagoons. Campsites (there's a charge) are available. The visitors' center is on the Newton B. Drury Scenic Parkway. *The park entrance is located six miles north of Orick; (707) 464-6101; www.parks. ca.gov/north/nerd/persp.htm*

BUNKING DOWN

KOA Kampground ★★★★/$

This site offers camping cottages. Also see "KOA Kamping in Kalifornia" on page 306. *4050 N. Hwy. 101, four miles north of Eureka; (800) KOA-3136; (707) 822-4243; www.koa.com*

FOSSIL RECORDS show that ancestors of the redwoods in these forests thrived during the Jurassic Period. Can you imagine dinosaurs roaming through forests of redwoods 160 million years ago?

Redwood National Park Hostel ★★★/$

This northernmost link in the California coast hostel chain is within Redwood National Park boundaries. Set in the historic 1890s pioneer DeMartin House, it has one group room that holds six people, and one private room for couples. A full kitchen and spectacular ocean views complete the list of amenities. Also see "Hosteling for Families" on page 215. *14480 Hwy. 101, Redwood National Park; (800) 909-4776, ext. 74; (707) 482-8265.*

Lassen Volcanic National Park

What kid doesn't love a volcano? Thrill yours with the chance to hike around on one of only two active volcanoes in the continental United States. (For inquisitive 6-year-olds, the other is Mount St. Helens in Washington State, which last erupted in 1980.) Though Lassen Peak is now dormant (it last

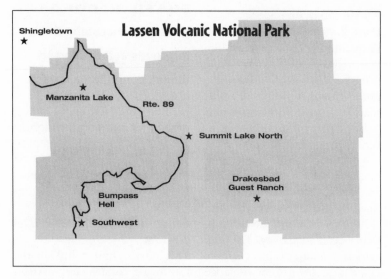

Lassen Volcanic National Park

★ Shingletown

★ Manzanita Lake

Rte. 89

★ Summit Lake North

Drakesbad
Guest Ranch
★

Bumpass
Hell

★ Southwest

erupted in 1914), its bright yellow and orange rocks, brilliant white and cerulean ponds, steaming fumeroles, and gushing hot springs provide plenty of action. The park is sometimes referred to as California's Yellowstone. Visit during summer, when the 35-mile road through the park is least likely to be closed by snow. In summer, guided hikes and campfire talks are scheduled. A free park newsletter/map orients visitors and lists daily activities. *The park headquarters is in Mineral; a visitors' center is located at Manzanita Lake (530/595-4444). From here, you can extend your excursion by continuing on up Highway 5 to the rustic, scenic wonderland of Mount Shasta; www.nps.gov/lavo*

JUST FOR FUN

Bumpass Hell
FamilyFun ★★★★/$

Wooden catwalks supplement the three-mile trail through this popular area of the national park. It features geological oddities such as boiling springs and mud pots, pyrite pools, and noisy fumaroles. The stinky springs where hydrogen sulfide is released are sure to evoke gleeful shrieks, while the "naughty" name usually elicits a few smirks and giggles. The trail is usually open

---

FamilyFun TIP

Do the Twist

Pipe cleaners have saved many a parent's sanity on long car trips. Kids can quietly fashion these building tools into an endless array of designs — from stick figures to animals to houses with furniture.

for only a few months during the summer, after the snow melts. Should you be here early in the season, you can usually see something from an overview in the parking lot. *In Lassen Volcanic National Park.*

Bunking Down

The park operates eight campgrounds. Sites are available on a first-come, first-served basis. *For information call (800) 365-2267 or log onto* www.reservations.nps.gov

Drakesbad Guest Ranch
★★★★/$$$
Located in a secluded, scenic mountain valley within the national park, this rustic resort is part dude ranch and part old-time resort. You and your family can enjoy luxury camping here in rustic cabins, bungalows, and lodge rooms. Most of the rooms lack electricity—kerosene lanterns are used for light, giving the kids a

glimpse of "what it was like in the olden days." Things are not *too* primitive, however—all rooms have private baths. Bounteous meals are included in the rate, and the dining room is used to high chairs and shrill voices. The ranch features a swimming pool, stables, and guided horseback rides into the national park. **NOTE:** You need to book far in advance—at least one year for prime summer-vacation periods. *At the end of Warner Valley Rd., 17 miles northwest of Chester, Lassen Volcanic National Park; (530) 529-1512;* www.calparksco.com

KOA Kampground
★★★★/$
The campground has 44 sites and four Kamping Kabins; there's a pool and volleyball court, plus a petting zoo and general store. *Located 20 miles east of Lassen National Park.* Also see "KOA Kamping in California" on page 306. *7749 KOA Rd., Shingletown; (800) KOA-3403; (530) 474-3133;* www.koa.com

The seacoast near Monterey is rocky, but you can still find places for your kids to build sandcastles.

Highway 1 South: Monterey Peninsula and Beyond

ONLY A THREE-HOUR drive south of San Francisco, the Monterey Peninsula is filled with family-friendly touring options. You can pet bat rays and starfish at the aquarium, picnic on the 17-Mile Drive, pedal a red-striped surrey along the scenic waterfront, and, from October to March, observe a multitude of migrating Monarch butterflies in Pacific Grove. From Big Sur, you can continue down the coast another 75 miles to the fairy-tale Hearst Castle, at which point you'll be halfway to Los Angeles. If you choose to continue south, you might want to plan a stop in Santa Barbara (see page 189), then zip on into L.A. Family fun here is ocean-centered.

THE **FamilyFun** LIST

MUST-SEE · MUST-SEE

Cannery Row (page 158)

Carmel Beach (page 167)

Dennis the Menace playground at El Estero Park (page 161)

Hearst Castle (page 174)

Monterey Bay Aquarium (page 159)

Pacific Grove Museum of Natural History (page 165)

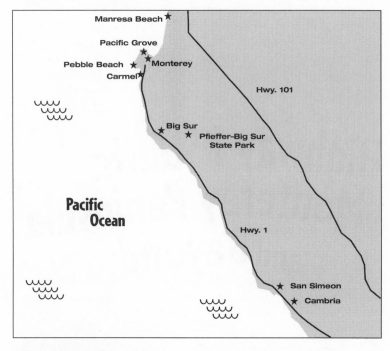

Monterey

The recently established Monterey Bay National Marine Sanctuary is the nation's largest protected marine area. The Monterey Bay Aquarium acts as its interpretive center, and a visit there will orient you and the kids to the area's wonders. The oceanside here is generally rugged, but youngsters can still find sand for digging. Bring along food for the seagulls, and you can enjoy an inexpensive and satisfying outing. You can usually spot shore birds and some seals at Fisherman's Wharf, a good place to find a reasonably

priced meal. The big city park that holds Dennis the Menace Playground is a great place to head when the natives get restless.

CULTURAL ADVENTURES

Cannery Row
FamilyFun ★★★★/Free
The fictitious focus of John Steinbeck's *Cannery Row*, this area, once booming with sardine

canneries, became a ghost town in 1945 when the sardines mysteriously disappeared from the area. Now Cannery Row houses restaurants, art galleries, shops, and—of greatest interest to the kids—the Monterey Bay Aquarium and Steinbeck's Spirit of Monterey Wax Museum *(see below)*. Moms and Dads who have read *Cannery Row* will want to check out the collection of shops. *By the Monterey Bay, from the aquarium to the Coast Guard pier, Monterey; (831) 373-1902.*

Monterey Bay Aquarium
FamilyFun ★★★★/$$

One of the nation's largest seawater aquariums, this spectacular structure provides a close-up view of the underwater habitats and creatures of Monterey Bay. Kids' favorite exhibits include a three-story-high kelp forest, a two-story tank filled with playful sea otters, and a walk-through aviary of shorebirds. Children especially enjoy the bat-ray petting pool (they're soft and slippery!) and the Touch Pool, where they can handle a variety of sea stars and other tide pool creatures. The new Splash Zone gallery, geared toward children 9 and under, offers hands-on activities. Your kids can pop up in a bubble window for a close look at black-footed penguins, and crawl through a tunnel with exhibits of live tropical reef fishes and giant clams. They can even get eye to eye with tropical

sharks with the help of a special mirror. Another newer section, The Outer Bay, features the world's largest acrylic window, which permits a peek into a simulated ocean filled with sharks, ocean sunfish, green sea turtles, and schools of tuna swimming in a million gallons of water. It's like scuba diving with your clothes on! This area also has a fabulous display of sea jellies (formerly known as jellyfish), including a tank filled with psychedelic orange sea nettles shown against a brilliant blue background. You'll need about three hours to see the aquarium, so you might want to plan a meal here—choices are a cafeteria and a pricier restaurant on the premises and picnic tables outside. Or you can get your hands stamped for reentry, eat somewhere nearby (First Awakenings restaurant is a good choice; see Good Eats), and return to meet more denizens of the deep after lunch. **NOTE:** The museum can get very crowded during vacation seasons

FamilyFun TIP

Guess My Name

In this acting game players imitate the motions, habits, and expressions of a famous person, such as an athlete, politician, musician, or actor. The clincher: No talking allowed! Players can ask Yes or No questions (which are met by a nod or a shake). The correct guesser does the next impression.

T's by the Sea

Here's a beach craft that will leave a lasting impression on your kids—or on their T-shirts, at least. Working right on the beach, you can use seashells and fabric paint (available at most art-supply stores) to print summery designs on a cotton shirt, hat, or beach towel.

First, clean each shell you plan to use and then press a ball of modeling clay onto its inner surface (this will serve as a convenient handle). Place newspaper between the front and back of the shirt to keep the paint from leaking through.

Next, pour some fabric paint onto a sponge. Press the outside of the shell into the paint and then onto the shirt. Repeat, experimenting with different colors (use a new shell and a clean portion of the sponge for each hue). At home, heat-set the dry paint according to the manufacturer's directions.

and on weekends. If you are planning a visit then, purchase tickets in advance so you won't have to wait in a long line with antsy kids. *886 Cannery Row, Monterey; (831) 648-4888; advance tickets, (800) 756-3737;*www.montereybayaquari um.org

Steinbeck's Spirit of Monterey Wax Museum ★/$

Here's an entertaining way for the family to learn a little area history. Local notables, including Robert Louis Stevenson and John Steinbeck, are depicted. The kids like the novelty of the wax figures, though the under-6 crowd might find it a bit spooky—the exhibits are basically dark. Nothing jumps out at you, though, and there is no House of Horrors. *700 Cannery Row, Monterey; (831) 375-3770.*

Monterey State Historic Park ★★★/$

Downtown Monterey is a state park that holds the largest collection of historic buildings west of Williamsburg— nearly 50 sites and preserved adobes. Kids usually enjoy touring the Stevenson House (as in Robert Louis), said to be haunted by a woman dressed in black, and the Cooper-Molera Adobe, a two-acre complex with chickens, sheep, carriages, and a visitors' center. The Path of History, a self-guided walking tour, follows gold-colored tiles embedded in the sidewalk to 46 other historic buildings and gardens. When you purchase your ticket, you'll be given a map that indicates where the various buildings are located. *20 Custom Plaza, Monterey; (831) 649-7118.*

JUST FOR FUN

El Estero Park
FamilyFun ★★★★/Free

The main reason you should seek out this bucolic park is the Dennis the Menace Playground by the lake on Pearl Street. Designed by former area resident Hank Ketchum, who created the *Dennis the Menace* comic strip, it is filled with colorful play equipment, including a hedge maze with a corkscrew slide in its center, a long suspension bridge, and an authentic Southern Pacific steam train engine for climbing. Kids 3 through 11 can play happily here for hours. Hike and bike on the trails here, too, and bring some crackers to feed the hungry ducks in the lake. You can also rent paddleboats in the park, and the kids can even drop a fishing line. *Bordered by Del Monte Ave., Camino El Estero, and Pearl St., Monterey; (831) 646-3866.*

Fisherman's Wharf
★★★/Free-$$

Look for the organ grinder at the entrance—his friendly monkey is happy to take coins from children's hands. Kids will also be delighted by the show-off sea lions that congregate around the wharf pilings. It's fun to just walk around the wharf, browsing the shops filled with kitschy souvenirs and picking a likely-looking dining spot for when hunger strikes. Oh, and try the attractions, too (fees). *Monterey; (831) 373-0600.*

Monterey Bay Kayaks
★★/$$$$

Here's a chance for young animal lovers to get nose-to-nose with some of the coast's most charming creatures. Guided tours on two-person kayaks allow adults and big kids (at least 54 inches tall) to observe sea lions and otters up close. Marine biologists guide the tours (near Fisherman's Wharf and along Cannery Row) and also provide safety instruction. No kayaking experience is required. *693 Del Monte Ave., Monterey; (800) 649-5357; (831) 373-KELP;* www.monterybaykayaks.com

Rent-A-Roadster
★★★★/$$-$$$

Imagine you and yours zipping down the coast or along the 17-Mile Drive in authentic reproductions of a 1929 Model A Ford Roadster. The autos rent by the hour, are easy to drive, and are perfect for an afternoon sight-seeing excursion. Roadsters seat four—two in the front and two in the popular rumble seat. It is well worth the price just to honk

161

the cranky, old-fashioned horn and watch the reactions of people you pass on the street. The whole family will have a blast. *229 Cannery Row, Monterey; (831) 647-1929.*

BUNKING DOWN

Clarion Hotel
★★★/$-$$$

The kids are going to love the indoor heated pool—it's a fabulous amenity in this often chilly area. This simple, well-priced 52-room motel also has two parent pleasers: a hot tub and a sauna. Some rooms have kitchens and gas fireplaces. Complimentary continental breakfast is included in the rate. *1046 Munras Ave., Monterey; (800) 252-7466; (831) 373-1337;* www.clarion hotelmonterey.com

Hotel Pacific
★★★/$$$-$$$$

The comforts of a B&B (complimentary breakfast and afternoon snack, plus fluffy feather beds and comforters), combined with the convenience of a motel (parking your own car, not dealing with a bellboy unless you want one), make this a good choice for traveling families. Situated near the Wharf, the comfortable 105-room property features spacious suites with VCRs and gas fireplaces. The open-style suites come equipped with either two double beds or a king-size bed and a

rollaway. Each has a half-wall separating the bedroom from the living room. The kids can romp in the attractive gardens, and the whole family can relax in the two hot tubs. *300 Pacific St., Monterey; (800) 554-5542; (831) 373-5700;* www.hotel pacific.com

Hyatt Regency Monterey
★★★★/$$-$$$

Two heated pools, two hot tubs, a fitness center, six tennis courts, and a jogging trail with exercise stations, plus volleyball, basketball, and croquet await you and your active offspring. On the outskirts of town, this quiet, luxurious 575-room resort is next to the scenic Old Del Monte Golf Course. Kids enjoy dining in casual Knuckles Historical Sports Bar, where 14 big-screen TVs are tuned to the action, a game room adjoins, and peanut shells can be dropped on the floor. Room service

includes special kid-friendly items. *One Old Golf Course Rd., Monterey; (800) 228-9000; (831) 372-1234.*

Monterey Bay Inn
★★★/$$$$

Within easy walking distance of the aquarium, this comfortable 47-room waterfront motel is a great place for families to spend the night. All rooms offer such family-friendly features as sleeper sofas, VCRs, and private balconies; some units also have a view of the bay, where you can often see otters and seals playing in the waves. Parents will want to unwind in the rooftop hot tub. Younger guests will appreciate the chocolate-chip cookies served in the lobby each afternoon. A complimentary continental breakfast is delivered to your room. *242 Cannery Row, Monterey; (800) 424-6242; (831) 373-6242.*

Motel Row

Modern motel accommodations can easily be found along Munras Avenue.

Spindrift Inn ★★/$$$$

Right in the heart of Cannery Row, two blocks from the aquarium, this tasteful lodging place has 42 comfortable rooms, many with bay views. All units have gas-fired fireplaces that accept wood, and the complimentary breakfast and newspaper is brought to your room on a silver tray. The inn's backyard is tiny

McAbee Beach, where kids can dig in the sand and get their tootsies wet. In the afternoon, munch on complimentary cookies and apple juice or tea before heading out to explore the Row. *652 Cannery Row, Monterey; (800) 841-1879; (831) 646-8900.*

GOOD EATS

Bubba Gump Shrimp Co.
★★★★/$$

Inspired by the Oscar-winning movie *Forrest Gump*, this informal, family-friendly spot is the first in the chain of seafood restaurants with a Gump theme. The place is packed with movie memorabilia, including script pages, storyboards, costumes, and photos. "Gumpisms" are scrawled on tabletops, and the movie plays continuously on video monitors. The children's menu offers corn dogs, burgers, pepperoni pizza, and deep-fried chicken strips, along with pictures to color and games to play. Make sure the kids know that the men's room is labeled "Bubba's" and the women's room "Jenny's." Also see Good Eats in San Francisco. *720 Cannery Row, Monterey; (888) 560-GUMP; (831) 373-1884;* www.bubba gump.com

First Awakenings ★★★★/$

A block north of the Monterey Bay Aquarium, in the American Tin Cannery Premium Outlet Mall, this place is perfect for grabbing a meal to break up your aquarium visit. (Just remember to get your hands stamped so you can get back in later.) Breakfast items include fresh fruit crepes and a variety of omelettes. Lunch brings on salads and sandwiches. All the family amenities are available (high chairs, booster seats, a children's menu), and on a warm day, the outdoor patio is a super place to have lunch with the kids. After you eat, wander through the industrial interior of the mall. Mom may want to stop at the Carter's outlet, while the kids will love the colorful merchandise at Come Fly a Kite. *125 Ocean View Blvd., Monterey; (831) 372-1125.*

Ghirardelli Chocolate Shop & Soda Fountain ★★★★/$

A much smaller version of the fountain in San Francisco, it serves up the same scrumptious sundaes and other ice-cream treats. *616 Cannery Row, Monterey; (831) 373-0997; www.ghirardelli.com*

Wharfside Restaurant ★★★/$$-$$$

It's time for the kids to learn that ravioli doesn't always come from a green-and-red can. If you're lucky, it will be ravioli-making day when you're here, and your Chef Boyardee fans can watch the cooks in the downstairs window prepare the seemingly endless varieties (meat and spinach, cheese, squid, salmon, shrimp, crab, lobster). Then head upstairs for dinner in the casual dining room, where you'll get great views of the bay. The menu also offers other pasta and seafood dishes and a children's menu featuring meat ravioli (of course), spaghetti and meatballs, fish-and-chips, and a burger. *60 Fisherman's Wharf #1, Monterey; (831) 375-3956.*

Pacific Grove

Just a few hops, skips, and jumps northwest of Monterey is Pacific Grove, also known as Butterfly Town U.S.A. Each October this community welcomes hundreds of thousands of stunning orange-and-black monarch butterflies that return from Western Canada and Alaska to winter on the needles of their favorite local pine trees. The insects stay until March, when they fly north again. It's a mystery how they find their way here each year, since their short life span (less than a year) means no butterfly makes the trip twice.

Your children are sure to be enchanted by the profusion of colorful flutterers in town; Monarch Grove Sanctuary and George Washington Park are particularly

FamilyFun **READER'S TIP** -

Tic-Tac-Tine

While my sister Barb and I and our seven kids were waiting for dinner at a restaurant recently, my nephew Josh, age nine, surprised me with a game he invented using dinner utensils and sugar packets. He set up forks, spoons, and knives in the traditional tic-tac-toe grid and gave me the choice of being the X's (regular sugar packets) or O's (artificial sweetener packets).

Soon everyone at the table was pairing off to play, and it was a fun way for us to pass the time before our meal arrived.

Theresa Jung, Cincinnati, Ohio

good viewing spots *(see below)*. The monarchs can't fly when temperatures drop below 55°, so look for them on sunny days between the hours of 10 A.M. and 4 P.M. On cold and foggy days they huddle together with closed wings, and you might easily mistake them for dead leaves. On such days be careful where you step. Monarchs that fly to the ground when the temperature drops sometimes find it too cold to fly back to their perch. And leave your butterfly nets at home. It is a misdemeanor carrying a $1,000 fine to molest a butterfly here.

To celebrate the annual return of the butterflies, a Butterfly Parade has been held in Pacific Grove every October since 1938, usually on a Saturday at the beginning of the month. Completely noncommercial, this delightful procession features local grade-school children marching down the street dressed as butterflies. Traditional bands and majorette corps from local schools also participate. The weather always cooperates: this parade has *never* been rained on.

The Pacific Grove Museum of Natural History *(see below)* can provide the family's scientists with all they want to know about the town's six-legged visitors. To receive a child's packet of information on the monarch, including stories and a coloring page, send a request and $1 for postage and handling to the nonprofit group Friends of the Monarchs at P.O. Box 51683, Pacific Grove, CA 93950-6683.

CULTURAL ADVENTURES

Pacific Grove Museum of Natural History ★★★/Free

Butterfly-related exhibits include photographs and displays, as well as an informative 10-minute videotape. The life history of the monarch is portrayed in drawings, and during the summer larvae are often on view. Milkweed—the only plant on which the female monarch will lay her eggs—attracts butterflies to a native plant garden outside the museum. In operation since 1882, this tiny museum also has exhibits of marine and bird life, native plants, seashells, and Native American artifacts. *Corner of Forest and Central Ave., Pacific Grove; (831) 648-5716.*

JUST FOR FUN

Monarch Grove Sanctuary
★★★★/Free

The densest clusters of monarchs congregate in the pine and eucalyptus grove behind the Butterfly Grove Inn. Guided tours are available from mid-October through mid-February. *1073 Lighthouse Ave., Pacific Grove; (888) PG-MONARCH; (831) 375-0982; www.pgmonarch.org*

BUNKING DOWN

Butterfly Grove Inn
★★★/$$-$$$

This 28-room complex has much to recommend it to butterfly-loving families. For starters, it's on a quiet side street adjacent to the Monarch Grove Sanctuary. It also has a heated pool and hot tub, and a school playground is just across the street. Accommodations are either two-bedroom family suites in a Victorian house or regular motel rooms; some units have kitchens and/or fireplaces. *1073 Lighthouse Ave., Pacific Grove; (800) 337-9244; (831) 373-4921.*

Carmel

Just a few miles south of Monterey, this well-established getaway is best known for its abundant shops, cozy lodgings, and (the main attraction as far as young visitors are concerned) its picturesque white-sand beach. The kids will be intrigued to see that this town has no street signs, streetlights, electric or neon signs, jukeboxes, parking meters, or buildings over two stories. The residential areas have no sidewalks, curbs, or house numbers. See if you can find any! But do be careful. Eccentric (though only loosely enforced) laws make it illegal to wear high-heeled shoes on the sidewalks, throw a ball in the park, play a musical instrument in a bar, or dig in the sand at the beach other than when making a sand castle. (Point this out when your kids complain that *your* rules are unreasonable!)

CULTURAL ADVENTURES

Mission San Carlos Borromeo del Rio Carmelo
★★★★/By donation

Also known as the Carmel Mission, this is the burial place of Father Junipero Serra. From this head-quarters, Father Serra managed the entire chain of California missions. Children enjoy the quadrangle courtyard garden, which has a fountain stocked with colorful koi. *3080 Rio Rd., Carmel; (831) 624-3600.*

JUST FOR FUN

Carmel Beach
FamilyFun ★★★★/Free

Let the kids run free across the white powdery sand at this world-famous beach. Time it right, and you can sit back and enjoy one of its equally famous spectacular sunsets. It's also the perfect place for a picnic or for flying a kite. But beware: swimming here is unsafe—the cold water is known for its riptides. Depending on the tides, the

Great Sand Castle Contest is held here each September or October. The castles produced are true works of art. *At the foot of Ocean Ave., Carmel; (831) 626-2522.*

Carmel River State Beach
★★★★/Free

Located behind the Carmel Mission, where the Carmel River flows into Carmel Bay, this beach is popular with both divers and families. It adjoins a freshwater lagoon where little ones can wade safely (swimming in the ocean is dangerous here). Also adjacent is a bird sanctuary where kids can look for sandpipers, brown pelicans, and assorted waterfowl. There are picnic facilities, too. *At the end of Scenic Rd., Carmel; (831) 624-4909; www.pointlobos.org*

Pebble Beach Equestrian Center
★★/$$$$

Unless there's a budding Tiger Woods among you, your family will probably not be playing at the legendary Spyglass Hill Golf Course. But you can enjoy an escorted horseback ride that takes you right past it, through the scenic Del Monte Forest, then down to the beach and over the sand dunes. You have a choice of English or Western saddles. Riders must be 7 or older, and reservations are required. *Portola Rd./ Alva La., Pebble Beach; (831) 624-2756; www.ridepebblebeach.com*

Point Lobos State Reserve
★★★★/$

This rustic, undeveloped area has been described as "the greatest meeting of land and water in the world." You'll see the flat-topped, gnarled-limbed Monterey cypress trees, which are native only to the four-mile stretch between here and Pebble Beach. You might be lucky enough to spot some sea otters frolicking in the protected waters. The self-guiding trails are easy enough for the youngest of hikers, and guided ranger walks are scheduled daily in summer. You and your kids can stop in the interpretive center, which operates inside a restored whaler's cabin built in 1851. There, artifacts and photographs describe the area's history. Dress warmly, and bring along binoculars, a camera, and perhaps a picnic, too. *Off Hwy. 1, three miles south of Carmel; (831) 624-4909;* www.pointlobos.org

17-Mile Drive ★★★★/$

This world-famous drive takes you past showplace homes, prestigious golf courses, and raw seascapes. Sights of particular interest to those in the backseat are: the Restless Sea, where several ocean crosscurrents meet; Seal and Bird Rock, where herds of sea lions and flocks of shoreline birds congregate; and the landmark Lone Cypress clinging to its jagged, barren rock base. Keep your kids from getting as restless as the aforementioned sea with stops along the way for a picnic or to walk the short trails found in several spots. If you splurge on lunch or dinner at one of the family-friendly ocean-view restaurants at the elegant Inn at Spanish Bay or Lodge at Pebble Beach, your gate fee (toll) will be reimbursed. *At Pebble Beach exit off Hwy. 1, between Carmel and Monterey.*

BUNKING DOWN

Carmel River Inn
★★★★/$$-$$$$

On the outskirts of town on the banks of the Carmel River, this property offers both motel rooms and larger one- and two-bedroom cottages with kitchens that are great for families. Some balconies or patios overlook the river. Kid pleasers: the 10-acre grounds offer plenty of room for running around, and the heated pool is kept at a comfy 85° F. *Hwy. 1 at bridge, Carmel; (800) 882-8142; (831) 624-1575;* www.carmelriverinn.com

Highlands Inn, A Park Hyatt Hotel ★★★/$$$$

Since it was built in 1916, this hotel has hosted many famous guests, including the Beatles and two presidents, Kennedy and Ford, though the kids will be more impressed by the heated pool. You can borrow bikes for a family ride during your stay. Parents might want to check out one of the three hot tubs and the fitness center. The 142 large, luxurious guest rooms all have ocean views and are sheltered by landscaping that provides plenty of privacy. Some have kitchens (handy when the kids are not up for another restaurant meal) and wood-burning fireplaces. The California Market has a fabulous ocean view and serves up casual fare, including a breakfast buffet and a hamburger at lunch; there's a children's menu, too. *On Hwy. 1, four miles south of Carmel; (800) 682-4811; (831) 620-1234;* www.highlands_inn.com

The Inn at Spanish Bay
★★★★/$$$$

For a luxury resort vacation the whole family will enjoy, you can't do much better than this spectacular oceanfront facility. Your little kids will want to spend as much time as possible in the heated pool, while preteens may join a parent on the tennis courts or the 18-hole golf course, and in the hot tub, sauna, fitness center, and health spa. The family can also rent bicycles (bikes for young children are available with 24-hour notice) and take a shuttle for day trips in Carmel and Monterey. All 270 rooms have VCRs and gas fireplaces; most have either a patio or balcony. Three restaurants are on-site, including lively Roys' at Pebble Beach featuring the strikingly colorful Euro-Asian cuisine of Hawaii-based chef Roy

FOOTPRINTS IN THE SAND

On beach vacations, sand seems to end up everywhere, especially between the toes. The simple plaster-casting project lets your child capture that sandy barefoot feeling — and a record of his feet.

MATERIALS
♦ Plaster of paris
♦ Small bucket
♦ Freshwater
♦ 4-inch lengths of string or wire (for hangers, if desired)

Choose a site to cast your molds—the moist, hard-packed sand near (but not too near!) the water's edge works best. Have your child firmly press both feet into the sand. The prints should be about 1½ to 2 inches deep. If your child can't press down that hard, he can use his finger to dig down into the print, following its shape. Mix up the plaster, according to the directions on the package, so that it has a thick, creamy consistency. Pour the wet plaster gently into the footprints.

If you want to make hangers, tie a knot about a half inch from each end of your pieces of string or wire. As the plaster begins to harden, push the knotted ends into the plaster and let dry. After 20 to 25 minutes, gently dig the footprints out of the molds and brush away any excess sand. Set sole-side up in the sun (away from the rising tide) for about an hour to let harden.

Yamaguchi. Kids get their own menu here, as well as coloring books and other distractions. As a bedtime treat, kids can order milk and cookies from room service. The nearby Lodge at Pebble Beach, with 161 rooms, is under the same management and also welcomes families. *2700 17-Mile Drive, Pebble Beach; (800) 654-9300; (831) 647-7500;* www.pebblebeach.com

Lamp Lighter Inn
★★★/$$-$$$

Both the village and the ocean are just a few blocks away in either direction from this enclave of nine charming gingerbread-style cottages that will fulfill your children's fairy-tale fantasies. One cottage, known as the Hansel and Gretel, has a special sleeping loft for kids. Cottages sleep up to six people, and several have kitchens. If your tots need a brief diversion, set them on a search for the 17 elves in the garden. There's no restaurant or pool. *Ocean Ave. near Camino Real, Carmel; (831) 624-7372.*

La Playa Hotel
★★★/$$$-$$$$

The largest hotel (80 rooms) and the only full-service resort in Carmel, this luxury Mediterranean-style property is a good choice for families who want to enjoy sightseeing and sand and surf. It's only two blocks from the beach and four blocks from town. Many guest rooms are quite large and can com-

fortably accommodate a family of four. The property also includes a group of charming, spacious cottages situated a block closer to the ocean. Some can accommodate up to eight people, and all but one have kitchens. Facilities include a heated pool and a casual restaurant. *Camino Real and Eighth Ave., Carmel; (800) 582-8900; (831) 624-6476;* www.laplayahotel.com

Lincoln Green Inn
★★★/$$$

On the outskirts of town, just a few blocks from the state beach and the point where the Carmel River flows into the ocean, this is a cluster of four English housekeeping cottages. Each features a living room with a cathedral-beamed ceiling and a stone fireplace, and all but one have a full kitchen. The comfortable cottages sleep up to four people and will serve nicely as your home away from home. *Carmelo St. and 15th Ave., Carmel; (800) 262-1262; (831) 624-1880;* www.vagabondshouseinn.com

Normandy Inn ★★/$$-$$$$

Right in town on the main shopping street and four blocks from the ocean, this inn accommodates families in comfortable suites and large cottages, some of which have wood-burning fireplaces and kitchens. Young guests (and their parents) enjoy the invitingly secluded heated pool. Continental breakfast is included in the rate, and in the afternoon there's sherry for adults, cookies and orange juice for the kids. *Ocean Ave. and Monte Verde St., Carmel; (800) 343-3825; (831) 624-3825; www.normandyinncarmel.com*

GOOD EATS

Carmel Bakery ★★★★/$
Buy your kids a caramel apple in Carmel—it might clarify any spelling confusions. *Ocean Ave. and Lincoln St., Carmel; (831) 626-8885.*

Em Le's ★★★/$
Football broadcaster John Madden is part-owner of this cozy, casual spot touted as a "vintage soda fountain." Breakfast is a particularly nice time for families to eat here because the morning menu offers lots of kiddie favorites (there's no special children's menu). A.M. options include wild blueberry pancakes and buttermilk waffles (kids like the fact that they have a choice of light- or dark-baked). Lunch and dinner bring on a really good hot dog, fried chicken, meat loaf, mashed potatoes, and apple pie. *Dolores St. and Fifth Ave., Carmel; (831) 625-6780.*

Toots Lagoon ★★★★/$$
You can count on plenty of noise here to cover up the sounds of cranky or rambunctious kids. The menu is famous for ribs, prepared with a choice of four sauces, but you'll also find brick-oven-baked

pizza, housemade pasta, and fresh fish, plus a special children's menu. It's a friendly, fun kind of place. *Dolores St. and Seventh Ave., Carmel; (831) 625-1915.*

Village Corner ★★★★/$$
The large patio, heated year-round, is just ideal for wiggly young diners, though the inside dining area here is also quite comfortable for families. The Mediterranean bistro menu offers bruschetta, deep-fried local calamari, pastas, and delicious Cajun-style blackened salmon. A kids' menu is available. *Dolores St. and Sixth Ave., Carmel; (831) 624-3588.*

SOUVENIR HUNTING

Cottage of Sweets
Chocolates? Gourmet jelly beans? Taffy? This candy cottage presents the sweet teeth in the family with some tough choices. But you can't really go wrong—everything is delicious. *Ocean Ave. and Lincoln St., Carmel; (831) 624-5170; www.cottageofsweets.com*

Sand Castles by the Sea
Promising "toys that build dreams," this shop delights kids with wooden toys, musical instruments, dress-up clothes, games, puzzles, and more. *In The Barnyard shopping center, Hwy. 1/Carmel Valley Rd., Carmel; (831) 626-8361.*

Big Sur

The rustic, rural town of Big Sur stretches along Highway 1 for six miles, offering a string of lodging places and restaurants. You can spend the night in a rustic cabin or in a luxury hotel—or save some money and camp out. The area has two state parks and a beach, and offers plenty of opportunities to enjoy the outdoors. Just south of town, the highway begins a 90-mile stretch of some of the most spectacular scenery in the United States.

JUST FOR FUN

Andrew Molera State Park ★/$

Located near the photogenic Bixby Bridge, this beach park has some short and easy hiking trails. The flat, two-mile (round-trip) Bluffs Trail follows the ocean to a promontory and is doable for children of any age. Kids should be 10 or so before they tackle the more challenging five-mile (round-trip) Bobcat Trail, which follows the Big Sur River through dense redwoods and involves some climbing. For a real treat, you and your children (7 and older) can go horseback riding on the beach. Walk-in campsites are available, too. *Hwy. 1, Big Sur. Park: (831) 667-2315. Horseback riding: (800) 942-5486; (831) 625-5486; www.molerahorsebacktours.com*

Pfeiffer Beach ★★★★/$

The only easily accessible public beach in the area is famous for being the spot where many years ago Elizabeth Taylor and Richard Burton acted out some love scenes in *The Sandpiper.* But your kids won't care (Elizabeth *who?*). They'll be much more impressed by the striking rock formations and arches carved out by the turbulent ocean. Make a game of giving the formations descriptive names as you walk along this sandy stretch. But don't go in the water—swimming here is unsafe. *To get here, watch for unmarked Sycamore Canyon Rd. on the west side of Highway 1, about 1.7 miles south of Fernwood Resort, and follow it to the beach.*

BUG BEGONE!

Although birds eat many insects, they have learned to steer clear of the monarch butterfly! Monarchs feed on milkweed plants, which contain a poisonous substance that tastes terrible to predators. The birds learn to recognize the monarch's bright coloring and even avoid butterflies that look similar, such as the viceroy.

Pfeiffer-Big Sur State Park
★★★★/$

A great place to enjoy the area's scenery, this expansive park offers hiking (an easy half-mile nature trail is fun with little kids), river swimming, and ranger-led nature walks and campfires. An open meadow is perfect for a game of baseball or for throwing a Frisbee. Campsites are available. *Hwy. 1, Big Sur; (831) 667-2315; www.parks.ca.gov*

BUNKING DOWN

Big Sur Lodge
★★★★/$$$-$$$$

Situated within Pfeiffer-Big Sur State Park, this comfy spot is composed mostly of spacious two-bedroom motel units distributed throughout the grounds. Some have kitchens and fireplaces, but there are no TVs. Facilities include a pleasant pool area and expansive grassy areas where deer are often seen grazing; a casual, moderately priced coffee shop serves meals all day. Guests also have access to the state park's facilities. *Off Hwy. 1, Pfeiffer-Big Sur State Park; (800) 4-BIG-SUR; (831) 667-3100; www.bigsurlodge.com*

Ripplewood Resort
★★★★/$-$$

Sixteen rustic, pleasantly decorated redwood cabins are both above and below the highway here. But the ones below, set in a dense, dark grove

of redwoods just a stone's throw from the Big Sur River, are the more desirable for fans of Grimms' fairy tales. The cabins, one of which can accommodate five people, have no TVs, but some have kitchens and wood-burning fireplaces. The resort's cafe serves breakfast and lunch. *Hwy. 1, Big Sur; (831) 667-2242; www.ripplewoodresort.com*

GOOD EATS

Nepenthe ★★★/$$

This famous restaurant, designed by a student of Frank Lloyd Wright as a cabin for Orson Welles and Rita Hayworth, is at the top of a cliff 808 feet above the ocean. In mild weather dine outside on the casual terrace so you can enjoy the breathtaking coastline view. (Keep a close eye on the kids, though. The terrace is safe, but there are drop-offs nearby.) The menu is simple: steaks, fresh seafood, roasted chicken, housemade soup, and a very good hamburger. The huge cold sandwiches are big enough for an adult to share with a child who has a small appetite. (There's no kids' menu.) Downstairs, Cafe Kevah is a choice spot to enjoy a quick snack, and the classy Phoenix gift shop provides pleasant browsing for the whole family. Careful—the children's section is filled with things they'll really, really want to possess. *On Hwy. 1, Big Sur; (831) 667-2345;* www.nepenthebig sur.com

FamilyFun SNACK

Gobbledy Gook

Place 4 cups oat or crispy-rice cereal, 1 cup chopped peanuts, 1 cup raisins or chopped apricots, 1 cup sunflower seeds, 1 cup chopped pretzels, and 3 tablespoons margarine, melted butter (optional) in a 2-quart plastic bag. Seal and then shake until well mixed.

San Simeon and Cambria

About 75 miles south of Big Sur, the small town of San Simeon is best known as the site of spectacular Hearst Castle, perched atop a reputedly enchanted hill. A few miles farther south, the tiny village of Cambria is filled with cute shops and restaurants and overflows with attractive lodging spots.

An alternative to driving to this area from San Francisco is the train package offered by Key Holidays *(800/783-0783)*. The leisurely rail excursion lets your family travel the way guests to San Simeon did in the 1920s and 1930s, when invitations to Hearst Castle always included train tickets. Amtrak's Coast Starlight transports you to San Luis Obispo, where you'll see the local sights; from there a bus takes you on a tour of the coast and then to Morro Bay to spend the night. The next day, you board a bus to the castle for a guided tour,

then head down scenic Highway 1 for a stop in the village of Cambria, and then back to San Luis Obispo for the return train trip. Meals are not included in the package. Special rates are available for children.

CULTURAL ADVENTURES

Hearst Castle
MUST-SEE FamilyFun ★★★/$

Kids will be amazed by the size and scope of this elaborate modern-day castle. The mansion took 28 years to build and is filled with art treasures and antiques from all over the world, gathered by newspaper czar William Randolph Hearst in the early part of the 20th century. (There are 22,500 pieces of art and antiques displayed at the castle now, which represent only 10 percent of the collection Hearst had at the time.) Though still unfinished, the estate contains 56 bedrooms, 102 bathrooms, 19 sitting rooms, a kitchen, a movie theater, two libraries, a billiard room, a dining hall, and an assembly hall. Colorful vines and plants grow in the lovely gardens, and wild zebras, tar goats, and sambar deer graze the hillsides—remnants of a private zoo that once also included lions, monkeys, and a polar bear. You can't really get close to the creatures, but there are a lot of them—see who can spot one first!

Five tours are available, all of which include a scenic bus ride up to the castle. (Children under 6 are admitted free only if they sit on a parent's lap during the bus ride.) Tour 1 is suggested for a first visit and includes gardens, pools, a guest house, and the ground floor of the main house. **NOTE:** Tours take approximately two hours and require walking about half a mile and climbing approximately 150 to 400 steps, so wear comfortable shoes. Strollers are not permitted, so this excursion may be too much for preschoolers. Picnic tables and a snack bar are near the visitors' center. Reservations are recommended, but you can sometimes purchase tickets at the visitors' center ticket office after 8 A.M. on the day of the tour. *750 Hearst Castle Rd., San Simeon. Reservations: (800) 444-4445; (805) 927-2020; www.hearstcastle.org*

JUST FOR FUN

William Randolph Hearst Memorial State Beach ★★/$

In addition to providing a very nice swimming beach, this park has a 640-foot-long fishing pier. You don't need a license to fish here, and you can rent your gear at Virg's Fishing, right on the pier. Your son or daughter may land a surf perch or halibut. *San Simeon.*

BUNKING DOWN

Bluebird Motel ★★/$-$$

Within easy walking distance of the village, this attractive 37-unit motel surrounds a landmark mansion dating from 1880. One large two-bedroom suite, perfect for families, is available. Several rooms also have connecting doors. Many rooms are creekside, with private balconies or patios. *1880 Main St., Cambria; (800) 552-5434; (805) 927-4634; www.bluebirdmotel.com*

Cambria Pines Lodge ★★★★/$-$$$

Perched on a pine-covered hill above town, this spacious 25-acre facility has 125 units. The rustic cabins sleep two to four people, or opt for one of the standard rooms; some have wood-burning fireplaces. The lodge, built in 1927 by an eccentric European baroness who wanted to

HEARST CASTLE was designed by Julia Morgan, the first woman ever to receive a degree in civil engineering from the University of California at Berkeley. Morgan was also the first woman to be granted an architecture certificate from the prestigious Ecole Nationale et Spéciale des Beaux-Arts in Paris.

live in opulent style near the Hearst Castle, now houses a moderately priced restaurant and a woodsy, casual lounge where live entertainment is scheduled every night in front of a large stone fireplace (kids are welcome). Active families appreciate the heated indoor pool and hot tub, the sauna, and the volleyball area; there's also a nature trail leading down into the village. A full buffet breakfast is included in the rate. *2905 Burton Dr., Cambria; (800) 445-6868; (805) 927-4200;* www.cambriapineslodge.com

Cavalier Oceanfront Resort
★★★/$-$$$
The only oceanfront resort in San Simeon, this contemporary 90-room motel features an expanse of ocean frontage. All rooms have VCRs, many have ocean views, and some also have private patios and wood-burning fireplaces. Facilities include two heated pools, a hot tub, a fitness room, and a restaurant. *9415 Hearst Dr., San Simeon; (800) 826-8168; (805) 927-4688;* www.cavalierresort.com

Fog Catcher Inn
★★★/$$-$$$
Situated across the street from the ocean, this pseudo English Tudor–style inn is great for traveling families. There are 60 oversized rooms as well as an even more spacious two-bedroom suite. All units have mini kitchens and gas fireplaces, and many have ocean views. Facilities include a heated pool and hot tub, and a complimentary continental breakfast is served each morning. *6400 Moonstone Beach Dr., Cambria; (800) 425-4121; (805) 927-1400;* www.fogcatcherinn.com

Motel Row
Numerous motels are located along scenic Moonstone Beach Drive in Cambria.

GOOD EATS

The Brambles Dinner House
★★★/$$$
A special room is set aside just for families at this restaurant featuring

international cuisine in an 1874 English-style cottage, and some very private booths are available as well.

House specialties include prime rib and traditional Yorkshire pudding, fresh salmon barbecued over an oak wood pit, and Greek dishes: a tasty salad with feta cheese, dolmathes (stuffed grape leaves), and saganaki (fried cheese). Steaks, chicken items, fresh seafood, and a hamburger are also on the menu, and kids' portions are available. A rich English trifle is among the desserts.

Expect to wait for a table if you arrive on a weekend night without a reservation. If your kids are old enough to handle the delay, you can spend the time exploring the rambling house, which has Victorian decor. *4005 Burton Dr., Cambria; (805) 927-4716;* www.bramblesdin nerhouse.com

Robin's
★★★/$$

Inside another converted house, Robin's has a kitchen that uses homegrown herbs in its delicious international ethnic and vegetarian dishes.

Though at first this might not seem like a place for children, the staff is very welcoming and the kids' menu offers a burger and a simple pasta dish. More adventuresome children can order from the regular menu. The salmon bisque is particularly good, and curries are prepared to order. Menu selections include salads, sandwiches and pastas, as well as

seafood and tofu dishes and house-made desserts. Seating is available on the heated patio. *4095 Burton Dr., Cambria; (805) 927-5007;* www.robins restaurant.com

Sebastian's General Store/Patio Cafe
★★★/$

Your hungry clan can chow down on short-order items in the outdoor café, where in winter you can sometimes spot monarch butterflies congregating in the adjacent eucalyptus and cypress trees. Located here since the late 1800s, the general store is a State Historical Landmark. Stocked with a wide assortment of stuff—including beach toys and an assortment of candy—it's a great place to browse. *422 San Simeon Rd., San Simeon; (805) 927-4217.*

SOUVENIR HUNTING

The Soldier Factory

An ideal souvenir stop, this shop offers everything from an inexpensive unpainted pewter animal to a dearly priced and elaborately painted Alice in Wonderland chess set. Assorted sizes and styles of pewter soldiers from various wars and nations are also for sale.

It's just possible that you will want to spend far more time here than your kids will. *789 Main St., Cambria; (805) 927-3804;* www. soldiergallery.com

SANTA CRUZ: A DAY AT THE BEACH

WHEN YOU AND YOUR family have had it up to here with the chilly San Francisco weather, set sail for Santa Cruz, where the sun shines 300 days each year (or so they say). A very Southern California–style, quintessential beach town, Santa Cruz is 80 miles south of San Francisco. If you leave really early, it can make a nice day trip; it's even nicer if you can spend the night. Or make it a stopover spot on your way to Monterey (Santa Cruz is 43 miles north). You'll know you're close when you see the police officers in shorts. Don't forget yours.

With the weather so reliably clear and sunny, Santa Cruz's main attractions are the beach and boardwalk. A half-mile-long concrete walkway parallels a clean, gorgeous stretch of fine sand and gentle surf. You'll find rest rooms and changing rooms on the boardwalk, and showers on the beach near the boardwalk bleachers. Lifeguards are on the beach all summer and some weekends in the spring and fall.

Built in 1907, this is the only beach boardwalk left on the West Coast; it's the home of the oldest amusement park in California *(400 Beach St.; 831/423-5590)*. Happily, neither has degenerated over the years. For kids, the combination of arcade games, fast-food stands (don't miss the salt-water taffy and caramel apples at Marini's), souvenir shops, indoor miniature golf, and amusement park rides (34 in all, including 11 kiddie rides) is hard to beat. Admission to the boardwalk is free. You just pay for individual rides, or you can purchase an all-day ticket. Thrill rides include the Giant Dipper, a rickety wooden roller coaster built in 1924 and rated by *The New York Times* as one of the ten best in the country, and Logger's Revenge, a refreshing water flume ride. A long-time family favorite is the Cave Train, recently refurbished but still featuring most of its original cast of cave characters. The old-fashioned merry-go-round, built in New Jersey by Charles Looff in 1911, is the largest of the four remaining classic carousels in Northern California. It features 70 hand-carved horses with authentic horsehair tails; two chariots; a rare, original 1894 band organ; and a ring toss—one of the few left in the world. There's also an old-fashioned Haunted Castle ride that most (but not all) kids enjoy—you'll know whether yours are up to it. Free band concerts are held on Friday nights in summer.

If there are surfers or boogie boarders in your group, head for the **Santa Cruz Surfing Museum** *(West Cliff Dr. at Lighthouse Point; 831/420-6289)*. The unique, one-room museum is housed in the small brick Mark Abbott Lighthouse. Hours are very limited, and exhibits are few—mostly surfboards and wet suits, but remember, it's free! A scenic three-mile bike and pedestrian pathway begins here. From nearby Steamer Lane, you'll be able to see surfers in action as well at Seal Rock, home to a herd of sea lions.

For a lesson in California history, visit **Mission Santa Cruz** *(126 High St.; 831/426-5686)*, a replica of a mission built here in 1794. A block away, in **Santa Cruz Mission State Historic Park** *(144 School St.; 831/425-5849)*, is the only remaining building from the original mission complex.

If you decide to spend more time in Santa Cruz, these are a few of our favorite sleeping and eating spots.

KOA Kampground
★★★★/$

This particularly posh campground has a heated pool, several hot tubs, two kiddie pools, and a water-fun playground. For more information, see "KOA Kamping in Kalifornia" on page 306. *1186 San Andreas Rd., near Manresa Beach, 13 miles south of Santa Cruz; (800) KOA-7701; (831) 722-0551;* www.koa.com

Seascape Resort
★★★★/$$$$

All of the 285 rooms at this cliff-top resort have two features much-loved by Moms and Dads—kitchens (fewer restaurant hassles!) and fireplaces (for those rare romantic moments). Many also offer expansive ocean views. There are plenty of places to play here—facilities include three pools, a hot tub, and a sauna, plus access to an adjacent 18-hole golf course and sports club with 12 tennis courts and a fully equipped fitness center.

Kids get a playground and, in summer, the inexpensive Seascape Kids Club for ages 5 through 10. But you and your kids will be most impressed being picked up by a bellman at your room in a golf cart who will whisk you to the beach, where he will build a fire and leave you with graham crackers, marshmallows, and chocolate bars—the makings for yummy, s'mores. *One Seascape Resort Dr., Rio Del Mar, about five miles south of Santa Cruz; (800) 929-7727; (831) 688-6800;* www.seascaperesort.com

Crow's Nest ★★★★/$$$

Fresh local seafood and steaks at reasonable prices, a kid-friendly attitude, and great ocean views make this a good choice for families. The children's color-in menu includes London broil as well as the usual suspects, and kids get to select a prize from the treasure chest. In good weather you can sit outdoors, protected by a glass shield, and watch yachts come and go from the Santa Cruz Yacht Harbor. *2218 E. Cliff Dr., Santa Cruz; (831) 476-4560.*

Summer activities at The Alisal Guest Ranch include the classic campfire marshmallow roast.

Solvang

Give your kids a glimpse of Denmark—without paying the transatlantic airfare. Founded in 1911 by Midwestern Danes, this replica Danish town, just 35 miles north of Santa Barbara, seems right out of a Hans Christian Andersen tale. Some people have described it as "more like Denmark than Denmark." Its downtown features authentic Danish architecture, complete with thatch-roofed buildings, hand-carved storks nesting by the chimneys, and windmills, all of which will be charming novelties to your children.

Many people come to Solvang just to go shopping, with hundreds of specialty shops offering a wide variety of gifts. Many of the boutiques operate inside buildings that are themselves interesting, with beams and other architectural details. Older children may enjoy checking out the buildings and purchasing souvenirs or holiday gifts in the shops. If your kids are very small or simply hate to shop, parents can take turns: one can browse in the stores while the other plays with the kids in Solvang Park.

Many local restaurants and outdoor cafés offer Danish menus, and

THE FamilyFun LIST

MUST-SEE · MUST-SEE

Hans Christian Andersen Museum (page 182)

Quicksilver Ranch (page 183)

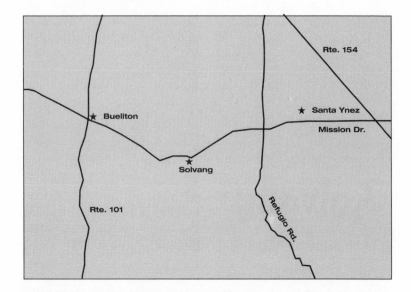

five thriving bakeries turn out excellent breads, cookies, and dessert pastries. You're never very far from a sweet and a cuppa here. Part of the fun is walking around and selecting an appealing spot to dine.

Benches are everywhere in this clean little town, making a visit especially easy on young children and/or grandparents. Pile the whole family onto a surrey-covered bike to tour the town, or ride the Honen—a replica 1800s Danish streetcar pulled by two blond Belgian draft horses. Don't miss touring Solvang again at night, when it is lighted up like a fairyland. The town stages a festive kid-oriented Danish Days celebration each September, when Solvang Park is filled with booths offering face-painting and other activities and games. There is even a tented area

where kids can play with Legos while the grown-ups rest and cool off.

Solvang is an especially satisfying destination around Christmas, when seasonal trimmings add to the festive air. Kids who are counting the days until Santa comes will be delighted by all the lights and decorations.

Cultural Adventures

Hans Christian Andersen Museum
★★★/Free

Located above The Book Loft—a wonderfully browsable bookshop with a superb children's section—this tiny museum holds the largest collection of Hans Christian Andersen books outside of Denmark. You'll see a ⅝-scale Gutenberg press built by a local craftsman as well as some journals and artwork by the well-known author. Don't leave the store without purchasing a souvenir book for the night's bedtime story, perhaps *The Ugly Duckling, The Little Mermaid,* or *The Princess and the Pea. 1680 Mission Dr., Solvang; (805) 688-2052; www.bookloftsolvang.com*

La Purisima Mission State Historic Park
★★★★/$

Located on 1,000 acres, this is the best preserved of the 21 California missions. It is completely restored, including its original aqueduct. The modern world will disappear as your family explores the expansive complex or hikes some of the 25 miles of trails. Swallows flock to the mission from March through October—you'll see more here than at San Juan Capistrano. *2295 Purisima Rd., near Lompoc; approximately 20 miles west of Solvang via Hwy. 246; (805) 733-3713.*

Old Mission Santa Inés
★★★/$

The 19th in the chain of 21 California missions is scenically located on the outskirts of town. Founded in 1804, it is fully restored and features hand-painted murals and lovely gardens. Recorded tours are

available. *1760 Mission Dr., three miles east of Solvang via Hwy. 246; (805) 688-4815; www.missionsantaines.org*

JUST FOR FUN

Nojoqui Falls Park
★★/Free

Let the kids run off some steam in this 60-acre park. The 168-foot Nojoqui (pronounced Na-hoo-ee) waterfall is at the end of a quarter-mile trail. There are picnic facilities, a ball field, and a playground. *On Alisal Rd., 6.5 miles south of Solvang; (805) 688-4217; www.caohwy.com/n/nojoqfcp.htm*

Quicksilver Ranch
MUST-SEE **FamilyFun** **MUST-SEE** ★★★/Free

You're welcome to visit the miniature horses (described in the ranch brochure as "bigger than a bread box but smaller than a Great Dane") at this expansive ranch. The kids will enjoy watching the small horsies get cleaned and clipped, but

---

FamilyFun TIP

A Tougher Tic-tac-toe

Make the classic game of tic-tac-toe a little more lively and a bit tougher with this one basic change: with each turn, *each* player can fill in the empty space of his choice with either an X or an O.

(due to liability restraints) no pet-
ing or riding is permitted. Many
people purchase these charming animals as pets, but you may want to
discourage the kids from putting
one on their Christmas list. Prices
start at $1,500 and go up to around
$7,500! *1555 Alamo Pintado Rd.,
about five miles from Solvang; (805)
686-4002;* http://ariel.syu.com/
qsminis/

Solvang Park ★★/Free
The large swath of grass surround-
ing a bronze bust of Hans Christian
Andersen is a nice place to relax.
Mission Dr. at First St., Solvang.

BUNKING DOWN

All but the first of these lodging
places are within easy walking distance of the village center.

The Alisal Guest Ranch
★★★★/$$$$
Life can be sweet on this classy,
woodsy 10,000-acre working cattle
ranch/resort that has been accommodating families for more than 50
years. A Western retreat with world-
class amenities, it boasts a heated
pool and hot tub, seven tennis
courts, two 18-hole golf courses, a
playground, a game room, a petting
zoo, a 100-acre spring-fed lake, and
a full equestrian center. In the summer, kids and teens (ages 3 through
19) can participate in supervised

activities. If that isn't enough to keep
everyone happy, you and your kids
can sail, fish, canoe, or kayak on the
lake, or tag along on a guided nature
hike. Children must be at least 7 to
ride the horses, but younger kids
can take cart rides pulled by miniature steeds. All guest rooms have
fireplaces, but no distracting telephones or TV sets. Breakfast and
dinner are included in the rate. *1054
Alisal Rd., Solvang; (800) 4-ALISAL;
(805) 688-6411;* www.alisal.com

Best Western
King Frederik Motel
★★/$-$$
This well-priced, modern, 45-room
motel has a very attractive pool and
hot tub area, earning it points with
kids and grown-ups alike. Children
under 12 stay free in their parents'
room, and continental breakfast is
complimentary. *1617 Copenhagen
Dr., Solvang; (800) 549-9955; (805)
688-5515;* www.bestwestern.com

Chimney Sweep Inn at
Tivoli Square ★★/$$-$$$
The quiet grounds here are beautifully landscaped with winding paths,
flower beds, and kid-pleasing fish
ponds, and the amenities include a
secluded Mom-and-Dad-pleasing
hot tub. Some of the 56 rooms have
fireplaces; others have kitchens. In
addition to motel units, several half-
timbered cottages are available and
are great for families. Equipped with
a sofa bed, they sleep four people

(one has two couches and sleeps six). Continental breakfast is included in the rate. *1564 Copenhagen Dr., Solvang; (800) 824-6444; (805) 688-2111;* www.chimneysweep.com

Inns of California
★★★/$-$$$

The indoor heated pool (the only one in town) and enclosed sunroom make this an especially inviting lodging place in winter. The 75-room contemporary motel has another feature that delights young guests: a game room complete with video games and a pool table. Continental breakfast is complimentary. *1450 Mission Dr., Solvang; (800) 457-5373; (805) 688-3210;* www.innsofcal.com

Royal Copenhagen Inn
★★★/$$

Resembling an Old World Danish village, with 48 rooms inside reproductions of actual Danish buildings, this charming motel will tickle the fancy of the whole family. There's an outdoor pool, and the complimentary continental breakfast is served at a nearby bakery. *1579 Mission Dr., Solvang; (800) 624-6604; (805) 688-5561;* www.royalcopenhageninn.com

Solvang Inn & Cottages
★★★/$-$$$

Located at the entrance to town, this half-timbered, 33-unit lodging spot offers a variety of accommodations. In addition to traditional motel rooms there are family units with a

shared entry but separate bedrooms and bathrooms, and cozy, self-contained cottages that sleep four (with sofa beds) and are equipped with kitchenettes. Have the kids look for the carved stork on each cottage's chimney. Facilities include a pool and hot tub, and the complimentary continental breakfast is served at the motel's own bakery across the street. *1518 Mission Dr., Solvang; (800) 848-8484; (805) 688-4702;* www.solvanginn.com

Solvang Royal Scandinavian Inn
★★/$$-$$$

Featuring Danish decor and a pool and hot tub area with a view of the surrounding hills, this property on the edge of town is a quiet, comfortable choice. The 133 guest rooms are spacious and attractive; some open onto the pool, others have private balconies. Children under 18 stay free. *400 Alisal Rd., Solvang; (800) 624-5572; (805) 688-8000;* www.royalscandinavianinn.com

Svendsgaard's Danish Lodge
★★/$-$$

This attractive, colorful, 48-room motel has a secluded outdoor pool area with a hot tub. Guest rooms are big (a plus for families) and some have fireplaces or kitchens (another plus). Continental breakfast is included in the rate. *1711 Mission Dr., Solvang; (800) 733-8757; (805) 688-3277.*

GOOD EATS

Andersen's Pea Soup Restaurant ★★★★/$

A reproduction of a Swiss chalet, this famous restaurant has been serving thick pea soup since 1924. But don't worry if your tots won't eat anything green. Young diners are given their own menu of standard favorites, along with a pea-green crayon to color it with. In addition to soup, the regular menu offers homemade breads, thick creamy milk shakes, and more substantial fare. The gift shop sells the famous house soup by the can or case, fresh from the pea soup factory in

Stockton. Outside, kids can ride coin-operated mechanical horses and cars. *376 Avenue of Flags, Buellton, three miles west of Solvang; (805) 688-5581;* www.andersens.com

Ingeborg's Danish Chocolate
★★★★/$

Let the kids pick out a sweet treat (most of the delicious chocolates and candies are made right on the premises) or opt for something from the soda fountain on the other side of the shop. If they've been really good and it's not too close to mealtime, maybe they can have *both! 1679 Copenhagen Dr., Solvang; (800) 621-1679; (805) 688-5612;* www.ingeborgs.com

Little Mermaid
★★★/$-$$

Your kids will love eating in this cute little cottage with its charmingly decorated interior and menu featuring Danish foods. Breakfast specialties include *aebleskiver,* which are sort of a Danish version of a doughnut; omelettes and scrambles and other popular morning items are also avail-

A Little Off the Top

Open-faced sandwiches are very popular in Denmark and in Solvang, so help your kids to make some themselves. Danish open-faced sandwiches are usually made with dark-rye bread, butter, and a wide variety of fillings on the sandwiches. Everything from meatloaf with cucumber salad to fried eggs and cold sausages is popular. Your children might be more comfortable with peanut butter and jelly, so use whatever ingredients you want. Just make sure not to spoil your open-faced sandwich by putting a piece of bread on top!

able. Lunch brings on open-faced sandwiches on pumpernickel bread, with a bland grilled cheese option for fussy kids. Dinner is meat and potatoes, as well as *hvidkaalsrouletter* (cabbage roll) and *kylling* (fried chicken). A peanut-butter-and-jelly sandwich is among the choices on the children's menu. *1546 Mission Dr., Solvang; (805) 688-6141.*

Paula's Pancake House
★★★★/$

If your kids get you up with the chickens, head on over to this eatery, which opens daily at 6 A.M. Windows, decorated cheerily with lace curtains, let you view the action on the town's main street. Standouts on the extensive and inexpensive menu include fresh-squeezed o.j., country sausage, whole-wheat and honey pancakes, and waffles. But the best item just might be the famous Danish pancake, a crepelike beauty that is so big it is served hanging over the plate, topped with fresh local strawberries and whipped cream. Kids are given crayons and crackers while they wait—and a number of tempting options. Should they order silver-dollar pancakes or the fabulous plate-size Mickey Mouse pancake with grape eyes, a strawberry nose, and a whipped-cream mouth? Breakfast is available

all day, and lunch items are added at 11 A.M. *1531 Mission Dr., Solvang; (805) 688-2867.*

Solvang Restaurant
★★★★/$

Home to Arne's famous *aebleskiver* (Danish pancake balls) and fresh-squeezed lemonade, this restaurant gives your family a choice. You can purchase some Danish fast food through a sidewalk window, or you eat inside, where the menu is extensive and seating is in charming Old Country-style wooden booths. Local specialties and coffee shop-style sandwiches and soups are on the menu, as are lots of pastries. The children's menu offers up the old reliables: hot dogs, hamburgers, and peanut-butter-and-jelly sandwiches. *1672 Copenhagen Dr., Solvang; (805) 688-4645.*

SOUVENIR HUNTING

The Storybook
This delightful shop has a selection of really cute stuffed animals, plus an unusual collection of toys. Little girls and their moms may find themselves longing for one of the boxed-china tea sets. *451 Second St., Solvang; (805) 688-5307; www.thestorybook.com*

See how many of the 100 varieties of palm trees
you can spot while paddling the waters
off of the Santa Barbara coast.

Santa Barbara

WARM SOUTHERN California weather and a gorgeous palm-lined, south-facing beach blend together in Santa Barbara to form a family vacation dreamland. Located approximately 360 miles south of San Francisco but just 105 miles north of Los Angeles, the city is a good stopover point on a trip down the coast—just take Highway 101 all the way. It's also a good getaway spot from L.A. If you'd rather not drive, Amtrak's Coast Starlight *(800/872-7245)* arrives from both San Francisco and Los Angeles daily.

Many of Santa Barbara's hotels are just across from the beach, where visiting families spend plenty of time. You can walk along the three-mile paved oceanfront path, palm-lined in parts, or rent a surrey bike and ride. If you seek calm swimming waters, head to West Beach, where lifeguards are on duty.

But the city offers other fun family activities beyond sand and surf. To learn a little about area history, take the 36-mile scenic drive, marked by signs around the city, past well-preserved adobe buildings from the

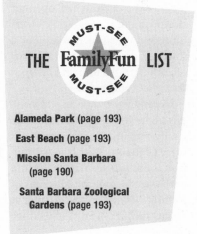

THE FamilyFun LIST

MUST-SEE
MUST-SEE

Alameda Park (page 193)

East Beach (page 193)

Mission Santa Barbara (page 190)

Santa Barbara Zoological Gardens (page 193)

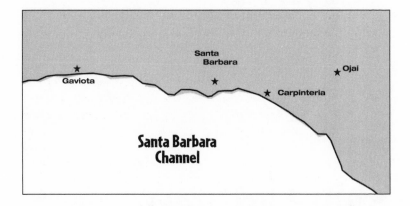

Santa
Barbara

★ Ojai

Gaviota

★

★ Carpinteria

**Santa Barbara
Channel**

Spanish and Mexican era. A 12-block downtown Red Tile Walking Tour (a map and details are included in the county visitors guide) leads you to the Santa Barbara Presidio, a partially reconstructed fort that dates from 1872, and other historic landmarks, including the beautiful Spanish-Moorish Courthouse. You'll find the lively city center along State Street between Ortega and Sola streets—it's filled with shops and inexpensive cafés. To relieve big and little tootsies alike, a free, open-air electric shuttle runs along the waterfront and downtown areas. For a small fee, the Santa Barbara Trolley offers a narrated tour and on-and-off sight-seeing privileges.

Depending on the ages and interests of the young sightseers in your family, you may want to check out some of the city's other top attractions, including Mission Santa Barbara, the zoo, the Museum of Natural History, and Sea Center at Stern's Wharf. And don't fail to spend at least some time enjoying the sun and the scenery in one of Santa Barbara's numerous lovely parks and gardens (see "Green Places" on page 194.)

The *Santa Barbara News-Press* includes a daily listing of events for children; events are also listed in the free weekly *Independent* newspaper.

CULTURAL ADVENTURES

Mission Santa Barbara
FamilyFun ★★★★/Free
In a beautiful residential section of town, this mission was established in 1786 and still functions as a parish church. You can take a self-guided tour that includes a typical bedroom and kitchen, a garden courtyard and chapel, and a cemetery with aboveground crypts. *2201 Laguna St., Santa Barbara; (805) 682-4713;* www.sbmission.org

Santa Barbara County Courthouse
★★★/Free

This Spanish-Moorish structure is considered to be one of the most beautiful municipal buildings—and jails—in the county. Your kids will be awed by the variety of colorful Moorish tiles, and the whole family is going to enjoy wandering through the porticos, arched doorways, and tropical gardens. Ride up to the observation deck of the 80-foot-tall clock tower to see how many of the city's approximately 100 different kinds of palm trees, most planted in the late 1800s, you and your kids can spot. *1100 Anacapa St., Santa Barbara; (805) 962-6464; www.sblocal.com/courthouse.htm*

Santa Barbara Museum of Art ★/$

Located downtown, this regional museum has a national reputation for its outstanding permanent collection of American, Asian, and European art. A new wing has a children's interactive gallery with special exhibits like the portrait studio, where kids can play dress-up in a mock artist's studio and then take a self-portrait. For maximum family fun, schedule your visit to coincide with the monthly themed Family Day celebration. Activities are seasonal and include storytelling and special performances. *1130 State St., Santa Barbara; (805) 963-4364; www.sbmuseart.org*

Santa Barbara Museum of Natural History
★★★/$

As far as most kids are concerned, the full-size model of a giant squid and the completely reconstructed skeleton of a 72-foot blue whale are the coolest things here. You can actually stand inside the whale's stomach! Kids also get a kick out of the colorful butterflies and the large collection of stuffed birds, nests, and eggs. But don't miss seeing the most complete skeleton of a pygmy mammoth in the world (found in the nearby Channel Islands). The Lizard Lounge, where live reptiles and amphibians are displayed, is particularly appealing to lovers of creepy-crawly things (though if the mere thought gives you chills, skip it). In the new Astronomy Center, filled with hands-on computers and educational activities, your kids can walk through a telescope and you can take their picture in front of a

Family First Fest

This festival features fun films for youngsters. It takes place on the first Saturday of each month, October through May.

Among the movies that have been shown are *Bedknobs and Broomsticks* and *Oliver!* Fiesta 5 theater, 916 State St., Santa Barbara; (805) 963-9503.

She Shows Seashells

My family loves to spend our vacations at the beach. We always collect many seashells that we think are pretty enough to frame so that we can make them part of our annual summer photo collage. Once we get home, Danielle, 9, and Tiffany and Stephanie, 7-year-old twins, pick out their favorite shells and glue them on the edge of an 8- by 10-inch frame. We cut up vacation photos and assemble the collage, then attach labels to caption the pictures. We hang the pictures proudly every year.

Lorene Hall, Starke, Florida

giant photograph of the moon. A small planetarium presents shows on weekend and Wednesday afternoon; they are recommended for kids ages 7 and older. A special *Magic Sky* show for kids ages 4 through 7 is shown on Saturday. Founded in 1916, this museum is housed in attractive adobe-style buildings in a shady canyon near the mission. It's a fun spot to get out of the sun for a while. Kids enjoy the outside areas, too, including a footbridge across a creek and a nature trail plus picnic tables. *2559 Puesta del Sol Rd., Santa Barbara; (805) 682-4711; planetarium, (805) 682-4711, ext. 405;* www. sbnature.org

JUST FOR FUN

Arlington Theater
★★★★/$

This vintage (1909) Spanish Revival movie palace now screens first-run films. Check the current listings and

cross your fingers: maybe the featured film will be rated PG or (better yet) G. Going to the movies here is a real treat—and a completely new experience for kids accustomed to the small screens and bland decor at modern multiplexes. Explore the beautiful tiled courtyard with its fountain before stopping to buy some popcorn in the lobby. Once in your seats, notice the theater walls, which are painted with a mural of a Spanish village, and the ceiling, which is studded with stars. The restored pipe organ, played before each movie, is another highlight here, as is the really big screen. Enjoy the show! *1317 State St., Santa Barbara; (805) 963-4408.*

Chase Palm Park
★★★/**Free**

This 10-acre waterfront park is dedicated to children. Along with a spectacular ocean view and plenty of space to romp, it features an antique carousel and the nautically themed

Shipwreck Park playground with a pirate ship play structure, a rubber rock, and whales that spout water, all of which your kids are sure to love. *323 E. Cabrillo Blvd., at Garden St., Santa Barbara; (805) 897-1982.*

East Beach
★★★★/Free

Thanks to its playground and volleyball nets, this well-equipped beach will quickly become your family's favorite. The Cabrillo Bath House here has beach chairs, umbrellas, and boogie boards for rent. *E. Cabrillo Blvd., east of Stearns Wharf, Santa Barbara.*

Kid's World Playground in Alameda Park
★★★★/Free

It's Kid's World that's the must-see here. A playground designed by kids, it will keep yours moving for as long as you'd like to take a rest to watch. See pages 194-195.

Los Banos del Mar ★★★★/$

This public swimming pool has a special shallow pool for your littlest offspring. It is open summer afternoons only. *401 Shoreline Dr., at W. Cabrillo Blvd., Santa Barbara; (805) 966-6110.*

Santa Barbara Zoological Gardens
★★★★/$

A visit to this nicely landscaped small zoo, on the site of a former palatial estate overlooking the Pacific Ocean, is a treat for the whole family. In addition to the standard zoo animals, most in re-created natural habitats, there's a farmyard animal petting area that's a surefire hit with the little ones. A grassy picnic area and playground designed for ages 3 through 10 are at the top of a hill, allowing adults to enjoy an excellent view of the city while the kids romp. There's a snack bar, so you can have an impromptu picnic. This picnic area is planted with a large variety of palm trees, all labeled (young horticulturalists can try to guess the names before checking the signs). A 15-minute ride on the zoo's miniature train is a must. The Andrée Clark Bird Refuge *(1400 E. Cabrillo Blvd.)*, adjacent to the zoo, has a scenic flat walking path; rare species of grackles and wood ducks can sometimes be spotted. *500 Niños Dr., Santa Barbara; (805) 962-5339; www.santabarbarazoo.org*

Stearns Wharf ★★/Free

Basically a three-block extension of State Street, this is the oldest working pier on the West Coast. It was once owned by Hollywood actor James Cagney and his brothers *(wharf info: 805/897-2683)*. Kids will have fun just walking and watching the boats sailing in and out, and a look at the Santa Barbara Channel affords them a chance to learn more about the area's marine life. *Foot of State St. at Cabrillo Blvd., Santa Barbara.*

GREEN PLACES

A CITY WITH 48 parks and 22,000 public trees, Santa Barbara is also known for its lush, exotic gardens. Pick one or two to visit with your children. Kids love the freedom a garden provides, but they can get a bit wild with all that open space. To tame yours and give yourself a few peaceful moments, why not pack along a small sketchbook for each child and hold a mini art contest? If you create enough categories, everyone can win.

Alameda Park
★★★★/Free

The city's oldest and most stately park is known for its rare and otherwise extinct trees and turn-of-the-century Victorian gazebo. But the real attraction for young visitors is Kid's World, a large, creative play-

ground designed by local children and built by volunteers. This exciting spot features turreted play structures and a shark to climb on. Kids can slide down an eel, step inside a whale's mouth, climb through a tree house, explore a haunted castle, cross a suspension bridge, and maneuver a maze. Yippee! *Micheltorena St. at Garden St., Santa Barbara.*

Ganna Walska Lotusland
★★★/$

Once a private estate, this flamboyant, eccentric, and even bizarre garden is named for the floating yellow, pink, and white lotuses that were planted in 1893 and now sprout each summer. The 37-acre exotic fantasyland holds 13 gardens of rare plants, including one of fast-growing prehistoric cycad palms that were once—listen up, kids—"dinosaur food." (On a related note, Steven *"Jurassic Park"* Spielberg has a home in the neighborhood.)

Though adults will appreciate this garden more, kids will enjoy the spacious expanses of grass and will definitely be impressed by the giant koi and the immense Amazon water lily with leaves five feet in diameter. The whole family can do some more palm-spotting, as over 75 different species grow here. You'll want to get each of your children the special Lotusland coloring book on sale in the gift shop, so they can relive their adventures and learn more about the exotic plants they saw as they color. Find out the times for the special family tours scheduled on the first and third Thursday of each month; reservations are required. *695 Ashley Rd., about five miles from town; (805) 969-9990.*

Moreton Bay Fig Tree
★★★/Free

Here's one for *Guinness Book of World Records* fans. This enormous fig was planted by a child in 1876. With branches now spreading an impressive 160 feet, it is the largest of its kind in the United States. It is said that 10,000 people could stand in its shade at noon. *Chapala St. at Montecito St., Santa Barbara.*

Santa Barbara Botanic Garden
★★★/$

Native California plants grow along the 5.5 miles of trails that meander through this 65-acre garden. Frolic with your kids in meadow, desert, arroyo (gulch) landscapes, and a redwood forest and check out a dam built by the Chumash Indians and mission padres on Mission Creek in 1807. Don't forget to bring along a picnic lunch or snack. You can take a docent-led tour and pick up a trail map and children's activity book at the gift shop. *1212 Mission Canyon Rd., Santa Barbara; (805) 682-4726; www.sbbg.org*

BUNKING DOWN
Camping

Carpinteria State Beach Park
★★★/Free-$

Camp out on what is said to be the world's safest swimming beach with few riptides and shallow areas for kids. Tide pools await exploration, and lifeguards are on duty in summer. Facilities include RV hookups, running water, picnic tables, pay showers and a visitors' center. Reservations are accepted. *Off Hwy. 101, 12 miles south of town, Carpinteria; (800) 444-7275; (805) 684-2811.*

Refugio State Beach
★★★/Free-$

You can pitch a tent right on the sand on this gorgeous beach. Facilities include RV hookups, running water, barbecue pits, trails, and a store. Reservations are accepted. *Off Hwy. 101 at Refugio Rd., 23 miles north of town, before Gaviota; (800) 444-7275; (805) 968-1033.*

Hotels

Fess Parker's Doubletree Resort
★★★/$$$

Built by the actor who made Davy Crockett famous, this sprawling 360-room resort is designed like a fortress (remember the Alamo?) and takes up several square blocks. It is quite controversial, with some people calling it atrocious and others singing its praises, but it is great for families. Rooms are spacious and some have ocean views. The many on-site facilities include two restaurants, a heated pool and hot tub, a fitness center, saunas, and three tennis courts with night lighting. *633 E. Cabrillo Blvd., Santa Barbara; (800) 879-2929; (805) 564-4333;* www.fpdtr.com

Four Seasons Biltmore
★★★★/$$$$
Built in 1927 in a fabulous oceanfront location across from Butterfly Beach, this palatial property was formerly a private estate. It offers guests a tony resort experience, hidden away from the masses—and yet it welcomes children with open arms. Kids under 18 stay free in parents' room, and facilities for family fun include two pools, tennis courts, croquet, badminton, a putting green, and several hot tubs. The Kids For All Seasons program offers activities for kids ages 5 through 12 daily in

---

FamilyFun TIP

Eco Etiquette
When snacking on the beach, make sure you throw away plastic bags and garbage, which can easily drift into the water. Eating garbage is one of the leading causes of death among aquatic animals. Turtles, sunfish, and other animals often mistake plastic bags for jellyfish.

---

summer and on weekends year-round, and the Star Fish program, also for ages 5 through 12, focuses on teaching kids to swim. An especially nice touch: all children find a welcoming cookie and glass of milk in their rooms. Room service has special kids' items, and your order arrives via a charming three-wheeled bicycle cart. The Patio, a sumptuous glass-enclosed courtyard restaurant has a special children's menu. *1260 Channel Dr., about five miles from downtown Santa Barbara; (800) 332-3442; (805) 969-2261;* www.fourseasons.com/santabarbara/

Harbor View Inn ★★/$$-$$$$
Situated across the street from Stearns Wharf, this attractive 80-room complex features a heated pool and hot tub fitness room as well as a large grassy area that's perfect for Frisbee-throwing and games of tag. Some rooms have private patios and harbor views. There's a new Four Diamond restaurant, but families might fare better at the Wharf. *28 W. Cabrillo Blvd., Santa Barbara; (800) 755-0222; (805) 963-0780.*

Hotel Oceana ★★/$-$$$$
All 42 rooms here have ocean views. Families can book a room with two queen-size beds; children stay free in parents' room. The kids will go for the heated pool; parents might head for the hot tub first. *202 W. Cabrillo Blvd., Santa Barbara; (800) 350-2326; (805) 966-9133.*

Hotel Santa Barbara
★★/$$-$$$

This well-priced, family-owned property is in a great location, right in the middle of the State Street action. A substantial old hotel with 75 rooms, it has been beautifully renovated and is a particularly good choice if you're not planning to spend all your vacation days on the beach. A filling continental breakfast is included and served in the marble entryway. **NOTE:** Although children are welcome, the atmosphere is sedate, and there is no pool or hot tub. *533 State St., Santa Barbara; (888) 259-7700; (805) 957-9300; www.hotelsantabarbara.com*

Motel 6 ★★/$

This was the very first Motel 6. Located right behind the Radisson Hotel, just one block from the beach, it offers a great location at bargain rates. The 51 rooms are basic and unembellished, but some have ocean views. And there's even a heated pool. Children 18 and under stay free in their parents' room. *443 Corona Del Mar, Santa Barbara; (800) 466-8356; (805) 564-1392; www.motel6.com*

Radisson Hotel Santa Barbara
★★★/$$$

Located just across the street from gorgeous palm-lined East Beach, considered the finest in the area, this is the perfect place for a family of beach lovers. The attractive,

Sculpt a Dune Buggy

A well-built sand castle is a joy to behold, but here's a beach craft your kids will really get into. This two-seater dune buggy has all the options: sand dollar headlights, a Frisbee steering wheel, a driftwood windshield, and a pebble license plate.

1. Get your assembly line rolling by helping your kids pile up a big mound of sand and pack it down firm. Now, start sculpting the body. Keep in mind the old artist's trick: working from the top down, carve away anything that doesn't look like a dune buggy.

2. Round out the car's hood and trunk, carve fat tires into the sides, and dig out a seat, a slanted dashboard, and a hole where the driver's and passenger's feet fit comfortably.

3. Once the basic shape is in place, your kids can add the trim: tire treads, driftwood windshield and bumpers, a shell hood ornament, a beach grass antenna, a towel seat cover, or whatever else they dream up.

4. As a last step, they can fill 'er up with shell gasoline, smooth out a highway, and hit the open road.

historic, 173-room Mission-style hotel offers large rooms—some with ocean views and some with kitchens—and convenient parking. Other pluses include a heated pool with an ocean view, an on-site restaurant that provides room service, an indoor hot tub, a sauna, and a fitness center. You can rent bikes on weekends and arrange to play golf or tennis at a nearby country club. Ask about packages. Smaller, budget-priced rooms are available at a nearby sister property, the Parkside Inn, whose guests have full use of all the main hotel's amenities. *1111 E. Cabrillo Blvd., Santa Barbara; (800) 333-3333; (805) 963-0744; www. radisson.com*

GOOD EATS

Acapulco Mexican Restaurant y Cantina
★★★★/$-$$

During mild weather you and the kids will enjoy eating at a table beside the soothing outdoor fountain. (In cooler weather, opt for the attractive interior space.) Lunchtime is especially nice here, and the midday specials include wonderfully seasoned chicken flautas (filled tortillas rolled up and fried). A kids' coloring menu comes with crayons and lists small portions of Mexican dishes as well as a hamburger and chicken strips. Complimentary, and delicious, fresh, thin tortilla chips and salsa give young diners something to munch on until the food arrives. A variety of fresh fruit margaritas are available. For a special treat, order virgin versions for the kids. *Salud! 1114 State St., Santa Barbara; (805) 963-3469; www.acapulcorestaurants.com*

Be Bop Burgers
★★★★/$

This cheap and casual spot has a lively 1950s decor. The fun starts in the parking lot, where spaces are "reserved" for famous era personalities like Elvis and Chuck Berry; see if you can park in Elvis's spot. Order your burger, sandwich, or salad from the back counter and then settle into a comfy oversized booth. Big shakes, flavored Cokes, and banana splits all help the good times roll. A jukebox awaits your selections, and a video game room beckons restless young 'uns. The grown-ups can sit and

Set Up a Souvenir Budget

The Howells of Morgan Hill, California, give their two kids a set amount of money for vacation souvenirs and let them choose how to spend it. Putting the kids in charge has eliminated those grating requests to Mom and Dad, and has also put the kids in touch with how much things cost. "They're more inclined to pinch pennies," mom Cindy says, "when it's their pennies."

munch while their offspring play. *111 State St., Santa Barbara; (805) 966-1956;* www.bebop burgers.com

California Pizza Kitchen
★★★★/$

Just about everyone likes pizza, and this place serves up just about every kind imaginable. For more details, see Good Eats in Los Angeles/ Beverly Hills. *719 Paseo Nuevo, on Chapala St., Santa Barbara; (805) 962-4648.*

Endless Summer Bar-Cafe
★★★/$$-$$$

Upbeat, efficient, and fabulously kid-friendly waiters and waitresses, plus free valet parking, make dining here easy. A good, reliable Big Kahuna burger and light beer-battered fish-and-chips await, along with a variety of fresh fish and meat dishes. Children get their own menu and crayons and will delight in feeding the birds out on the deck. For dessert they can choose vanilla, chocolate, or the day's special ice cream. Yum! After your meal you can enjoy a walk along the breakwater. **NOTE:** The Santa Barbara Maritime Museum is also found on the main floor of this building. *113 Harbor Way, Santa Barbara; (805) 564-4666;* www.endlesssummerbarecafe.net

Enterprise Fish Co.
★★★★/$$-$$$

This lively eatery has a nautical atmosphere and a menu to match. It features large portions of simply prepared fresh fish, most grilled over mesquite, and a variety of seafood salads. Fish-phobic kids can order hamburgers. *225 State St., Santa Barbara; (805) 962-3313.*

La Super-Rica ★★★/$

Step into the usually long line to order extraordinary soft tacos at this inexpensive, locally popular spot. (Don't worry—the line moves quickly, and kids can sit at a table with one parent while the other waits to order.) The tacos are served flat and topped with a variety of tasty grilled meat fillings; the tortillas are made fresh and taste like it. One taco is enough for most children, but adults will want several. You can sip your drinks while waiting for your order on the casual enclosed patio. Children like the tasty home-made *horchata* drink flavored with vanilla, rice, and cinnamon. Cash only—no credit cards. Food is served on paper plates, and customers bus their own debris—but even local resident and chef Julia Child puts up with it all because the food is so good. *622 N. Milpas St., at Ortega St., Santa Barbara; (805) 963-4940.*

Moby Dick's ★★★★/$

Perched near the end of Stearns Wharf and offering great harbor views, this casual, nautical spot with rough-hewn wooden floors and beams is a great place for breakfast, lunch, *or* dinner. The regular

menu of coffee-shop fare includes plenty of things kids like. There's also a special menu just for them, offering fish-and-chips and other popular items in smaller portions. Dining here permits you to park free on the wharf. *Stearns Wharf, Santa Barbara; (805) 965-0549.*

Sambo's ★★★★/$

This Sambo's was the first in what was once a large chain, and it is now the last. It has been owned and operated by the same family since 1957. You can sit at a counter, in comfy booths, or outside. Breakfast is served until 9 P.M., and menu specialties include huevos rancheros (a delicious beans, cheese, and eggs concoction), a tostada salad, and a California veggie sandwich. Kids get their own activity menu with yummy, budget-friendly options

such as blueberry pancakes, a corn dog, and an Oreo shake. *216 W. Cabrillo Blvd., Santa Barbara; (805) 965-3269.*

Santa Barbara Cinnamon Rolls ★★★/$

This is a hole-in-the-wall, with no phone or address, but it serves up tasty and gigantic cinnamon rolls. With coffee and milk, they make a terrific bargain-basement-priced family takeout breakfast. You can all just stroll across the street to the beach to munch and watch the free entertainment provided by cyclists and joggers. Outdoor seating is also available on the premises. *On Cabrillo Blvd. between Helena and Anacapa Sts., Santa Barbara.*

SOUVENIR HUNTING

Big Dog Sportswear

The cute company logo—a big dog with a red tongue—appears somewhere on most of the garments made by this popular local sportswear manufacturer. This is the place to pick up a colorful souvenir T-shirt or beach towel, but you and yours will also be tempted by the baby bibs, stuffed doggie slippers for humans, and toys for dogs. *136 State St., Santa Barbara; (805) 963-8728; www.bigdogs.com*

AN OJAI ESCAPE

LOCATED 30 miles south of Santa Barbara and 14 miles inland, the idyllic **Ojai Valley** has attracted visitors since the Chumash Indians discovered it 8,000 years ago. The Chumash named it *ojai* (pronounced oh-high), meaning nest, because of the way the mountains encircle the valley.

The tranquil valley offers many enticements to day-tripping families. A small village features a Spanish mission-style arcade filled with interesting shops, and a park with a colorful playground. There's also hiking, fishing, boating, golfing, horseback-riding, mountain-biking, and Jeep-touring. But it would be a shame not to stay long enough to enjoy at least one of Ojai's peaceful nights.

For a real splurge, book a room at the **Ojai Valley Inn & Spa** *(Country Club Rd.; 800/422-OJAI; 805/646-5511)*, which offers plenty of pampering for both parents and kids—for a price ($$$$). The 206 rooms are large and comfortable, and many feature small open-air patios. In the former hacienda that is the property's core, the Vista dining room offers a well-priced buffet breakfast each morning; the Oak Cafe has both outdoor terrace and indoor fireside seating and views of the scenic golf course. Special kids' menus are available at both, and children under 3 eat free. A room service children's menu features inexpensive things kids like to eat, like Mickey Mouse waffles and a Red Baron mini pepperoni pizza.

The Camp Ojai children's program has a staff of trained counselors to supervise potty-trained children ages 3 through 12. Activities include art projects, Native American stories, and pony rides.

Among the resort's recreational facilities are a tennis center with eight courts, an 18-hole golf course, two heated swimming pools and a hot tub, a spa with another pool plus a fitness center, bikes to use on the area's extensive off-road bike trails, and a stable with both scenic trails for guided horseback riding and a children's petting farm. Kids also like to visit the large cage filled with colorful birds.

To make a trip to Ojai even more interesting for children ages 4 through 11, pick up a copy of *Tessa on Her Own* by Alyssa Chase (Marsh Media). The story of a fox that learns how to live on her own in Ojai is the perfect story to read before, during, or after a trip to this scenic area. Another children's book that mentions Ojai is *The Worry Stone* by Marianna Dengler (Northland Publishing/Rising Moon). This folktale picture book should appeal to children ages 8 through 11.

Grab a boardwalk snack after riding on Santa Monica Pier's antique carousel and solar-powered Ferris wheel.

Santa Monica

THIS OCEANSIDE CITY, where the sun shines more than 300 days each year, has long been a favorite with active families. You'll all get plenty of exercise here. Located just west of Los Angeles, Santa Monica enjoys mild, humidity-free weather year-round, with temperatures usually between 53° F and 67° F in winter. That makes it a perfect place for walking, biking, skateboarding, and in-line skating. You can also swim in the ocean, play volleyball, or fly kites on the fabulous sand of the West Coast's widest beach, or take advantage of the paved South Bay Bicycle Trail that runs along the beach for 22 miles. The nearby coastal mountains, boasting waterfalls and hiking trails, are another area venue for outdoor adventures.

Though Santa Monica measures eight square miles, most of the major hotels and attractions are concentrated within a 14-block radius. In addition to the beach, the city offers family teatime in a toy museum, kid-oriented magic and puppet shows,

THE **FamilyFun** LIST

MUST-SEE
MUST-SEE

Magicopolis (page 205)

Puppet & Magic Center (page 205)

Santa Monica Pier (page 206)

Will Rogers Beach State Park (page 207)

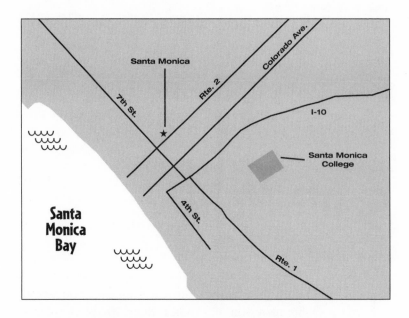

some slick airplanes to check out, and rides on an old-time carousel. And keep your eyes open for movies in the making. This city issues more than 1,000 filming permits annually, so your odds of coming across a movie shoot are good.

If you want to ditch your car, the electric Tide Shuttle runs every 15 minutes and costs only 25 cents per person. It loops south along the beach, up Main Street, and around Santa Monica Place at the south end of the Third Street Promenade shopping area, stopping at many hotels and attractions. The Big Blue Bus makes longer trips, including stops at UCLA, the L.A. airport, and the J. Paul Getty Museum in Los Angeles. For shuttle and bus information, call (310) 451-5444.

CULTURAL ADVENTURES

Angels Attic
★★/$

An eclectic collection of antique toys and dolls is displayed in this charming museum. Located on the outskirts of downtown, it's set in a Queen Anne house, one of the last two Victorians left in this city. Little girls of a certain age (7 or 8 is ideal) will go nuts, and so will many mommies. Reserve ahead if you want to take afternoon tea on the glassed-in front porch; it's served from 12:30 to 3:30 on the days the museum is open (Thursday through Sunday) and is open only to museum-goers.

A nice selection of miniatures is for sale—your daughter is sure to find something she likes for her own dollhouse. This charming spot is a nonprofit corporation that contributes to the support of the Julia Ann Singer Center for Autistic and Developmentally Handicapped Children. *516 Colorado Ave., at Fifth St., Santa Monica; (310) 394-8331.*

Magicopolis
FamilyFun ★★★/$$
Some of the best professional magicians in the world perform live on the stage of this charming small theater. Seats are steeply tiered so everyone gets a good view. Your kids will love watching the magician pull a rabbit out of a hat and meeting a stuffed goose that can read their minds. An ornate door handle from Houdini's home is displayed here; it's said that if you hold it for 10 seconds, you will experience a "magical moment" sometime during the day. (Kids are sure to find something magical about the ensuing 24 hours.) Both matinee and evening hocus-pocus performances

are scheduled on Friday, Saturday, and Sunday. They are always family-oriented and appropriate for all ages. Call for a schedule and to make reservations. *1418 Fourth St., at Broadway, Santa Monica; (310) 451-2241; http://www.magicopolis.com*

Puppet & Magic Center ★★★/$
FamilyFun
Children will be enchanted by the pretend performers and performances held here. The 40-seat theater stages a puppet show with magic and surprises, followed by a puppetry demonstration (in which some secrets are revealed) and a question-and-answer session. Arrive early to check out the center's collection of more than 500 puppets, marionettes, and ventriloquist figures. *1255 Second St., at Arizona St., Santa Monica; (310) 656-0483;* www.puppetmagic.com

JUST FOR FUN

Bright Child
★★/Free-$
This children's activity center has an innovative indoor playground with slides and an area especially for toddlers. Young athletes can shoot hoops at the pint-size basketball court, and then sink a few balls at the mini putting green. A room devoted to arts and crafts and a selection of keyboards for little musicians rounds out the fun. Socks are required throughout this shoe-free

Top Air Travel Tips

◆ Book early for good seats.

◆ Order kids' meals when you make your reservation.

◆ Stuff your carry-on for every contingency: pack medications, extra kids' clothes, diapers, baby food, and formula. And be sure the kids' toys are in their carry-ons.

◆ Bring international currency for overseas layovers.

◆ Make each child who is old enough responsible for his own luggage.

◆ Check luggage curbside.

◆ Let kids work off energy in the lounge — save sleepy moments for the plane.

◆ To quell plane fears, explain each step of the flight to first-time fliers so they understand that sudden noises and shaking do not signal an imminent crash.

◆ Locate pillows and blankets as soon as you board.

environment. A café serves snacks that appeal to kids. *1415 Fourth St., at Broadway, Santa Monica; (310) 393-4844.*

Palisades Park
★★/Free

Located north of the pier, this ribbon of grass and shade trees runs along the top of cliffs overlooking the ocean. It is the perfect jogging, biking, and walking path. Pack along your kids' in-line skates and they'll soon be one of the gang. You might even run into a movie set, as this is a particularly popular filming site. *From Colorado Ave. to San Vicente Blvd., Santa Monica.*

MUST-SEE FamilyFun MUST-SEE Santa Monica Pier
★★★★/Free-$$

Dating from 1909, this wooden wharf, now a pleasure pier, holds several restaurants and attractions. But as far as most kids are concerned, the highlight here is Pacific Park, the West Coast's only amusement park on an oceanfront pier (fees). Your kids can pick and choose from among this newly renovated park's 11 rides, including an antique carousel with two hand-carved chariots and 56 hand-carved horses, a nine-story solar-powered Ferris wheel (the largest on the West Coast), and a unique seven-story column-suspended roller coaster. There's a charge for rides, but access to the pier is free. A food court and assorted shops and boardwalk games round out the fun, and free concerts are scheduled in the summer. Just beneath the carousel is another kid pleaser: the **UCLA Ocean Discovery Center** (*310/393-6149; www.odc.ucla.edu/*). Open only on weekends, it features touch tanks filled with sea stars, sea urchins, hermit crabs, and such, and aquariums that are home to sharks, stingrays, and more than 50 kinds of sea jellies (aka jellyfish). Kids can also view specimens under microscopes, and on Saturday they might get to watch the shark having lunch. The pier is also a nice place to teach your kids to fish. You can rent poles inexpensively and do not need a license. *End of Colorado Ave. at Ocean Ave., Santa Monica; (310) 458-8900.*

Carousel rides at the Santa Monica Pier cost just a quarter for kids and fifty cents for adults.

Venice
★★★★/Free

Begun in 1904, this town was the result of one man's effort to replicate that other Venice—in Italy. At that time the town boasted 16 miles of 40-foot-wide canals, with Venetian-style bridges, and gondolas were actually used as transportation. Eventually a seaside amusement park also opened here. The gondoliers are gone now, and only six small canals and bridges remain. But Ocean Front Walk, along the edge of the beach and ocean between Venice Boulevard and Rose Avenue, is as popular a promenade today as it was back then, when it was Coney Island West. Known locally as the Venice Boardwalk, this sun-drenched area offers some of the world's best people-watching. Even preschoolers will get a kick out of the passing parade—and older kids will want to look in every direction at once. (You may have to remind them that it's not polite to stare.)

You'll see just about anything imaginable and some things unimaginable here, including bikini-clad in-line skaters and muscle-bulging bodybuilders. It is *very* California. Countless movie scenes have been filmed here—when you get home, you'll all start recognizing it in movies and on TV shows. Stalls sell things you never knew you needed, and you can stop for a snack at Big Daddy's, where everything—cheese pizza, French fries, etc.—is just $1. *Off Pacific Coast Hwy., a few miles south of Santa Monica.*

Will Rogers Beach State Park
MUST-SEE **FamilyFun** **MUST-SEE**
★★★★/Free

Everything you need for a perfect day in the sun is at this popular beach. In addition to sand and surf, it has a playground, volleyball courts, and picnic facilities. *Pacific Coast Hwy., Sunset Blvd., Santa Monica;* http://www.caohwy.com/w/wilrogsp.htm

BUNKING DOWN

Best Western Ocean View Hotel
★★/$$-$$$$

A big selling point for this place is that it's just one block from the beach. The basic—but very nice—hotel has 60 rooms, some with ocean views and private balconies. There's no pool or restaurant, but the location is great and the price is right. *1447 Ocean Ave., Santa Monica; (800) 452-4888; (310) 458-4888; www.bestwestern.com*

Comfort Inn ★★/$-$$

About 10 minutes from the beach but in a good, central location, this attractive 101-room motel is a bargain. There's a large swimming pool, and some rooms have spacious private patios. Complimentary continental breakfast is included; it's another money-saving plus. *2815 Santa Monica Blvd., near 26th St., Santa Monica; (800) 228-5150; (310) 828-5517; www.comfortinn.com*

Fairmont Miramar Hotel
★★★★/$$$$

Ideally located, this stately 302-room hotel is just across the street from Palisades Park, where kids can skate, run, and ride bikes, and is only a block from Third Street Promenade. It has been a celebrated resort for decades, and now you and your offspring can splash in the same swimming pool that has held Hollywood royalty such as Marilyn Monroe, Cary Grant, and Doris Day (tell the kids they were the Jennifer Love Hewitt, Adam Sandler, and Cameron Diaz of the olden days). This is also where former President Clinton stays when he is in town. There's a fitness center, and the beautifully landscaped grounds, with vibrant flowers, exotic trees, and tropical ferns, are a delight to stroll through. Children love watching the daily koi feeding and will be wowed by the century-old, 80-foot-high Moreton Bay fig tree that welcomes guests at the entrance. *101 Wilshire Blvd., Santa Monica; (800) 866-5577; (310) 576-7777; www.fairmont.com*

Hotel Oceana ★★★★/$$$$

Located in a residential area across the street from the ocean and just three blocks from the Third Street Promenade, this stylish, vibrantly colorful all-suite hotel, a converted condominium complex, makes a great family home away from home. The 63 units are wrapped around a center courtyard with an inviting pool. (Prediction: the kids will be splashing away minutes after you check in.) Some units in the front boast ocean views; those in the back have roomy Adirondack chairs on their doorstep that you and your kids can lounge in while watching your neighbors frolic in the pool. All the suites are spacious, painted in sun-drenched colors, and equipped with full kitchens. A particularly

handy feature: the full-size fridge is stocked with goodies for sale, including frozen pizza. Though the whole family shares one bathroom in even the most expensive units, they are marble-lined and deluxe; some have deep Jacuzzi tubs. Twenty-four-hour room service is from Wolfgang Puck's Cafe. *849 Ocean Ave., Santa Monica; (800) 777-0758; (310) 393-0486;* hoteloceana.com

Loews Santa Monica Beach Hotel ★★★★/$$$$

Children under 18 stay free in their parents' room, which is only one of a number of reasons this quietly elegant hotel is a great place for families. For starters, it is just across an alley from a clean, sandy beach with playground equipment. Most of the 349 tastefully decorated rooms offer ocean views; all are furnished with terry robes, three phones, and a bathroom TV (turn on the Disney channel and the kids will stay in the tub until their fingers wrinkle). At check-in time, young guests are welcomed with something special (like a puzzle, book, beach ball), and com-

plimentary cookies and milk are brought to kids' rooms each night. The all-day Splash Club for children 4 through 12 offers age-appropriate activities, including a lot of time at the beach and pool and at nearby attractions. It operates during the summer and holidays. An evening program sometimes operates on Friday and Saturday, and a video room on the ground floor is always open. Mom and Dad will appreciate the spa/fitness center and oversized indoor hot tub, and the whole family will want to put in some time at the large indoor/outdoor pool. The casual café has a kids' menu, and the lobby bar has live music on weekends and serves a variety of virgin drinks that make little ones feel grown-up and special. Be on the lookout for familiar faces. Borderline famous people (bit actors, character actors, directors) who can *almost* be recognized hang out seemingly everywhere—reading scripts and being interviewed by the press. *1700 Ocean Ave., Santa Monica; (800) 23-LOEWS; (310) 458-6700;* www.loewshotels.com

THE SANTA MONICA PIER has always been popular, but severe storms and heavy use nearly caused its demise. In 1959, the city council ordered the deteriorating pier to be demolished, but the city residents fought back by launching a "Save Our Pier" initiative. Today, the pier hosts three million visitors per year.

Santa Monica Hostel
★★/$

Just a block from Third Street Promenade and two blocks from the beach, this 200-bed hostel offers free airport pickup and runs regularly scheduled trips to Disneyland and Universal Studios. Nine private family rooms are available; reservations are accepted. For more information about hostels, see "Hosteling for Families" on page 215. *1436 Second St., Santa Monica; (310) 393-9913.*

Santa Monica Travelodge
★/$$-$$$

In a great location overlooking the ocean and pier, this simple 29-room motel has a pleasant pool area and offers free parking. *1525 Ocean Ave./Broadway, Santa Monica; (800) 578-7878; (310) 451-0761;* www.santamonicatravellodge.com

GOOD EATS

Border Grill
★★★★/$$

Kids love watching tortillas being made from scratch in the front window of this brightly painted, funky, loud restaurant. Located just one block from Third Street Promenade, this fun place is owned by Mary Sue Milliken and Susan Feniger, the authors of a cookbook and hosts of the TV series *Too Hot Tamales.* From among the authentic Mexican dishes here, your family can easily create a fabulous meal to share by selecting some of the smaller items from the *entradas* (appetizers) menu plus one or two entrées. (The green corn tamales, plantain empanadas, and *panuchos* are all exceptional.) Soft tacos and quesadillas, beloved by most kids, are available. There's also a children's menu with some inexpensive items, including a $1 taco. Save room for dessert; choices include Mexican chocolate cream pie, assorted flans, and Mexican sugar cookies. Yum! After your meal, take a stroll along the block, which holds the Bright Child activity center and Magicopolis (see page 205) as well as a branch of Toys 'R' Us. *1445 Fourth St., at Broadway, Santa Monica; (310) 451-1655;* www.bordergrill.com

Broadway Deli ★★★/$$

Basic deli fare is served up at this spacious spot, which consists of one huge open room. Even really big families can sit together in the oversized booths while feasting on bagels, blintzes, salads, and sandwiches. *1457 Third Street Promenade, Santa Monica; (310) 451-0616.*

Chandni Restaurant
★★/$$

With its big, comfortable booths and welcoming atmosphere, this is a good spot to introduce your offspring to the joys of Indian cuisine. The entire menu is vegetarian, and the fare is generally mild flavored. If your children are willing to try new dishes, they will probably find several that they like. For starters, kids usually appreciate the puffy *puris* (deep-fried bread) and *samosas* (little pies with potato-pea filling). The entrées are all quite good—just pick your favorite ingredients. Leave room for dessert; which might include *kheer* (a rice pudding) which is a popular choice. And for a beverage, perhaps the little lad or lassie would like a mango or mint *lassi* (a rich yogurt drink). *1909 Wilshire Blvd., Santa Monica; (310) 828-7060.*

Crocodile Cafe
★★★★/$-$$

Whether you choose one of the comfy booths inside or one of the patio tables with a view of the ocean across the highway, you'll get a good meal here. The very L.A. menu offers a variety of salads, sandwiches, pizzas, calzones, and pastas, plus oakwood-grilled meats. A kids' coloring menu has all the usual suspects—but where are those crocodiles? *101 Santa Monica Blvd., at Ocean Ave., Santa Monica; (310) 394-4783; www.crocodilecafe.com*

Earth, Wind & Flour
★★★★/$

Chow down on inexpensive fare, chosen from an eclectic menu. For additional details, see Good Eats in Westside/Los Angeles. *2222 Wilshire Blvd., at 26th St., Santa Monica; (310) 829-7829.*

El Cholo Cafe
★★★★/$-$$

Large, yet still cozy, this place is famous for its immense fruit-infused margaritas, available in both familiar and unusual flavors. How about a prickly pear, sweet corn, or green apple one? The kids and any nondrinkers can have virgin margaritas in strawberry and peach. Kids can order à la carte items or select from their own coloring menu, which includes Mexican dishes as well as hamburgers, spaghetti, and chicken nuggets. **NOTE:** There is usually a long wait for a table; you're given a beeper that goes off when one is available. In the meantime, you all can wander around the waiting room and courtyard and check out the exhibits about the restaurant's history. For additional details, see Good Eats in Downtown/Los Angeles. *1025 Wilshire Blvd., at 11th St., Santa Monica; (310) 899-1106.*

Enterprise Fish Co.
★★★★/$$-$$$

Reliable seafood is served in a family-friendly environment. For additional details, see Good Eats in Santa Barbara. *174 Kinney St., at Neilson Way, Santa Monica; (310) 392-8366.*

Fritto Misto
★★★/$-$$

This neighborhood Italian café is known for its low prices and large portions. In addition to the traditional Italian favorites, there is an extensive selection of vegetarian items such as sweet potato ravioli and gnocchi gorgonzola. Kids really like the "create your own pasta dish" option. The only negative is that sometimes there is a wait—but there isn't a waiting area. *601 Colorado Ave., at Sixth St., Santa Monica; (310) 458-2829.*

Jamba Juice
★★★/$

Branches of this happening juice bar chain seem to be everywhere, perhaps because it offers a treat that really is both delicious and nutritious. Jamba Juice serves a variety of custom-blended smoothies.

Growing preteens might opt for the stomach-stretching 24-ounce portion, perhaps spiked with some very trendy wheatgrass. Smaller portions are available for smaller appetites. There are also some soups on the menu, but juice is the main attraction here. Show health-conscious kids the nutrient analysis guide, which lists exactly what is in each drink (and provides far more information than most people really want). *304 Santa Monica Blvd., Santa Monica; (310) 656-2411. Another branch that offers particularly good stargazing is at 1426 Montana Ave., Santa Monica; (310) 656-3434.*

Louise's Trattoria
★★★★/$-$$

Great house pizza and chopped salad are served at this small branch of a local chain. For additional details, see Good Eats in West Hollywood/Los Angeles. *1008 Montana Ave., Santa Monica; (310) 394-8888. Also at 264 26th St., Santa Monica; (310) 451-5001;* www.louises.com

---

FamilyFun **READER'S TIP**

Fledgling Photographers

Last summer, I put an extra flash in our vacation. Instead of having grown-ups be the only photographers, I bought each of our five children, whose ages range from 7 to 19, a 24-exposure disposable camera and let them snap their own pictures. The kids loved it, and we were able to see our vacation through their eyes. Plus, since they were inexpensive cameras, I didn't worry about them being dropped or lost. For very little money, these simple cameras brought our family a lot of smiles.

Kathi Kanuk, Chardon, Ohio

Lula Cocina Mexicana ★★★/$$

All the usual suspects appear on the extensive, interesting menu, but many have an unusual twist: tacos stuffed with shrimp or fish, for example, and burritos made with filet mignon. The appetizer selection is exceptional, and it is possible to put together a great meal of small dishes. Order up some margaritas (virgin versions for the kids) and you've got a memorable family dinner. The dining room is colorful and comfortable, and children fit in well in the casual, jovial atmosphere. The kids' menu offers smaller and milder burritos, enchiladas, quesadillas, and tacos. *2720 Main St., Santa Monica; (310) 392-5711.*

Polly's Bakery Cafe ★★★★/$

Famous for its pies, this old-fashioned coffee shop has plenty of family-friendly booths. The inexpensive menu features a homey chicken pie and rotisserie-chicken dinner, a wide variety of sandwiches, burgers, and specialty salads, and an array of breakfast items. The kids' menu includes a corn dog, macaroni and cheese, and a chicken drumstick. Consider yourself warned: leave room for dessert! Pies include creams and meringues, fresh and baked fruit, and even some more unusual versions such as candy bar (with Snickers) and German chocolate. *501 Wilshire Blvd., at Fifth St., Santa Monica; (310) 394-9721; www.pollyspies.com*

Schatzi on Main ★★/$$-$$$$

Kids acting up? Take them to this spot owned by tough-guy Arnold Schwarzenegger and his wife. A casually elegant restaurant, it has an international menu featuring Austrian dinner specialties such as Wiener schnitzel and wild boar. But don't worry: the kids' menu offers pizza, chicken fingers, pasta, and a grilled cheese sandwich. There's Charly Temmel gourmet ice cream for dessert. Prices are reasonable, and the place is open daily for breakfast, lunch, and dinner. *3110 Main St., Santa Monica; (310) 399-4800; www.schatzi_on_main.com*

Trastevere ★★★/$-$$$

The dining room of this trattoria-pizzeria feels so Italian you might think you actually are in the Roman neighborhood it's named for. But part of the fun here is watching the street parade, so if the weather is good, seat your family outside. After ordering, stave off kiddie hunger with the complimentary basket of delicious breads and a chopped-olive spread. Lunch—you can order a sandwich or a pizzetta—is a bargain. Dinner is pricier, but the pizzas, pastas, and grilled meats are very good, and kids can share. A bowl of wonderful amaretti cookies arrives with the check. *1360 Third Street Promenade, Santa Monica; (310) 319-1985; www.trastevereristorante.com*

FamilyFun GAME

Word Stretch

Give your child a word challenge by asking her to make as many words as she can from the letters in a phrase such as "Are we there yet?" or "When will we be at the zoo?"

Wolfgang Puck Cafe
★★★/$$

More casual than some of Puck's other places, this family-friendly spot serves up the celebrity chef's famous wood-fired pizzas, plus pasta, rotisserie chicken, salads galore, and sandwiches. *1323 Montana Ave., Santa Monica; (310) 393-0290;* www.wolfgangpuck.com

Wolfgang Puck Express
★★★★/$

More casual and more family-friendly even than Wolfgang's café (above), the star chef's fast-food eatery guarantees that you'll get in and out in short order. The menu is the same, though served with less panache: pizza, pasta, roasted chicken, salads. Kids can choose cheese pizza or chicken fingers with French fries from a special menu. (For details, see Good Eats in Hollywood/Los Angeles.) Once everyone has their food, you can all sit outside on the patio and feast your eyes on the sidewalk scene. *1315 Third St., Second Level, Santa Monica; (310) 576-4770.*

SOUVENIR HUNTING

There are four areas in Santa Monica where shops and restaurants can be found. Check out Main Street, with its trendy boutiques and one-of-a-kind restaurants; Montana Avenue, with upscale specialty shops and restaurants; Santa Monica Place at Third Street and Broadway, a traditional retail mall with department stores and a family-friendly food court; and Third Street Promenade, a three-block pedestrian shopping street running from Broadway to Wilshire and featuring bookshops, alfresco cafés, and a weekly farmers' market. Third Street Promenade is the most fun for families with little ones because it's blocked off to traffic. The following shops are of particular interest to visiting kids and their parents.

Aahs!

Kids and adults alike are tickled by the kitschy items here. Things you never knew you needed are found in endless supply. In addition to fur-covered frames and funny greeting cards, the store stocks popular candies and gross gums. *3223 Wilshire Blvd., Santa Monica; (310) 829-1807;* www.aahs.com

Color Me Mine

The whole family can paint souvenirs for themselves here. Just select an unfired item and add your own artwork. (Arnold Schwarzenegger, a Santa Monica resident who frequents the store, favors flowers, hearts, and butterflies.) Kids particularly enjoy decorating figures of dinosaurs and bugs. It takes time for the pottery to be fired (baked), so you have to wait a few days before you can pick up your finished masterpiece. If you leave town while it's still only half-baked, shipping can be arranged. *1109 Montana Ave., Santa Monica; (310) 393-0069; www.colormemine.com*

Puzzle Zoo

If you have a kid who collects action figures, they're going to go nuts when they see this store's vast selection. *1413 Third Street Promenade, Santa Monica; (310) 393-9201; www.puzzlezoo.com*

HOSTELING FOR FAMILIES

Stretch your family's vacation budget with a stay at one of American Youth Hostel's affordable accommodations. In addition to the separate men's and women's dormitory-style rooms commonly associated with hostels, many now have special family rooms that you can reserve in advance. Most also have fully equipped communal kitchens where you can prepare meals, and some even add a touch of luxury with hot tubs or saunas. In the interest of keeping costs down, accommodations are simple. Guests provide bedding and linens (sleep sets can be rented inexpensively), bathrooms are shared, and all guests are expected to do a chore. (Surprisingly, kids often like this, especially when they are permitted to choose what they will do.) Lights go out at 11 P.M., and hostels are closed during the day, usually from 9:30 A.M. to 4:30 P.M.

Rates for members of the AYH organization vary from $10 to $25 per night per adult; children's rates are usually discounted—or kids stay free. Nonmembers may stay in the hostels, but must pay a surcharge of $3 to $5 per night. Note that many hostels do not accept credit cards. For further information and a brochure listing all the hostels in Northern California, call (415) 863-1444. For a free Hostelling Map of the USA, call Hostelling International at (800) 444-6111 or (202) 783-6161.

NORTHERN CALIFORNIA
Redwood National Park Hostel
(see page 153)
San Francisco Hostels (Fisherman's Wharf and Union Square)
(see pages 62 and 70)
SOUTHERN CALIFORNIA
Santa Monica Hostel (see page 210)
San Diego (downtown) Hostel
(see page 309)
San Pedro Hostel (see page 280)
HAWAII
Holo Holo In Hostel (see page 371)
Waikiki Hostel (see page 342)

At the George C. Page Museum, kids can check out skeletons of mammoths, giant sloths, and an ancient human excavated from the La Brea Tar Pits.

Los Angeles

THE SECOND-LARGEST CITY in the country, sprawling Los Angeles attracts 50 million visitors each year. They come to enjoy the good weather (the area averages 329 days of sunshine each year), to visit the area's myriad attractions, and to see some movie stars. Your family can do all of the above, plus have a blast watching surfers, swimming at picture-perfect beaches, seeing the latest movies in the best theaters, visiting thrilling theme parks, and maybe doing some shopping. (L.A. has the largest concentration of retail stores per resident in the nation.) Los Angeles is a great destination for a family vacation, and kids are welcome almost everywhere. For information on current kid-oriented special events, check out the "kid stuff" guide in the current issue of *Los Angeles* magazine.

This sprawling city is broken into large subareas, and some communities that are generally thought of as part of Los Angeles are, in fact,

THE **FamilyFun** LIST

Carole & Barry Kaye Museum of Miniatures (page 230)

Grauman's Chinese Theatre (page 235)

La Brea Tar Pits and George C. Page Museum/Hancock Park (page 233)

Universal Studios Hollywood (page 236)

separate municipalities. This chapter covers a mix of such neighborhoods and towns: downtown Los Angeles; Beverly Hills and Century City; Hollywood; West Los Angeles; and the West side, which comprises Westwood, Brentwood, and Bel Air. Other chapters are devoted to Santa Monica and to the beach towns to its north and south.

There is a downtown Los Angeles, but it is located far to the east of the city's center; for that reason, Melrose Avenue feels more like the heart of L.A. As you bop around town from place to place, you'll frequently travel along Wilshire and Sunset boulevards, both of which are interesting to drive end to end.

Keep in mind, as you plan your itinerary, that the southland (as it's called) is so spread out that travel-ing from one area to another can be daunting, and in general L.A. drivers are more combative than most. They honk if you don't start up immediately, run in tight packs, and refuse to let cars merge—a gen-eral road rudeness that is chilling. To keep car travel at a minimum, con-sider clustering your activities in a particular neighborhood so that you can walk to at least some of your des-tinations. Because distances are so great here and the freeways are often congested (and sometimes actually stopped), be prepared with car activ-ities and tapes and CDs for the kids.

When you do drive, you'll find valet parking everywhere in L.A.—at hospitals, grocery stores, movie the-aters, and even coffee shops. Everyone offers this service in this car-glutted city, even when it's not really needed.

At posh restaurants, valets charge you to park your car in adjacent lots! After a while you get used to it, and you might as well do as the natives do. It's fun, and kids really do seem to enjoy the fuss. (Just remember to tip the valet a buck or two, or your memories might not be so pleasant.)

You also might want to make use of the Metro Red Line, this city's newish subway system. Each station is decorated with the works of a different artist, making them interesting as well as functional. Stops include Hollywood and Vine (across the street from the Pantages Theater, where family-oriented musicals are often staged), Hollywood/Highland (near Grauman's Chinese Theatre), and Universal City Studios.

You won't starve in this town, but you will have to search out really good restaurant food. Like many things here, the surface often looks good but you're sometimes disappointed by what is found just beneath. Still, there's no shortage of choices. In this most ethnically diverse city in America (people from 140 countries live here), you'll find a dizzying selection of ethnic restaurants. That's good news for families, as these spots are usually inexpensive and very welcoming of children.

So put on your sunglasses, slather on the sunscreen, and get ready for some fabulous family fun in this famously city of Angels.

Downtown

Though this is Los Angeles's historic core, business and financial district, and the largest government center outside Washington, D.C., it is also so far away from the city's big-draw attractions that many people, including local residents, never get here. That is unfortunate, as there is plenty to see and do. Children tend to like tall buildings, and downtown is home to the tallest office tower west of the Mississippi (the 73-story First Interstate World Center). The world's shortest incline railway, another kid pleaser, is here, too. Your family can visit a museum designed especially for children, walk the streets where L.A. started, and shop for bargains until you drop.

CULTURAL ADVENTURES

El Pueblo de Los Angeles State Monument
★★★★/Free
This is where the city of Los Angeles originated. Located across the street from Union Station, it is home to the Avila Adobe, the oldest house in

L.A.; Firehouse No. 1, the city's first firehouse, now a museum displaying fire-fighting equipment; Old Plaza Church, the oldest Catholic church in Los Angeles; and the elegant Italianate Pico House hotel. The kids will particularly enjoy festive, pedestrian-only Olvera Street, which is lined with inexpensive taco stands and colorful shops selling Mexican imports such as paper flowers and huge sombreros. There are also bakeries and candy stalls, and kids will gobble down the *alfajor* (a coconut bar), the *jamoncillo* (like vanilla fudge), *viznaga* (cactus candy), and yummy *churros* (long, thin, and delicious Mexican-style doughnuts). You can take free guided walking and bus tours. *Visitors' center: 622 N. Main St., Los Angeles; (213) 628-1274;* www.cityofla.org/elp/

Exposition Park
★★★/Free

About five minutes south of the Convention Center and across the street from the University of Southern California campus, this expansive park holds the Romanesque Coliseum that was host to the Olympics in 1932 and 1984, and the Los Angeles Sports Arena. You can also stroll through a large sunken Rose Garden with more than 200 varieties of roses and visit the California African-American Museum, the California Science Center, and the Natural History Museum of Los Angeles County

(see below). Bordered by Exposition Blvd., Figueroa Blvd., South Park Dr., and Menlo Ave., Los Angeles; http://www.usc.edu/dept/CCR/theme/expo.html

California African-American Museum ★★/Free

This small museum has rotating exhibits of photographs, artifacts, and videos that focus on African-American contributions to world history and culture in both ancient and modern times. *600 State Dr., Los Angeles; (213) 744-7432;* www.caam.ca.gov

The California Science Center
★★★★/By donation

A surefire hit with the grade-school set, this exciting discovery museum is filled with interactive exhibits. It is the second-largest science/technology museum in the United States (the Smithsonian Institution in Washington, D.C., is the largest). Your son might find himself pedaling a bicycle across a 43-foot-high wire to demonstrate the principle of gravity and counterweights, while your daughter gets strapped into a space simulator to sample zero gravity. The innovative science center also has a fascinating Air & Space Gallery and an IMAX theater that shows both regular and 3-D movies. Before you leave, visit the World of Life Exhibition Hall to make sure you're still breathing and that your heart is still pumping, and stop in to Creative World, which examines the environment and communications technologies. Mom and Dad might learn a thing or two, too. *700 State St., Los Angeles; (323) 724-3623; www.casciencectr.org*

Natural History Museum of Los Angeles County
★★★★/$

Here's something your sixth grader can relate to: the first science fair west of the Mississippi was held here in 1952. Housed in a lovely Spanish Renaissance building dating from 1913, this is the third-largest natural science and cultural history museum in the country. Your whole family will enjoy the outstanding exhibits, including the spectacular Schreiber Hall of Birds, with 27 learning stations and three walk-through habitats; an Insect Zoo that's home to red-kneed tarantulas, hissing cockroaches, and other creepy crawlers (cool!); and a two-story replica of a Pueblo cliff dwelling showcasing Native American baskets and beadwork. Kids also like the gallery of dinosaur fossils and the impressive gemstone display, and they can dig for fossils and touch live animals in the hands-on Discovery Center. Special programs and classes especially for children are scheduled regularly. *900 Exposition Blvd., Los Angeles; (213) 763-DINO; www.nhm.org*

JUST FOR FUN

Fashion District of Los Angeles ★/Free

The largest concentration of clothing-related businesses outside of Manhattan, this district comprises 56 blocks of stores and outlets. The bargains are tremendous and include kids' clothes and toys. However, most shops are open only Monday through Friday, and many don't sell to the general public, so do your homework. The Cooper Building *(860 S. Los Angeles St.)* holds 50 shops and is a good bet for one-stop shopping. On weekends, festive, bazaarlike Santee Alley, running between Santee Street and Maple Avenue from Olympic to Pico, is full of bargains, including kids' clothes and backpacks. Call for a free map, or drop by the promotions office *(110 E. Ninth St., Suite C625)* and pick one up. Or call for the schedule of the guided

FamilyFun GAME

Thumb Wrestling

When you crave an active car game, pack up the books and puzzles and thumb wrestle. Two players sitting next to each other hook the four fingers of their right hands together so both of their right thumbs are sticking straight up. The object is to pin down your opponent's right thumb using your right thumb.

one-hour Trolley Tour *(213/488-1153)* of the fashion district and reserve your free seats. *The Fashion District is bounded by San Pedro Street, Spring and Main Streets, Fifth Street, and the Santa Monica Freeway. Los Angeles;* www.fashiondistrict.org

BUNKING DOWN

The New Otani Hotel & Garden
★★★/$$-$$$$

This deluxe, 434-room hotel is within an easy walk of the Little Tokyo shopping area. Kids will enjoy (and maybe even be soothed by) the half-acre rooftop Japanese garden modeled after a 400-year-old garden at a sister hotel in Tokyo. Featuring tranquil pathways, ponds, and waterfalls, it is an oasis of serenity amidst the bustling city. Both Japanese-style and Western-style rooms are available. Opting for the

former gives you the opportunity to introduce the whole family to an additional bit of Japanese culture. All rooms have coffeemakers and some are equipped with VCRs. A spa, fitness center (but no pool), and three restaurants, including the traditional Japanese-style A Thousand Cranes with its unusual tempura bar, are on the premises. Child care can be arranged. Local experts demonstrate such arts as *ikebana* (flower-arranging), kimono-wearing, and calligraphy. Call for a schedule. *120 S. Los Angeles St., Los Angeles; (800) 629-1200; (800) 639-6826;* www.newotani.com

GOOD EATS

Clifton's Brookdale Cafeteria
★★★★/$

With its interior waterfall and faux forest, the largest public cafeteria in the world doesn't look much like your kids' school lunchroom. But all the old-fashioned cafeteria selections are available, including kids' favorites like Jell-O and pudding. Prices are bargain-basement cheap, and include daily specials such as cube steak with mashed potatoes, spaghetti, and baked halibut. Open every day from 6:30 A.M. to 7 P.M., this place has been serving shoppers since it opened in 1935. They just don't make them like this anymore. *648 S. Broadway, Los Angeles; (213) 627-1673.*

Sign Language

The "HOLLYWOOD" sign in the Hollywood Hills stands 50 feet tall, stretches 450 feet across, and weighs 450,000 pounds. It was originally constructed in 1923 to promote a real estate development; at that time, the sign read "HOLLYWOODLAND." It was only meant to last for a year and a half, but the sign endures. The "LAND" portion was removed in 1949, leaving us with the familiar image we know today.

El Cholo ★★★★/$-$$

Opened across the street from its present site in 1927, this popular spot is said to be L.A.'s oldest Mexican restaurant. Set inside a converted bungalow house decorated like a Spanish hacienda, it also has a family-friendly patio area. On Mondays, mariachis serenade diners—kids will enjoy the show. Famous for its margaritas, nachos, guacamole, and green-corn tamales, the eatery also prepares crab taquitos, a selection of fajitas (including the house specialty shrimp version), and the typical combination plates. Kids' portions and specialty drinks are available. Reservations are advised. Also see Good Eats in Santa Monica. *1121 S. Western Ave., at Pico, Los Angeles; (323) 734-2773;* www.elcholo.com

Grand Central Market ★★★★/$

Just across the street from the base of Angel's Flight, this enclosed marketplace has been operating here since 1917. It features vegetable stands as well as an array of stalls dispensing prepared international foods. Among them you'll find some of the best and cheapest Mexican food in town, plus some tasty shakes that are also good for you (don't tell the kids). Each member of the family can pick what he or she wants, and then you can all sit down at one of the tables to eat together. Mariachi music often adds to the festive air. Two entrances: *317 S. Broadway, and Hill St. at Fourth St., Los Angeles; (213) 624-2378.*

The Original Pantry ★★★/$

Eating here is like walking into a time warp. Open 24 hours a day *every* day, this old-time dining spot, now a landmark, still has its original fixtures. Because the word has been out for quite some time (the restaurant opened in the 1930s), you'll probably have to wait in line if you arrive before 2:30 or after 5, as no reservations are taken. But it is worth the inconvenience to chow down on big helpings of bargain-priced, good old American food served at breakfast, lunch, and dinner. Lots of stars have eaten here, and the restaurant is currently owned by former L.A. mayor Richard

Riordan. Next door, the Pantry Bake & Sandwich Shoppe serves up almost the same menu but is open fewer hours. *877 S. Figueroa St., at Ninth St., Los Angeles; (213) 972-9279. Sandwich shop: 875 S. Figueroa St., Los Angeles; (213) 627-6879.*

Philippe the Original
★★★/$

Kids will love the candy counter and sawdust on the floor of this budget self-service cafeteria, which dates back to 1908. The restaurant is famous for inventing French-dip sandwiches and for its 10-cent cup of coffee. Across from Union Station, between Olvera Street and Chinatown, it has communal tables and a lively atmosphere. It's open daily for breakfast, lunch, and dinner. *1001 N. Alameda St., Los Angeles; (213) 628-3781;* http://www.philippes.com/

TOT ★★★/$$

Located in Little Tokyo, this simple contemporary spot displays modern art on its walls. Families might appreciate being tucked away in one of the cozy wooden booths, but in general the atmosphere is welcoming of young guests. Kids can order French fries or a bowl of plain noodles, but more adventuresome diners can explore the extensive, inexpensive menu, which includes a wide variety of noodle and curry bowls, plus salads and cutlets and several types of tempura. *345 E. Second St., Los Angeles; (213) 680-0344.*

Beverly Hills and Century City

Though Beverly Hills doesn't leap to mind when you're considering family-friendly vacation destinations, it is a place that excites interest in all ages. Its glitz and glamour, famous faces, grand mansions, long cars, and tall palm trees intrigue just about everyone. Even the very youngest travelers are capable of enjoying the scene from their strollers. (Have the kids look for the city's exclusive platinum fire hydrants that indicate you really are *here*.) You'll want to at least window-shop along luxurious Rodeo Drive, lined with boutiques and restaurants between Wilshire and Santa Monica boulevards, and perhaps mail a letter at the post office, where you can have your car valet-parked if you'll be a while. A ride on the inexpensive open-air Beverly Hills Trolley *(310/285-2438)* is a fun way for families to get the lay of the land. Catch it at the corner of

Rodeo Drive and Dayton Way, across from Louis Vuitton.

Century City, located between Beverly Hills and the Westside, was once the back lot of Twentieth Century Fox. It was sold and then developed into a commercial center. The Century City Shopping Center has a multitheater movie complex and an international food court that is great for families. The Shubert Theater at the shopping center often stages family-oriented live productions.

JUST FOR FUN

Tipperary ★★/$$
If it's time for a haircut, call ahead for an appointment here. Located just across the street from Il Fornaio restaurant, this is where the stars take their kids for grooming and pampering. Head shots of famous kids as well as the kids of the famous decorate the walls. Don't forget your camera to document your child's new Beverly Hills 'do. *9422 Dayton Way at Beverly Dr., Beverly Hills; (310) 274-0294.*

BUNKING DOWN

Beverly Hills Hotel
★★★★/$$$$
Located in the legendary 90210 zip code, this 203-room landmark hotel, nicknamed the Pink Palace, sprawls

across 12 lushly landscaped acres of prime residential real estate and is famous for hiding away celebrities in its 21 unique private bungalows. In fact, Elizabeth Taylor honeymooned with six of her eight husbands here. The hotel also welcomes families with an outdoor pool and hot tub. Suites are equipped with refrigerators and microwaves, and all rooms have coffeemakers, VCRs, and CD players. Children who stay here are given a logo teddy bear and other children's goodies. For a casual meal with kids in tow, try the tucked-away Fountain Coffee Shop, where they serve up a good cheeseburger and a shake made with homemade ice cream. *9641 Sunset Blvd., Beverly Hills; (800) 283-8885; (310) 276-2251.*

Beverly Hills Plaza Hotel
★★★/$$$-$$$$
This attractive low-rise hotel is actually between Westwood and Beverly

Hills, but it's close enough to be included here. A converted apartment building, the comfortable hotel has 116 suites, all with kitchens and some with more than one bedroom. Kids really like the centrally located pool. Other on-site facilities include a hot tub, fitness center, and restaurant. *10300 Wilshire Blvd., at Comstock Ave., Westwood; (800) 800-1234; (310) 275-5575; www.beverlyhillsplaza.com*

The Beverly Hilton
★★★/$$$-$$$$
Owned by ex-talk-show-host and wealthy entrepreneur Merv Griffin, this 581-room hotel is in the exclusive 90210 zip code. Because of its unimpressive exterior, the elegant marble lobby with its colorful chandeliers is quite a pleasant surprise. Poolside garden rooms are particularly nice for families. Children under 19 stay free in their parents' room. Facilities include two swimming pools, one with a fountain in the center, and a poolside fitness center. Complimentary shuttle

service is provided to destinations within three miles of the hotel. This is popular as a venue for star-studded events, so keep your eyes open wide. *9876 Wilshire Blvd., Beverly Hills; (800) HILTONS; (310) 274-7777;* www.hilton.com

Century Plaza Hotel and Tower
★★★★/$$$$
Situated on the former back lot of Twentieth Century Fox studios (the property was sold off after *Cleopatra* bombed at the box office), this 727-room high-rise hotel is set on 10 acres of gardens and reflecting pools. Cribs, high chairs, strollers, potty seats, step stools, and other bulky necessities that you don't want to drag along from home are available, too. Rooms, especially those on the north side of the tower, offer great views. All are equipped with coffee-makers, refrigerators, and microwaves, and you can rent VCRs. Hotel facilities include two swimming pools, two outdoor fitness centers, and an adjacent tennis club. Complimentary town car service is

Rent a Classic Car
What kid—or adult who still has an inner child with needs—wouldn't get excited about driving down Sunset in a Corvette or a Ferrari? Delight all the kids in the family by renting an exotic car from the unsurpassed selection at Budget. This Beverly Hills outfit offers a wide range of luxury and "exotic" vehicles. Flashy convertible choices include Corvette and Porsche Speedsters and the very popular Mustang GT. You'll all look so cool that no one will suspect that you're tourists. *9815 Wilshire Blvd., Beverly Hills; (800) 227-7117; (310) 274-9173;* http://www.budgetbeverlyhills.com/

provided to any destination within a 10-minute radius of the hotel. The Century City Shopping Center and its movie theater complex is just across the street. Across the street in another direction are more movie theaters (this *is* the movie-making capital of the world) and the Shubert Theater, which sometimes stages family-friendly musicals. *2025 Ave. of the Stars, Century City; (800) WESTIN-1; (310) 277-2000;* http://www.centuryplazala.com/

Four Seasons Hotel at Beverly Hills
★★★★/$$$$

Classy and expensive, the only Beverly Hills accoutrement this 285-room hotel lacks is the zip code. It's 90048—not the famous 90210. But it is *close* to Beverly Hills, and it has a luxurious, pampering ambience. Even kids are impressed with the many phones plugged in by the rooftop pool's lounge chairs. Children under 18 stay free in their parents' room and there are plenty of family-friendly extras: children get complimentary milk and cookies on their first night; baby shampoo, playpens, and vaporizers are available by request at no charge; and car seats, strollers, and children's videos and board games can be borrowed. Both the hotel restaurants and room service offer an extensive children's menu, and the Sunday brunch has a special children's buffet table decorated to please kids

and groaning with an eye-popping selection of items such as chicken fingers, pizza, and chocolate candies. *300 S. Doheny Dr., Beverly Hills area; (800) 332-3442; (310) 273-2222;* www.fourseasons.com

GOOD EATS

California Pizza Kitchen
★★★★/$

The first California Pizza Kitchen opened in Beverly Hills. Now this casual, well-priced chain is all over the western United States. It's particularly popular with families because it is usually equipped with plenty of comfortable booths, and the menu offers a vast variety of pizzas as well as soups, salads, pastas, and sandwiches. *207 S. Beverly Dr., Beverly Hills; (310) 275-1101;* www.cpk.com

Century City Food Court
★★★★/$

When everyone wants something different, head for this busy, cheery spot, located in a corner of a very upscale shopping center. You can have diner food in Johnny Rockets (for details, see Good Eats in West Hollywood), fill your own burritos and pay by the weight at Bueno Bueno, bliss out on Ben & Jerry's ice cream, or order smoothies and candy apples at Kelly's Coffee & Fudge Factory. The Stage Deli, a branch of the New York institution, is also here, or try the Chinese, Italian, and Japanese

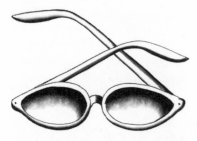

fares. For entertainment, you can select from 14 movies at the adjacent AMC Theaters, or browse the shops. *Century City Shopping Center, 10250 Little Santa Monica Blvd., at Ave. of the Stars, Century City; (310) 277-3898; www.westfield.com*

The Cheesecake Factory
★★★★/$$

A block over from Rodeo Drive, this wildly popular restaurant offers an extensive eclectic menu and, as might be expected from the name, a large selection of cheesecake. Save room for a slice of Oreo, or maybe white chocolate raspberry truffle. With a menu so large it is bound like a book, you'll be able to find something for even the pickiest eaters. It's a great spot for either a snack (the avocado egg rolls are great) or a full meal. Kids will like the omelettes, pizzas, and burgers, but there are plenty of pasta dishes, salads, and sandwiches, too. There are fabulous espresso drinks for the grown-ups and frozen, smoothie-style drinks for everyone. *364 N. Beverly Dr., Beverly Hills; (310) 278-7270; www.thecheesecakefactory.com*

Chin Chin ★★★★/$-$$

Kids love the dumplings, rolls, and noodle dishes served here. Also see Good Eats in Westside. *206 S. Beverly Dr., Beverly Hills; (310) 248-5252; http://www.chinchin.com*

Il Fornaio
★★★/$-$$$

Because you can park here easily on the street before 10 A.M., breakfast is a particularly good meal to enjoy at this popular and trendy spot, just one block from Rodeo Drive. Though the smallish tables and chairs can be uncomfortable for a family, the menu has simple things that kids love as well as more exotic fare for Mom and Dad. And the people-watching is incomparable. Also see Good Eats in San Diego. *301 N. Beverly Dr., at Dayton Way, Beverly Hills; (310) 550-8330; www.ilfo.com*

Islands ★★★★/$

This is an outer island in the chain that serves up sandwiches in a tropical atmosphere. Also see Good Eats in West Los Angeles. *350 S. Beverly Blvd., Beverly Hills; (310) 556-1624; www.islandsrestaurants.com*

Johnny Rockets ★★★★/$

A tad more interesting than the Golden Arches, this inexpensive burger joint is cheap and kid-pleasing. Also see Good Eats in West Hollywood. *474 N. Beverly Dr., Beverly Hills; (310) 271-2222; www.johnnyrockets.com*

Louise's Trattoria
★★★★/$-$$

The whole family will eat heartily on pizza and salad (unless they won't touch salad). Also see Good Eats in Hollywood. *10645 W. Pico Blvd., Rancho Park (near Beverly Hills); (310) 274-4271;* http://www.louis es.com

Nate 'n Al's ★★★★/$

In business since 1945, this bustling deli has a loyal clientele. You usually have to wait to get in, but comfortable booths and good menu choices for kids make it popular with families. Keep your eyes peeled—it's popular with movie stars, too. *414 N. Beverly Dr., Beverly Hills; (310) 274- 0101.*

SOUVENIR HUNTING

Little Folk Art

This is where the stars go to outfit their offspring. Take yours in for some trendy Tinseltown duds. Only a few items won't bust the bank, so be careful with the plastic. And keep your eyes open—that just could be Maria Shriver or Madonna in the next aisle. *205 N. Robertson, Beverly Hills; (310) 860-9872;* www.littlefolkart.cc\

Hollywood, West Los Angeles, and Environs

Although most of the major movie studios have moved elsewhere, the name "Hollywood" still evokes the glamour of the movie-making business. Few families travel to L.A. without checking out the famous Hollywood Walk of Fame and the foot- and handprints of stars in front of Grauman's Chinese Theatre. You can also take the kids to such attractions as the Hollywood Wax Museum, the Hollywood Entertainment Museum, the Hollywood Guinness World of Records Exhibition, and Ripley's Believe It or Not! Odditorium. They may be touristy, but most kids love them, and (admit it) their parents do, too.

Hollywood's fabled Sunset Strip has been home to glittering and brash nightlife for more than three-quarters of a century, but there's not much there for young children. Trendy West Hollywood offers numerous hotels, restaurants, and quite a few alluring shops. Your 10 and up crowd will want to soak up some of the glamour in a coffee-house or restaurant, but the little guys may get bored. Try to keep younger siblings occupied with a game of "Count the Limos."

West Los Angeles, just south of Hollywood, is best known for the Miracle Mile. A one-mile stretch of Wilshire Boulevard from La Brea Avenue to Fairfax Avenue, it was once Los Angeles's most glamorous boule-vard, lined with upscale department stores. It is now the site of La Brea Tar Pits, which are sure to intrigue fans of dinosaurs, mastodons, and other prehistoric beasts; the Carole and Barry Kaye Museum of Miniatures, a must-see for dollhouse fans; and the Petersen Automotive Museum, which will please lovers of cars and trucks.

Also covered in this chapter is Griffith Park, just northeast of

Hollywood and site of the Griffith Observatory and Planetarium and the Los Angeles Zoo, among other attractions. West of the park is Universal City, where you'll find Los Angeles County's top tourist attrac-tion—the Universal Studios Holly-wood movie studio/theme park. And north of Universal Studios is Burbank, home of NBC.

CULTURAL ADVENTURES

Carole & Barry Kaye Museum of Miniatures
★★★/$$

Crammed full of tiny versions of almost everything, this two-floor museum has the largest and most comprehensive collection of minia-tures in the world. It all started when Mrs. Kaye's 5-year-old grandson vis-

---

DAY TRIP

A Dino Day in L.A.

10 A.M. Arrive at the **La Brea Tar Pits** to check out the grime and the scene of the crime, where so many animals got stuck so many years ago.

After about a half hour of this, stroll on over to the **George C. Page Museum** (closed Wednesday) and see some of the reconstructed skele-tons of animals found in the pits. Allow time for the kids to get

involved in some of the hands-on activities.

Noon Lunch at **Farmers Market**.

1 P.M. Continue on to the **Natural History Museum,** for dinosaur fos-sils galore—this museum's phone number is *(213) 763-DINO.* Check out some of the other popular exhibits, too, including the Insect Zoo and the gemstone gallery.

ited her in L.A., and they decided to make a miniature house. Then she made six more and became so addicted that her collection outgrew her Century City house. To make a long story short, the Kaye collection now includes everything from a mini tree laden with mini tree houses to a re-creation of the O.J. Simpson trial courtroom to a *Titanic* model made with 75,000 toothpicks and two gallons of glue. The museum also holds an elaborate collection of palaces created with the help of artists from around the world. It includes The Vatican, Hampton Court Palace, and Fontainebleau, complete with real silver embellishments. Little boys as well as little girls like this place, which has a large car collection. To get the most out of your visit, ask for a free copy of the *Discovery Guide* for each of your children when you arrive. Before leaving, check out the well-stocked Petite Elite Gift Shop, where prices range from $1.50 to $100,000. But be careful. You might get yourself started on a hobby that could eventually crowd you out of your own house! *5900 Wilshire Blvd., at Spaulding St., West Los Angeles; (323) 937-MINI.*

El Capitan Theatre ★★/$

This beautiful old movie palace hosted the world premiere of Orson Welles's *Citizen Kane*. It now shows only Disney movies. Short, live shows are often presented before films. *6838 Hollywood Blvd., Hollywood; (323) 467-7674.*

Egyptian Theatre ★★/$

Another beautifully renovated and restored movie palace, the Egyptian has a King Tut–ish theme, with sphinxes and winged cobras as part of the decor. *Forever Hollywood,* an hourlong documentary film

---

3 P.M. Hit the freeway for Universal Studios Hollywood. Before entering, have a snack at **Universal CityWalk.**

4 P.M. Spend the rest of the day at **Universal Studios.** The fabulous attraction stays open until 10 P.M. in the summer, 7 P.M. the rest of the year. But today you and your young dinosaur fans are specifically here to experience Jurassic Park—The Ride. Said to be one of the most technically sophisticated rides ever created, this raft adventure is filled with special effects. After a smooth beginning, things get rougher as you are swept by rapids into Carnivore Canyon and a gang of velociraptors (children under 5 might be frightened). Fortunately, you'll all be saved by an unexpected hero. If you liked the movie, you're going to love the ride. But be prepared—you're going to get wet.

about Hollywood's history, is shown during the day; it will interest preteen movie buffs, but bore their younger brothers and sisters. Come back in the evening to see feature films. *6712 Hollywood Blvd., at N. Las Palmas Ave., Hollywood; (323) 466-FILM; www.egyptiantheater.com*

Griffith Park ★★★★/Free

You can easily spend all day in this 4,107-acre park in the Hollywood Hills. It's the largest city park in the country and offers a plethora of things to do. In addition to the Autry Museum of Western Heritage, Los Angeles Zoo, and Travel Town *(see below for details)*, it has more than 50 miles of hiking trails, 28 tennis courts, four golf courses, riding stables, and a public swimming pool. The little guys will like the kiddie rides—a miniature train, a carousel, a simulator that provides a virtual ride on a roller coaster and airplane, and *real* ponies. *Entrances on Los Feliz Blvd. and Zoo Dr., Los Angeles; (323) 913-4688; http://www.city ofla.org/RAP/grifmet/griffith.htm*

Autry Museum of Western Heritage ★★★/$

Got a kid who won't go anywhere without his cowboy hat? Mosey on over to this museum, which tells the story of the Old West through murals, movies, and hands-on exhibits. One of the most comprehensive collections of American Western artifacts, it includes displays of firearms, tools, clothing, toys, and furnishings. Contrary to what you might expect, there is little here that commemorates the legendary cowboy Gene Autry, save a bronze statue and one display case. If possible, time your visit for a weekday afternoon; on weekday mornings the museum is usually crowded with school groups, and the place is also generally busy on weekends, when Western films are screened for a small additional charge. *4700 Western Heritage Way, Griffith Park, Los Angeles; (323) 667-2000; http://www.autry-museum.org*

Griffith Observatory and Planetarium ★★/$

Following a multimillion-dollar renovation this first-rate attraction, whose centerpiece is the Foucault pendulum, is scheduled to reopen in 2004. *2800 E. Observatory Rd., Los Angeles; (323) 664-1181; www.grif fithobs.org*

Los Angeles Zoo ★★★★/$

Animals from five continents can be seen here, living in environments that resemble their natural habitats. The Winnick Family Children's Zoo lets the whole family get up close and personal with goats and sheep in a separate "contact" area. An indoor "kids place" features storytelling, puppet shows, and more up-close encounters with animals. Children seem to particularly enjoy the nocturnal exhibits, including the very popular Koala House. There are bird

Terrific Task Masters

When our family goes on vacation, we assign each of our seven children an important task for the duration of the trip, one that will make each child an active part of planning. On a trip to Orlando, Florida, these were their assignments. Sylvia, age 15, navigator and accountant, kept track of mileage, maps, and money; TamiSue, 13, photographer, had to use two rolls of film a day; Joshua, 10, auto mechanic, pumped gas and checked oil and tire pressure; Bryan, 7, mailman, got postcards and stamps and mailed the cards kids write to themselves each day; Libby, 7, dietitian, made sure the cooler was stocked; Andrew, 6, activities coordinator and music director, was solely in charge of the tape player; and Katie, 5, referee, settled all road disputes.

Wendy Lira, Alma, Kansas

and animal shows. Plan on at least a full morning or afternoon to see the entire zoo; morning is the best time to visit, as the animals are most active and vocal then. *5333 Zoo Dr., Los Angeles; (323) 644-6400; www.lazoo.org*

Travel Town ★★★/Free

This tiny outdoor transportation museum includes several retired L.A. streetcars. Best of all, you and your kids are welcome to climb aboard. A miniature quarter-scale train ride operates nearby. The kids will be distracted by the choo-choos, but adults can enjoy breathtaking city views, too. *5200 W. Zoo Dr., Los Angeles; (323) 662-5874; www.cityof la.org/RAP/grifmet/tt*

Hollywood Entertainment Museum ★★/$

The exhibits and videos here will enhance your kids' (and your) understanding of Hollywood—the place and the industry. When you visit the museum, you get a tour of a studio back lot and a visit to the actual sets used for *Cheers* and *Star Trek*. Special events, including screenings and children's programs, are held here regularly. *7021 Hollywood Blvd., Hollywood; (323) 465-7900; www.hollywoodmuseum.com*

 **La Brea Tar Pits and George C. Page Museum/ Hancock Park**

★★★★/Free-$

Junior paleontologists won't want to miss the black gooey pools found in otherwise unremarkable Hancock Park. Thousands of years ago, many now-extinct animals were fooled into thinking these tar pits, covered by a thin layer of water, were watering holes. As they got stuck, they

233

KIDS CAN MAKE their own impressions with a tray of sand and some plaster of paris (similar to the hand and foot prints in front of Grauman's Chinese Theatre). However, unlike the Hollywood stars, your child can take her handprint home! See "Footprints in the Sand," page 169.

attracted predators, which also became stranded, and they all sank into the ooze, slowly. Yuck. Kids love the somewhat grisly history of the pits and, at the adjacent Page Museum, the reconstructed skeletons of the creatures that met their end in them. Skeletons of mammoths, giant sloths, and saber-toothed cats are displayed, along with the only human skeleton ever found in the pits, a female victim of a 9,000-year-old murder. The museum also offers an orientation film, exhibits depicting prehistoric Los Angeles, and a working paleontology lab. There are hands-on activities for kids, too. *5801 Wilshire Blvd., West Los Angeles; (323) 934-PAGE;* www.tarpits.org

Los Angeles County Museum of Art ★/$

This large, eclectic museum is composed of five buildings and a sculpture garden surrounding a central court. Its collection spans the ages. Family activities are offered every weekend, and Family Sundays are held regularly. Taking part in the hands-on activities at these special events is a great way to introduce children to the pleasures of visiting a great art museum. Unless you've got a budding Titian in tow, don't expect your kids to last more than a couple of hours (at most) here. Call for a schedule. *5905 Wilshire Blvd., West Los Angeles; (323) 857-6000;* www.lacma.org

Petersen Automotive Museum ★★/$

The car is one of those things that can capture the interest of kids and parents alike. That's why this museum, which is a sort of a road map to the history of the car in Los Angeles, is such a good place to take your family. Exhibits on the first floor trace the history of the automobile and explain how the car shaped the culture of Los Angeles and drove (no pun intended) the area's commerce with gas stations, roadside diners, and the world's first shopping district. Kids will particularly like the top floor, where classic automobiles, motorcycles, and hot rods are displayed. The May Family Children's Discovery Center uses cars to teach basic scientific principles. Don't forget your camera—the photo opportunities are choice. To park your car, enter the attached garage off Fairfax Avenue. *6060 Wilshire Blvd., at Fairfax Ave., West Los Angeles; (323) 930-CARS;* www.petersen.org

Ripley's Believe It or Not! Odditorium ★★/$

Who can resist a name like that! Inside this enormous two-story museum you'll see more than 300 exhibits. Among the oddest are a picture of John Wayne made out of laundry lint, shrunken heads from South America, two-headed goats, and cows with six legs. Yuck! Best for kids 8 and older. *6780 Hollywood Blvd., Hollywood; (323) 466-6335;* www.hollywoodripleys.com

JUST FOR FUN

Grauman's Chinese Theatre
★★★/Free-$

You can try matching your hands and feet to impressions of some of the biggest stars—Marlon, Liz, Duke—left behind in cement in front of Grauman's Chinese Theatre, where movies are still shown. You might be able to pick up some free tickets to TV tapings (there are age requirements for children; check beforehand), as the studios often send representatives here to give them away. *6925 Hollywood Blvd; (323) 464-8111* www.manntheatres.com

Hollywood Boulevard
★★★★/Free

Take the family for a stroll on this storied street, where you can see Hollywood's most famous movie-related attractions. The famous **Hollywood Walk of Fame** is a sidewalk embedded with brass-trimmed pink terrazzo stars honoring hundreds of celebrities. It runs along Hollywood Boulevard from Gower to Sycamore and along Vine Street from Yucca to Sunset. Marilyn Monroe's star is at *6744 Hollywood Boulevard*, Elvis Presley's is at *6777*, and James Dean's is at *1719 Vine Street. For information on upcoming induction ceremonies, call (323) 469-8311.*The 6700 block of Hollywood Boulevard also holds the **Hollywood Wax Museum** *(6767 Hollywood Blvd.; 323/462-8860)*, where you'll see all the big stars looking strangely smaller than life.

Hollywood Guinness World of Records Exhibition ★★/$

Located within the refurbished Hollywood Theatre, Hollywood's

first movie house, are these exhibits that bring record-breaking feats and achievements vividly to life. The amazing (though not particularly useful) information your kids learn here will probably stay with them longer than last week's math or history lesson. *6764 Hollywood Blvd., at N. Highland Ave., Hollywood; (323) 463-6433.*

NBC Studios Tour
★★★★/$

Touted as the world's largest television studio, and home of *The Tonight Show with Jay Leno*, this studio is also where many popular game shows and series are taped. Take the tour—it's designed to demonstrate how a television show is put together. It begins in a mini studio where your kids will have the chance to see themselves on TV, then continues backstage with stops at the wardrobe department, prop and set storage area, and maybe the Jay Leno set. You might even be lucky enough to spot a star. The tour is open to all ages, but doesn't offer much for the *Blue's Clues* crowd. *3000 W. Alameda, Burbank; (818) 840-3537.*

 **Universal Studios Hollywood**
★★★★/$$$$

In the old days you had to know somebody to get a behind-the-scenes studio tour. Now you don't, but you do have to wait in lines. Your family will be playing "Hurry Up and Wait" the entire time you're here, so just breathe easy and plan on spending a whole day at this movie studio/theme park, the top tourist attraction in Los Angeles County. The guided Backlot Tram Tour is a favorite feature and is fun for kids of all ages. You ride through the studio's back lots and see actual sets, including the *Psycho* house and Amity Island from *Jaws*. You'll also visit a number of soundstages and learn about some of the technical aspects of filmmaking. Then it's on to the blockbuster rides based on blockbuster movies, including the chilling, awesome, dinosaur-filled raft adventure Jurassic Park—The Ride, the flying bicycles of E.T. Adventure, and the sizzling-hot walk-through

My Sweet

You don't need to lug toys from the car when you stop to eat. Just grab the sugar packets on the table and try these sweet games:

Arrange 12, 16, 20, or 24 packets on the table in straight lines of four. Now have two players take turns removing one, two, or three packets at a time. The player who picks up the last packet loses.

Or, hide an even number of pennies, nickels, dimes, and quarters under the packets and take turns trying to find matching pairs.

demonstration of Backdraft. The Terminator 2: 3-D is the world's most technically advanced and visually spectacular film-based attraction. It's a multisensory virtual adventure created by *Titanic* director James Cameron. Some of the rides and attractions are too scary for small children, but all ages enjoy the live shows, including the new Spider-Man Rocks! adventure show, Nickelodeon Blast Zone, in which kids can play messy games, and the Animal Actors Stage, where four-legged stars rehearse hilariously for their next role. Be ever-vigilant, as celebrities are often sighted here. And don't forget your camera. There are photo ops galore. *100 Universal City Plaza, Universal City; (818) 622-3036;* www.themeparks.universal studios.com/hollywood

Universal CityWalk
★★★★/Free

Take the kids for a day at Universal Studios and then have dinner here before you head home. This glimmering "urban entertainment center" is lined with shops, restaurants, and clubs. It refers to itself as "the coolest street in America," and, with an 18-screen movie theater complex and an IMAX-3D screen among its many amenities, it just might be. Rock music plays loud, and the latest videos are shown on oversized outdoor screens. Restaurants include branches of Buca di Beppo, Gladstone's, the Hard Rock Cafe, Jerry's

Famous Deli, and Wolfgang Puck Cafe. It is easy to spend an entire afternoon or evening here. *100 Universal City Plaza, Universal City; (818) 622-4455.*

BUNKING DOWN

Best Western Hollywood Plaza Inn
★★★/$$

This very attractive 82-room property abuts the Hollywood Hills and is within walking distance of many of the Hollywood Boulevard sights. Rooms are equipped with refrigerators, and your family will enjoy the nice pool area after a day of sightseeing. You don't even have to go out to eat: a small coffee shop off the lobby serves inexpensive meals. *2011 N. Highland Ave., Hollywood; (800) 232-4353, (800) 528-1234; (323) 851-1800;* www.bestwestern.com

Days Inn Hollywood ★★/$$

This branch of the reliable, well-priced chain has 74 rooms and features a comfortable lobby where you can watch the Sunset street action. Deluxe and kitchenette rooms are equipped with refrigerators and microwaves; other family-friendly pluses include a heated swimming pool and complimentary deluxe continental breakfast. *7023 Sunset Blvd., at La Brea Ave., Hollywood; (800) 325-2525; (323) 464-8344;* www.daysinn.com

Holiday Inn Walk of Fame
★★★/$$

Within walking distance of many of the Hollywood Boulevard sights, this well-located, 160-room hotel has a small pool and a hot tub, a fitness center, and a cheery, full-service café. Children under 18 stay free in their parents' room. *2005 N. Highland Ave., Hollywood; (800) HOLIDAY; (323) 850-5811; www.basshotels.com/holiday-inn*

Hollywood Roosevelt Hotel
★★★/$$-$$$

Tell the kids to be on the lookout—the stargazing is usually very good here. Opened in 1927 and the site of the first Academy Awards ceremony in 1929, this historic 328-room property is located in the center of old Hollywood. It is built in a stately Spanish-Moorish style, and facilities include a large courtyard with a hot tub and an Olympic-size pool decoratively painted by artist David Hockney. Rooms are equipped with coffeemakers, and you can rent a refrigerator or VCR. *7000 Hollywood Blvd., Hollywood; (800) 950-7667; (323) 466-7000; http://www.hollywoodroosevelt.com/*

Motel Row

There's good pickings on Sunset near La Brea.

Sheraton Universal
★★★★/$$$

Billed as the hotel of the stars, this comfortable 436-room lodging place is just down the hill from Universal Studios (a tram will drop you there) and a 10-minute drive from the legendary corner of Hollywood and Vine.

Some ground-level rooms are particularly convenient to the pool and hot tub. All rooms have coffeemakers, and you can rent refrigerators and VCRs. Find out about packages that include parking and two tickets to Universal Studios. *333 Universal Terrace Pkwy., Universal City; (888) 627-7186; (818) 980-1212; www.sheraton.com*

GOOD EATS

Canter's
★★★★/$

Open round the clock, this very large, popular, old-time deli has plenty of spacious, comfy booths as well as counter seating. Families fit right in with the din. Or order food to go and have a picnic. There's something on the menu to please even picky eaters. In addition to an extensive selection of deli items, the regular menu offers kid-pleasing Belgian waffles, hot dogs, hamburgers, peanut-butter-and-jelly, and pastas, plus an array of side dishes. Special meals for "little fressers" include a drink and potato chips. Free parking is available in their corner lot. *419 N. Fairfax Ave., at Oakwood Ave., West Los Angeles; (323) 651-2030.*

Carneys Express Limited
★★★/$$

The kids will get a bang out of eating in an authentic Union Pacific railway car sitting on actual train tracks. You can even watch the fancy car parade on Sunset while you dine. It's self-service for the inexpensive, simple fare of burgers, hot dogs, sandwiches, tacos, and pasta salads. Ice-cream bars and gigantic frozen chocolate-dipped bananas make for chillin' desserts. *8351 Sunset Blvd., Hollywood; (323) 654-8300; www.carneytrain.com*

Chin Chin ★★★★/$-$$

For some sumptuous noodle and dumpling dishes, this is a must. Also see Good Eats in Westside. *8618 Sunset Blvd., in Sunset Plaza, West Hollywood; (310) 652-1818; www.chinchin.com*

Duke's Coffee Shop
★★/$

Though it's not much to look at, this cheap, cozy, casual spot gives you a choice of sitting at a counter or at a communal table—the kind you see in New York delis—for your cup of coffee or cocoa. You can't miss it. It's across the street from Larry Flint's Hustler adult store (some eye-shielding may be required) and next door to the legendary Whiskey A Go Go, where Jim Morrison and the Doors played way back when. Though this wouldn't be a place with kids at night, in the morning it's interesting, and

High-Flying Games

Games that use a pen or pencil are perfect to play on airplanes, since you can lean on the tray top. The following ideas are especially enjoyed by players who are sitting in a row. Unlike backseat games, which can get fairly boisterous, these airplane pastimes are a bit quieter, so you won't make enemies of your fellow fliers.

CRAZY CREATURES

Create strange-looking people, beasts, or any combination of both by folding a piece of paper into three equal sections. One person draws the face in the top section, then folds down the paper so the next person can't see it. That person then draws the midsection of the body, folds down the paper, and passes it to the third person, who sketches the legs in the bottom section. Finally, unfold the paper and name your creature.

TOUCHY TELEPHONE

This is a good game for people sitting in a row. Player 1, on one end, thinks of a word. Player 2, next to 1, closes his or her eyes and holds out an arm. Using a finger, Player 1 "writes" the word on Player 2's arm. The word gets passed down the row — and maybe across the aisle — until it reaches the last person in your party. That person says the word he thinks was written on his arm out loud, and Player 1 says the original word. Let Player 2 start the next round, and so on.

the coffee shop serves great, big breakfasts—fluffy pancakes, three-egg omelettes and scrambles, excellent blintzes, French toast, muffins, and plenty more. The kid-friendly menu also lists grilled cheese sandwiches, a large variety of burgers, and yummy shakes, smoothies, and desserts. And it's popular with the stars, whose photos cover the walls. *8909 Sunset Blvd., West Hollywood; (310) 652-3100.*

Farmers Market ★★★★/$

Since 1934, when it opened as a market for farmers to sell their produce to the public, Farmers Market has emerged as more than just a popular eatery. Movie moguls and film stars have gathered regularly to talk deals and plan projects. Even Walt Disney sat at the market while preparing designs for Disneyland. Your children will salivate watching the fudge and candy being made or as some of the 1,000 daily doughnuts emerge from the oven at Bob's Doughnuts. You probably won't get out without buying something from the Ultimate Nut & Candy stall, which has been around for over 60 years. From pancakes and waffles to pasta and pizza to Chinese food favorites, it's all here. You'll also want to browse the two dozen or so stores that sell gifts, gadgets, and assorted, souvenirs. Don't forget to stop in Kip's Toyland. **NOTE:** The parking lot is between the food stalls and most of the shops. It is very busy, so

watch children extra carefully. *6333 West Third St., at the corner of Fairfax Avenue in West Los Angeles. Look for the clock tower; (323) 933-9211; www.farmersmarketla.com*

Hamburger Hamlet
★★★/$

This popular chain has an extensive kid-pleasing menu that includes a wide variety of hamburgers plus chili, rotisserie chicken, steaks, and ice-cream sundaes. *9201 Sunset Blvd., West Hollywood; (310) 278-4924. A branch with a view of Grauman's Chinese Theatre is at 6914 Hollywood Blvd., Hollywood; (323) 467-6106.*

Hard Rock Cafe
★★★★/$-$$

Located near Beverly Hills, this link in the chain has the usual Cadillac crashing through the roof and loud rock and roll music. Kids get coloring books and crayons and a menu that includes a burger, grilled cheese, and barbecued chicken. They can check out the displays of rock memorabilia when they get restless. Also see Good Eats in San Francisco. *Beverly Center, 8600 Beverly Blvd., at La Cienega Blvd., West Los Angeles; (310) 276-7605; www.hardrock cafe.com*

Hoys Wok ★★★/$

Delicious Chinese food is prepared in a health-conscious manner here and served in simple surroundings. All the usual suspects are on the menu, everything is deliciously fresh, and kids can share. *8163 Santa Monica Blvd., at Crescent Heights, West Hollywood; (323) 656-9002. Also at 7105 Sunset Blvd., at La Brea Ave., West Los Angeles; (323) 850-6637.*

Islands ★★★★/$

You and the kids can pretend that you've been whisked away to a tropical island when you dine in this atmospheric spot. Servers wear Hawaiian shirts, and faux palm trees decorate the room. The food is the kind kids like best—hamburgers, tacos, fries. There are some adult-pleasing sandwiches and salads, too, and they have cute names: the Hula is a mushroom burger with Swiss cheese; the Sandcastle is grilled cheese on egg bread. Small portions are available on the Gremmie Menu for surfers 12 and under. A full bar can prepare any libation Mom and Dad might fancy—perhaps a margarita or piña colada (it's vacation!)—as well as special kids' drinks. Soft drinks, tea, and coffee are served with budget-stretching, eye-popping "endless" refills. *10948 W. Pico Blvd., at Veteran Ave., West Los Angeles; (310) 474-1144;* www.islandsrestaurants.com

Jerry's Famous Deli
★★★/$

There's something for everyone on the menu at this popular deli. *8701 Beverly Blvd., West Hollywood; (310) 289-1811.*

Johnny Rockets ★★★★/$

This inexpensive burger joint seems to be everywhere now, but this, the original location, is probably the best. You can sit either at the popular counter inside and watch the preparations, listening to rock from the 1950s, or outside under umbrellas and soak up the rays while watching the sidewalk fashion show. Chili dogs, sandwiches, and fountain items are also on the menu, and kids can order peanut-butter-and-jelly sandwiches or indulge in the chili fries favored by older folks. The waiters here have been known to make your life truly carefree by pouring your ketchup for you. *7507 Melrose Ave., West Hollywood; (323) 651-3361;* www.johnnyrockets.com

Louise's Trattoria
★★★★/$-$$

You can easily fill up on the complimentary pizza bread and fabulous dipping oil that the waitstaff brings to the table, but do save room for the top-notch handmade Neapolitan-style pizza topped with homemade pizza sauce and whole-milk mozzarella. Order one pie plus a fabulous chopped salad, and you'll fill the average family of four. Homemade pasta and assorted chicken dishes round out the menu. A special children's coloring menu offers smaller portions for kids. This location is a favorite because you can sit outside pretty much year-round and catch a glimpse of the wild Melrose street scene while you dine. *7505 Melrose Ave, West Hollywood; (323) 651-3880; www.louises.com*

Lucy's Cafe El Adobe
★★★/$

Situated across the street from Paramount Studios, this unassuming spot serves simple, reliable fare and sometimes attracts a star or two. Keep your eyes open while you indulge in the house specialties: *arroz con pollo* (chicken with rice), *ropa vieja* (a Cuban dish—shredded beef in a sauce), and *gallina en mole* (chicken in smoky mole sauce). Comfortable booths and special children's plates are pluses for families. *5536 Melrose Ave., West Hollywood; (323) 462-9421; www.lucyseladobe.com*

The Old Spaghetti Factory
★★★★/$

This family-friendly chain seems to turn up in every big city. Oodles of spaghetti noodles are served with a choice of sauces, and kids' meals are available. If you're lucky, you might

get a table inside the 1918 trolley. Reservations are not accepted, so expect a wait at prime dining times. Also see Good Eats in Silicon Valley-San Jose. *5939 Sunset Blvd., West Los Angeles; (323) 469-7149;* http://www.osf.com/

Pink's Famous Chili Dogs
★★★/$

Open from early in the morning into the wee, wee hours (around 3 A.M.), this famous hot dog stand has been serving movie stars and everyone else since 1939. The people in line are a cross-section of the town's population. Some wear suits, others chat on cell phones. And kids, not surprisingly, love it as much as adults. It's nothing to look at from the outside, so the hot dogs had better be good—and they are. Many people consider them to be the best in town. The chili dog is what the place is best known for, but do consider the foot-long jalapeño dog, chicken fajita burritos, and chili tamales. Hamburgers, turkey burgers and more fast foods are also on the menu, and the potato salad is excellent. The service is fast, another big plus when you've got hungry customers. *709 N. La Brea Ave., between Santa Monica Blvd. and Melrose Ave., West Hollywood; (323) 931-4223.*

Roscoe's House of Chicken 'n Waffles ★★/$

The outside of this very small café is deceptive. Lacking windows, it resembles a bar, and you simply must go inside to see what's up. Once you're in, you might as well pick a table and order up some fried chicken and biscuits. Or a buckwheat waffle and syrup. Or team them both up on one plate. Southern side goodies include red beans and rice, grits, corn bread, and sweet-potato pie. For the hard to please, a few sandwiches also grace the menu. This place has been around forever and is said to be patronized by plenty of stars, probably because everything is so delicious. For a southern-style picnic, order your meal to go. *1514 N. Gower St./Sunset, West Hollywood; (323) 466-7453. There are branches at 5006 W. Pico Blvd. at LaBrea Ave., West Los Angeles (323/934-4405), and 106 W. Manchester Blvd., at Main St., downtown (323/752-6211).*

Tail O' The Pup
★★/$

Located within sight of the Beverly Center, this hot dog stand is literally as famous as some of the stars who line up in front. It's shaped like a giant hot dog, which is sure to tickle your child's funny bone. In addition to dogs, the bill of fare includes hamburgers, chili fries, and, for breakfast, a fried egg sandwich and doughnuts. Though most people eat their purchases on the run, you can sit at one of the few outdoor tables. *329 N. San Vicente Blvd., at Beverly Blvd., West Hollywood; (310) 652-4517.*

Wolfgang Puck Cafe
★★★/$$

Pizza, pasta, and salad is served up here in a colorful contemporary setting. Also see Good Eats in Santa Monica. *8000 Sunset Blvd., at N. Laurel Ave., Hollywood; (323) 650-7300; www.wolfgangpuck.com*

SOUVENIR HUNTING

Aahs!
Kids get a kick out of the kitschy gifts sold here; there are cards and candy, too. *8878 Sunset Blvd., West Hollywood; (310) 657-4221.*

Hollywood Toys & Costumes
You'll know you're here when you spot the Mister Rogers star on the sidewalk in front. Inside, you'll find just what the name promises. In addition to toys galore, huge stuffed animals, and magic props, you can get everything you need for next Halloween. Let the whole family go wild selecting their dream look from a fabulous assortment of wigs, hats, and accessories. Elaborate complete costumes are available, and the vast selection of masks includes everything from KISS to O.J. And though it would be hard to do, don't miss the "skeleton" buried under glass in the center of the store. (This is *not* the place to bring little ones who think there are monsters under their beds.) *6600 Hollywood Blvd., Hollywood; (800) 554-3444; (323) 464-4444.*

Melrose Avenue

Catering to a contemporary, off-beat audience, and selling everything kooky, zany, and left-of-center, you'll find a batch of imaginatively named stores here, such as Aardvark's and the Wound & Wound Toy Co., where the owner is a World War II flying ace and the inventory includes windup toys as well as tin toys and Pez dispensers, are fun for everyone. The kids won't be the only ones overstimulated by the sights and sounds. Pick one of the area's many restaurants for some R&R.

Moletown

The real business here, since 1926, is making lighting equipment for "the industry." But in addition, this huge warehouse is filled with all kinds of official logo items—T-shirts, baseball caps, mugs, jackets—from a diverse selection of movie and television productions. You can get *Friends* everything, as well as cool

desk lamps that look like miniature movie lights, and there are plenty of items from kids' programs, too. *900 N. La Brea Ave., at Melrose Ave., West Los Angeles; (323) 851-0111; www. moletown.com*

Storyopolis

Half art gallery, half bookstore, this spacious store is filled with children's books, framed and unframed art from storybooks, and plenty of related and unrelated toys. It is the perfect spot to select items to enhance your child's home library, and the knowledgeable staff is ever ready to help you choose the perfect book. Special events and book signings are scheduled regularly. *In Robertson Plaza A, 116 N. Robertson, West Los Angeles; (310) 358-2500; www.storyopolis.com*

Westside: Westwood/ Brentwood/Bel Air Area

This area is more casually tony than Beverly Hills. Home to UCLA, it caters to students on a budget as well as to movie stars with deep pockets. Sunset Boulevard is more or less the divider between the two

worlds. North of Sunset is movie-star land; south of Sunset is where folks with more modest incomes tend to congregate. It's a good area for shopping and dining and absolutely great for driving around and gawking at mansions. You'll pass the occasional park where you can let the kids frolic with the locals.

CULTURAL ADVENTURES

The J. Paul Getty Museum
★★★/Free

While art museums and kids usually don't mix, this magnificent new facility just might be an exception to the rule. For some kids, simply getting here is half the fun: visitors board a computer-operated, emission-free electric tram for the five-minute scenic ride from the parking lot up into the Santa Monica Mountains to the museum's central plaza. The extensive art collection is split among five buildings. You might want to rent the audio guide, which has a special track designed to generate discussion between children and adults. When children have looked at enough pictures, you can herd them outside to the Central Garden, with its cascading waterfall and seasonal plants, or for a snack and to enjoy the magnificent city view from the terrace café. Don't miss the Family Room, where hands-on activities and games help children connect with the objects they see in the galleries. You can check out "The Getty Art Detective" here, which takes you on a treasure hunt through the galleries. There's a bookstore for children, too.

Among the special family programs is Adventures for Families, a gallery talk every Saturday and Sunday at 2 P.M. Though admission to the museum is free, you must make advance parking reservations for weekdays (reservations are not required on weekends) and pay a $5 parking fee when you arrive—unless you're traveling with a college student with current ID, in which case parking is free and reservations are not needed. Alternatively, you can take Metro Bus #561, the Santa Monica Big Blue Bus #14, or a cab. *West of I-5, 1200 Getty Center Dr., Bel Air; (310) 440-7300;* www.getty.edu/

UCLA Campus Tour ★/Free

It's never too early to get kids interested in college. Start now with a guided tour of this beautiful campus. Of greatest interest to college-bound teens and preteens are the tours given here on weekdays only; reservations are necessary. Before, after, or instead of the tour, you can visit the Franklin D. Murphy Sculpture Garden, where art meets nature. Kids can romp among the displays, and you'll have some great photo ops. The Mildred E. Mathias Botanical Garden, which specializes in subtropical and tropical plants that are usually only seen in the United States in greenhouses, is also a good place to skip and stroll. *10945 Le Conte Ave., at Gayley Ave., Westwood; (310) 825-8764;* www.ucla.edu/

BUNKING DOWN

Century Wilshire Hotel
★★★/$$-$$$

On an impressive stretch of Wilshire Boulevard, near UCLA and Westwood, this well-located low-rise offers families a tasteful, comfortable retreat. Originally an apartment house, it has been converted into 99 rooms with half-kitchens and charming lace curtains. The large pool, which has a shallow area for children, is in a garden setting with palm and banana trees. Free parking and a continental breakfast are included. *10776 Wilshire Blvd., Westwood; (800) 421-7223; (310) 474-4506;* www.centurywilshire hotel.com

Doubletree Hotel
★★★★/$$$-$$$$

This well-equipped 295-room hotel is in a superb location right in the thick of the Wilshire glitz. Complimentary transportation is provided to the UCLA campus, from there it's $7 per person round-trip transportation to the Getty Museum. Facilities include a year-round heated outdoor pool and hot tub, a sauna, a fitness center, and an inexpensive café. *10740 Wilshire Blvd., Westwood; (800) 472-8556; (310) 475-8711;* www. doubletreelawestwood.com

W Los Angeles
★★★/$$$-$$$$

Located on a tree-lined residential street that is an extension of UCLA's sorority row, this stylish, all-suite hotel has 258 units and provides families with a comfortable home base in L.A. Parents can tuck kids into the living room's sofa bed, maintaining their privacy in a separate, luxuriously appointed bedroom. On-site extras include two acres of landscaped gardens, two outdoor pools (one with private cabanas), and a state-of-the-art fitness center. Not touted by the hotel,

---

The Postcard Flip-Book
AGES 3 TO 7

Simplicity is the key to this young kids' souvenir. Before you leave home, go to a stationery store and buy a standard hole punch and two large silver rings. Each day of the trip, select a postcard and let your child dictate to you (or write, if he's old enough) a favorite memory of the place it depicts. Punch two holes in the top of the postcard and slip it onto the rings. You will return home with a colorful flip-book of the trip — pictures on one side, the child's memories on the other.

As hard as it seems, resist the urge to censor the child's commentary. Take pleasure in your child's unique perspective on your family vacation. His favorite memory of the zoo may be the green soap in the bathroom dispenser, so let him write that on the card.

but well worth mentioning, is that guests can hear the soothing hourly chimes of the bell tower from the church across the street. *930 Hilgard Ave., Westwood; (877) W-HOTELS; (310) 208-8765;* www.whotels.com

GOOD EATS

Apple Pan ★★/$

Looking a bit like the subject of the popular children's story *The Little House,* this tiny restaurant has been here since 1947 and now sits amid the big Westside Pavilion shopping center and office buildings. It offers only swivel-stool counter seating, which kids usually enjoy (keep an eye on the little ones). The menu is limited—burgers, sandwiches, fries—and everything is served on paper plates. But the price is right, and there is apple, cream, and pecan pie for dessert. *10801 W. Pico, at Westwood Blvd., Westwood; (310) 475-3585.*

Cheesecake Factory ★★★★/$$

This branch of the chain has inviting outdoor patio seating that is popular in warm weather. Also see Good Eats in Beverly Hills. *11647 San Vicente Blvd., Brentwood; (310) 826-7111;* htttp://www.thecheese cakefactory.com/

Chin Chin ★★★★/$-$$

Americanized Chinese food prepared L.A.-style dominates the menu at this cheerful and noisy spot with comfy booths and patio seating. Among the dim sum items are a variety of dumplings and rolls, including ever-popular potstickers. You'll also find soups, salads, classic stir-fried dishes, and lots of noodle dishes, plus a good selection of vegetarian items. Most kids like the noodles with peanut sauce. *In San Vicente Plaza, 11740 San Vicente Blvd., Brentwood; (310) 826-2525;* www.chinchin.com

The Coffee Bean & Tea Leaf ★★/$

This casual, extremely popular coffeehouse is omnipresent in Los Angeles. Kids are seen hanging out with their parents on weekends at this location, which is also frequented by students and starlets, all of whom chat on cell phones as they wait in the (also omnipresent) line. The chain is famous for delicious flavored lattes and specialty coffee drinks, but the younger set usually prefers to get their jolt from hot chocolate and a sweet roll. An outdoor seating area provides room for kids to wiggle. *11698 San Vicente Blvd., at Barrington Ave., Brentwood; (310) 442-1019;* www.coffeebean.com

Earth, Wind & Flour ★★★★/$

Kids love the pizzas here, and the rustic decor, with sawdust on the floors, seems to welcome them. Parents like the low prices, big

A STARGAZING GUIDE

ARE YOU AND your offspring interested in the lifestyles of the rich and famous? There are several ways to try to get a glimpse at some Los Angeles celebrities and/or their expensive homes.

First, you can just drive aimlessly through Beverly Hills, following any street north off of Sunset Boulevard, and be satisfied by anonymous mansion sightings. A better method is to buy one of those maps to the stars' homes that seem to be sold on every corner, though they're often out of date.

If your children are 8 or older, the best stargazing approach of all is a tour given by a professional guide versed in the latest real estate developments. Call **L.A. Tours** *(323/460-6490)* and a knowledgeable guide in a small van will pick you up at your hotel and give you an intimate guided tour. Among the possibilities on these ever-changing tours is seeing Marilyn Monroe's grave and glimpsing Barbra Streisand way back behind the security gate of her estate. These tours also inform you about little-known and very interesting facts about Beverly Hills: that there are different kinds of trees planted on every block (and that there are no elm trees on Elm Street or maple trees on Maple Street); that in the city's 5.6 square miles there are 155 jewelry stores; that Beverly Hills High School has an operating oil well on its campus. And sometimes they dispense intriguing rumors: that the fire department uses Perrier to put out fires, and that the police department has an unlisted number, to name just two.

Another way for your family to see some movies stars is just to follow the big trucks that transport filming equipment. Los Angeles is really just one giant film set, and one movie or another is being shot somewhere in the city practically every day. You might also try to watch a TV show being taped. Some studios give away free tickets to tapings—the easiest way to get them is at a kiosk outside Universal Studios or in front of Grauman's Chinese Theatre. **NOTE:** Most shows don't permit young children in the audience, with minimum ages ranging from 12 to 16. On the other hand, kids of all ages are welcome on the NBC Studio Tour (see page 236) and at Universal Studios Hollywood theme park (see page 236), where stars are sometimes seen.

Whatever star-searching approach your family takes, you must be very alert. It can be almost as difficult to recognize a star—out of context and looking much smaller than he or she does on the screen—as it is to get near one.

portions, and vast variety of pastas, salads, burgers, and sandwiches. *1776 Westwood Blvd., at Santa Monica Blvd., Westwood; (310) 470-2499;* www.earthwindandflour.com

Palomino
★★★★/$$$$

It's upscale, but family-friendly nonetheless. Young diners enjoy pasta or pizza while their parents feast on fish or spit-roasted meat. Also see Good Eats in San Francisco. *10877 Wilshire Blvd., Westwood; (310) 208-1960;* www.r-u-i.com

Souplantation
★★★★/$

The expansive buffets here make mealtime easy, offering a wide choice of soups, salads, pastas, and plenty more. Kids can pick and choose their food, and everyone leaves full and happy. *11911 San Vicente Blvd., Brentwood; (310) 476-7080.*

SOUVENIR HUNTING

Aahs!

Kids and adults find plenty of things they don't need but want anyway, including kitschy gifts, comic cards, and candy. *1090 Westwood Blvd., Westwood; (310) 824-1688.*

Brentwood Country Mart

Located off the main drag, this red barn of a building houses a variety of shops and restaurants and is a pleasant spot to shop and lunch. Preschoolers can indulge in several kiddie rides nearby. The Hansel and Gretel kids clothing store is also worth a browse, and kids will want to check out Country Mart Toys, which is noisy and full of things they'll like. *225 26th St., at San Vicente Blvd., Brentwood; (310) 395-6714.*

South Barrington Place, Brentwood

This shopping enclave has lots of stores that appeal to kids and parents alike. Ruby Slippers *(171 S. Barrington Pl.; 310/476-0699)* sells really cute children's shoes. A few doors down, Ragg Tattoo *(133 S. Barrington Pl.; 310/440-2989)* has "hot styles for sophisticated kids." For the grand finale, cross the street and reward your kids with a purchase at Star Toys *(130 S. Barrington Pl.; 310/472-2422).*

Summers at Disneyland mean nightly fireworks over Sleeping Beauty Castle.

Anaheim

BEST KNOWN FOR ITS TWO world-famous amusement parks, Disneyland and Knott's Berry Farm, the Anaheim area is chock-full of family activities and familiar fast-food restaurants. Located in Orange County, it is 28 miles south of downtown Los Angeles. There's fun galore here, but when you've had your fill of man-made attractions, you'll find just as many opportunities to commune with nature.

Beach towns are close by, with plenty of spots where kids can explore tide pools and play tag with gentle waves. Bike paths abound, and you can arrange boat excursions. The mountains are also close, with hiking trails and other facilities, and your kids might well want to drop by the several spots that offer miniature golf and ice-skating.

THE **FamilyFun** LIST

MUST-SEE · MUST-SEE

The Disneyland Resort
(page 253)

Knott's Berry Farm
(page 255)

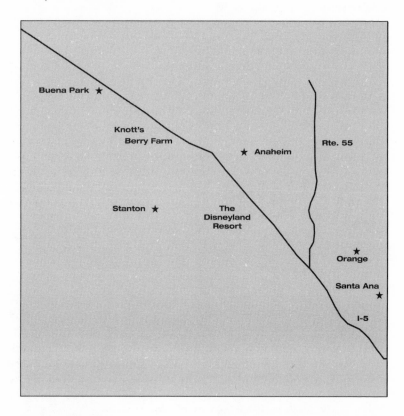

CULTURAL ADVENTURES

Discovery Science Center
★★★/$

To find this "amusement park for your mind," just 10 minutes south of Disneyland, have the kids see who's the first to spot the giant tilted cube on its roof. Kids can run around here unrestrained; exhibits are completely hands-on and interactive. Among those unique to this place are the Shake Shack, where your youngsters can experience three different simulated earthquakes (Newport Beach's 4.7, Santa Barbara's 5.1, and Long Beach's 6.4), and the Bed of Nails, in which kids lie down on a wooden table embedded with 3,500 nails and are then lifted up on the nails (don't worry: it doesn't hurt, and they will discover why). The new Solar Fountain lets them increase and decrease the water level of fountains by moving solar panels, something they'll really go for—especially on a hot summer day. When hunger strikes, pick up a kid- and budget-friendly meal at one of the on-site fast-food restaurants: Pizza Hut or Taco Bell. *2500 N. Main St., Santa Ana; (714) 542-CUBE;* www.discoverycenter.org

JUST FOR FUN

The Block at Orange
★★/Free-$

This mega-entertainment complex, just two miles from Disneyland, is a happenin' place. Its super design means that all you have to do to see everything is follow one circular path. The Block is the site of 100-plus shops, 30 movie screens, and more than 25 eateries, including branches of Jamba Juice and the Wolfgang Puck Cafe. Kids old enough to be on their own while Mom and Dad shop can spend some time Rollerblading and skateboarding at Vans Skate Park. Video games fans will love Powerhouse, a vast space filled with the hottest interactive games (fees for all attractions). *20 City Blvd. W., Orange; (714) 769-4000;* www.theblockat orange.com

The Disneyland Resort
FamilyFun ★★★★/$$$$

When the "happiest place on earth" opened in 1955, it had 20 attractions. Today it has more than 65—including the separate Disney's California Adventure theme park—more than you'll be able to experience in one day. Do some pretrip planning: let the whole family vote on their absolute-can't-leave-here-without-it must-sees—also see "Some Disneyland Tips" on page 265.

The fairy-tale village of Fantasyland appeals to the child in everyone, but your little kids, especially, will love its tame rides. Snow White's Scary Adventures, Mr. Toad's Wild Ride, Peter Pan's Flight, and Pinocchio's Daring Journey (be warned, preschoolers sometimes exit this ride crying) are all enhanced by the original movie sound tracks. The Mad Tea Party, a wild, spinning teacup ride based, of course, on *Alice in Wonderland,* is here. The It's a Small World ride is here as well. Children 6 and under love it; most adults get a kick out of it the first time (be prepared: your little ones will want to go round and round on this one). Check this one out during the winter; the ride and its famous song are sometimes transformed for the holidays.

Disneyland has three well-disguised roller coasters, all of which can be scary for your preschoolers but will delight bigger kids. They go fast, but don't have any steep drops; even scaredy-cat adults who usually hate roller coasters often find themselves enjoying these. Big Thunder Mountain Railroad mimics, with appropriate scenery, a runaway mine train. It's fast, but stays low to the ground. The Matterhorn Bobsleds is a more traditional coaster that whips through a series of tunnels; riders don't see its skeletal frame and so don't reel from the sensation of being up high. Space Mountain, one of the park's most popular rides, is a speed demon of a coaster that flies through a dark, starlit space inside a man-made mountain structure. **NOTE:** It is not for the timid, weak of heart, or pregnant.

Other attractions include Star Tours, a simulated ride through space designed by movie mogul George Lucas (it cost more to build than the entire park did in 1955!); Mickey's Toontown, where everything is askew—preschoolers will like these rides—and the Indiana Jones Adventure, a Jeep ride that is eerily like the movie. To get a sense of Disneyland's awesome size, take a trip on either the monorail or the Disneyland Railroad. In summer, you'll want to stay around for the nighttime parade and fireworks that close each day.

The newest theme park, **Disney's California Adventure,** is adjacent to the existing park. Celebrating the special magic of the California dream, its three themed lands focus on the beach, moviemaking, and the state's natural wonders. Among the regional adventures is a beachfront boardwalk and a white-water rafting expedition; for those who can't bear to leave, the new 750-room Grand Californian destination resort hotel is inside the park. Your littlest ones will enjoy Flik's Fun Fair featuring a mini railroad, bus-themed car ride, and a playground with sprinklers. Disneyland and Disney's California Adventure are connected by a public esplanade lined with shops and restaurants.

As you might expect, all the restaurants at Disneyland offer lots of children's favorite eats. And the addition of Disney's California Adventure has really upped the quotient of Mom and Dad eats. Breakfast is a piece of cake, or a pancake, because the lines haven't started yet. You can have a buffet breakfast with the Disney characters at the Plaza Inn on Main Street, U.S.A. or grab something quicker and get a jump on the rides. At lunch, you can try the Cafe Orleans in New Orleans Square, where a terrace overlooks the main waterway. The River Belle Terrace in Frontierland is another good lunchtime choice, with cafeteria service and a good view of the action. For dinner, the best restau-

Tuesdays, Wednesdays, and Thursdays are **Disneyland's** least-crowded days.

rants are the priciest and the most crowded. Avoid the rush by dining before 6 or after 8. Or take the monorail to the Disneyland Hotel and choose from among the half dozen restaurants there. (See Good Eats for some recommended dining spots.)

Moms and Dads are in for a pleasant surprise when potty time rolls around. The rest rooms are immaculate and equipped with changing tables and diaper machines. Stop at the Baby Care Center to prepare formulas, warm bottles, and change infants; you can buy baby paraphernalia, too, and rent strollers just outside the main entrance. *1313 Harbor Blvd., Anaheim; (714) 781-4565; www.disneyland.com*

Knott's Berry Farm
FamilyFun ★★★★/$$$$

Your older kids may be interested in the story behind this, the nation's oldest theme amusement park. It all began back in the 1920s when Walter Knott's neighbor, a Mr. Boysen, began trying to develop a cross between the blackberry, loganberry, and red raspberry, which he called the boysenberry. Boysen abandoned the project, but Knott took up where he left off and then began selling the delicious new

berry variety to the public. During the Depression, Knott's wife, Cordelia, began serving chicken dinners at the couple's boysenberry farm. By the 1940s the meals were famous, attracting long lines of diners. So Mr. Knott built a replica of an Old West town on his property to entertain people during their long wait to eat. In 1966, the family decided to enclose and expand the park and charge admission—and Knott's Berry Farm was born.

About 15 minutes north of Disneyland in the town of Buena Park, Knott's Berry Farm is a low-key and less congested place than its more famous neighbor. Still owned by the Knott family, it has a homier feel. The Magic Kingdom is a hard act to follow, but the Farm can stand on its own. Just don't visit the day after a visit to Disneyland, because you'll find yourselves simply too tired to take full advantage of all that Knott's has to offer.

Your kids can pan for real gold, snack on old-time funnel cakes, and ride in an authentic Butterfield Stagecoach through a dusty 1880s Old West Ghost Town. At Camp Snoopy, your preschoolers can try the tame rides and visit an old-fashioned petting farm, as well as the Huff and

CORDELIA KNOTT served her first chicken dinners to the public on her wedding china. The meals cost each customer just sixty-five cents.

Puff car ride and Woodstock's Airmail, a mini-Supreme Scream drop ride for little thrill-seekers. The lovable beagle and his friends will pose for pictures, too. The Kingdom of the Dinosaurs showcases 21 fully animated figures on a seven-minute ride. Sprinkled throughout these theme areas is an assortment of live shows plus hair-raising roller coasters, including Montezooma's Revenge, which goes from 0 to 55 mph in less than five seconds, and the new Excellerator. The hideous, 30-story Supreme Scream drop ride is the tallest structure in Orange County; fearless preteens and teens will love it, but it's much too stomach-turning for anyone else. Ghost-Rider, which resembles a precarious toothpick sculpture, is the tallest (118 feet) and longest (1,511 yards) wooden roller coaster in the West and might also be the most thrilling. The newest ride to cause a splash is Perilous Plunge—the tallest and steepest water ride in the world. If you visit during October, your kids can enjoy Halloween Haunt at Knott's Scary Farm, when the park is transformed into a spooky, but fun, nighttime adventure. In September and October your preschoolers can head right to Camp Spooky, a nonscary Halloween celebration for ages 3 through 11 (costumes are encouraged for this age group only). There are also nearly 20 places to eat, including sit-down restaurants and fast-food places.

8039 Beach Blvd., Buena Park; (714) 220-5200; www.knotts.com

Soak City U.S.A.
★★★★/$$$

This new 13-acre water adventure park, directly across the street from Knott's Berry Farm, has 21 themed water rides and attractions for all ages. Wet and wonderful highlights include 16 slides, a giant wave pool, the three-story Toyota Beach House water fun house, the Gremmie Lagoon kids' water playground, and a Lazy River that's a third of a mile long. *8039 Beach Blvd., Buena Park; (714) 220-5200;* www.knotts.com

Movieland Wax Museum
★★/$$

Don't have time to hit Hollywood? Take the short tour—where you can guarantee the kids that they'll see a star or two. Just a block from Knott's Berry Farm, this wax museum displays more than 400 lifelike figures of famous movie and TV stars that the grade-school crowd will especially enjoy (ages 6 through 13). Bring your camera so the kids will be able to amaze their friends with pictures with their favorite celebrities. If you have preschoolers or fearful older kids, skip the Chamber of Horrors and its displays of Dracula, Frankenstein, and Jason. The well-stocked candy concession within the gift shop is another maybe yes/maybe no stop. Pooped parents take note: a Starbucks is out front inside an odd round building. You can get combination tickets with Ripley's Believe It or Not! Museum *(see below). 7711 Beach Blvd., Buena Park; (714) 522-1154;* www.movie landwaxmuseum.com

Ripley's Believe It or Not! Museum
★★/$

Here are the biggest, smallest, tallest, strangest, and most bizarre things you'll ever see. Your kids (and maybe you, too) might be interested to know that Mr. Ripley, who was a famous cartoonist in his time, was a believe-it-or-not kind of guy in real life. To wit: he was born on Christmas Day at the beginning of the last century; he drew his cartoons with his art board upside down (starting at the bottom of the drawing and finishing at the top) and only between the hours of 7 and 11 A.M.; he owned five cars but didn't drive; and he visited 198 countries in search of the unique, bizarre, and beautiful. While touring this collection of curiosities, be on the lookout for the educational (primitive currency), the bizarre (shrunken heads), the entertaining (a work of art made with clothes-dryer lint), and the unique (a cow with two heads and a man with four eyes). The little ones might find some stuff too strange and scary, but kids ages 6 through 13 will love it. *7850 Beach Blvd., Buena Park; (714) 522-7045;* www.ripleysbuenapark.com

Bunking Down

In Disneyland

For information on Disneyland hotels, call *(714) 781-4565.* To make reservations at any Disneyland hotel, call *(714) 956-MICKEY.* For information on Disneyland vacation packages, call *(877) 700-DISNEY.*

The Disneyland Hotel
★★★★/$$$

This first-class Official Hotel of the Magic Kingdom gives you and your kids the convenience and fun of entering and leaving Disneyland by monorail. It is modern, luxurious—and expensive. Located on what was formerly an innocuous grove of

FamilyFun GAME

Color Safari

This all-ages game is easily adaptable to your kids' attention spans and the amount of time you have to play. All you do is agree on a basic color—such as red, blue, green, or yellow—and challenge your kids to find 100 items that are this color. Younger kids can play a shortened version—counting items to 10 or even 25; older kids will be challenged if you set a time limit and make them race against one another. You can also give each player a different color to search for.

orange trees, the huge resort complex boasts 990 rooms and could easily qualify as a vacation destination in its own right. Your kids will love the huge new, lushly landscaped, tropical Never Land pool, with its wood-and-rope suspension bridge, a bubbling Jacuzzi with a mermaid statue, and 100-foot-long water slide through Skull Rock. Another children's pool is landscaped to resemble a Tahitian beach, complete with real sand and palm trees. There's also a 165-foot waterfall on the grounds, and at scheduled times children and enthusiastic adults can take a fistful of fish food, put their hands right into the koi pond, and let the fish suck up their meal in a feeding frenzy. It's a memorable and very photogenic experience! Room TVs are hooked up to the Disney Channel, and Mickey Mouse provides the morning wake-up call. The family-oriented hotel has supervised recreational activities for kids ages 4 through 12 each night from 6 to 11 P.M. Children's menus,

high chairs, and booster seats are available in the hotel's restaurants. Family-friendly? You bet! *1150 W. Magic Way, Anaheim; (714) 956-MICKEY;* www.disneyland.com

Disney's Grand Californian Hotel
★★★★/$$$-$$$$

This deluxe, 750-room destination resort hotel, located inside Disney's California Adventure, is done up in Craftsman style, resembling a massive national park lodge. A "boulder" wall dominates the vast, open lobby. Some rooms have balconies overlooking the park, and some have bunk beds. All have luxurious marble baths, minibars, coffeemakers, and robes (children's robes are provided upon request); portable cribs are also available. Facilities include two heated pools with a water slide, two hot tubs, a children's pool shaped like Mickey Mouse, and a fitness center. The kids will also enjoy breakfast with Chip 'N' Dale in the Storytellers Café. *1600 S. Disneyland Dr., Anaheim; (714) 956-MICKEY;* www.disneyland.com

Disney's Paradise Pier Hotel
★★★★/$$$

Next door to the Disneyland Hotel and part of the Disneyland Resort complex, this hotel has 502 spacious and comfortable rooms that have either two double beds or a king-size bed plus a sofa bed. All have coffeemakers. You can easily reach the monorail ride into Disneyland after you've entered the park via the main gates. The pool and a hot tub are great for refreshing after-the-theme-park dips and soaks, and Mom and Dad can try the fully equipped fitness center. Take the kids to a traditional English "Practically Perfect Tea" in a Victorian-style tearoom, with entertainment by everyone's favorite nanny, Mary Poppins. You'll need to call ahead for a reservation for this one *(714/956-6755)*. *1717 S. Disneyland Dr., Anaheim; (714) 956-MICKEY;* www.disneyland.com

Near Disneyland

Anaheim Plaza Hotel & Suites
★★/$-$$

Currently right across from the Disneyland entrance (although this could change), this well-priced 300-room hotel has spacious grassy grounds with a pool, a hot tub, and a video-game room. Some family suites can accommodate up to eight people, and all rooms have a coffeemaker and small refrigerator. The seven two-story buildings are spread over nine acres landscaped with flowers and mature palms. You get a free hookup to the Disney Channel, too. The Parkside Grill has a view of the park. *1700 S. Harbor Blvd., Anaheim; (800) 532-4517; (714) 772-5900;* www.anaheimplazahotel.com

Castle Inn & Suites
★★★/$$

The whole family will feel like roy-alty here. Across the street from Disney's California Adventure, this colorful 200-room motel resembles a medieval castle. Larger families will appreciate the two-room family suites, and Mom and Dad will like the complimentary morning coffee. Transportation is available to Disneyland. There's a heated pool, hot tub, and children's wading pool, too. *1734 S. Harbor Blvd., Anaheim; (800) CASTLE-0; (714) 774-8111;* www.castleinn.com

Embassy Suites
★★★/$$-$$$

Two Embassy Suites hotels are within convenient commuting distance of Disneyland. The 222-room Disneyland branch is six miles from Disneyland, and you get complimentary shuttle service to the theme park. The 201-room Buena Park branch is five miles from Disneyland and also provides a free shuttle; right across the street from Movieland Wax Museum, it is within walking distance of five major attractions, including Knott's Berry Farm. Perfect for families, both hotels offer spacious two-room suites (a bedroom plus a separate living room with a sofa bed). Each unit has two TVs and a kitchenette with a coffeemaker and a refrigerator. The kids will love the indoor heated pool and hot tub; there's a sauna and a fitness center to soothe and stretch grown-up muscles. Take advantage of the free cooked-to-order breakfast. An

Travel Trivia

My husband and I wanted our family trip to be both educational and fun for our 9 and 11 year old boys. To engage their interest, we devised a game to play while sightseeing. Every morning I would give my sons three questions pertaining to the places we would visit that day. If they answered all three they could order the dessert of their choice at dinner. They could use any resource, including a plaque at the site, a tour guide, brochures, and the like. They thought it was great fun to win a dessert off Mom and Dad, and they were so successful that we bought a round every night. Websites and guide-books were our sources for the questions. With that little bit of preparation, our kids ended up not only having a great time but learning a lot, too.

Kathy Davis, Charlotte, North Carolina

evening cocktail reception for all ages includes snack foods. *3100 E. Frontera, Anaheim; (714) 632-1221. Also at 7762 Beach Blvd., Buena Park; (714) 739-5600; (800) EMBASSY (for both);* www.embassysuites.com

Hilton Anaheim
★★★/$$-$$$$

Just two minutes from Disneyland (transportation is available; there's a fee), this 1,600-room megahotel has a rooftop recreation deck with an outdoor pool and hot tub; a fitness center with an indoor pool, four hot tubs, and a basketball court; a spa; a three-story atrium lobby; and seven restaurants. All rooms have coffeemakers, and you can request a small refrigerator. The Vacation Station program allows kids ages 5 through 12 to register at their own desk; they are given a membership button that gets them

free movies and more. **NOTE:** This place is so big that even adults can get lost, so keep an eye on wandering little ones. *777 Convention Way, Anaheim; (800) HILTONS; (800) 222-9923; (714) 750-4321;* www. hilton.com

Holiday Inn— Anaheim at the Park
★★★/$$

Just across the freeway from Disney-land, this hotel offers some fun of its own. The nicely landscaped pool area has a children's dancing water foun-tain (they can try to catch the water before it catches them) and there's a small video-game room that is open around the clock. Transportation to Disneyland is available (there's a fee). All rooms have coffeemakers, and you can get a refrigerator for a small fee. Kids eat free at the convenient Poppy Cafe, which is just off the lobby. *1221 S. Harbor Blvd., Anaheim; (800) HOLIDAY; (714) 758-0900;* www.6continents.com; www.holiday-inn.com/anaheim-park

Motel Row

Motels line Katella Avenue and Harbour Boulevard in Anaheim.

Portofino Inn & Suites
★★★/$-$$

Bargain prices are the lure here, just across from Disneyland. Or you can pay a little bit more for a Kid's Suite; it sleeps six, with a separate room with a king-size bed for the grown-ups, and a kids' room with bunk beds. All rooms have coffeemakers, and you can request a small refrigerator. The kids will go for the heated pool and hot tub, a fitness center, and a video arcade; grown-ups will appreciate the restaurant, free parking, and a shuttle to Disneyland ($2 for anyone age 9 or over). *1831 S. Harbor Blvd., Anaheim; (800) 482-8389; (714) 491-2400;* www.portofino-inn.com

Sheraton Anaheim Hotel
★★★/$$-$$$

Built to resemble a medieval castle, this attractive, plush, well-equipped and nicely landscaped 489-room hotel has a really nice central courtyard pool area, a fitness center, two restaurants, and shuttle service to Disneyland. All rooms are equipped with coffeemakers; some open onto grassy expanses. In addition to the pool, the kids will particularly like the indoor-outdoor koi pond and the stream that meanders through the lobby. *909 S. Disneyland Dr., Anaheim; (800) 325-3535; (714) 778-1700;* www.sheraton.com

At Knott's Berry Farm

Radisson Resort Knott's Berry Farm
★★★★/$$$

Situated just a few steps from the Farm, this deluxe 321-room hotel offers extra-special Camp Snoopy rooms in a soundproofed section that is painted in primary colors. Kids can play in the cozy halls, featuring Snoopy characters on the walls and green carpet "grass" on the floor. The rooms are done in Snoopy-theme decor and accessories, and each family gets one plush Snoopy to take home. Upon check-in, every child also gets a miniature stuffed Snoopy and a cup that can be filled endlessly with soft drinks at the hotel restaurant. *Shhhhh!* Don't tell the kids: you can order the Snoopy Sleep Tight service, and at bedtime Snoopy will show up with a chocolate dog bone and a hug for your child (have the camera ready). Other pluses on the premises is a pool, a hot tub, two lighted tennis courts, a fitness center, and an arcade game room. The Cucina Cucina Italian Cafe serves up pizza and more, and the Citrus Café is open for light fare. Bowling to the competition, the hotel provides a free shuttle to Disneyland. A variety of packages are available. *7675 Crescent Ave., Buena Park; (800) 333-3333; (714) 220-5130;* www.radisson.com

GOOD EATS

At Disneyland

Blue Bayou Restaurant
★★/$$

Located next to the Pirates of the Caribbean ride, this popular place re-creates a starlit Louisiana bayou and serves up classic chicken, fish, and beef entrées. *New Orleans Square, Disneyland;* www.disneyland.com

French Market ★★/$$
Also in New Orleans Square, this eatery offers chicken, ribs, and

---

Castle, Sweet Castle

Sleeping Beauty Castle is significantly smaller than any of the other Disney theme park castles because during its construction, Walt Disney had recalled stories concerning the building of European castles. Often, the huge castles were built to intimidate the peasants. Walt believed a smaller castle would be a friendlier castle.

---

shrimp dishes as well as some Cajun-style specialties. A Dixieland jazz band plays on the terrace throughout the evening. *New Orleans Square, Disneyland;* www.disneyland.com

Goofy's Kitchen
★★★★/$$$

Featuring appearances by Disney characters, this breakfast and lunch buffet is open in summer and during holidays. Your kids can collect autographs and you can take pictures in between tanking up on made-to-order omelettes and Mickey pancakes and waffles. Disney music classics play in the background, and the kids can eat and stare in awe and wander freely. But whatever you do, don't mix up Pluto and Goofy, or you might suffer a noisy lick. Reservations are advised. *Disneyland Hotel, 1150 Magic Way, Anaheim; (714) 956-6510;* www.disneyland.com

Disney's PCH Grill ★★★★/$$$
This comfortable restaurant in the Disney's Paradise Pier Hotel offers sophisticated California-style family dining in the evening. The kid's Magical Meals menu offers the popular Pluto's Pizza: kids shape a ball of pizza dough, add toppings of their choice, and then deliver it to the chef for baking. Some parents find themselves barging in to help—don't you be one of them. The Mom-and-Dad menu includes main courses such as baby back ribs, wood-fired designer pizzas, and fish and steak

items. This is really one happy, happy place. In the morning, this is the site of the buffet Breakfast with Minnie & Friends. *Paradise Pier Hotel, 1717 S. Disneyland Dr., Anaheim; (714) 956-6510;* www.disneyland.com

At Knott's Berry Farm

Mrs. Knott's Chicken Dinner Restaurant
★★★★/$-$$

Begin your day with a hearty farm breakfast—eggs and pancakes and cereal and baskets of buttermilk biscuits served with plenty of butter and Knott's berry preserves. Note that the restaurant is outside the entrance to Knott's Berry Farm, so you can eat here whether you actually visit the theme park or not. Also, stop in for one of the famous fried chicken lunches or dinners. The bargain-priced dinner consists of homemade chicken noodle soup or a green salad, homemade biscuits, real mashed potatoes with gravy, super-delicious fried chicken, and a hunk of boysenberry pie. More than 1.5 million of these dinners are served annually, so there's usually a line. It starts getting long at around 5 P.M., and reservations are not accepted. A kids' menu offers the usual small-fry alternatives, including an American cheese sandwich on white bread with potato chips and strawberry gelatin. Yum. *8039 Beach Blvd., Buena Park, in the Marketplace; (714) 220-5080;* www.knotts.com

Elsewhere in the Anaheim Area

Medieval Times
★★★★/$$$$

As if Los Angeles weren't bizarre enough, enter Medieval Times—a "dinner and jousting tournament." It is practically across the street from Knott's Berry Farm and ten minutes from Disneyland.

Jousting is a sport in which, according to one ad, "knights on horseback compete at breakneck speed in tournament competitions that end with a clash of swords and breathtaking battles." Here they do all this and more while the audience, seated in a large amphitheater, munches on dinner in between cheering for their assigned knight of the evening.

As the pageantry begins, dinner is served by a bevy of serfs and wenches. Kids love the idea that the four-course feast consists of finger foods, so they don't have to use any utensils—they feast on roasted chicken, ribs, and baked potatoes and then, stuffed to the brim, anxiously await dessert. (Some of the "battles" might be too intense for children under 8.) The audience really gets into booing and cheering, making a hectic family dinner at home seem tame by comparison. Reservations are required. *7662 Beach Blvd., Buena Park; (800) 899-6600; (714) 521-4740.*

Spaghetti Station Restaurant and Old West Museum
★★★/$-$$

Situated inside a rustic wood building and featuring an Old West theme, this place knows how to please the whole family. The Young 'Uns Menu offers a Pony Pizza (with pepperoni and mozzarella) and a Sugarfoot Sal (spaghetti with tomato sauce), while the regular menu offers 14 kinds of spaghetti. It's a popular place, and takes reservations only for groups of eight or more, so expect a wait in the evening. *999 W. Ball Rd., Anaheim; (714) 956-3250.*

The Train McDonald's
★★★★/$

One block north of Knott's, this very big branch features a gift shop selling collectible McDonald's plates. The big excitement for kids, however, is watching the three trains chug around the establishment. *7861 Beach Blvd., Buena Park; (714) 521-2303; www.mcdonalds.com*

Wild Bill's Wild West Dinner Extravaganza
★★★★/$$$$

At this Western-themed dinner theater you'll get a four-course dinner and loud family entertainment that is squeaky clean. The show includes cancan dancers, Native American dancers, sensational rope tricks performed by a smiling cowgirl, and a very funny comedian. There are

buckets filled with a delicious beef-barley soup, buttermilk biscuits with whipped honey butter, tossed salad, fried chicken and barbecued ribs, plus sides of corn on the cob and baked potatoes. Reservations are advised. *7600 Beach Blvd., Buena Park; (800) 883-1546; (714) 522-6414.*

SOUVENIR HUNTING

Of course, Anaheim's two main attractions, Disneyland and Knott's Berry Farm, have plenty of places to buy gifts and mementos of your visit.

Hobby City

Everyone in your family will find something of interest in this collection of crafts and collectibles shops. The complex includes the American Indian store in a real log cabin and the Doll and Toy Museum and gift shop, housed in a half-scale model of the White House. Hobby City: *1238 S. Beach Blvd., Anaheim; (714) 527-2323.*

After shopping, you can have some fun next door at low-key Adventure City (*10200 S. Beach Blvd., Stanton; 714/236-9300*), a three-acre theme park designed for kids 2 through 12 and their families. It has 17 attractions, including kiddie rides, an interactive live theater, and a petting farm.

SOME DISNEYLAND TIPS

- Friday is generally the lightest attendance day; Saturday is the heaviest. The week before Thanksgiving is said to have the lightest crowds of the year, with the week before Christmas also said to be light. Plan accordingly.
- When you make your lodging reservations, inquire about packages.
- To save money, stay in a nearby motel with shuttle service to the park. But be aware that not all shuttles are the same. Some hotels provide dedicated shuttles that service only their guests. Others subscribe to a service that stops at a series of hotels on the way to and from the park.
- Note that Disneyland keeps changing its gate location. Booking into a motel that is across the street from the entrance is only helpful if you're sure the entrance won't be moved again before you arrive.
- Arrive at the park when the gates open, go back to your hotel for a nap or a swim when the park gets hot and crowded in the afternoon, and then return to the park refreshed for dinner in the evening.
- Go on as many rides as is humanly possible before 11 A.M.,

when everything starts getting crowded.
- Plan to eat at off times, as park food lines can be ridiculous.
- Bring along bottled water. You can purchase cute souvenir straps to hold them.
- Don't miss Disneyland at night. The atmosphere is totally different than during the day. The very popular parade of Disney characters is a must for preschoolers, and there's often live band music geared to pre-teens and teens. The fabulous fireworks display will thrill everyone.
- Disneyland does have a lot of lines. Plan to use the waits to engage in some of that "quality time" we parents hear so much about but usually have so little actual time for. To paraphrase John Lennon, life is what happens while you're waiting in line for the ride.
- Accept that you can't possibly see and do everything in one day. You'll simply have to save something for next time.
- For a special thrill, your children won't soon forget, secretly purchase a postcard depicting their favorite Disney character. Compose a message from the character and mail it to your home before you return.

For some classic Americana, put the top down and cruise the Pacific Coast Highway.

Southern California Beach Towns

P ERHAPS THE BEST way to arrive at a Southern California beach town is in a convertible, or at least in a car with all the windows open, and with a tape or CD blaring Beach Boys music. Children will love the catchy tunes, even if they're hearing them for the first time. Leave Los Angeles via Sunset Strip, winding past the mansions of Beverly Hills, past the UCLA campus, past Dead Man's Curve (which Jan and Dean warned about in a famous sixties song), on through the exclusive Pacific Palisades residential area, and then to the splendid blue expanse of the Pacific Ocean at Pacific Coast Highway.

From here you can head up the coast to Malibu, where the stars have homes hugging the beaches and the hills—but where anyone can plop a beach blanket down wherever they

THE **FamilyFun** LIST

MUST-SEE ★ MUST-SEE

Aquarium of the Pacific
  (page 278)

Mission San Juan Capistrano
  (page 287)

The Queen Mary (page 277)

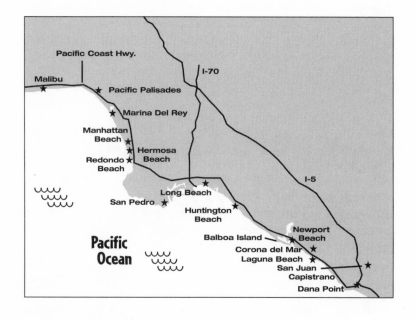

Pacific Coast Hwy.
Malibu
Pacific Palisades
I-70
Marina Del Rey
Manhattan Beach
Hermosa Beach
Redondo Beach
Long Beach
I-5
San Pedro
Huntington Beach
Pacific Ocean
Newport Beach
Balboa Island
Corona del Mar
Laguna Beach
San Juan Capistrano
Dana Point

find space. Try stopping for necessities at one of the shopping malls in these parts—it's fun. Who is that familiar-looking person studying the Band-Aid box?

After (or instead of) a trip to Malibu, head south down the coast from L.A. A string of tiny beach towns—Hermosa Beach, Huntington Beach, Laguna Beach—lines the Pacific Ocean here, and each offers fun, fun, fun for beach boys and girls of all ages.

Either way, your family can look forward to leisurely days together on the beach—dodging waves, building sand castles, boogie-boarding, taking long walks, or just digging holes in the sand and watching them fill with water. Don't forget the sunscreen!

Malibu

Beginning eight miles northwest of Santa Monica, the Malibu strand hugs the sea for 25 miles, extending inland about three miles. The ulti-

mate beach, this area is home to some of the richest and most famous people in Hollywood—people whose names your young movie buffs will recognize. The landmark Malibu Pier, about 12 miles from Santa Monica, is at its center. To reach Malibu, follow the Pacific Coast Highway north. Many of the area's mega-homes are invisible from the road—your kids will be asking about who lives in the "castles." Leave your windows open on the ocean side, the better to hear the waves. You can stop in many spots and be right on the beach in minutes.

NOTE: Around these parts, people in the know refer to the Pacific Coast Highway as P.C.H., so we will, too.

Just for Fun

Malibu Lagoon State Beach
★★/Free

In this wild and wonderful spot, your kids will enjoy hiking the nature trails, searching the tide pools, watching the surfers, and picnicking. Surrounded by a magnificent ornate brick fence, the property has an almost castlelike appearance. Wednesday through Saturday your family can tour the historic Moorish-Spanish Colonial Revival–style Adamson House on the grounds. The house is famous for its special custom-built features and lavish use of exquisite ceramic tiles, all made in Malibu in the 1920s. The adjoining Malibu Lagoon Museum ($) tells the area's history through artifacts and photographs. Just north of the lagoon is the Malibu Colony, a pricey, gated residential enclave

No Time to Spend the Night?

Here's a suggested itinerary for a day trip to Malibu from Los Angeles.

9:30 A.M. Beat the beach crowds by getting up early and having breakfast at **Gladstone's 4 Fish** in Malibu.

10:30 A.M. Drive up Pacific Coast Highway, stopping at the **Malibu Pier** for a stroll.

11:30 A.M. Drive farther up the highway to one of the **pocket beaches.** Park your car and select your sunning spot. (Don't forget sunscreen and snacks.)

1:30 P.M. Pack it up and head to the **Malibu Country Mart** for a late lunch. You can hang out at the Coffee Bean and do some shopping—and perhaps some star-spotting.

3 P.M. By now you've probably had enough sun. Head back to Los Angeles via Sunset Strip, getting off at the **UCLA campus.** This is a great spot to rest on the grass for a while.

5 P.M. Return to your hotel. Rest up and then off to dinner.

almost as famous as its celebrity residents. *23200 P.C.H., Malibu; (310) 456-8432;* www.adamsonhouse.org

Pocket Beaches
★★★/$

As you drive along the P.C.H., have your kids keep their eyes open for the turnoffs to these delightful little beaches. Among the best bets are El Matador, La Piedra (the foot—see if the kids can figure out where the name came from), and El Pescador beaches. You'll have to pay for parking, so you might as well plan to stay a while. *(805) 488-1827.*

Surfrider Beach
★★/Free

Tucked into a cove between Malibu Pier and Malibu Lagoon State Beach, this famous surfing spot is great for people-watching both on the surf and on the sand. *P.C.H./Sweetwater Canyon Rd., Malibu.*

BUNKING DOWN

Casa Malibu
★★/$$-$$$

Though it has very little street appeal, once you're in the lobby you'll quickly see that this standard motel has been turned into something much more. It's a tropical fantasyland, with thriving plants aplenty. The 19 rooms and two suites have tasteful cottage decor; some have full kitchens or fireplaces. Some of the rooms adjoin—handy for families. Though well- priced garden-view rooms are available, and all the rooms are just a few steps from the beach, consider splurging on a beachfront room with a private deck. *22752 P.C.H., Malibu; (800) 831-0858; (310) 456-2219.*

GOOD EATS

Duke's Malibu
★★★/$$-$$$

Great food in great surroundings, not to mention a killer view, are reason enough to stop here for a relaxing meal. Also see Good Eats in Huntington Beach. *21150 P.C.H., Malibu; (310) 317-0777;* www.hulapie.com

Gladstone's 4 Fish
★★★/$$

The sawdust on the floors bodes well—this place is kid-friendly. The large wooden booths are prime real estate—and even better when they are windowside, with a view of the ocean. In good weather take everybody to a table on the outside deck. The menu for all three meals is available all day. This means that kids can order up scrambled eggs for dinner (the grown-ups may prefer seafood, the house specialty). Get a head start on the crowds by stopping here for breakfast, or plan on dinner (and lots of company) on your way back down the coast. Reservations are accepted. *17300 P.C.H./Sunset Blvd., Malibu; (310) GL-4-FISH; www.gladstones.com*

Inn of the Seventh Ray
★★★/$$-$$$

A few miles inland from Pacific Coast Highway in rural Topanga, this magical natural foods restaurant is reached via a winding back road. Your family will love it for lunch or weekend brunch—but avoid the evenings, when it's hopelessly romantic with incense and fairyland lights, and much less fun with kids along. Prices are quite reasonable, considering that all foods are house made and the cooks use no preservatives, food colorings, sugar, or bleached flour. Normally hyper kids might actually come away feeling calm. Pick a creekside table outdoors under the sycamore trees, where birds chirp happily, and just sit back and delight in the good vibes. Many people take streamside strolls after their meal, and deer sometimes show up at dusk. You can get delightful vegetarian, vegan, and macrobiotic dishes, along with chicken and fish. For lunch, try the salads or sandwiches; sometimes fondue is available, the perfect dish for a family to share. Brunch brings on omelettes and waffles and sweet rolls. It's surprising to find valet parking in this rural area, but remember, this is still L.A. (FYI: Topanga Canyon is known as a UFO hot spot. Older kids might relish the area's creepy claim to fame; younger kids might not.) *128 Old Topanga Canyon Rd., Topanga Canyon; (310) 455-1311; www.innoftheseventhray.com*

Paradise Cove Beach Cafe
★★★★/$$

Drive off the highway and down a narrow road to reach this gem of a spot on the beach. Kids can grab some peanuts from the barrel by the door to tide them over until their meals come. The veritable sea of comfy booths all have ocean views. Standard breakfast and lunch fare are kid-friendly, and at dinner you'll find pricier entrées. Children's choices include chicken fingers, grilled cheese,

Beach Butterflies

Before summer flies by, turn your family's beach finds into colorful keepsakes. For each butterfly, you'll need a matching pair of small or medium-size clean, dry mussel, clam, or oyster shells. Arrange the pair side by side with the inner surfaces facedown and the hinged edges flush. Hot-glue the hinged edges together (a parent's job), creating a strong bond. Then bend a 6-inch pipe cleaner length into a V and curl the tips to create antennae. Hot-glue the base of the V to the top of the glued joint. Flip over the butterfly, and your child can paint the inner shells with a distinctive wing pattern.

and peanut-butter-and-jelly, and all come with fries, a drink, and ice cream (there are seafood dishes for Mom and Dad). You get three hours of free parking, so use the rest of the time to frolic on the sandy beach. *28128 P.C.H., Malibu; (310) 457-2503.*

PierView Cafe & Cantina
★★★★/$-$$

On a nice day, you can enjoy a casual breakfast or lunch seated on a deck abutting the beach. But even on cooler days you get a great ocean view from inside, where there's kid-friendly sawdust on the floor. Lots of appetizers and specialty bar drinks make it a great place just to stop just for a snack. The menu is simple—salads, sandwiches, pizza, hamburgers—and the kids' coloring menu includes peanut-butter-and-jelly sandwiches and spaghetti, and the like. *22718 P.C.H., Malibu; (310) 456-6962.* www.pierviewcafe.com

SOUVENIR HUNTING

Malibu Colony Plaza

Even the rich and famous some-times need to shop at a grocery store, stop at the drugstore, or pick up a video—and this is where they go in Malibu. While they're here, they sometimes pop into Coogie's Beach Cafe *(310/317-1444),* a simple coffee shop that serves great whole-wheat pancakes. Steven Spielberg, Danny DeVito, and Ron Howard

have all been spotted here. *23700 P.C.H., on the ocean side, Malibu;* http://www.seeing-stars.com/Shop/MalibuPlaza.shtml

Malibu Country Mart

The town has no center, but this informal town square is a bustling hub, with restaurants, a busy playground, and picnic tables. Residents come here to buy both necessities and luxuries in a shopping complex that resembles a spiffed-up Third World bazaar. It sprawls on both sides of the road and includes a branch of Coffee Bean, the very trendy L.A. coffeehouse chain, and a bargain taqueria that uses organic beans and plenty of vegetarian options. The movie theater sometimes screens children's films, and the stars, including Cher and Bob Dylan, have been seen bringing their offspring here for a flick. The whole family will enjoy stopping at the mart for a snack. Keep your eyes peeled. The stars are here. *3835 Cross Creek Rd., on mountain side of P.C.H., Malibu.*

Marina Del Rey

Los Angeles's version of the French Riviera, Marina Del Rey is where the stars anchor their yachts. Boasting the world's largest man-made small-craft harbor, the town is home to 6,000 in-the-water private yachts. Activities here are simple. Rent bikes or roller skates and explore some of the 22 miles of scenic off-road trails. Put on your swimsuits and soak up some rays. Stroll around and look at the neat boats. Have fun.

Marina del Rey is a quiet retreat from the frenetic pace of L.A. proper, yet is only an easy 20-minute drive away (when the traffic is moving normally). It's also a convenient 10-minute taxi ride north of Los Angeles International Airport, making it a good spot to visit during layovers.

BUNKING DOWN

Jamaica Bay Inn
★★★/$$-$$$

With only 42 rooms, this small, two-floor hotel overlooks what is known as Mother's Beach—a waveless, placid section of the marina bordered by a groomed stretch of sand. The property also has a pool and hot tub plus a popular beachfront café. All rooms have refrigerators and microwaves, and children under 17 stay free. And even this modest inn

attracts stars. On one splendid afternoon here, a commercial for a soft drink was being filmed by the pool, and Gena Rowlands was spotted out

A Watery Wonderland

If you're in Marina Del Rey in December, you can watch the **Tournament of Lights Holiday Boat Parade**—in which local boats don their holiday finery. Held at Christmastime for more than three decades, the fabulous, and free, two-hour display of festively decorated and lighted vessels begins with a fireworks display. It's quite a sight. Some of the boats are strung with twinkling lights, while others are decorated elaborately in theme, perhaps with live bands, caroling groups, or costumed characters such as Santa and Frosty on board. Kids from northern climates will get a big kick out of seeing such warm Christmas festivities. Best viewing spots are from Burton Chace Park, which has a playground in its center, and Fisherman's Village, a themed shopping center with cobblestone walkways and a miniature lighthouse. *(310) 822-9455.*

FamilyFun TIP

Essentials

The Magellan's catalog (800-962-4943) has inflatable pillows (saving graces on long trips) and a variety of light, durable travel essentials, such as hair dryers, luggage straps, alarms, adapter plugs, and clothing organizers.

front in her long, sleek, black roadster. *4175 Admiralty Way, Marina Del Rey; (800) 528-1234; (310) 823-5333;* www.bestwestern.com

Marina Del Rey Hotel
★★★/$$$
On the main canal of the area's harbor, this well-priced hotel features water views from most of its 160 rooms and has a wind-sheltered pool with a large shallow area for children. Bathrooms are done in marble, you can request an in-room refrigerator, parking is free, and the restaurant has waterfront views. Kids under 12 stay free in their parents' room. *13534 Bali Way, Marina Del Rey; (800) 882-4000; (310) 301-1000;* www.marinadelrey.com

The Ritz-Carlton ★★★★/$$$$
All rooms in this 306-room luxury waterfront hotel boast marble bathrooms, three phones, weighty plush terry bathrobes, private balconies, and a partial or full marina view. Under the hotel's Protect Our Little Ones program, a specially trained

bellman will install safety features to protect guests under 5 from injury. Electric outlet plugs, a tub spout cover, and a night-light are included, and you'll even be given a basic first-aid kit. Then you can all relax and enjoy the facilities, which include a swimming pool and hot tub (always 80° F and always open—24 hours a day!), a fitness center with sauna, two tennis courts with night lighting, bicycle rentals, and a basketball court. (If the pool looks familiar, you might have seen it in the remake of *The Parent Trap*.) A fabulous Sunday brunch with a kids' buffet is served on select holidays. *4375 Admiralty Way, Marina Del Rey; (800) 241-3333; (310) 823-1700;* www.ritzcarlton.com

GOOD EATS

California Pizza Kitchen
★★★★/$
The family-friendly menu lists a vast variety of pizzas as well as soups, salads, pastas, and sandwiches. Also see Good Eats in Beverly Hills/Los Angeles. *Marina Waterside Center, 13345 Fiji Way, at Lincoln Blvd., Marina Del Rey; (310) 301-1563;* http:/www/desertdiningguide.com/c alpizza.html; www.cpk.com

The Cheesecake Factory
★★★★/$$
Choose a cheesecake from a staggering variety of mouthwatering flavors—perhaps Milky Way

Chocolate, Adam's Peanut Butter Cup Fudge Ripple, or Peach Bellini—and enjoy a marina view while you indulge. There's also a heap of kid-friendly "healthy" fare here. Also see Good Eats in Beverly Hills/Los Angeles. *4142 Via Marina, Marina Del Rey; (310) 306-3344; www.thecheesecakefactory.com*

Chin Chin ★★★★/$-$$

Your kids will love the dumplings and rolls, including ever-popular potstickers, and the oodles of noodle dishes that are served here. Also see Good Eats in Westside/Los Angeles. *13455 Maxella Ave., at Del Rey Ave., Marina Del Ray; (310) 823-9999; www.chinchin.com*

Islands ★★★★/$

This is an outer island in a chain of eateries that serves up burgers and sandwiches in a tropical atmosphere. Also see Good Eats in West Hollywood/Los Angeles. *404 Washington St., at Via Dolce, Marina Del Rey; (310) 822-3939; www.islandsrest aurants.com*

Jerry's Famous Deli
★★★/$

Lots of generic deli food is the order of the day at this very popular chain. Also see Good Eats in Westside/Los Angeles. *13181 Mindanao Way, Marina Del Rey; (310) 821-6626; www.jerrysdeli.com*

Ruby's Diner
★★★★/$

The whole family can sit in an extra-comfy oversize booth in this old-fashioned diner. The menu is real simple, featuring such items as veggie burgers and French-fried onion rings. *In Marina Marketplace, 13455 Maxella Ave., Marina Del Rey; (310) 574-7829.*

Souplantation
★★★★/$

What kid doesn't like a buffet? They can check out the possibilities first and pick something that's just right. Also see Good Eats in Westside/Los Angeles. *In Marina Marketplace 13455 Maxella Ave./Lincoln Blvd., Marina Del Rey; (310) 305-7669.*

Hermosa Beach

Between Manhattan Beach and Redondo Beach, only 10 minutes from LAX and 30 minutes south of Santa Monica via the miserable, tight-laned 405 Freeway, this small beach town is in a time warp.

Hermosa Beach was home to Ozzie and Harriet and the boys in the 1950s, so it makes sense that families find it alluring. (Other famous past residents include Dizzy Gillespie, Errol Flynn—who wasn't rated G in his personal life—and Charlie Chaplin.) At many Southern California beaches, sewage pipes empty into the ocean, but not here. Spend some time frolicking in the clear water, as well as sunbathing and making castles on the meticulously clean sand. Anytime is a good time to visit, but summer is prime, with festivals and volleyball tournaments galore. When the sand volleyball courts are empty, you can start up a family competition.

BUNKING DOWN

Beach House
★★★/$$$

With is dazzling oceanfront location and 54 spacious, well-equipped suites, this is a great place for a family to settle in for some serious beaching. Each loft suite has a separate living room and bedroom area, a private balcony, and a wood-burning fireplace. Each is also equipped with a wet bar, microwave, refrigerator, CD player, and stereo. A 26-mile paved path known as The Strand runs right in front of the hotel. You can walk or bike or stroller it all the way to Malibu, if you have the stamina—or just go as far as you like and turn around. Enjoy the complimentary continental breakfast of croissants and muffins and coffee and milk in your suite—that is, if someone goes to the breakfast room and gathers up a tray. That way you and the kids

can have a more leisurely start to the day and spend even more time looking at that beautiful ocean. *1300 The Strand, Hermosa Beach; (888) 895-4559; (310) 374-3001;* www.beach-house.com

GOOD EATS

Hennessey's Tavern
★★★★/$

Your hungry family will have a relaxing meal here. In true pub fashion, it is cozy to the max and has an inexpensive sandwich menu that will satisfy everyone. Just outside the restaurant, the pedestrians-only Pier Plaza is ringed with more shops and restaurants. You can check out the bronze statue of local lifeguard/surfer legend Tim Kelly (who now wears droppings from disrespectful seagulls on his head). *8 Pier Ave., Hermosa Beach; (310) 372-5759;* www.hennesseystavern.com

Long Beach

About 10 miles down the coast from Hermosa Beach you reach Long Beach, the place to go for water-related activities. On these six miles of beaches, you and the kids can learn to windsail, scuba dive, and sail—or just splash in the water and dig in the sand. Charter firms offer sportfishing expeditions and seasonal whale-watching cruises. You can take a narrated cruise of the harbor, or a water taxi to Shoreline Village to shop or dine, and the kids can ride the vintage hand-carved Looff carousel.

CULTURAL ADVENTURES

The Queen Mary
MUST-SEE FamilyFun ★★★★/$$
MUST-SEE

Now permanently moored in Long Beach Harbor and operating as a hotel and tourist attraction, the *Queen Mary* is said to be one of the largest and most luxurious ocean liners ever to sail the seas, bigger even than the *Titanic.*

The *Queen Mary* crossed the Atlantic between the United States and Britain 1,001 times before she was retired, carrying such well-known passengers as Greta Garbo, Spencer Tracy, Bob Hope, Bing Crosby, and the Duke of Windsor.

She normally held 2,000 passengers and 1,200 crew members. In 1967 the ship was purchased by the city of Long Beach and refitted into a 365-room hotel.

The best way to appreciate the *Queen Mary* is to take a tour, which you can do even if you don't spend the night. The standard admission fee covers a self-guided Shipwalk Tour, with a multi-image show detailing the ship's history; a visit to the Hall of Maritime Heritage, with models of many famous ships; a lifeboat drill demonstration; and the new Ghosts and Legends Tour of the *Queen Mary*—a 30-minute walk-through exhibit that focuses on spirit sightings aboard the ship. You'll also see replicas of original staterooms, crews' quarters, and the children's playroom.

Live entertainment is scheduled on board during holiday periods, and fireworks are presented on Saturday nights in summer. Kids of all ages enjoy touring the Cold War–era submarine *Scorpion* moored next to the ship. Pay separately or get a combined-admission ticket. *1126 Queens Hwy., at the end of the 710 Freeway, Long Beach; (800) 437-2934; (562) 435-3511;* www.queenmary.com

You can get good family fare lunch or dinner at the Promenade Cafe, or sample snacks from the ship's delicatessen.

JUST FOR FUN

Aquarium of the Pacific
★★★★/$$

Kids love to look at fish and they'll see more than they can count here. Celebrating the astonishing treasures found in the planet's largest, most diverse body of water—the Pacific Ocean—this new aquarium concentrates on the waters of Southern California/Baja Pacific, the Northern Pacific, and the Tropical Pacific. Your kids will be wowed by the aquarium's size—as big as three football fields—and by the 88-foot-long sculpture of a blue whale and her 21-foot-long calf. Cafe Scuba is an indoor/outdoor restaurant good for family dining. *100 Aquarium Way, Long Beach; (562) 590-3100; www.aquariumofpacific.org*

Planet Ocean ★★/Free

Lovers of sea creatures will be thrilled by this huge mural at Rainbow Lagoon Park Marine by noted marine artist Wyland. The world's largest mural at 122,000 square feet, it depicts life-size gray whales and dolphins. *E. Shoreline Dr. and S. Linden Ave., Long Beach.*

BUNKING DOWN

Dockside Boat & Bed
★★★★/$$$-$$$$

Here's your chance to spend the night on a yacht. (It's a fantasy com-

Catalina Island

Just 26 miles and a one-and-a-half-hour boat ride across the sea, as the Four Preps' song promises (never mind, kids, it's way before your time), delightful Catalina Island is fun for a day and even more fun if you have time to spend the night.

Catalina Island is often compared to Italy's Isle of Capri. You and your kids can swim in crystal-clear waters and sunbathe and build sand castles on sandy beaches, but you can also go horseback riding, bicycling, scuba diving, and golfing. Fish-watching on a glass-bottom boat is a particularly appropriate activity here—this is where glass-bottom boats originated.

Wrigley Memorial Botanic Garden—a 38-acre memorial to the chewing-gum baron who originally developed the island—showcases plants native to the island. As for animals, a herd of buffalo—descendants of animals brought here by a film crew in 1924—roams the remote parts of the island, and buffalo burgers are a popular item on the town's fast-food menus.

In the sleepy town of **Avalon**, named for the mythical island where

mon among Moms and Dads—if not their kids.) In Rainbow Harbor, just 500 yards from the aquarium, this unique B&B usually has up to a dozen vessels available for overnight lodging. Some have several staterooms and are particularly comfortable for families. Each is equipped with a VCR and galley, and you get free continental breakfast before you go ashore in the morning. Book the Snooze and Cruise package and a captain will take you all out for a ride. Also see Bunking Down in San Francisco. *316 E. Shoreline Dr., Long Beach; (562) 436-3111; www.boatandbed.com*

The Queen Mary
★★★★/$$-$$$$

For a truly memorable experience,

spend a few nights aboard this grande dame of the sea, now a 365-room hotel. First-class cabins retain the charm of a bygone era with Art Deco carpeting, natural wood walls, and porthole windows. Some of the smaller second- and third-class rooms have been converted into spacious family units with two double beds and private bathrooms. The casual, medium-priced Promenade restaurant offers fresh fish, pasta, and sandwiches and a children's menu that includes all their favorites. Several more upscale restaurants and bars and an assortment of informal snack spots, including a bakery, pizza parlor, and ice-cream stand, are also on board. The ship's original first-class dining room has a Sunday brunch with a special children's buffet. But

King Arthur's body was buried. Keep your eyes open for celebrities, as they often moor their yachts in Avalon's harbor. The island is most crowded on summer weekends and when cruise ships are in port.

Only local vehicles can drive Catalina's hilly streets, so you can't rent a car. But it doesn't really matter, since most sights are easily reached on foot, and you can take shuttle buses when your tootsies get tired. You can also rent a golf cart or bikes to tour the island.

You'll find many inexpensive family-friendly lodgings and restaurants on the island. So if this West Coast

"Isle of Capri" captures your fancy, check with the **Catalina Island Visitors Bureau** *(310/510-1520)*. Several boat lines offer frequent year-round service to Catalina Island.

♦ **Catalina Express** *(310/519-1212; 800/995-4386)* has departures from San Pedro, Long Beach, Newport Beach, and San Diego.

♦ **Catalina Passenger Service** *(949/ 673-5245)* departs from Newport.

You can fly, too, from Long Beach and San Pedro via **Island Express** *(310/510-2525)*.

be aware that the vintage ocean liner has no swimming pool, game room, or other kid-favored features. *1126 Queens Hwy., Long Beach; (800) 437-2934; (562) 435-3511;* www.queen mary.com

San Pedro Hostel ★★/$

Located in Angel's Gate Park, this seaside hostel offers a million-dollar view. Beaches and tide pools are within walking distance. Private rooms for families are available. Also see "Hosteling for Families" on page 215. *3601 S. Gaffey St. #613, San Pedro, Long Beach; (310) 831-8109;* www.hiayh.org

GOOD EATS

Johnny Rockets ★★★★/$

This 1950s diner is fun for kids. Also see Good Eats in Los Angeles/West Hollywood. *245 Pine Ave., Long Beach; (562) 983-1332;* www.john nyrockets.com

Polly's Bakery Cafe ★★★★/$

Famous for its pies, this café is also not expensive. Also see Good Eats in Santa Monica. *3490 Atlantic Ave., Long Beach; (562) 595-5651. Also at 4680 Los Coyotes Diag., Long Beach; (562) 597-6076.*

Huntington Beach

In Orange County, about 35 miles south of L.A., this sunny beach town is surf central. Indeed, the city has proclaimed itself the Surfing Capital of the World. Palm-lined Main Street, which is two compact blocks of restaurants and shops, leads to California's longest pier, and surfing competitions are held here year-round. The town even has a Surfing Walk of Fame. Family members who'd like to give surfing a try can rent surfboards and take lessons; boogie boards are available for little wave-riders. The surf is fine (not too rough) for swimming, too. So inhale the salty air, slather on some sunscreen, and jump right in.

JUST FOR FUN

Adventure Playground ★/$

Located in Central Park and open in summer only, this special spot lets children play the day away digging in dirt, floating on Tom Sawyer–style rafts, sliding down muddy embankments, and building their own forts. Is it any surprise that it is also known as Mud Park? Dress the kids in old clothes and bring along towels. Outdoor showers are available. Park in the library lot. *Five miles inland from the beach, on Talbert Ave. at Gothard St., Huntington Beach.*

Bolsa Chica Ecological Reserve
★/Free

This 185-acre restored coastal salt marsh is home to birds both rare and common. The whole family will enjoy the one-and-a-half-mile self-guided nature walk and a visit to the interpretive center. *3842 Warner Ave., Huntington Beach; (714) 846-1114.*

Huntington State Beach
★★★/Free-$

Beautiful and extremely popular, this three-mile-long beach runs the length of the town of Huntington Beach and is California's second-most popular state park. Some 2.5 million people visit every year—and with good reason. Your family will get the full California beach experience here, as there is plenty going on, including the occasional free beachside concert and surfside volleyball tournament. Lifeguards are on duty and snack stands are available. You can surf, too. There's a fee for parking. *Huntington Beach; (714) 536-1455.*

International Surfing Museum
★/By donation

If your kids weren't interested in surfing before, they will be after a day or two in Surf City U.S.A. So you may want to stop in at this downtown museum, which chronicles the history of the sport. Housed inside a former Art Deco movie house is a collection of surfing artifacts that spans nearly a century. Surfing music

FamilyFun SNACK

Bag o' Bugs

Place a few graham crackers in a plastic bag, seal it shut, and crush the crackers into a fine sand using a large spoon. Add a few raisins and let your kids dig for bugs in the sand. Experiment with other tasty critters: dried cranberry ladybugs, chocolate or carob-chip ants, even gummy worms.

plays softly as you study the displays, including a bust of Duke Kahanamoku, who is credited with introducing surfing to California. Young skateboarders and snowboarders will be interested in the exhibit showing how surfing evolved into those popular land sports. Outside, a colorful surfing mural adorns one of the walls, and live surfing music is presented in the parking lot on most Sunday afternoons from 1 to 3 P.M. Call for museum hours. *411 Olive Ave., Huntington Beach; (714) 960-3483; www.surfingmuseum.org*

BUNKING DOWN

Hilton Waterfront Beach Resort
★★★★/$$$-$$$$

Your family will find lots to like at this 290-room resort hotel: a large landscaped ocean-view pool and hot tub, a fitness center, a lighted tennis court, a sand volleyball court,

Eating an Alphabet

and a basketball court. The ocean-view restaurant is particularly nice for families at Sunday brunch, when kids under 5 eat free and the Li'l Surfers Buffet caters to the tastes of young children with everything from corn dogs to Jell-O. But perhaps the best family-friendly amenity is the Beach Cookout package, which includes everything you need for a picnic by the ocean's edge: food, firewood, a blanket, and a ride over to the beach. *21100 P.C.H., Huntington Beach; (800) 822-SURF; (800) 445-8667; (714) 960-SURF;* www. hilton.com

Quality Inn ★★/$$

This nice-looking budget hotel has 50 rooms, some with an ocean view. Though it has no swimming pool, it does have a rooftop hot tub with a 360-degree view, and the beach is just across the street. Start the day with the complimentary continental breakfast. An operating oil well (that fascinates kids) and a Taco Bell are both just next door. *800 P.C.H., at Eighth St., Huntington Beach; (800) 228-5151; (714) 536-7500;* www.qual ityinn.com

GOOD EATS

Duke's Huntington Beach
★★★★/$$-$$$

One young customer said it all: "This restaurant is good, dude!" At the base of the pier, with a fabulous view of the beach and a surf-theme decor of Koa wood paneling and tropical plants, this outpost of the popular Oahu restaurant combines California and Hawaiian flavors in a creative, tasty, and well-priced surf 'n' turf menu. (Mom and Dad: the beach drinks are good here, especially the Lava Flow—a piña colada with strawberry puree that tastes Hawaiian.) The Keiki menu ("keiki" means child in Hawaiian) lists a cheeseburger, spaghetti, and cheese pizza as options. But save some room for the signature dessert—a giant piece of the gooey ice cream concoction known as Hula Pie, with enough spoons for the whole family. Valet parking is convenient and adds to the fun. *317 P.C.H., Huntington Beach; (714) 374-6446;* www.hula pie.com

Polly's Tasty Food and Pies
★★★★/$

Pies are the draw at this inexpensive café. Also see Good Eats in Santa Monica. *9791 Adams Ave., Huntington Beach; (714) 964-4424.*

Ruby's Surf City Diner ★★★★/$

Perched on the end of the pier, this colorful diner dishes up soda-fountain treats as well as great burgers, sandwiches, and soups and salads. Kids' meals are available. *On Huntington Beach Pier, Huntington Beach; (714) 969-RUBY.*

Wahoo's Fish Taco
★★★/$

This place is as casual as it gets. Place your order at the back, and then select one of the mismatched Formica tables. The kids can watch one of the TVs playing overhead while you wait for your Mexican fast food. Choose from a variety of burritos and other standard Mexican items, plus Hawaiian-style plate lunches and the namesake fish taco. *120 Main St., Huntington Beach; (714) 536-2050;* www.wahoos.com

Newport Beach

Only 14 miles from Disneyland, this is the largest small-boat harbor in the world. It's *the* place for your family to enjoy all things boat-related—gondola rides, ferry trips, boat rentals. Watch for the public playgrounds with brightly colored play equipment. The local police patrol on cute little dune buggies.

JUST FOR FUN

Balboa Fun Zone
★★★/Free-$$

Wheee! Kids of all ages can ride a Ferris wheel, carousel, and bumper cars (fees) at this small waterfront park. You can also rent pedalboats and pontoons, try your luck at a variety of arcade games, or play miniature golf (fees for all). If the gang gets hungry, you can pick up some fast food—including the chocolate-and-sprinkle-covered ice cream treats known as Balboa Bars. The Catalina Island excursion boat leaves from here, and you can also catch a boat to Balboa Island. *400 E. Bay Ave., Balboa Peninsula, Newport Beach; (949) 673-0408;* www.the balboafunzone.com

Balboa Pier
★★★/Free

A beach with a playground is at the beginning of the pier. About 900 feet out, at pier's end, you'll find a Ruby's Diner *(1 Balboa Pier; 949/644-7829; also see Good Eats* in Marina Del Rey) done up in chrome and lipstick-red vinyl, serving hearty breakfasts in the morning and ample hamburgers and shakes in the afternoon. *Balboa Peninsula, Newport Beach.*

Duffy Electric Boat Co.
★★/$$$$

Rent an electric boat with a surrey on top and putter the family around the harbor for a while. This business also manufactures the boats and will sell you one if you and the kids become attached. *2001 State 1, Newport Beach; (949) 645-6427; www.duffyboats.com*

Newport Dunes Resort
★★★/Free-$

Situated on a large lagoon, this family-friendly beach offers calm waters and all the beach games and equipment you could want for rent:

pedal boats, kayaks, sailboats, bikes, horseshoe sets, hammocks, barbecues, and umbrellas. Lifeguards are on duty in summer, and whale floats mark a special children's swimming area. Barbecue grills, campsites, RV parking (fee), and a playground equipped with a whale and pirate ship to climb on are other family-friendly amenities. *1131 Back Bay Dr., Newport Beach; 949-729-DUNE; www.newportdunes.com*

Upper Newport Bay Ecological Reserve
★★★/Free

Hike, bike, or kayak through Southern California's largest estuary. This quiet saltwater marsh ecosystem teems with wildlife and birds. You can take walking tours and family campfire programs. *Off Backbay Dr., Newport Beach; (949) 640-6746.*

BUNKING DOWN

Balboa Inn
★★/$$$-$$$$

In a great location near the Balboa Pier, this historic landmark has 34 rooms, some with ocean or bay views. The oceanfront suites are particularly nice for families; they're equipped with small refrigerators, coffeemakers, and whirlpools. The property also boasts a pool and a hot tub. **NOTE:** You must pay an additional fee to park in a city lot across the way. *105 Main St., Balboa*

Peninsula, Newport Beach; (877) BALBOA-9; (949) 675-3412; www. balboainn.com

Best Western Bay Shores Inn
★★★/$$-$$$$

Just one block from the bay in one direction and from the ocean in the other, this simple 25-room motel has a few rooms equipped with full kitchens and some with ocean views. There's no pool, unfortunately, but you can see the bay and ocean from the rooftop sundeck. Rooms have VCRs with free movies. Free continental breakfast and afternoon cookies add to the family-friendly atmosphere. You can borrow beach toys and equipment, including umbrellas and boogie boards, free. *1800 W. Balboa Blvd., Balboa Peninsula, Newport Beach; (800) 222-6675; (949) 675-3463; www.bestwestern.com*

Four Seasons Hotel
★★★★/$$$$

The atmosphere may seem a little fancy for kids, but this elegant 285-room luxury hotel welcomes families with special services. When you reserve you'll be asked the names and ages of your children, and at check-in time they'll be greeted with a special goodie bag filled with age-appropriate items and a kid-size terry robe. Board games, jump ropes, and baby equipment such as strollers and car seats may be borrowed at the concierge desk. Dress is casual, and

the restaurants and room service have a special dinosaur-theme children's menu that doubles as a coloring book. Everybody will like the tropically landscaped pool and hot tub area and the fitness center. *690 Newport Center Dr., Newport Beach; (800) 332-3442; (949) 759-0808; www.fourseasons.com*

Hyatt Newporter
★★★★/$$$-$$$$

This luxury resort is across the street from the Newport Dunes aquatic park and the Upper Newport Bay Ecological Reserve wildlife sanctuary. There are three swimming pools (one heated, one unheated, and one just for children) and plenty of space for sunbathing, three hot tubs, a nine-hole golf course, tennis courts, a shuffleboard court, and expansive gardens. *1107 Jamboree Rd., Newport Beach; (800) 233-1234; (949) 729-1234; www.hyatt.com*

Newport Beach Marriott Hotel & Tennis Club ★★★★/$$$

This link in the always family-friendly chain is a monster 578-room high-rise hotel equipped with two swimming pools, two hot tubs, and eight lighted tennis courts. All rooms are equipped with coffeemakers, and you can request a small refrigerator or VCR. Room service has special kids' items at prices that will make your heart sing. *900 Newport Center Dr., Newport Beach; (800) 228-9290; (949) 640-4000; www.marriott.com*

Portofino
Beach Hotel
★★/$$$-$$$$

Across a parking lot from the ocean near Balboa Pier, this cozy 20-room European-style hotel offers a few larger beach apartments with kitchen facilities and one cottage—both are fine choices for families. Several rooms have ocean views. *2306 W. Oceanfront Blvd., Balboa Peninsula, Newport Beach; (800) 571-8749; (949) 673-7030; www. portofinobeachhotel.com*

GOOD EATS

Anthony's
Riverboat Restaurant
★★★★/$$-$$$

It's like dining in a real riverboat. This replica stern-wheeler—it actually floats on the water—sports southern decor, including a grand staircase leading up to the dining rooms. The kitchen specializes in large portions of surf and turf. The kids' menu also has plenty of fun drinks. *151 E. Coast Hwy., Newport Beach; (949) 673-3425; www.river boatrestaurant.com*

Caffe Panini
★★★/$-$$

Parents and kids both like the Italian-style grilled sandwiches, gourmet pizzas, pastas, and salads. *2333 Pacific Coast Highway, Corona del Mar; (949) 675-8101.*

The Cannery
★★★/$$-$$$

This historic waterfront building, once a fish cannery, is now a bustling restaurant perfect for family dining. The bill of fare includes monster lobsters, abalone, and fresh fish as well as kid-friendly hamburgers. Sunday champagne brunch is a relative bargain, with special prices for kids. Reservations are advised. This restaurant also books harbor meal cruises. *3010 Lafayette Ave., Newport Beach; (949) 566-0060.*

Cheesecake Factory
★★★★/$$

Your whole family will love the large portions of delicious food and fabulous selection of cheesecakes. Also see Good Eats in Beverly Hills/Los Angeles. *Fashion Island, 1141 Newport Center Dr., Newport Beach; (949) 720-8333; www.thecheese cakefactory.com*

SOUVENIR HUNTING

Teddy Bears &
Tea Cups

You'll find everything bear- and tea-related in this absolutely charming shop. Take tea in the back room on Wednesday afternoon and some holidays. You'll be unbearably disappointed if you forget to make reservations. *225 Marine Ave., Newport Beach; (949) 673-7204; www.teddybearsandteacups.com*

Laguna Beach

Often called California's Riviera, this sunny beach town and artists' colony is halfway between Los Angeles and San Diego. Art galleries, specialty boutiques, and restaurants crowd the streets, but Laguna Beach's biggest attraction is the lovely Mission San Juan Capistrano. There's not much else in the way of sight-seeing here, so you can look forward to some real downtime on the gorgeous beach.

CULTURAL ADVENTURES

Mission San Juan Capistrano ★★★★/$

Go just a few miles south of town to the spot where hundreds of swallows return each March, around the 19th. Birds fly in all the way from Goya, Argentina, and their arrival is celebrated with a traditional Mexican fiesta. Called the Jewel of the Missions, this is the premier cultural attraction of the area. It was built in 1776 and houses the oldest building still in use in California. Call for the schedule of Living History Days, when docents dress is historical costumes and demonstrate crafts.

There are also summer children's programs, including Discovery Camp where your kids can spend a week enjoying learning Native American and Spanish songs, dances, stories, and cultures. *Camino Capistrano/Ortega Hwy., San Juan Capistrano; (949) 234-1300;* http://missionsjc.com

BUNKING DOWN

Laguna Cliffs Marriott Resort ★★★★/$$-$$$$

Standing on a bluff above Dana Point, this low-key 346-room resort features lots for kids to do—two swimming pools and areas for basketball, volleyball, Ping-Pong, and croquet. Rent beach gear—boogie boards, jet skis, windsurfing and scuba equipment, as well as bicycles. A kids' camp for children ages 5 through 12 operates on weekends June through August. Nearby, Lantern Bay Park features 42 acres of parkland with jogging and bicycle trails, and Doheny State Beach is just a little farther down, at the base of the hill. *25135 Park Lantern, Laguna Beach; (800) 533-9748; (949) 661-5000;* www. marriott.com

The Ritz-Carlton Laguna Niguel ★★★★/$$$$

This ultraluxurious resort is a popular destination for vacationing families. The honor bar in each room can be emptied for service as a small

In Search of Frozen Bananas and Balboa Bars:

A DAY TRIP TO BALBOA ISLAND

A CTUALLY COMPOSED OF several tiny islands that were created when Newport Harbor was dredged in the early 1920s, Balboa Island calls to mind the beach towns of New England. You can rent a cottage and spend the entire summer or visit just for the day, as most people do.

It is possible to drive to the main island, Balboa, via a small bridge off Bayside Drive. But traffic and parking are usually difficult on this tightly packed island, so consider leaving your car at the pier and taking the tiny, vintage, three-car ferry that leaves from the Balboa Peninsula near the pier. Allowing time for window-shopping and a Balboa Bar ice cream or frozen banana on Marine Avenue, you can "do" the island in about an hour. But you might want to stay longer and rent bikes or skates.

About those Balboa Bars: there seems to be a dispute as to which island shop has been serving the chocolate-and-sprinkle-covered ice-cream bars the longest. There's also some disagreement about who made the first frozen banana (some people say it was created right on this island). Perhaps you should patronize both of the title contenders and

decide for yourself which one tastes the best:

Sugar 'n' Spice *(310 Marine Ave.; 949/673-8907)* is credited with creating the world's first frozen banana. The little sugar shack still sells them in small, medium, and large sizes (the large is very large) as well as rolled in chocolate and your choice of crumb topping. The place also claims to have been making Balboa Bars since 1945. You can get other fun foods here, such as corn dogs, ice creams, and waffle cones. Service is through a window, and you dine on street benches outside.

Practically next door, the upstart **Dad's** *(318 Marine Ave.; 949/673-8686)* has been serving up pretty much the same things as its neighbor since 1960, although here you can also purchase bakery items and doughnuts.

For real food, go to **Wilma's Patio** *(203 Marine Ave., Balboa; 949/675-5542)*. With its farmhouse atmosphere and decor, this friendly place specializes in casual family dining. Indeed, anything your kids might want is probably on this menu. There are soups, salads, sandwiches, burgers, Mexican items, pasta dishes, and more, and breakfast is served all day.

refrigerator, and your kids can rent VCRs and Nintendo games at the concierge desk. After check-in, your kids will become the excited recipients of a special gift delivered to your room, and you can opt to treat them to cookies and milk from room service at bedtime. Facilities include two swimming pools, two hot tubs, four tennis courts, a health club with sauna and steam room, and two miles of public beach. Ritz Kids, an all-day children's program, operates daily in summer, and on Friday and Saturday evening, a three-hour Kids' Night Out treats children ages 5 through 12 to dinner and a movie. **NOTE:** This being the Ritz, pack your spiffiest attire. *1 Ritz-Carlton Dr., Dana Point; (800) 241-3333; (949) 240-2000;* www.ritzcarlton.com

Vacation Village
★★★/$$-$$$$

With its own private beach, this 130-room hotel offers a casual family atmosphere and views that stretch all the way to Catalina Island. Oceanside rooms have private balconies; some units have kitchens. The kids will like the two swimming pools, a hot tub and sauna, a kids' game room, and a beachfront restaurant. *647 S. Coast Hwy., at Sleepy Hollow La., Laguna Beach; (800) 843-6895; (949) 494-8566;* www.vacationvillage.com

GOOD EATS

Ruby's ★★★★/$

This 1940s-style diner has a patio with an ocean view. Also see Good Eats in Marina Del Rey. *30622 South Coast Hwy., Laguna Beach; (949) 497-RUBY.*

Wahoo's Fish Taco
★★★/$

Bring the family here for Mexican fare in very casual surroundings. Also see Good Eats in Huntington Beach. *1133 S. Coast Hwy., Laguna Beach; (949) 497-0033.*

During special programs at the San Diego Zoo and Wild Animal Park, your kids just might get the opportunity to feed a giraffe.

San Diego

I N SAN DIEGO, families mix learning about California's historical beginnings with the pleasure of sunning on beautiful beaches and the adventure of visiting the world's largest zoo. It is the home of the Pacific fleet, and so has a fabulous kid-pleasing collection of military ships. Your children will also enjoy getting to know a few of the city's approximately 90 museums. Good Mexican food is easily found, and many of the restaurants prepare dishes that you don't often see. (See if you can get the kids to try some of them.) The state's fastest-growing city is also its second largest, and the eighth largest in the United States. Renowned for excellent weather, San Diego boasts an average year-round temperature of 70° F. Though summer is the most popular time to visit, the consistent good weather

THE **FamilyFun** LIST

Balboa Park (page 292)

Gaslamp Quarter (page 300)

San Diego Aerospace Museum (page 296)

San Diego Model Railroad Museum (page 297)

San Diego Wild Animal Park (page 301)

San Diego Zoo (page 301)

SeaWorld Adventure Park San Diego (page 302)

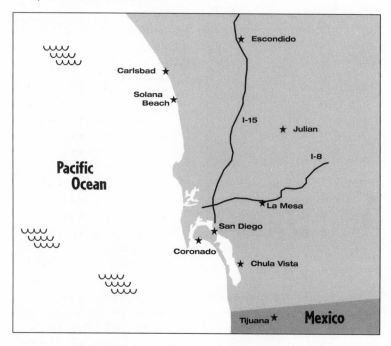

Escondido

Carlsbad ★

Solana
Beach ★

I-15

★ Julian

I-8

**Pacific
Ocean**

★ La Mesa

San Diego

★
Coronado

★ Chula Vista

Tijuana ★ **Mexico**

makes it a pleasant place to vacation any time. Be aware, though, that this generally sunny town does get summer fog, and is famous among the locals for its "June gloom." However, summer is the time of year when the jacaranda trees bloom, and the gorgeous lavender blossoms more than make up for a little chilly mist. You will need a car for convenient access to the many nearby recreational areas, which include ocean, mountains, and desert, and you're going to love the fact that parking is free almost everywhere. Train lovers (including most kids) are also going to enjoy the many required stops at clanging railroad crossings, complete with flashing lights.

CULTURAL ADVENTURES

★ Balboa Park
FamilyFun ★★★★/Free-$

You would need to spend several days or more to see everything in this 1,200-acre recreational wonderland. Larger than New York's Central Park and older than San Francisco's Golden Gate Park, Balboa Park is one of the largest city cultural complexes in the United States. On weekends, street performers entertain in El Prado, the central plaza area, and on Sunday afternoon at 2 P.M. you can take your kids to the free concerts of performances on the world's largest outdoor pipe organ. Younger children especially enjoy the weekly shows at the Marie Hitchcock Puppet Theater (*619/685-5045;* there's a fee), and older kids appreciate the entertainment presented year-round in the three theaters comprising the Old Globe Theatre (*619/239-2255;* fees). On Sunday afternoons, the interesting House of Pacific Relations (*619/ 234-0739*) hosts informal exhibits depicting the traditions and customs of an assortment of foreign countries. In the Spanish Village Art Center (*619/233-9050*), you'll see interesting craft shops where the artists work and demonstrate their skills. An immense Moreton Bay fig tree is nearby. Children especially enjoy riding the miniature train and the hand-carved animals on the 1910 carousel—on which they can also still grab for the brass ring.

In addition to the famous San Diego Zoo (see page 301), this fabulous park is also home to a host of fascinating museums, most of which are found along the Prado—a sort of Museum Row. To avoid getting "museumed out," punctuate your gallery-going with garden-strolling. If you plan on visiting more than a few museums, look into the money-saving Passport to Balboa Park, which includes admission to 12 participating museums and is valid for a week. *The park is bordered by*

Way Out in the Desert

Located about two hours northeast of San Diego *(Hwy. 8 east, to 79 north, to 78),* **Anza Borrego Desert State Park** *(760/767-5311)* encompasses 600,000 acres, making it California's largest state park. The geologic formations, plants, and animals there are found nowhere else. The best time to visit (because the weather is most comfortable for humans and because you can see more creatures) is October through May. Kids will be agog at viewing a "living dinosaur," one of the rare desert pupfish found in the area, or (careful!) a real, live scorpion. Should you decide to spend the night, there are some hotels in the area, and campsites are available. On the way to or from the park, stop at **Palomar Observatory** *(760/742-2119),* which holds the country's largest telescope; it's reached by the steep switchbacks of the Highway to the Stars. Admission is free. Also on the way is the colorful 1870 **gold-mining town of Julian**, more famous now for its quaint cafés serving home-made apple pie. *For information on all, call the Julian Chamber of Commerce, (760/765-1857).*

Sixth Ave., 28th St., Upas St., and Russ Blvd., San Diego; (619) 239-0512; www.balboapark.org

Botanical Building ★★★/Free

This grand old building—250 feet long, 75 feet wide, and 60 feet tall—was the largest wood lath structure in the world when it was built in 1915. It houses more than 2,100 tropical plants along with a changing display of seasonal flowers. The gorgeous reflecting pond filled with lilies and turtles attracts kids like a magnet; they get mighty excited when they spot a few ducks doing a dive-bomb landing in front of them. *On the Prado, west of the San Diego Museum of Art, San Diego; (619) 239-0512; www.balboapark.org*

Children's Museum/ Museo de los Niños ★★/$

Located in a colorful building near Seaport Village (see Souvenir Hunting, page 312), this hands-on spot is designed to please children of all ages. Kids can get really creative in the Art Zone, and toddlers have an area designed especially for them. To allow for paint-drying time, head

for the art activities first. After seeing the museum, stop at the adjacent children's park. *200 W. Island Ave., San Diego; (619) 233-KIDS.*

Junipero Serra Museum and Park ★★/$

Located just above Old Town, on the original site of the San Diego Mission, this museum has a lovely 40-acre hilltop setting. Kids enjoy climbing the steep tower stairs and looking through the unusual narrow windows set in thick, castlelike walls. Adults appreciate the breathtaking panoramic view. Exhibits feature mission and Native American artifacts. Plan a picnic and let your kids run loose on the expansive grassy grounds. *2727 Presidio Dr., San Diego; (619) 297-3258; www.sandiegohistory.com*

Marine Corps Recruit Depot Command Museum ★★★/Free

The Marines have been a visible presence in this city since 1846. This museum documents the history of the Corps, with detailed exhibits on all the U.S. wars. An entire room is devoted to the Marine Raiders, who trained at Camp Elliot in San Diego and participated in some particularly brutal Pacific battles in World War II. While you may not want to expose the youngest and most impressionable members of the family to the harsh realities of war, the museum is a good place to foster in grade-schoolers an appreciation of those who have dedicated their lives to protecting our country. Kids particularly like the authentic Jeeps and the colorful medals. A bonus here is that the museum is on a military base; most kids like to see men and women in uniforms, and there are plenty here. You can take guided tours by prior arrangement. If you come on Friday morning, you can also see the U.S. Marine Boot Camp Graduation Ceremonies and "Pass in Review" Parade, held at the base most Fridays at 10 and to which you and every other American are invited *(619/524-8720);* www.merdsd. usmc.mil *Off I-5 at Old Town exit, follow the signs; Marine Corps Recruit Depot, Bldg. 26, San Diego; (619) 524-6038;* www.usmchistory.com

Mission San Diego de Alcala (San Diego Mission) ★★★/$

Founded in 1769, this was the first California mission. It has been rebuilt several times and is now in Mission Valley, six miles from its original site. For a pittance you can rent a portable audiotape tour, which kids ages 7 and up particularly enjoy. *10818 San Diego Mission Rd., San Diego; (619) 281-8449.*

Museum of Photographic Arts ★★/$

If your budding photographers see the world through the eyes of master photographers, they might be inspired to go out and capture the

Let's Go to LEGOLAND!

If your kids love building things with tiny plastic bricks—or if they can never get their fill of amusement parks—plan on driving 30 miles north of San Diego.

The first LEGO theme park in the United States, and the third in the world (the first is in Billund, Denmark, the second in Windsor, England), LEGOLAND is designed especially for children ages 2 through 12 and is about as kid-friendly as a place can get. The big attractions here are miniature versions of five regions of the United States, with 1,000 buildings and famous landmarks built to 1:20 scale using 20 million LEGO bricks. Fully animated with cars and people and sound effects, the mini cities light up at night.

The amusement park offers 50 rides, including a boat cruise through fairy-tale lands and three mild roller coasters, including one that travels through a castle, complete with a dungeon and fire-breathing dragon. Most attractions are designed to be operated by kids, who find pleasure in pedaling fiercely to make the monorail go faster and in stomping on colored tiles to produce a musical tone from a fountain's spurting waters. Special features include restaurant menu boards posted at a child's eye level and tyke-size rest room facilities. Can you guess what the perfect LEGOLAND souvenir is?

LEGOLAND California, 1 LEGO Dr., Carlsbad; 877/534-6526; 760/919-LEGO; www.legoland.com

world as they see it. Get them a kid-friendly camera (a disposable one will do). Exhibits change frequently. *In Casa de Balboa, 1649 El Prado, San Diego; (619) 238-7559;* www.balboapark.org

Old Town State Historic Park
★★★★/**Free**

Site of the first European settlement on the West Coast, this 12-acre park was the center of town in the mid-1800s. It now houses a pleasant mixture of museum displays, shops, and Mexican restaurants. Your family can take the ranger-guided tour scheduled daily at 2, or you can opt for a self-guided tour using an inexpensive map. Kids especially enjoy the Wells Fargo History Museum *(619-238-3929)*, where they can see a stagecoach and telegraph, and the 1865 Mason Street School, where they can sit at an old-time desk. *The park is within the six blocks bounded by Taylor, Juan, Twiggs, and Congress Sts.; park headquarters is at 4002 Wallace St., San Diego; (619) 220-5423.*

Palm Canyon
★★★/**Free**

Don't miss this chance to see 450 palms in one spot. An original group of Mexican fan palms dates back to the early 1900s. The kids will love being able to run relatively free in a beautiful garden area. *Located south of the House of Charm, San Diego;* www.balboapark.org

Reuben H. Fleet Science Center
★★★★/**$$**

This Science Center—a mini version of San Francisco's Exploratorium—promises and delivers you and your kids an out-of-this-world experience. You won't find velvet ropes or DO NOT TOUCH signs here; instead, look for plenty of hands-on exhibits demonstrating physical principles. An IMAX theater and SciTours simulator ride round out the (educational) fun. *1875 El Prado, San Diego; (619) 238-1233;* www.rhfleet.org

San Diego Aerospace Museum ★★★★/**$**

Any aircraft fans, old or young, are going to get pretty excited when they see this gigantic museum, which documents the history of powered flight and displays full-size planes. The hangarlike space is packed with over 65 U.S. and foreign aircraft. They hang from the rafters and are parked on the floor. Kids find the helicopter with a turning blade in a central courtyard especially thrilling. And all the while jets are taking off and landing at the nearby San Diego Airport, adding realistic sound effects. *2001 Pan American Plaza, San Diego; (619) 234-8291;* www.aerospacemuseum.org

San Diego Automotive Museum
★★/**$**

This welcoming museum says, "Kids love cars. Come see ours." Take them up on it, and you'll take your family on a trip through automotive history. Highlights include horseless carriages of the 1920s, cruisers of the '50s, and one of the largest motorcycle collections on the West Coast. *2080 Pan American Plaza, San Diego; (619) 231-AUTO;* www.sdautomuseum.org

San Diego Maritime Museum
★★★/$

Three historic vessels make up this floating museum: the 1898 ferryboat *Berkeley*, the 1904 English luxury steam yacht *Medea*, and the steel-hulled, handmade 1863 sailing ship *Star of India*—the oldest merchant sailing vessel still afloat. Kids have a blast exploring them, and parents have fun, too. *1492 N. Harbor Dr., San Diego; (619) 234-9153;* www.sdmaritime.com

San Diego Model Railroad Museum
★★★★/$

This is the largest operating model railroad exhibit in the United States. Hundreds of volunteers have spent countless hours constructing the numerous displays here, and they also are on hand to operate them. Kids' eyes will pop when they see the huge layouts and moving trains, and they'll go positively bananas when they find the buttons that let them operate some of the features themselves. The gift shop has the perfect souvenirs, including Oshkosh caps and overalls, and "Thomas" trains.

FamilyFun TIP

Layover Plans

If you get stuck with a long layover, give your children a portable tape recorder so they can interview family members or fellow travelers about their destinations. Also, make sure favorite travel games, toys, and books are packed in their carry-on luggage.

In Casa de Balboa, 1649 El Prado, San Diego; (619) 696-0199; www.sdmodelrailroad.com

San Diego Museum of Man
★★★★/$

The dioramas of cave people are a hit with children at this museum, which features anthropological displays and local history exhibits. Kids also enjoy the Native American crafts and tools. Check to see if they're holding the frequently scheduled demonstrations of such things as weaving from Oaxaca (Mexico) and making traditional Mexican tortillas. The Children's Discovery Center (additional fee) offers a variety of hands-on activities that tap into kids' apparently endless interest in ancient Egypt. *1350 El Prado, San Diego; (619) 239-2001;* www.museumofman.org

San Diego Natural History Museum ★★★★/$

The museum opened 125 years ago, but the exhibits are totally contem-

A SAN DIEGO SAFARI

Located 30 minutes north of the San Diego airport, in the foothills of the San Pasqual Mountains, the **San Diego Wild Animal Park** *(15500 San Pasqual Valley Rd., Escondido; 760/747-8702)* is a magnificent 1,800-acre wildlife preserve. It is the sister facility of the San Diego Zoo (both attractions are owned and operated by the non-profit Zoological Society of San Diego), but here the people are in the "cages" (in this case, moving ones) and the animals roam free. Visitors take a five-mile narrated monorail ride that lasts almost an hour through a magnificent open area that is home to herds of uncaged animals. With older kids, you can also walk a 1.75-mile foot trail through this area as well as stroll through an Australian Rain Forest.

Young children especially enjoy the animal shows and petting area, and everyone in the family will be totally won over by the instant gratification of the lorikeet enclosure. Hold out a tiny cup of nectar and you'll soon have a host of riotously colored birds crowding together on your hands. The new Heart of Africa exhibit permits you to take a safari in search of many more unusual animals and birds such as secretary birds, bat-eared foxes, and aardvarks (ask your kids if they know that Arthur of TV and literary fame is

really an aardvark); your kids will get giddy with delight when they hand-feed a Baringo giraffe. The new Condor Ridge exhibit has the famed California Condors. A winding trail takes you through a variety of African habitats that include a dense forest, flourishing wetlands, sprawling savannas, and open plains. No passports or shots are required for this exciting expedition, but you should pack binoculars and a camera.

This park shares the San Diego Zoo's goal of increasing breeding among animals in captivity—particularly endangered species. Perhaps one of the reasons it has been so successful in achieving this goal is that its climate and terrain are very similar to that of the animals' native Africa and Asia. Call for information on how to join a photo caravan, take a behind-the-scenes tour, or spend the night on a Roar & Snore campout on a hill above the East Africa exhibit *(800/934-CAMP)*; www.wild animalpark.org

If you'd like to spend some time in the area, check into the **Rancho Bernardo Inn** *(17550 Bernardo Oaks Dr.; 858/675-8500; 800/896-6934)*. This posh resort makes a comfortable base for an excursion to the nearby wild animal park. On-site recreational facilities include two pools and seven hot tubs, an 18-hole championship golf course, 12 tennis courts, a fitness center, a grass volleyball court, table tennis, and jogging trails. Spa treatments are also available. There are several camps, including Camp RBI, which offers separate supervised activity programs for children ages 5 through 11 and 12 through 17, operates from 9 A.M. to 9 P.M. during all of August, part of December, and on holiday weekends. The program is flexible, with full- and half-day rates available. Activities include water Olympics, talent shows, and arts and crafts as well as the occasional Make-A-Movie and Casino Party. Kids also like attending the teas scheduled each Wednesday and Saturday afternoon; www.ranchobernardoinn.com

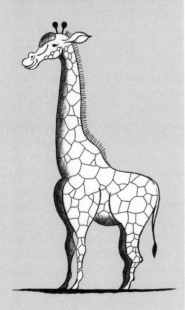

porary. In addition to the more traditional dinosaur skeletons and a Foucault pendulum, innovative exhibits include displays on the area's animal and plant life with plenty of child appeal. Many exhibits invite kids to get involved and to touch a variety of artifacts. The Desert Ecology area has creative displays with stuffed birds and animals, and your preschoolers will appreciate it that many exhibit windows are at their eye level. The gift shop is filled with stones and bugs and other things kids love; look for the wildly popular lollipops with worms in them (not real ones). Call for information on family programs and children's classes. *1788 El Prado, San Diego; (619) 232-3821;* www.sdnhm.org

JUST FOR FUN

Belmont Park ★★/Free
Admission to this old-fashioned beachside amusement park is free, then you and your children can pick and choose what to spend your money on. Perhaps the fully restored, Pepto-Bismol–pink Giant Dipper wooden roller coaster, whose roaring sound will punctuate your visit here (it is a National Historic Landmark?). Or maybe the small Liberty Carousel, the bumper cars, or one of the assorted arcades? The youngest family members will enjoy the kiddie rides—stuff like Baja Buggies and Thunder Boats. The

Plunge, which opened in 1925, was once the largest indoor saltwater swimming pool in the world. It is still the largest in Southern California and is a beautifully restored facility with original tile and an island that kids can rest on in the shallow end. Also part of Belmont Park is Pirate's Cove indoor playground *(see below)*. And then there's the beach, the beautiful, beautiful, free beach. *3146 Mission Blvd., San Diego; (619) 491-2988.*

Pirate's Cove ★★/$

The kids will like going through the underground passage that's the entrance to the indoor playground here. They can enter through an in-wall slide tube and climbing net. Once inside, they can wander through mazes, climb on cargo nets, crawl through ball pools, and swirl down a four-story spiral slide. Parents can play, too. This is a particularly good place for a rainy day. *3106 Mission Blvd., San Diego; 858/539-7474; www.giantdipper.com*

Cabrillo National Monument ★★★/$

Located at the tip of Point Loma, the monument commemorates Portuguese explorer Juan Rodriguez Cabrillo's exploration of the California coast and discovery of San Diego Bay in 1542. Kids love exploring the tiny restored Old Point Loma Lighthouse and walking and running and hollering along the rustic trails in

this wide-open space. You'll all have a chance to get in touch with nature—there are lots of trilling birds—and spectacular views of San Diego and the Pacific Ocean are an added delight. During the winter, this is a prime spot to watch the annual gray whale migration. The scenic drive out here takes you past part of Fort Rosecrans naval base and its picturesque and somber national cemetery, lined with row after heartbreaking row of white headstones. *1800 Cabrillo Memorial Dr., San Diego; (619) 557-5450; www.nps.gov/cabr/*

Gaslamp Quarter
MUST-SEE FamilyFun **★/Free**

This 16-block area of downtown, now a National Historic District, is filled with art galleries, specialty shops, and restaurants—all housed in beautifully restored Victorian Florentine, Romanesque, and Italianate buildings. You can take guided walking tours, but kids and parents both will probably have more fun just browsing at their own pace. Plan a stop in for some dessert at Ghirardelli Soda Fountain *(645 Fifth Ave.; 619/234-2449).* You can also stop in at the Children's Museum when you are here (see page 294). Kids might be interested to learn that though this is a very charming area today, San Diego never had any real gas lamps in the years before electricity. *Between Fourth and Sixth Aves. and Broadway and L St., San Diego; (619) 233-5227.*

ON AUGUST 21, 1999, the San Diego Zoo hosted the first giant panda birth in the Western Hemisphere in almost ten years. The new giant panda is a girl named Hua Mei. Her mother and father, Bai Yun and Shi Shi, have lived at the zoo since 1996. As of press time, all three pandas are on loan from the People's Republic of China.

Harbor Excursion
★★★★/$$

What kid doesn't like a boat ride? These one- and two-hour narrated tours are a good way to get oriented to the harbor area. You'll get a close-up look at merchant vessels and Navy ships, including frigates, ammunition ships, helicopter carriers, and destroyers, as well as the occasional tug and tuna trawler. The world's largest hospital ship, *The Mercy*, is usually in port and hard to miss—she's painted white and decorated with a huge red cross. *1050 N. Harbor Dr., San Diego; (800) 44-CRUISE; (619) 234-4111*; www.sdhe.com

Mission Bay Aquatic Park
★★★★/Free

Families have much to choose from at this 4,600-acre aquatic playground: 27 miles of public beaches and every kind of water sport (waterskiing, sailing, swimming, powerboating, and fishing each have separate designated public areas), plus a bike trail (rentals available), campsites, and golf courses. An assortment of bay cruises is also offered. *2688 E. Mission Bay Dr., San Diego; (619) 275-8259.*

 ## San Diego Wild Animal Park
★★★★/$$

You don't have to go to Africa to take a walk on the wild side— giraffes, condors, and colorful birds are right here. For more information, see "A San Diego Safari" on page 298.

San Diego Zoo
★★★★/$-$$

The city's most popular attraction, this famous zoo is known for its large, diverse, and rare collection of animals—most of which are housed in attractive habitat enclosures. It is home to almost 4,000 rare and exotic animals, including giant pandas from China, koalas from Australia, pygmy chimpanzees from Central Africa, and Komodo dragons from Indonesia. Natural habitats include the Sun Bear Forest, Gorilla Tropics, and Tiger River, a three-acre simulated

The Fleet's In

Held annually in October, **Fleet Week** celebrates the U.S. Navy. The festivities are similar to those in San Francisco (see page 54), and many are free, including a Sea-N-Air Parade on San Diego Bay and naval ship tours.

ecosystem in which you walk along pathways past plants and animals living much as they would in the wild. Your kids will go ape at the Polar Bear Plunge and at the hippo exhibit in Ituri Forest, where those hefty animals can be viewed swimming under water. The new Owens Rain Forest Aviary simulates the sights and sounds of a Southeast Asian jungle and gives you a close-up look at more than 200 birds. This zoo is also a botanical garden with more than 6,500 species of flora represented, including many unusual tropical and subtropical plants and flowers. Because the zoo covers 100 acres, especially if you have young children in tow, begin a visit with the 40-minute bus tour. You can then return to areas of particular interest. The refreshing Skyfari Aerial Tramway is another way to give your family's tootsies a rest. Be sure to allow time for the trained seal show and the Children's Zoo, which features a popular animal petting area and has ducks running loose for kids to meet. For a fabulous sou-

venir, let your kids pick out a favorite animal in stuffed format; a zoo coloring book is a good choice, too. Be sure to buy desired items when you see them at the small gift stands spread throughout the zoo, as the gift shop by the main gate does not stock everything. If you're traveling with a baby, note that changing tables are available in both the women's and men's rest rooms. You can also rent strollers. Daily in summer, the zoo gates open at 9 A.M. and stay open until 10 at night (it may be way past your kids' bedtime, but it's playtime for the zoo's nocturnal creatures). Special summer day camps are held for kids in kindergarten through grade 12 *(619/557-3963). Park Blvd./Zoo Pl., San Diego; (619) 231-1515;* www.sandiegozoo.org

 **SeaWorld Adventure Park San Diego**
★★★★/$$$-$$$$

Your kids are dying to come here and (admit it) so are you. You can see and even touch dolphins, whales, sharks, and other amazing creatures of the sea. What could be more exciting? Located on the south shore of Mission Bay, the ocean-side 150-acre marine zoological park is the world's largest and offers a variety of aquariums and water shows. You'll see Shamu, a trained two-ton killer whale at Shamu Stadium, the world's largest live shark display, The Shark Encounter, and Manatee

Rescue—the only display of these rare sea mammals outside of Florida. The sea lion-feeding pool will amaze the whole family, and you'll all be surprised at how soft the dolphins are after spending time at the dolphin petting pool. Other attractions include the refrigerated Penguin Encounter, which re-creates the South Pole and is home to six species of Antarctic penguins, a two-acre playground, and a game and video arcade. *500 Sea World Dr., San Diego; (619) 226-3901; www.seaworld.com*

Silver Strand
★/Free

This nine-mile-long peninsula is only a quarter-mile wide. A highway and bicycle path runs its length, and it holds Silver Strand State Beach, which boasts lifeguards and rest rooms and lots of seashells. The U.S. Naval Amphibious Base, home of the Navy SEALs, is also here (it's not open to the public). *On Coronado Island; (619) 435-5184.*

BUNKING DOWN

Bahia Hotel
★★★★/$$$-$$$$

Situated on its own peninsula jutting out into Mission Bay, just a few blocks from Belmont Park, this 325-room resort hotel has a lot to offer a vacationing family: a private bay beach with boat rentals, a heated outdoor pool with a lifeguard, a hot tub, a fitness center, two lighted tennis courts, and a restaurant. Kids of all ages are agog at seeing real seals swimming around in the seal pool, and older children quickly take to the game room. The resort's stern-wheeler, the *Bahia Belle*, is shared with the Catamaran Resort Hotel and offers special family boat trips out on the bay *(858/539-7779)*. Accommodations are in a five-story tower as well as attractive one- and two-story buildings across the street from the bay. Some rooms open right on the bay beach, others onto a garden area, and some have bay or ocean views. All are equipped with coffeemakers, and most have small refrigerators, too. *998 W. Mission Bay Dr., San Diego; (800) 576-4229; (858) 488-0551; www.bahiahotel.com*

Best Western Blue Sea Lodge
★★★/$$-$$$$

With a fabulous beachfront location on the Pacific Ocean (as opposed to one of the area's bays), this comfortable 100-room motel is a super deal for families. Rooms have patios or balconies, as well as coffeemakers, microwaves, and small refrigerators. The second-floor pool and hot tub area has an ocean view. *707 Pacific Beach Dr., San Diego; (800) BLUE-SEA; (858) 488-4700; www.bestwestern.com*

Catamaran Resort Hotel
★★★★/$$$$

Here, your family's biggest decision

Hola Tijuana

Another country and a different world lie just 16 miles south of San Diego. A day trip to Tijuana offers the chance, if time permits, and you have the correct documentation, to do a little shopping in a foreign country and perhaps, to have an authentic Mexican lunch.

Tijuana is known for its shopping values. Many people also come to see the jai alai, horse races, and bullfights. Photos of your children wearing sombreros and seated on "zonkys"—burros painted to look like zebras—make classic souvenirs. It's a good idea to avoid street food, except maybe for the electric-yellow peeled mangoes on a stick. For lunch, try a taco platter at comfortable, clean, entirely green Tilly's Fifth Avenue *(1109 Ave. Revolucion; 01152-6646-859015)*; or a Mexican plate and Caesar salad at Caesar's Palace *(1071 Ave. Revolucion; 01152-6646-384562)*, the place where that salad was invented. Or try one of the familiar American-style fast-food outlets.

Be aware that visiting Tijuana is not always pretty. If you wander from the main thoroughfare you'll run into dirty, dusty streets and young children selling gum instead of begging (be sure to buy some). But it will open your own children's eyes in important ways and might provide the fodder for some soul-searching family discussions.

each day will be whether to go to the pool, the hot tub, or the beach. This bayfront hotel boasts a heated outdoor pool and hot tub as well as a fitness center. The kid-friendly establishment also has a video arcade, sports equipment rentals (in-line skates, bikes, boogie boards, etc.), and an inexpensive, informal summer activities program that offers kids the chance to meet their peers at ice-cream socials, volleyball games, and the like. The grounds feature lush gardens enhanced with rare tropical plants, and an authentic stern-wheeler is berthed at the hotel pier when not out cruising Mission Bay. All of the 312 rooms have coffeemakers and most have small refrigerators as well. *3999 Mission Blvd., San Diego; (800) 288-0770; (858) 488-1081;* www.catamaranresort.com

Dana Inn & Marina
★★★/$$-$$$
Though the 196 rooms at this well-priced two-story hotel are simple, the list of facilities that families seek is fairly complete: a heated outdoor pool, a hot tub, rental boats and bikes, bayside jogging paths, shuffleboard courts, two tennis courts, and a restaurant. Another big plus: it's within walking distance of SeaWorld. Some bayfront rooms are available, and all rooms are equipped with coffeemakers and small refrigerators. *1710 W. Mission Bay Dr., San Diego; (800) 445-3339; (619) 222-6440;* www.danainn.com

Embassy Suites
★★★/$$$$

Located close to downtown, this 12-story, 337-suite link in the chain is also within walking distance of the Seaport Village shopping and dining complex. Accommodations are in spacious two-room suites (a bedroom plus a separate living room with a sofa bed) that are great for families. Each unit is equipped with two TVs and a kitchenette with a coffeemaker and a refrigerator. On-site facilities include an indoor heated pool, a hot tub, a sauna, and a fitness center. The room rates include a cooked-to-order breakfast served in a lush tropical atrium and evening cocktails for the grown-ups, plus soft drinks and snacks for everyone. *601 Pacific Hwy., San Diego; (800) EMBASSY; (619) 239-2400; www.embassysuites.com*

Hotel del Coronado
★★★★/$$$$

This exceptional hotel is a must-see, even if you don't stay overnight. Twelve U.S. presidents have visited here, and author L. Frank Baum is said to have modeled the Emerald City in *The Wizard of Oz* after the brightly lighted hotel at night. Located out on Coronado Island, the luxury 26-acre, 700-room oceanfront property is seven miles from downtown and reached by a dramatic 2.3-mile bridge. Built in 1888, the Victorian gingerbread main building is both a state and

national historic landmark. Facilities include a heated outdoor pool, tennis courts, and a spa and fitness center with a hot tub; there are also five restaurants. The hotel is right on the beach, and the sprawling grounds offer plenty of space to run around; you can also rent bicycles and explore the island's 15-mile dedicated bike path. Tent City Kids Camp offers special programs for children 4 through 12, while Tent City Tykes Camp caters to 3- and 4-year-olds. Overnight programs are available for kids ages 8 through 12, and teens can take kayaking and surfing lessons with Kahuna Bob. The Family Package includes a beach bucket filled with beach toys, recreation vouchers, and a picnic basket filled with goodies for a family picnic on the beach. *1500 Orange Ave., Coronado; (800) HOTEL-DEL; (619) 435-6611; www.hoteldel.com*

Humphrey's Half Moon Inn & Suites
★★★/$$$-$$$$

Located across the street from a beach on San Diego Bay, this pleasant 182-room Polynesian-style hotel has a plethora of facilities on its spacious grassy grounds. You and yours can enjoy a heated outdoor pool with waterfall, a hot tub, a children's play area, a Ping-Pong table, a putting green, and bicycle rentals. An on-site restaurant and room service are other pluses, and all rooms are equipped with coffeemakers and small refrigerators. During the summer, a Concerts by the Bay series brings in big-name entertainers such as John Lee Hooker and the Righteous Brothers (check for schedules). *2303 Shelter Island Dr., San Diego; (800) 345-9995; (619) 224-3411;* www.halfmoon.com

InnSuites Hotels— San Diego Balboa Park Hotel & Suite Resort
★★★/$$-$$$$

Resembling an old Southern mansion and listed on the National Register of Historic Places, this 147-room hotel originally opened in 1946 as Imig Manor. Entertainer Bob Hope was its first guest, and many other stars of the era also stayed here (each of the suites is now named for one). Family-friendly features include a large outdoor heated pool and hot tub, a fitness center, a small playground, an activity room with video games and a pool table, and an expansive complimentary breakfast buffet. Rooms have refrigerators stocked with complimentary juice and bottled water and microwaves. Just off the lobby, the Red Fox Steak House operates in an old inn that originally stood in Surrey, England. **NOTE:** This hotel

KOA KAMPING IN KALIFORNIA

If your family is longing for an outdoors camping vacation, but you don't own a tent or an RV, head for a KOA campground. The Kampgrounds of America chain is the largest campground franchise operation in the United States, with 500 campgrounds, 30 of which are in California. Your family can book a rustic "kamping kabin" for $25 to $50 a night and have all the fun and excitement of camping out with all the security and comfort of sleeping in. Each one-room cabin sleeps four, with a double bed and a kid-pleasing bunk bed. A two-room cabin sleeps six. You need bring only sleeping bags and cooking gear. A few KOA locations also have "kamping kottages," complete with fully equipped kitchenette and bathroom.

If you do own a tent or RV, you can still camp at KOA sites. Most of the campgrounds in the chain have swimming pools, and some offer additional recreational facilities. The particularly posh KOA Kampground near Santa Cruz has a heated pool, several hot tubs, two kiddie pools, and a water playground. To get a KOA directory, send $3 to: KOA Directory, P.O. Box 30558, Billings, MT 59114-0558.

CALIFORNIA KOA KAMPGROUNDS

Chula Vista (see page 307)
Eureka (see page 153)
Santa Cruz (see page 179)
Shingletown (see page 155)
Volcano (see page 136)

is several miles from Balboa Park, but the neighborhood is pleasant to come back to each day after sightseeing. *2223 El Cajon Blvd., San Diego; (877) DIEGO-4-U; (619) 296-2101;* www.innsuites.com

KOA Kampground
★★★/$

Located eight miles from downtown San Diego, this facility has over 275 campsites and cabins. Recreational facilities include a pool, hot tub, playground, bike rentals, and a rec room with video games, a pool table, horseshoes, and Ping-Pong. Also see "KOA Kamping in Kalifornia" on page 306. *111 N. Second Ave., Chula Vista; (800) KOA-9877; (619) 427-3601;* www.koa.com

Loews Coronado Bay Resort
★★★★/$$$-$$$$

Set on the calm San Diego Bay side of the Silver Strand, this posh, isolated 440-room low-rise resort has an elegantly charming chintz-and-wicker decor and a lobby with an expansive ocean view. But the kids will care more about the three connected swimming pools and hot tubs, the marina with rental sailboats and Wave Runners, the five bayside tennis courts, and the fitness center. The resort welcomes young guests—its Loews Loves Kids program includes a complimentary gift bag for kids under 10, childproofing kits for families traveling with children under 4, and children's menus

in the restaurant and from room service. The Commodore Kids Club offers activities for children ages 4 through 12. Water-taxi service is available to Coronado and San Diego. *4000 Coronado Bay Rd., San Diego; (800) 23-LOEWS; (619) 424-4000;* www.loewshotel.com

Marriott Hotel & Marina
★★★/$$$$

Located downtown, across from the bay and near the Seaport Village shopping and dining complex, this 1,354-room hotel is the second-largest Marriott on the West Coast. Many rooms have private balconies and bay views, and all are equipped with coffeemakers. Kids will particularly like the video game room and the two pools. Also on the premises are three restaurants, two hot tubs, six tennis courts, a sauna, a fitness center, and a marina with related activities and boat rentals. The Coronado Island Marriott Resort San Diego *(2000 Second St., Coronado; 619/435-3000),* a sprawling sister property, is directly across the bay in Coronado. A hotel boat ferries guests between the two properties. *333 W. Harbor Dr., San Diego; (800) 228-9290; (619) 234-1500;* www.marriott.com

Paradise Point Resort
★★★★/$$$-$$$$

Fronting Mission Bay near SeaWorld, this beautifully landscaped resort is on a 44-acre private island that looks like the tropical

Shangri-la that its name promises. The uncrowded layout holds 462 spacious, colorful guest rooms and suites in one-story bungalows. All rooms have small refrigerators and coffeemakers, and some units have kitchenettes. There are plenty of amenities to keep everyone busy and happy: five outdoor pools, a hot tub, a fitness center and sauna, an 18-hole putting green, a full-service marina, six tennis courts, a volleyball court, a croquet lawn, a 1.3-mile jogging path, bicycle rentals, and two restaurants. In summer, a recreation program offers fun themed activities for kids ages 3 through 12. Activities for the whole family include nature walks, pool games, and beach bonfires, with a view of the SeaWorld fireworks. Children under 17 stay free. *1404 W. Vacation Rd., San Diego; (800) 344-2626; (858) 274-4630;* www.paradisepoint.com

Ramada Limited Old Town, San Diego
★★/$$-$$$

This well-priced, well-located 125-room hotel is in a quiet part of San Diego near Old Town. It has an attractive hacienda-style decor, with blue-tiled fountains and an invitingly landscaped central courtyard. An outdoor pool and hot tub will please the kids, and complimentary continental breakfast will make mornings a little easier. Each room is equipped with a small refrigerator, a microwave, and a coffeemaker.

3900 Old Town Ave., San Diego; (800) 451-9846; (619) 299-7400; www.ramada.com

San Diego Hilton Beach & Tennis Resort
★★★★/$$$-$$$$

Do your kids have a lot of energy? Let them burn it off at this elegant 354-room high-rise resort. The list of facilities is long: a heated outdoor pool, a heated children's wading pool, several hot tubs, a half-mile-long private beach, a playground, jogging trails, a fitness center with sauna and hot tub, three putting greens, five lighted tennis courts, rental bikes, and a children's game room. A complimentary supervised children's program, Kids Klub Vacation Station, operates daily in summer and on weekends the rest of the year. Parents must stay with children under age 6, and kids 6 to 12 can participate for as little as an hour. Special family programs and meals are scheduled in summer, and children of any age stay free in their parents' room. There's an on-site restaurant with a children's menu, too. *1775 E. Mission Bay Dr., San Diego; (800) HILTONS; (619) 276-4010;* www.hilton.com

San Diego Hostel (downtown) ★★/$

You can't ask for a better location than this one in the historic Gaslamp Quarter. For more information on hostels, see "Hosteling for Families" on page 215. *521 Market St., San Diego; (619) 525-1531.*

Sheraton San Diego Hotel & Marina ★★/$$-$$$$

They do things in a big way at this 1,045-room hotel. A huge aquarium is positioned behind the concierge desk (sure to become your kids' favorite hangout), and the really big main swimming pool is landscaped with rocks and waterfalls. The property also has two more pools, a hot tub, a fitness center and health spa, tennis courts, bicycle rentals, jogging paths, and three restaurants. Every room has a private balcony with a view of the bay. All rooms have a coffeemaker, and you can rent a small refrigerator. *1380 Harbor Island Dr., San Diego; (800) 325-3535; (619) 692-2200;* www.sheraton.com

GOOD EATS

Anthony's Fish Grotto ★★★★/$$

Everyone and their auntie comes here for the superfresh seafood, the great water view, and the reasonable prices. Kids enjoy watching the boats and planes, and can usually find something they like on the children's coloring menu, which offers grilled cheese, pasta, pint-sized fish items, and drinks in a nice souvenir cup. Those with more mature palates can order anything from fresh mahimahi to lobster thermidor; the place is famous for hand-battered fish-and-chips and Louis salads. Unfortunately, no reservations are accepted, so expect to wait. A simpler menu, quick service, and patio dining are available out front at the Fishette. Time your visit to coincide with the open hours at the adjacent Maritime Museum, and you can tie in a tour of the vessels. *1360 N. Harbor Dr., at Ash St., San Diego; (619) 232-5103;* www.gofishanthonys.com

Buca di Beppo ★★★★/$-$$

Southern Italian immigrant cuisine is served in an irreverent atmosphere at this Gaslamp Quarter eatery, part of a local chain. For more details, see Good Eats in San Francisco. *705 Sixth Ave., San Diego; (619) 233-PAPA.*

Crocodile Cafe ★★★★/$-$$

The regular menu offers typical California fare: meal-size salads, sandwiches, pizzas, calzones, and pastas, plus oakwood-grilled meats. A kids' coloring menu has all their favorites. For more details, see Good Eats in Santa Monica. *7007 Friars Rd., San Diego; (619) 297-3247.*

Clap, Tickle, Tug

It's the sitting—and sitting and sitting—that gets to kids on the road. Get their belted-in bodies moving with this game of competitive copycat. The first player makes an expression or a movement, such as a hand clap; the next player repeats that movement and adds another; and so on. Kids will be pulling on their ears, sticking out their tongues, tipping back their heads, holding their elbows—and smiling! When a player forgets a movement, he's out. When everyone's out, start over.

Hard Rock Cafe ★★★★/$-$$

This branch of the worldwide chain is downtown in the Gaslamp Quarter. For more details, see Good Eats in San Francisco. *801 Fourth Ave., San Diego; (619) 615-7625;* www.hardrockcafe.com

Il Fornaio Coronado
★★★/$$-$$$

This splendid harborfront restaurant on Coronado Island offers fabulous views over to San Diego. It is especially gorgeous at night, when you can watch the lights come on. Families gravitate to the waterfront deck, where kids can move around in the open air; inside, you can dine in comfortable booths. It's easy to fill up on the wonderful housemade breads for which this chain is famous, but leave some room for a delicious pasta, rotisserie-roasted chicken, specialty pizzas, and fresh fish. After your meal, take a stroll on the promenade in front of the restaurant—it's the perfect place to snap a souvenir family photo with the San Diego skyline in the background. If you're staying in San Diego, consider taking a water taxi over for lunch or dinner. *1333 First St., Coronado; (619) 437-4911;* www.ilfornaio.com

The Old Spaghetti Factory
★★★★/$$

Located in the Gaslamp Quarter, this popular restaurant is inside an antiques-filled warehouse. The spaghetti dinner offers a choice of many toppings and is very filling. Note that reservations are not taken, and service can be very slow. For more details, see Good Eats in Silicon Valley/San Jose. *275 Fifth Ave., at K St., San Diego; (619) 233-4323;* www.osf.com

Sammy's Woodfired Pizza
★★★★/$-$$

You can choose between cozy booths and outdoor sidewalk seating (in nice weather) at this Gaslamp Quarter spot near Horton Plaza. It's very popular with locals, and you'll see why when you order up one of the pizzas. Pastas, salads, rotisserie chicken, fresh fish, and grilled bratwurst are also on the bill of fare.

OLD TOWN MEXICAN RESTAURANTS

FAMILY-FRIENDLY Mexican restaurants abound in the Old Town section of San Diego. Here are three that you can count on.

Casa de Pico
★★★★/$-$$

Located within the park in festive Bazaar del Mundo, a courtyard rimmed by colorful shops, this casual outdoor restaurant is famous for potent margaritas, strolling mariachis, and classic Mexican cuisine. Try the enchiladas verdes topped with green tomatillo sauce, or the fish taco plate. Children's portions are available. The dining area is ablaze with vividly colored piñatas, Mexican paper flowers, and shady umbrellas. *Juan St. at Wallace St., San Diego; (619) 296-3267.*

Casa de Bandini
★★★★/$$

Operating within a beautifully appointed 1829 adobe home that was once the town's social center, this spot, near Bazaar del Mundo, features out-of-the-ordinary Mexican cuisine. Sit in one of the graceful interior rooms or on the more casual patio with a cascading central fountain that is as loud as a waterfall and draws kids like a magnet. The Mexican seafood items and Mexican specialties, including a chimichanga (a deep-fried burrito) and tamales, are noteworthy. For dessert, get a *bunuelo* (a crisply fried tortilla topped with ice cream) to share. *2754 Calhoun St., San Diego; (619) 297-8211;* www.casadebandini.com

Casa Guadalajara
★★★★/$-$$

Across the street from Bazaar del Mundo, this comfortable spot is decorated like a Mexican hacienda, with adobe walls, tile floors, and heavy wooden furniture. Seating is available both indoors in an expansive, colorful room, and outdoors in a quiet sheltered courtyard. The children's coloring menu offers familiar items such as a cheese enchilada and bean burrito. Those with more adventuresome palates will want to try "armadillo eggs" (deep-fried jalapeños stuffed with cream cheese), dishes made with spicy mole sauce, and seafood Mexican style. Mexican breakfast items are also available until 2 P.M. For dessert, the whole family can easily share an order of deep-fried ice cream. Kids' dessert choices include a churro (a long Mexican doughnut) and the Cup of Mudd (chocolate pudding with crushed Oreo cookies and gummy worms). Mariachis perform on Friday, Saturday, and Sunday evenings. *4105 Taylor St., San Diego; (619) 295-5111;* www.casaguadala jara.com

The children's coloring menu offers simple pasta dishes, five-inch pizzas, and mugs of ice cream. The grown-ups may want to save room for a Messy Sundae, featuring hot fudge overflowing its dish. *770 Fourth Ave., at F St., San Diego; (619) 230-8888.*

Tom Ham's Lighthouse
★★/$$-$$$$

Arrive here before sunset to take full advantage of the spectacular water view. Later, when the dramatic lights of the city take over, the view acquires a more romantic tone. It's a fairly formal place, but your family will probably be most comfortable tucked into one of the oversize, half-moon-shaped booths; call ahead and reserve one. Lunch choices include a kid-friendly bargain buffet served from a full-size rowboat; the children's dinner menu has smaller portions of some of the adult menu items as well as a reliable burger and kid-pleasing fish-and-chips. The regular lunch menu offers seafood as well as salads and sandwiches. If you arrive before 6 P.M. Sunday through Friday, you can take advantage of a well-priced early-bird menu. *2150 Harbor Island Dr., San Diego; (619) 291-9110;* www.tomhamslighthouse.com

SOUVENIR HUNTING

Basic Brown Bear Factory

Can your kids bear the thrill of stuffing their own teddy? Then bring them to this Old Town shop, where teddy bears are born. For more details, see Souvenir Hunting in San Francisco. *2375 San Diego Ave., San Diego; (877) 234-BEAR;* www.basicbrownbear.com

Horton Plaza

Your family can browse the more than 140 shops and restaurants in this festive, colorful, neon-drenched shopping center, including a Sanrio Gift Gate, which specializes in Hello Kitty and other Japanese-cartoon-character merchandise. An outdoor food court has something to please everyone, with indoor seating available when the weather turns cool. There are two performing-arts theaters and a 14-screen cinema, too. *Broadway and G St., San Diego; (619) 238-1596;* www.hortonplaza.shoppingtown.com

Seaport Village

This shopping and dining complex is designed to look like a quaint fish-

WHO AM I? Do an impression of someone whom everyone else in the car knows. It could be a neighbor with an accent or a movie character. The first person to guess correctly gets the next turn at trying an impersonation.

ing village, with winding paths, gurgling fountains, and rides in horse-drawn carriages. It's not your average mall—there's not a Gap in sight. Stores are more distinctive and quirky; the Apple Box, for example, specializes in wooden toys. Street performers sometimes entertain, and children can look forward to a ride on a turn-of-the-century Looff carousel, originally from Coney Island, featuring hand-carved horses and animals and a 1914 band organ. They also can play on a grassy, eight-acre waterfront park (one parent can shop while the other supervises the outdoor fun). In addition to several restaurants, there's an inexpensive food court dispensing tacos, deli items, and ice cream, candy, and caramel apples, with plenty of seating and space for kids to move. *W. Harbor Dr. and Kettner Blvd., San Diego; (619) 235-4014; www.seaportvillage.com*

Trains are Good!

As you may have guessed, everything in this Old Town store is related to railroads. You'll find train videos and books, rubber stamps, T-shirts, and plenty of Thomas the Tank Engine train pieces to add to your kids' collection. (According to the store owner, "By age three kids can name all twenty of the Thomas locomotives, but they often can't tell you the name of their sibling.") Children have their choice of four train play tables, and there is a rest room for customers. Storytime is held weekly; call for schedule. *2802 Juan St. #10, San Diego; (619) 294-8372; www.trainsaregood.com*

The floors of the Palm Springs Aerial trams slowly rotate riders 720° during the trip up and down Mount San Jacinto.

The Desert: Palm Springs and Environs

WHEN YOU PLAN on a vacation in Southern California, you expect it to be sunny. But even in this region, which is famous for its fine weather, clear skies are not guaranteed. Except, perhaps, in Palm Springs. While elsewhere in California you may run into rain and cool temperatures (especially in winter), this is one place where dry days are practically a given. In Palm Springs, it is said, the sun shines 354 days a year.

It should be noted, however, that while it is invariably sunny here, it isn't always hot. In October the temperature in Palm Springs ranges from a low of 63° F to a high of 93° F; in January temperatures range from 43° F to 69° F.

It's actually rather fitting that families travel to Palm Springs in search of nice weather: that's exactly why

THE **FamilyFun** LIST

Boomers Park (page 319)

Children's Discovery Museum (page 318)

Covered Wagon Tours (page 319)

The Living Desert Wildlife & Botanical Park (page 320)

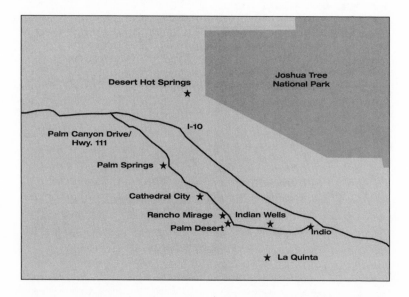

the area was settled in the first place. In 1884, San Franciscan John Guthrie McCallum traveled here with his family, hoping that the dry desert air would be beneficial to his tubercular son. The McCallums were the area's first permanent non-Indian residents.

An oasis in the arid area east of Los Angeles known as the Colorado Desert, the Palm Springs region is a favorite destination of folks looking to get away from the big city scene. Of course, the big city can be found here, too—on Palm Canyon Drive, where there is a gathering of boutiques and art galleries—but you could easily eliminate this part of town from your itinerary. You and your children can just concentrate on the area's natural beauty and the many fun outdoor activities and

attractions. Take time while you're in Palm Springs to learn more about its Native American history, to hike along old Indian trails, and to enjoy a quiet night of stargazing. Conditions here are prime for such simple pleasures.

One popular way to enjoy the wonderful weather and natural attractions of Palm Springs is to vacation at one of the area's many resorts. Once upon a time the resorts in Palm Springs were exclusively for the rich and famous, who came here for seclusion and solitude. Most regular folks settled for less fancy accommodations. Time has changed this. Now there are plenty of "democratic" luxury resorts, many of them gigantic megaresorts, that welcome everyone and their children. Many even offer kids' programs that allow parents some adult time together. (Note that the children's programs do not always operate regularly. Be sure to confirm details of programs when you make a reservation.) Once settled into one of these fabulous resorts, many families just stay put and take advantage of all the facilities, venturing out for only the occasional meal or special activity.

But staying at a resort is not the only way to enjoy the area's attractions. On a tight budget? You can still bring your family to Palm Springs. Economy hotels and special packages are available year-round. After Memorial Day, when some businesses actually roll up the carpet for the long hot summer and head for the coast, significantly reduced off-season rates prevail at most lodging places. The rising temperature and dropping prices make for a bargain family vacation, but you'll find the dry desert heat is actually quite tolerable when you have access to air-conditioning and a pool.

Beyond the resorts' pools and tennis courts, Palm Springs offers an assortment of museums, parks, a great zoo, a cooling IMAX theater, and outdoor family recreation galore—miniature golf, bumper boats, and Jeep tours. There's much more to do than you'll have time for.

Palm Springs is approximately 107 miles east of Los Angeles, about a two-hour drive. You'll know you're close when you drive through the San Gorgonio Pass, site of an impressive "wind farm" of 4,500 wind turbines that generate electricity for 93,000-plus homes. (Expect "wows!" from the backseat.) After whizzing through the striking desert terrain on relatively unbusy Highway 111 and viewing the gorgeous, rocky San Jacinto Mountains up close, you'll find yourself pulling into Palm Springs.

The Palm Springs Desert Resorts Area (as it is sometimes called) is composed of eight cities: Cathedral City, Desert Hot Springs, Indian Wells, Indio, La Quinta, Palm Desert, Palm Springs, and Rancho Mirage. Palm Canyon Drive (Hwy. 111) is the major route that connects all eight. It won't take long for the kids to figure out how the road got its name. Parts of it are lined with a stunning collection of palm trees, including an impressive palm tree forest in Indian Wells.

Tree Trivia

Joshua trees grow in the Mojave Desert region of southwest California, Nevada, Utah, and Arizona. It is thought that the tree was named by early Mormon settlers who believed that its long, upright branches looked similar to the Old Testament prophet Joshua waving people on toward the promised land.

CULTURAL ADVENTURES

Children's Discovery Museum ★★★★/$

This happy place encourages children to learn about themselves by exploring their environment. The more than 50 hands-on exhibits are designed especially for kids ages 2 through 10. They can dig for replicas of Cahuilla Indian artifacts, paint an old VW Beetle, and play grocery store with mini carts and a fully equipped checkout area. There's also a dress-up area and a mini climbing wall. It's a great spot on a hot or wet day, and adults seem to have as much fun as their children. Be sure to pick up a *Museum Guide*, which explains all the exhibits and gives you ideas on how to increase your child's enjoyment of them. *71–701 Gerald Ford Dr., Rancho Mirage; (760) 321-0602;* www.cdmod. org

---

FamilyFun TIP

Tour Guides on Tape

Ride With Me tapes (800-752-3195) are cassettes keyed to common roadways. Put in a tape at the prescribed mile marker, and it's like having a guide versed in history, geography, and trivia along as you drive through a state. (But you won't have to give up an extra seat or share your lunch.)

Palm Springs Air Museum
★★★/$

Model-airplane builders and kids who want to be pilots when they grow up will be in heaven here. Located near the airport, this collection of 27 World War II aircraft is one of the world's largest. In addition to the vintage planes, there are photo and art displays and continuous movies and videos chronicling the European and Pacific theaters of that war. Flying demonstrations are sometimes scheduled. Children's programs and activities are scheduled regularly, and A Wild Goose Hunt activity sheet, appropriate for grade-schoolers, encourages kids to open their eyes and use their imaginations. Younger ones will just like being so close to the airplanes. Lots of fun souvenirs in the gift shop. *745 N. Gene Autry Trail, at Vista Chino, Palm Springs; (760) 778-6262;* http://palmspringsairmuseum.org

Palm Springs Desert Museum
★★/$

Classic Western American art and contemporary California art are exhibited in this downtown facility, but your children may be more interested in the changing natural science exhibits. They include a desert display complete with live local creatures as well as the occasional dinosaur program. Kids also really like the Leo S. Singer Miniature Room Collection, where the realistic, carefully crafted miniature rooms illustrate how people have done their laundry through the centuries and around the world. When you arrive, ask for the children's work sheet for your kids to fill out. Special family days are usually scheduled on the first Friday of each month, when admission is free. *101 Museum Dr., Palm Springs; (760) 325-0189;* www.psmuseum.org

JUST FOR FUN

★ Boomers Park
FamilyFun ★★★★/Free-$

Operating within a faux fortress beside a grove of palms, this center is a great spot in the cool of the morning or evening, when the miniature-golf course, bumper boats, and batting cages (fees) are a lot of fun. In the heat of the day, you'll want to head for the indoor game pavilion. Go-carts and an outdoor rock-climbing wall are also available (fee for attractions). *67–770 E. Palm Canyon Dr., at Crosby Rd., Cathedral City; (760) 770-7522;* www.boomersparks.com

★ Covered Wagon Tours
FamilyFun ★★★★/$$$$

This guided tour lets your family explore the desert beyond the resorts and golf courses. In a mule-drawn covered wagon (albeit one with padded seats and pneumatic tires), you'll tour the beautiful Coachella Valley Preserve and

travel along the San Andreas Fault line for a look at how earthquakes have changed the desert's face. You'll also pass through two oases. Wagons are covered on top but open on the sides, allowing for good views, and because they are slow and quiet, your kids (and you) might get to see some of the area's wildlife, including snakes, coyotes, and jackrabbits. After the tour, you'll chow down at an old-fashioned chuck-wagon cookout dinner, complete with a sing-along. Reservations are required. *In La Quinta; call for directions; (800) 367-2161; (760)-347-2161;* www.cov eredwagontours.com

Desert Adventures
★★★★/$$-$$$$

The kids will love cruising around in one of this outfit's bright red Jeeps. You'll be picked up at your hotel for a bouncy ride along an old Indian trail into the ruggedly beautiful backcountry of the Santa Rosa Mountains. The ecotour focuses on rare wildflowers and an assortment of native animals that are sure to please the critter lovers in the crew. The children also will be fascinated by tales about the area's Cahuilla (pronounced Ka-wee-ya) Indians, who are descendants of the Shoshone and Aztec peoples and who own more than 42 percent of the valley. And the impressive demonstrations of the guides will amaze you all. One guide has been known to pluck a long thorn from a cactus,

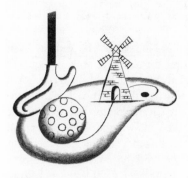

peel it using two hands and his teeth, and then do a little sewing with the resulting very, very sharp needle that has been self-threaded with the plant's fiber. *67–555 E. Palm Springs Canyon Dr. #A-104, Cathedral City; (888) 440-JEEP; (760) 324-JEEP; www.red-jeep.com*

Desert IMAX Theatre
★★★★/$

Do take in one of the special 3-D movies or regular (2-D) first-run feature films that alternate here on a six-story-high screen. Watching a movie while fortified with a large soft drink is a particularly refreshing way to spend a hot afternoon. By the time you exit, things may have cooled off outside. *68–510 E. Palm Canyon Dr., Cathedral City; (888) 340-2460; (760) 324-7333; www.desertimax.com*

Indian Canyons ★★★★/$

Kids—especially ones from the country's colder regions—tend to be impressed by palm trees. If your clan doesn't see the tropical trees very often, you'll enjoy a hike through these lush canyons, which shelter North America's largest natural palm oases. More than 5,000 Washingtonia filifera palms—the only palms native to this continent—grow along the waterfall-fed streams. These scenic canyons are also the ancestral home of the Agua Caliente Band of Cahuilla Indians, whose name means "hot water." *Located at the end of South Palm Canyon Dr., five miles from Palm Springs; (800) 790-3398; (760) 325-3400; www.indian-canyons.com or www.aguacaliente.org*

Knott's Soak City
★★★/$$$

The 21-acre water playground has 18 attractions, including 12 water slides (seven for big kids and five for the grade-schoolers), a lazy river innertube ride, and California's largest wave pool. A family water playhouse and lagoon will provide plenty of moist activities. *1500 Gene Autry Trail, Palm Springs; (760) 327-0499; www.soakcityusa.com*

The Living Desert Wildlife & Botanical Park ★★★★/$

MUST-SEE FamilyFun MUST-SEE

This spectacular, beautifully landscaped zoo is home to animals from the deserts of North America and Africa. The zoo's premier exhibit, Eagle Canyon, displays mountain lions and a golden eagle in a state-of-the-art habitat with the actual desert as a backdrop. The newest exhibit is Village Wa Tu Tu, an authentic reproduction of a trading village in Northern Kenya that includes two dromedary camels and a petting kraal (corral). Also noteworthy is the Indian Ethno-Botanic Garden, which displays various local plants and explains how the local Indians used them in their daily lives. You'll also get a close-up view of bighorn sheep, which are native to this area but rarely spotted by visitors. Probably the most illuminating experience for young and old, however, will be walking out of the searing dry desert heat into the dramatic, cooling shade of a real oasis. **NOTE:** In the hot, hot summer the zoo opens at 8 A.M. and closes at 1:30 P.M. *47-900 Portola Ave., Palm Desert; (760) 346-5694;* www.livingdesert.org

Moorten Botanical Gardens
★★/$

Especially nice in the morning, this funky private arboretum is a good place for the kids to let off a little steam while the whole family views more than 3,000 varieties of rare and unusual desert plants. It claims to be the world's first "cactarium." Your crew will find the giant cactus forest and the dinosaur footprints in rocks awesome. You'll also see birds, both caged and wild, plus caged tortoises and iguanas and assorted relics. For an appropriate souvenir of your visit, let each of the kids purchase a pet cactus to take home and care for. *1701 S. Palm Canyon Dr., Palm Springs; (760) 327-6555.*

Palm Springs Aerial Tramway
★★★/$$

Palm Springs' oldest attraction, this fun ride travels through five climatic zones on its ascent up Mount San Jacinto, providing a fabulous view of the valley along the way. State-of-the-art, 80-passenger tram cars were recently installed; using the latest ropeway technology, the floors of the trams slowly rotate—turning full circle twice per trip—as the cars ascend and descend the mountain, giving passengers 360-degree views. At the top, depending on the weather, you can hike or take a nature walk with your children. Cross-country skiing is offered in the winter. **NOTE:** This is not a fun ride for folks, big or little, who fear heights. *1 Tramway Rd., Palm Springs; (760) 325-1391; (888) 515-TRAM;* www.pstramway.com

Also, Top of the Tram restaurant is a good place for lunch, with burgers available for kids. For dinner it is a little more on the elegant side.

Shields Date Gardens
★★/Free

When your family is looking for an unusual outing and a cooling treat, head down the major thoroughfare that is Highway 111 in search of one of the area's authentic date gardens. (Some 95 percent of U.S.-grown dates come from this area.) The first one you'll come to is Shields Date Gardens, where your older kids will willingly enter the tantilizingly titled film *The Romance and Sex Life of the Date;* it's shown in a cool, dark room inside the café/gift shop. Although it sounds a bit like an X-rated movie, it would probably only merit a G. The presentation will tell you and your children everything you want to know about how dates are hand-pollinated and harvested. Purchase several varieties of dates before you leave so you can do some taste testing. The kids may be surprised to discover that there is indeed a difference in taste between one date variety and another. Most people prefer the most expensive variety—the delicious Royal Medjool. *80–225 Hwy. 111, Indio; (760) 347-0996; www.shieldsdates.com*

BUNKING DOWN

Doral Palm Springs Resort
★★★★/$$$-$$$$

Formerly a Doubletree hotel, this 285-room lodging place is relatively modest. But it has a large pool and hot tub area and offers access (for an additional fee) to the facilities of the adjacent Desert Princess Country Club, including its 27-hole golf course, 10 tennis courts, and racquetball courts. If your family is large, check out the one-, two-, and three-bedroom condominiums with fully-equipped kitchens. The Fun Factory offers kids ages 3 through 11 full- or half-day programs of activities based on themes such as Arctic Explorers and Old-Fashioned Fun. A morning session is available Wednesday through Sunday, and on Saturday an afternoon and evening session are also available. *67–967 Vista Chino, at Landau Blvd., Cathedral City; (888) FUN-IN-PS; (760) 322-7000; www.doralpalmsprings.com*

Embassy Suites Palm Desert Resort
★★★/$$-$$$$

Thanks to its spacious accommodations, this desert-gold-colored resort, decorated with Mexican tiles and fountains and tucked away amid a nine-acre date grove, is perfect for families. Each of the hotel's 198 guest rooms is a suite that consists of a bedroom plus a separate living room with a sofa bed. All the units have two TVs and a kitchenette with a coffeemaker and a refrigerator. On-site facilities include an outdoor pool and hot tub, an 18-hole putting green, six tennis courts with night-lights, and a fitness center. The room rate includes a cooked-to-order breakfast and cocktails for the grown-ups, plus soft drinks and snacks for the kids. *74–700 Hwy. 111/Monterey Ave., Palm Desert; 800-EMBASSY; (760) 340-6600; www.embassysuites.com*

Hyatt Grand Champions Resort
★★★★/$$$$

Famous for its super tennis facilities, this elegant, 338-unit, all-suite luxury retreat has lots to keep guests of all ages amused, even if they never swing a racquet. Camp Hyatt offers activities for children 3 through 12 and operates daily and Friday and Saturday evening. (An additional evening program is available by the hour.) While the children are playing with kids their own age, parents can indulge in spa treatments, use the fitness center or hot tubs, golf on the two 18-hole championship golf courses, or play tennis on one of the several courts. For another fun family excursion, take advantage of the hotel's rental bikes. There are two hotel restaurants, giving you the choice of upscale and casual. *44–600 Indian Wells Lane, Indian Wells; (800) 233-1234; (800) 55-HYATT; (760) 341-1000;* www.hyatt.com *or* www.grandchampions.hyatt.com

Lodge at Rancho Mirage
★★★★/$$$-$$$$

Well equipped for families, this sumptuous 240-room gem is nestled in the rugged foothills of the Santa Rosa Mountains, high above the desert floor. It is adjacent to the Bighorn Institute, and you can sometimes see bighorn sheep on the property. You might also see roadrunners scurrying hilariously across the manicured lawns, with toddlers in giggling pursuit. Movie stars hang out here, too. Was that actress Ellen Barkin seen slurping ice cream with her kids by the hot tub? The Ritz Kids program operates daily from 9 A.M. to 1 P.M. for children ages 5 through 12. Facilities include a pool,

Pet Savvy

It's easier than ever to bring your pet along on vacation. A number of hotels now accept pets, and some even offer exercise areas and pet room service. (A few go so far as to bring dog biscuits and bottled water to your room on a silver tray!)

Ready Buddy for travel by making sure his ID tags are complete and by taking him on short trips close to home (so he doesn't think getting in the car means going to the vet). Try calling these hotel and motel chains to find out their pet policies: Best Western *(800-528-1234);* Four Seasons *(800-332-3442);* Holiday Inn *(800-465-4329);* Loews *(800-235-6397);* and Motel 6 *(800-466-8356).*

tennis center, croquet, spa, fitness center, and playground, plus three restaurants. Kids' videos are available upon request. *68900 Frank Sinatra Dr., Rancho Mirage; (760) 321-8282; www.rockresorts.com*

Marriott's Desert Springs Resort & Spa
★★★★/$$-$$$

The largest megaresort in the area, it boasts 884 rooms and suites and sprawls over 400 lushly landscaped acres. As you might expect from a resort so large and luxurious, there's a lot to keep the troops amused here. Kids get saucer-eyed when they see the cascading waterfall and lake in the lobby, and are really wowed by the chauffeured boats that stop in the lobby and then continue outdoors, circumnavigating the property. Facilities include two 18-hole golf courses, an 18-hole putting course, 20 tennis courts, a health spa and fitness center, six swimming pools,

volleyball and basketball courts, lawn croquet, and seven restaurants. And as if that weren't enough, the Kid's Klub has activities for guests ages 4 through 12; the program operates daily from 10 A.M. to 5 P.M. *74855 Country Club Dr., Palm Desert; (800) 331-3112; (760) 341-2211; www.mariottdesertsprings.com*

Motel Row

Numerous moderately priced motels are in the area. Just drive along Palm Canyon Drive from one end to the other.

Rancho Las Palmas Marriott Resort
★★★★/$$$-$$$$

There's lots to recommend this family-friendly, 260-acre, 450-room resort, including a lovely hacienda-style decor, fabulously landscaped golf greens, and a long list of facilities. But as far as the kids are concerned, the supercool pool is the

---

FamilyFun **READER'S TIP** -

The Gasoline Log

It's a rare child who isn't motivated by the jingling of change. In the McComas family of Reistertown, Maryland, 12-year-old Joshua has a shot at hitting it big once a month, but only if he does his math. "He's in charge of the gas log," explains his mom, Melissa. "Every time I get gas, I make sure he is in the car. He has to record the mileage, gas price, gallons added, price paid, and miles the car got per gallon." At the end of the month, when they figure the totals, Joshua pockets any money left over in the McComases' gas budget. He's become an expert on math, budgeting, town gas prices, and local short-cuts. "I end up spending the same amount of money each month," says Melissa. "He just helps to figure out how much he gets to keep."

selling point here. Dubbed Tortuga Island, it features a 100-foot water slide, pop-jets, and squirting turtles. More info for Mom and Dad: the spacious, adobe-style guest rooms accommodate families comfortably, and an assortment of informal children's activities are scheduled every day. There are also organized children's programs for kids ages 5 through 12: the Cactus Kids Camp operates on Saturdays and Sundays from 9:30 A.M. to noon (if a minimum of two children signs up), and the Sundown Kids Camp from 5 P.M. to 8 P.M. Resort facilities include three pools, two hot tubs, a full-service spa, a fitness center, a jogging trail, 27 holes of golf, and 25 tennis courts. The on-site Madeira restaurant is especially nice at breakfast. *41000 Bob Hope Dr., Rancho Mirage; (800) 458-8786; (800) 228-9290; (760) 568-2727; www.marriott.com*

Renaissance Esmeralda Resort
★★★★/$$$-$$$$

You can tell you're headed somewhere special when you drive up the palm-lined entry here. This very smart, elegant, upscale resort is basically a 560-room mini city—and also happens to be kid-friendly. Your children will just adore the pool complex, which is the largest in the area. It has a waterfall, a section where floating on rafts is permitted (kids are partial to rafts), a shallow toddler pool with a sandy beach area complete with

pails, shovels, and other toys, and several hot tubs. A Kids Camp has organized activities for children ages 5 through 12. Guests happily spend their time on the two tennis courts, two 18-hole golf courses, and health spa and fitness center. Guarantee: you will not hear the words "I'm bored" here. *44-400 Indian Wells Lane, Indian Wells; (800) 552-4386; (800) HOTELS-1; (760) 773-4444; www.renaissanceesmeralda.com*

GOOD EATS

California Pizza Kitchen
★★★★/$

Come here for every kind of pizza imaginable. For details, see Good Eats in Los Angeles/Beverly Hills. *123 N. Palm Canyon Dr., in Palm Desert Fashion Plaza, Palm Springs; (760) 322-6075. Also at 73-080 El Paseo, Palm Desert; (760) 776-5036; www.cpk.com*

Elmer's Pancake and Steak House ★★★★/$

Always filled with families, and particularly popular in the morning, this coffee shop has great food at bargain prices. In addition to the usual breakfast items, the menu offers Swedish crepes with lingonberries, Snoqualmie Falls oatmeal with bananas, plus every kind of pancake you can imagine. The kids' menu is on the back of a booklet filled with games, and they get a box of crayons, too, plus a balloon and lollipop when they leave. Adults might find themselves envious of some of the kiddie choices: chocolate chocolate-chip pancakes, bow wow corn pups, steamin' mac & cheese. Yum. Reservations are not accepted, so expect a wait at prime dining times. *1030 E. Palm Canyon Dr., at Camino Real, Palm Springs; (760) 327-8419.*

Hadley Fruit Orchards
★★/$

The kids won't beg to come here for date-tasting, but bring them in anyway. They'll love the date milk shake, and you can pick up some fresh trail mix, dried fruit, and candy. *122 La Plaza, Palm Springs; (760) 325-2160.*

Hamburger Hamlet
★★★/$

This more upmarket alternative to the Golden Arches specializes in all kinds of burgers. For details, see Good Eats in Los Angeles/ Hollywood. *123 N. Palm Canyon Dr., Palm Springs; (760) 325-2321.*

Islands
★★★★/$

This is one of a chain of "Islands" that serves up burgers and sandwiches in a tropical atmosphere. For details, see Good Eats in Los Angeles/Hollywood. *72–353 Hwy. 111, in Desert Crossing Center, Palm Desert; (760) 346-4007;* www.islands restaurants.com

John's
★★★★/$

Place your order at the window, then select one of the comfy booths. The menu at this coffee shop includes eggs Benedict, bicuits and gravy, and huevos rancheros in the morning along with the more common breakfast items. Lunch and dinner bring on a wide variety of hamburgers, sandwiches, and salads. The informal atmosphere is fine for kids, and although there's no children's menu, prices are so reasonable that you can afford to order a regular meal for them. *900 N. Palm Canyon, Palm Springs; (760) 327-8522. Also at 74–601 Hwy. 111, Palm Desert; (760) 346-3352.*

Las Casuelas Nuevas
★★★★/$-$$

In balmy weather, you can't beat dinner on the outdoor patio at this unique local restaurant, but the festive, hacienda-style interior is inviting as well. The whole family will love being serenaded by mariachis while dining on Mexican food. Start with a round of specialty margaritas—you can order a virgin version for the tykes. (Be forewarned: some of the drinks have risqué names.) Plenty of chips and salsa will keep everyone busy until your meal arrives. The kids' menu offers a beef or chicken taco, a cheese enchilada, and mini versions of a cheese quesadilla and a burrito—all served with beans and rice. More unusual items for grown-ups include crab and shrimp enchiladas and *pollo en mole poblano* (chicken in a wonderful exotic chili-nut sauce). Though there are several branches of this restaurant in the area, this is the one to head for. Make reservations or expect a long, long wait. *70–050 Hwy. 111, Rancho Mirage; (760) 328-8844.*

Palomino Euro Bistro
★★★/$$$$

The kids can enjoy pasta or pizza while Mom and Dad feast on more inspired cuisine at this stylish desert oasis. For details, see Good Eats in San Francisco. *73–101 Hwy. 111, Palm Desert; (760) 773-9091.*

Sammy's Woodfired Pizza
★★★★/$-$$

The wood-fired ovens here are operated at 800° F, giving the pizza a distinctive toasty taste. The children's coloring menu offers pasta dishes in addition to pizza, and the regular menu lists pastas, salads, rotisserie chicken, fresh fish, and grilled bratwurst, too. It's upstairs at the Gardens shopping enclave on an upscale shopping street. For additional details, see Good Eats in San Diego. *73–595 El Paseo at Larkspur, Palm Desert; (760) 836-0500.*

Taqueria **★★★★/$$-$$$**

Hey, Mom and Dad—it's your vacation, too. Why not spend some of it sitting on the open-air patio on a warm evening, listening to live music while munching on handmade tortilla chips and sipping a potent margarita? Luckily, kids also love it here, and with all the din, no one even notices when a child is not on his or her best behavior. All the usual suspects are on the menu, along with lobster tacos, baby back ribs, and paella. A kids' menu offers French fries and Jell-O as well as tacos. On Wednesday nights kids eat free (one kid per adult). *125 E. Tahquitz Way, Palm Springs; (760) 778-5391. Also at 72–286 Hwy. 111, Palm Desert; (760) 776-8240;* www.palmsprings taqueria.com

TGI Friday's **★★★★/$$-$$$**

A huge menu, cheery staff, and bustling atmosphere make this chain a hit with families. For details, see Good Eats in San Francisco. *72–620 El Paseo, Palm Desert; (760) 568-2280;* www.fridays.com

SOUVENIR HUNTING

Dollsville Dolls & Bearsville Bears

Britain's Rarest Bear—the only one left out of 12 red teddies made there way back in 1918—is part of a teddy-bear exhibit at this shop, which stocks a choice collection of dolls and stuffed animals. There are also fabulous Barbies and Disney collector dolls. *292 N. Palm Canyon, Palm Springs; (800) CAL-DOLL; (760) 325-2241;* www.dollsville.com

Hawaii

SET IN THE MIDDLE OF the vast Pacific Ocean, the Hawaiian Islands consist of 132 islands formed 40 million years ago by a series of volcanic eruptions. Today, eight of these intriguing islands are inhabited, and six cater to visitors in general—and families in particular. Hawaii's wonderful beaches, warm waters filled with colorful fish, lush rain forests that are home to still more colorful and interesting creatures, exciting volcanoes and waterfalls, laid-back tropical ambience, and interesting culture and history make it a natural destination for a family vacation.

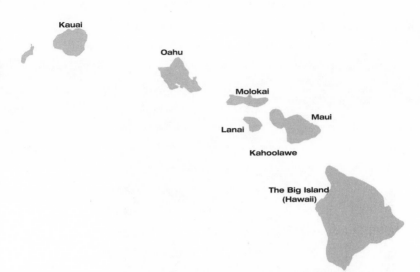

Kauai

Oahu

Molokai

Maui

Lanai

Kahoolawe

The Big Island
(Hawaii)

When making lodging reservations, always ask about packages. Hawaiian resorts are extremely family-friendly, and almost always have some kind of deal going.

To save even more money, look for condominium resorts, which are an especially good choice for families. For still more information on affordable options, see "Family-Friendly Lodging Chains and Touring Companies" on page 368.

Beaches are the main attraction here, but be cautious about swimming in unguarded waters. Undertows and strong currents can be dangerous. On most islands, you can take tours by helicopter, boat, and Atlantis submarines. You can also go horseback riding, snorkeling, and kayaking.

Now there's only one thing left for you to do: enjoy!

ATTRACTIONS

$	under $5
$$	$5 - $10
$$$	$10 - $20
$$$$	$20 +

HOTELS/MOTELS/CAMPGROUNDS

$	under $100
$$	$100 - $200
$$$	$200 - $300
$$$$	$300 +

RESTAURANTS

$	under $10
$$	$10 - $15
$$$	$15 - $25
$$$$	$25 +

FAMILYFUN RATED

★	Fine
★★	Good
★★★	Very Good
★★★★	FamilyFun Recommended

Aspiring dancers can attempt to master the hula with lessons at the Bishop Museum—or just improvise at the ocean.

Oahu

OAHU IS THE CENTRAL island in the Hawaiian chain and has been a gathering place since the days when Polynesian chiefs made it their home. Today, many visitors to Hawaii decline a stopover in Honolulu, the southernmost state capital in the United States, in favor of heading directly to an outer island. Don't be one of them. You won't be sorry that you scheduled two or three nights on Waikiki Beach, the famed beach/resort area of Honolulu. While some kids have actually been heard to complain that the outer islands are "boring," no one would ever say that about Waikiki.

Described by one worldly sixth grader as "New York on the beach," Waikiki nonetheless deserves its reputation as one of the world's finest sandy shorelines. Granted, it

THE **FamilyFun** LIST

MUST-SEE
MUST-SEE

Bishop Museum (page 333)

Honolulu Zoo (page 336)

Kodak Hula Show (page 334)

Sea Life Park (page 336)

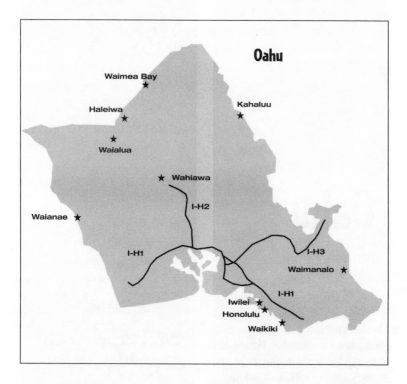

is crowded, and high-rises pack the shoreline, but the sand is clean (the powdery white stuff is barged in from Molokai), the water warm, and the overall effect gorgeous. Upon arrival, pick up a free copy of *This Week Oahu* for useful maps, money-saving coupons, informative ads, and information on attractions.

As your family will soon find out, there's much more to do here than lie on the beach and splash in the surf. You'll want to plan a few excursions to the other side of Honolulu—perhaps to see the seashell collection at the Bishop Museum—or out to the east side of the island to Sea Life Park,

home of the world's only "wholphin." Although you may want to rent a car for a day (see "A Drive Around Oahu" on page 340) you won't need your own wheels to hit the highlights of Waikiki and downtown Honolulu. You can use Honolulu's excellent public transportation system (known as TheBus) or take cabs (fares are reasonable for families). Or wow your kids by springing for a limo cab—they cost the same as a regular taxi.

Get off the plane and see what all the fuss is about. You can do Oahu *wikiwiki* (fast) with your *keiki* (kids) and then depart for a quieter outer island.

CULTURAL ADVENTURES

 **Bishop Museum**

FamilyFun ★★★★/$-$$

The romantics in the family will be interested in the story behind this museum of Hawaii's natural and cultural history. And children will be won over by the wonders of Kidspace *(see below)*. The museum was founded in memory of a Hawaiian princess, Bernice Pauahi, by her mourning husband, Charles Reed Bishop, to display the artifacts she had collected during her lifetime. Opened in 1889, it now holds more than 20 million items. The century-old gray, Romanesque-style building is in the scenic residential area of Kalihi, about a 20-minute ride by cab or car from Waikiki, and is fun to get to by TheBus. The whole family will be delighted by the three-story Great Hawaiian Hall, which exhibits historical and cultural artifacts. Highlights include portraits of Hawaiian monarchs framed with feather *kahili*, and the skeleton of a 50-foot sperm whale that "swims" overhead. More halls highlight other Polynesian cultures, displaying restored outrigger canoes, brightly colored royal feather capes, and historic surfboards.

In Kidspace, children can put together a canoe, create a "feather"

Fly Time Scavenger Hunts

You end up with a lot of idle time when you travel by air. Scavenger hunts are an easy way to spend those hours calmly.

IN THE AIRPORT

You don't want anyone lost in the crowd, so set off in parent-child teams to find the following:

♦ A child holding a doll
♦ A person carrying four pieces of luggage
♦ An abandoned sports section of *USA Today*
♦ 4 pilots
♦ 2 courtesy carts

ON THE AIRPLANE

Find these items individually or together:

♦ Cars
♦ Railroad tracks
♦ A cloud
♦ Another airplane
♦ A mountain range below
♦ Someone speaking in a foreign language
♦ A father holding a baby
♦ A person in an apron
♦ Somebody sleeping
♦ A laptop computer
♦ A mustache
♦ A briefcase
♦ A Walkman radio
♦ A pillow and blanket
♦ Candy
♦ A blue tie

cape using felt, try on an authentic Hawaiian sea turtle shell, play native musical instruments, and explore drawers filled with Hawaiian seashells. Hula lessons are scheduled each day at 1 and 3 in the afternoon, and there are ongoing demonstrations of native crafts such as making quilts and feather leis. Kids will also enjoy the Planetarium, which features shows about the sky and the planets; special shows are scheduled daily and telescopes are available in the observatory for afternoon solar observing. *1525 Bernice St., in Kapalama/Kalihi, Honolulu; (808) 847-3511;* www.bishopmuseum.org

Iolani Palace
★★/$$

Surrounded by a spacious park that is perfect for a relaxing family picnic (plan it for Friday at noon and you'll get free entertainment provided by the Royal Hawaiian Band), this palace was once the official residence of King Kalakaua and Queen Liliuokalani, the last monarchs of Hawaii. It is also one of only three

official palaces in the United States (the other two are the Queen Emma Summer Palace in Nuuanu, also on Oahu, and the Hulihee Palace in Kailua-Kona on the Big Island). A guide dressed in a muumuu will take you on a journey back in time to the 1800s. Your kids might be interested to learn that the king was so impressed when he saw electricity in Paris that he converted this palace from gaslight to electricity before either Buckingham Palace or the White House did. Children under 5 are not permitted, and reservations are advised. *King St. and Richards St., downtown Honolulu; (808) 522-0832.*

Kodak Hula Show
FamilyFun ★★★★/Free

This colorful, free production has been performed in the Waikiki Shell since 1937, making it Hawaii's longest-running show. Kids love watching the dances, performed with a backup chorus of "aunties" dressed in riotously colorful muumuus and looking as if they

Paper Leis

It wouldn't be a true Hawaiian celebration without colorful flower leis. You can either make them before your vacation, or provide the supplies during the trip so kids can make their own. First, trim the tops of colorful cupcake liners to resemble scalloped-edged flowers. Then cut a bunch of drinking straws into 1-inch lengths for spacers. Using a wide-eyed embroidery needle and twine, alternately sew through the centers of a bunch of flowers and string on straw sections. When the strand is long enough, tie together the strong ends, and the lei is ready to wear.

just got back from a shopping binge at Hilo Hattie. The souvenir stalls outside are almost as impressive as the show. You can pick up brightly painted wooden earrings in tropical parrot and fish shapes for just $1, and shiny black kukui-nut necklaces (worn by both girls and boys) for under $10. The Honolulu Zoo (see page 336) is just across the street. *In Kapiolani Park, Waikiki; (808) 627-3379.*

Mission Houses Museum
★★/$

The three saltbox-style frame houses here were built in New England and shipped to Oahu to house missionaries. The 1821 Frame House is the oldest existing house in Hawaii. Two other houses here were constructed from bricks made by hand from coral. Kids enjoy checking out the island's original schoolhouse, and they especially like the Living History Program on Wednesday, when guides dress in period costumes. Tours last about one hour, and you don't need reservations. Don't miss the huge Kawaiahao Church across the street. It was built entirely of coral by missionaries between 1838 and 1842. *553 S. King St., downtown Honolulu; (808) 531-0481;* www. missionhouses.org

Polynesian Cultural Center
★★/$$$$

This is a great place for kids and adults to get an overview of the music, crafts, and dance of the South Pacific. The center is divided into seven separate villages, each representing a Polynesian island group—Tahiti, Tonga, Samoa, New Zealand, Fiji, Marquesas, and Hawaii. Begin with the canoe ride, which will give you an overview of the place, and then walk through and explore the various buildings and villages more thoroughly. Two IMAX films and Hawaii's only canoe pageant are included in the general admission price, but the evening Polynesian revue and luau are optional and cost an additional fee. A new children's program, Keiki Activities, features 20 ancient Polynesian games and dances. Kids are shown how to play the games and do the dances and are then let loose to try it for themselves. Though you can drive here if you have a car, you'll have a better experience if you take the shuttle (additional fee). It picks you up at your hotel, and a guide narrates the trip and provides important background information that will help your family make the most of your visit. Remind your kids that this is not a theme park but a cultural show, and things sometimes move slowly; visitors can explore the exhibits at their own pace, but you sometimes have to wait for the next show or activity to start. Most grade-schoolers would enjoy a visit here, but even younger kids will have a good time, especially if they're with older siblings. A variety of packages is available. *In Laie, 35 miles from Waikiki; (800) 367-7060; (808) 293-3333;* www.polynesia.com

JUST FOR FUN

Honolulu Zoo
FamilyFun ★★★/$

Princess Kaiulani's pet peacocks were among the first residents in this zoo when it was established in 1914. Today the compact 43-acre park is home to more than 1,250 animals of some 300 different species. The tropical bird collection is a highlight here—your kids can see the nene, Hawaii's state bird, as well as rarely exhibited (other than in Hawaii) birds of paradise. It is the only place in the islands where you will see a snake. You can also go on a family safari through the ten-acre African Savanna exhibit, which replicates the natural habitats of African wildlife. Special programs for families include Snooze in the Zoo and Breakfast with the Keepers (reservations required; *808/971-7195).* A legendary Art Mart, where original art and framed photographs are sold, is held outside the zoo fence on Wednesday, Saturday, and Sunday. Kids might enjoy having a caricature portrait rendered on the spot. *151 Kapahulu Ave., Waikiki; (808) 971-7174;* www.honolulu zoo.org

Sea Life Park
FamilyFun ★★★/$$$

Built on the east side of the island at Makapuu Point, this aquarium displays hundreds of species of sea creatures. Kids will get the giggles as they try to pronounce the tongue-twisting names of two specimens found in the 300,000-gallon Hawaiian Reef Aquarium: the humuhumunukunukuapua'a (the state fish) and the lauwiliwilinukunukuoioi (also known as the long-nosed butterfly fish). They'll also be impressed by the 36-foot sperm whale skeleton, and Kekaimalu, the world's only real live "wholphin"— a cross between a false killer whale and an Atlantic bottle-nosed dolphin. Most exciting of all, kids at least 40 inches tall can interact with bottle-nosed dolphins at Splash U (additional fee; reservations required). Round-trip shuttle service is available from select locations in Waikiki. *41–202 Kalanianaole Hwy., in Waimanalo; (808) 259-7933.*

Waikiki Aquarium
★★★/$

Known for having Hawaii's most extensive collection of tropical Pacific marine life, this aquarium opened in 1904 and is the third oldest in the United States. Youngsters enjoy seeing the endangered sea creatures, including the cute Hawaiian monk seal. Don't miss the kid-pleasing Jet Set gallery featuring creatures (the nautilus, cuttlefish, octopus to name a few) that jet-propel themselves through water. *2777 Kalakaua Ave., Waikiki; (808) 923-9741; www.waquarium.org*

BUNKING DOWN

The Breakers ★★/$$

It's located at the north end of Waikiki, just behind the Hilton Hawaiian Village. But in exchange for walking a block to the beach, your family gets comfortable accommodations at bargain-basement rates. Set in a low-rise building that encircles a tropically landscaped pool, the 81 rooms here have a Polynesian flavor and lots of space. Every unit is air-conditioned and has a kitchenette. Garden suites, which have a bedroom with a queen-size bed plus a sitting room with two twin beds, accommodate up to four people. There's a café on the premises, too. *250 Beachwalk, Waikiki; (800) 426-0494; www.breakers-hawaii.com*

THE ONLY WAY TO GO

One of Oahu's best buys, "TheBus" (aka the #2 bus) will transport your family to many of Oahu's main attractions: downtown Honolulu, Chinatown, the Iolani Palace, the Bishop Museum, the Kodak Hula Show, and the Honolulu Zoo. *On Kuhio Street in Waikiki, the fare is just $1 per person; (808) 848-5555.*

Hawaiiana Hotel ★★/$$

Located next door to The Breakers *(at left)*, this appealing 95-room bargain hotel is similar to its neighbor, with two courtyard pools in a garden setting. Every room is air-conditioned and has a kitchenette, and the one-bedroom suites are extra-comfortable for a family of four. You'll be presented with a fresh pineapple upon arrival, and Kona coffee and pineapple juice are served poolside in the morning. Other nice extras are a poolside barbecue where you can prepare evening meals, convenient coin-operated washers and dryers, and Hawaiian entertainment on Sunday evening. You can even borrow beach mats. *260 Beach Walk, Waikiki; (800) 367-5122; (808) 923-3811; www.hawaiianahotelatwaikiki.com*

Hilton Hawaiian Village
★★★★/$$$$

With more than 3,000 rooms, this is the largest resort hotel in Hawaii

337

and the only true self-contained resort on Waikiki. At 22 acres, it is so big and so well equipped that you could easily spend your entire vacation on the premises and never get bored. Families always give it rave reviews. In the mornings, the spectacular palm-studded beach and adjacent saltwater lagoon beckon. You'll also want to spend some time in the gorgeous 10,000-square-foot "super pool," landscaped with lava rock waterfalls and flowering native plants. And don't forget to check out the lobby areas, where your kids can get an up-close look at 60-plus species of tropical birds, including black-footed penguins, African red-winged flamingos, and black swans. The resort has more than 20 restaurants and lounges and 90 shops. Of special note are the ethnic shops in the one-story-high Rainbow Bazaar, which also houses a Thai temple, a 50-foot-high replica of a Japanese pagoda, and an authentic Japanese farmhouse.

The Hilton's daily Rainbow Express program for children ages 5 through 12 operates year-round with full- and half-day sessions. Children can also sign up and participate in the King's Jubilee parade or take a wildlife tour. Still in search of something to do? On Friday nights, the free King's Jubilee Hula and Fire Dancing Show is followed by a spectacular fireworks display. All rooms in the Rainbow Tower and most rooms in the beachfront "vil-

lage" have ocean views; all units are also equipped with handy coffeemakers and refrigerators. Children stay free in their parents' room. *2005 Kalia Rd., Waikiki; (800) HILTONS; (808) 949-4321; www.hiltonhawaii.com*

Hyatt Regency Waikiki Resort & Spa
★★★/$$$$

A great choice for beach-loving families, this resort lets you keep the ocean in view all the time. In the heart of Waikiki, right across the street from the beach, the 1,230-room hotel has a pool and sundeck on the third floor overlooking the sand and surf. The three-level open-air atrium lobby features an indoor waterfall, tropical landscaping, and the occasional colorful parrot. The rooms and suites are set in two 40-story towers; all are equipped with coffeemakers and refrigerators, and you can rent VCRs. Regency Club guests have access to a rooftop sundeck and hot tub. Camp Hyatt, for kids ages 3 to 12, features Hawaiian activities, stories, and crafts, and operates daily in summer and on Friday and Saturday the rest of the year. For a quick lesson in Hawaiian culture, take the kids to the second-floor lobby, which has a display of historical Hawaiian arts and crafts and memorabilia, including antique hula dolls and ultratiny Chinese women's shoes. More than 65 shops are found on the first three floors. And Moms take note: the resort boasts Waikiki's first full-service spa, which has an ocean view. There are several restaurants, including the award-winning and sophisticated Ciao Mein (see Good Eats). *2424 Kalakaua Ave., Waikiki; (800) 55-HYATT; (808) 923-1234;* www.hyatt.com

Pacific Beach Hotel
★★/$$$-$$$$

Across the street from the beach, this 841-room hotel offers three restaurants (including Oceanarium; see Good Eats), a lap pool and hot tub on a fourth-floor sundeck, a fitness center, rooftop tennis courts, and a spa. The Keiki Korner children's program for ages 6 through 11 offers island crafts, swimming, tide pool fish-gathering, and hula lessons. *2490 Kalakaua Ave., Waikiki; (800) 367-6060; (808) 922-1233;* www. pacificbeachhotel.com

Royal Hawaiian
★★★/$$$$

Sometimes referred to as the Pink Palace of the Pacific, this very pink, Moorish-Mediterranean–style hotel dates from 1927 and offers old Hawaiian ambience. Upon arrival, all guests are given a lei—a once-traditional greeting that is now rare. There are 528 rooms and suites; those in the old section are spacious and unfussy, with high ceilings and windows that open to the trade winds. All units have coffeemakers, and some have refrigerators, too.

The children's Keiki Aloha program, which operates at the nearby Sheraton Waikiki, includes snorkeling and boogie-boarding as well as excursions to the Waikiki Aquarium and Honolulu Zoo; an evening program offers crab hunting and a hotel scavenger hunt. The open-air, beachside Surf Room is a choice spot for breakfast or lunch, and the Surf Bar, also open-air and beachside, is perfect for a sunset drink. Kids can order Pink Palace ice cream, made exclusively for this hotel with pink rose-petal extract. An elaborate luau—the only one on Waikiki—is held on the hotel's oceanside lawn

Hawaii's State Symbols

STATE MARINE MAMMAL
the humpback whale

STATE BIRD
the nene (or Hawaiian goose)

STATE FISH
the humuhumunukunukua-pua'a, a colorful triggerfish. (Not to be confused with the long-nosed butterfly fish, or lauwiliwilinukunukuoioi!)

STATE FLOWER
the yellow *Hibiscus Brackenridgei.* (There are 25 shapes and colors of hibiscus.)

every Monday night. *2259 Kalakaua Ave., Waikiki; (800) 325-3535; (808) 923-7311,* www.royal-hawaiian.com

Sheraton Moana Surfrider
★★★/$$$$

Built in 1901 on the site of the 19th-century home of King Kamehameha the Great, this wedding-cake-white, 793-room beachfront property is the oldest hotel on Waikiki. It's right in the middle of everything—

Waikiki just grew up around it. The rooms and suites are spacious, decorated in low-key style with Hawaiian touches such as locally made quilts and seashell-shaped soap, and equipped with coffee-makers and refrigerators. Some packages include a lei greeting at check-in. Kids can frolic on the beach (parents appreciate the life-guard station located right in front of the hotel). There's also a pool and

---

DAY TRIP
A Drive Around Oahu

This route takes you north through the center of Oahu and then follows the coast around the island's east edge. The drive will give your family a glimpse of the wildly scenic "real" Oahu, although parts of it are as crowded and congested as Honolulu.

For the best rates, reserve a car as far in advance as possible; you might want to ask about two- and three-day packages. Cars are sometimes available at the last minute, but the price of such rentals is high. Most of the big rental agencies have satellite offices in Waikiki where you can pick up and return your vehicle.

The night before, arrange at your hotel for a picnic lunch.

9 A.M. Pick up your picnic lunch and depart Waikiki. You'll be driving north on the Nimitz Highway (Hwy.

92) toward the airport, taking the H-1 to the H-2 to Highway 99. You'll then take Highway 83 up to the northern tip of the island and down to Highway 72, which leads back to Waikiki. Your car rental agency will provide a good map, and you can't get too lost—there aren't enough roads on the island.

9:30 A.M. Stop at **Sam Choy's** in Iwilei for breakfast, then visit **Hilo Hattie** to pick out matching aloha outfits for the whole family.

11:30 A.M. Get lost in the world's largest maze at the **Dole Plantation** in Wahiawa *(64-1550 Kamehameha Hwy./Hwy. 99; 808/621-8408),* 26 miles/45 minutes from Waikiki. Spread over two acres, the six-foot-high maze has a 1.7-mile-long path to its center. Instead of a traditional English hedge, this maze is planted with 11,400 colorful pink Hawaiian hibiscus and fragrant

fitness center on the premises. The daytime and evening Keiki Aloha program for kids ages 5 through 12 operates at the nearby Sheraton Waikiki, if you want to immerse your children in Hawaiian culture. Even if you don't stay overnight, stroll through the second-floor rotunda gallery of historic photographs and memorabilia (kids will laugh at the itchy woolen swimsuits that people wore in the 1930s) and

take the free historical hotel tour scheduled Monday through Friday at 11 A.M. and 5 A.M. *2365 Kalakaua Ave., Waikiki; (800) 782-9488; (808) 922-3111; www.sheraton.com*

Sheraton Princess Kaiulani
★★★/$$$

Located across the street from the Sheraton Moana Surfrider, this top-notch 1,150-room hotel offers the same amenities as its beachfront

plumeria plants. The least amount of time it has taken anyone to make it through so far is six minutes; the longest is 1½ hours, and the average is 45 minutes. (If you really do get lost, you can open an emergency map.) While here, your kids can also explore a pineapple garden growing 21 varieties. There's also an interesting historical train tour of the plantation. Don't miss the unusual graffiti-laden leaves on the Autograph Tree just outside the visitors' center. Messages carved into the round leaves last about one year. Inside, you can purchase a coconut "postcard" (you can mail it up the road in Haleiwa, or at any post office) and snack on a waffle cone filled with pineapple whip.

1 P.M. Stop in **Haleiwa**, the gateway to Oahu's North Shore. This quiet, rustic town has quaint shops, modest restaurants, and plenty of art galleries. It also has some great shave

ice. Give the kids lunch backward, with dessert first, here at the **M. Matsumoto Grocery Store.** You'll know you've arrived at the right place when you see people sitting on the bench out front, holding neon-bright cones with equally bright, colorful puddles at their feet.

2 P.M. After leaving Haleiwa, you'll drive past the legendary North Shore surfing beaches: **Sunset, Banzai Pipeline, Waimea Bay.** All are great spots to have your picnic and catch some rays while watching the surfers.

4 P.M. Start back to Waikiki, driving the scenic route back via the eastern shore.

5:30 P.M. Arrive back at your hotel. Rest for a while and freshen up. If you've rented a car just for the day, head out to a restaurant you need to drive to. Take advantage of having wheels!

sister properties, but costs less. The rooms and suites have coffeemakers and refrigerators, and kids like the large pool area. They can also participate in the Keiki Aloha program for children ages 5 through 12 at the nearby Sheraton Waikiki. The whole family will enjoy the cocktail and buffet dinner show scheduled five nights a week, most of the year. For a little history lesson, check out the portraits and artifacts relating to the hotel's namesake princess that decorate the lobby. *120 Kaiulani Ave., Waikiki; (800) 782-9488; (808) 922-5811;* www.sheraton.com

Sheraton Waikiki
★★★/$$$$

This 1,852-room behemoth is the second-largest hotel on the islands. It has two pools, direct beach access, and a fitness center. Eighty percent of the rooms and suites have ocean views; all are equipped with coffeemakers. Young guests love the glass elevator, which takes you to the top of the 31-story tower for a spectacular view of the area. The Keiki Aloha program for kids ages 5 through 12 is the only such program in Hawaii offered year-round. (The Sheraton piloted resort children's programs in Hawaii, introducing theirs in 1988.) At some of the hotel's restaurants, kids 12 and under receive free meals

when with a paying adult. The oceanside Sand Bar has a delicious view of Diamond Head and is a great spot to stop for cocktails and pupus. Hawaiian entertainment is presented on the main pool stage every evening from 6 to 8. *2255 Kalakaua Ave., Waikiki; (800) 325-3535; (808) 922-4422;* www.sheraton.com

Molten rock below the surface of the Earth that rises in volcanic vents is known as **magma**, but after it erupts from a volcano it is called lava.

Waikiki Hostel
★/$

Located just two blocks from the famous Waikiki beach, this peaceful retreat is in the center of all the action. Private rooms that can accommodate up to four family members are available; reservations are advised. For more information on staying in youth hostels, see "Hosteling for Families" on page 215. *2417 Prince Edward St., at Kaiulani St., Waikiki; (808) 926-8313.*

GOOD EATS

Bubba Gump Shrimp Co.
★★★★/$$

Dine on everything shrimp at this popular *Forrest Gump*–themed restaurant. Also see Good Eats in San Francisco. *1450 Ala Moana Blvd., in Ala Moana Shopping Center, Honolulu; (808) 949-4867;* www.bubbagump.com

California Pizza Kitchen
★★★/$

This branch of the casual, well-priced chain has a full bar. The menu offers pizzas, soups, salads, pastas, and sandwiches. Also see Good Eats in Los Angeles/Beverly Hills. *Also in Kahala Mall, 4211 Waealae Ave., downtown Honolulu; (808) 737-9446;* www.cpk.com

Cheeseburger in Paradise
★★★★/$

Burgers and breezes, plus fish and salads, are the specialties of this popular place. Hot dogs and cheeseburgers are available for children by request, and live music is scheduled nightly from 4 to 11. Also see Good Eats in Maui. *2500 Kalakaua Ave., Waikiki; (808) 923-3731.*

Ciao Mein
★★★/$$$-$$$$

Located in the Hyatt Regency Waikiki Resort, this award-winning and sophisticated restaurant features both Italian and Chinese fare as well as fusions of both (spicy ginger-garlic shrimp with angel hair pasta). The spring rolls, prize-winning

Szechuan eggplant, and Chinese salad are particularly delicious. Everything is served family style. Young diners are accommodated nicely with their own activity menu offering pasta or cheese pizza. *2424 Kalakaua Ave., Waikiki; 808-923-CIAO;* www.ciaomein.com

Duke's Waikiki
★★★★/$$-$$$

The Outrigger Canoe Club was established here in 1908 to perpetuate ancient Hawaiian water sports. It lives on in this casual dining venue, where the family can learn about the history of surfing through photos and memorabilia decorating the walls. Named for surfing legend Duke Kahanamoku, who was once an Outrigger Canoe Club member and lived nearby, the place is almost a museum, with displays of antique surfboards and a koa outrigger canoe. Adding to the Hawaiian atmosphere are koa walls, palm-thatched palapas, and lauhala-weave ceilings. Situated on the beach, the eatery has a no-shoes-required policy, allowing you and your kids to walk in right off the sand. And the food is good, too. The all-you-can-eat buffet breakfast is a bargain. Light lunches are also served, and at dinner it's Hawaiian fish, steak, pizza, pasta, burgers, and the house specialty, Hula Pie, made with vanilla ice cream, macadamia nuts, and chocolate syrup. The keiki menu offers spaghetti and a cheeseburger. Service is good, though the servers tend to look and act as though they could star in a movie titled *The Stepford Waitstaff.* Be here at sunset to catch live slack-key guitar. The restaurant also hosts a Concerts on the Beach series, with top island entertainers on Friday, Saturday, and Sunday afternoons from 4 to 6. *In the Outrigger on The Beach Waikiki, 2335 Kalakaua Ave., Waikiki; (808) 922-2268;* www.hulapie.com

Hard Rock Cafe
★★★★/$$

Since it's located away from the beach, on the outskirts of Waikiki, the best way to get to this popular spot is by cab. The menu offers a variety of American favorites. The tropical mixed drinks are outstanding (kids can indulge in virgin versions), and you'll all be entertained by the music, the rock memorabilia, and the trade-

---

FamilyFun ACTIVITY

Wind Bags

Getting a homemade kite off the ground doesn't get much easier than this quick trick. First, tie together the handles of a plastic shopping bag with an end of a ball of string. Staple a few 2-foot lengths of ribbon to the bottom of the bag for kite tails. Now find a windy spot outdoors and start running. As the bag fills with air, slowly let out the string and the kite should begin to soar and dive.

---

mark car decoration—here it's a real Cadillac "woody" station wagon suspended over the bar. Also see Good Eats in San Francisco. *1837 Kapiolani Blvd., Honolulu; (808) 955-7383;* www.hardrockcafe.com

Hau Tree Lanai ★★★/$$

Adjacent to a sandy beach on the quiet southern end of Waikiki, this restaurant has an expansive patio under an old banyan tree. It's especially nice for breakfast or lunch, when the inexpensive menu offers plenty of things kids like. Dinner is pricier, and there is no children's menu. If you do dine here, arrive by cab or bus, then take a nice leisurely walk back to central Waikiki, perhaps stopping off at the zoo or aquarium on the way. (That way you can eat before anyone gets too hungry or too tired.) *In the New Otani Kaimana Beach Hotel, 2863 Kalakaua Ave., Waikiki; (808) 921-7066;* www.kaimana.com

Keo's ★★/$$$

The sumptuous orchid-filled dining room of this Thai restaurant is popular with locals and celebrities alike: Elton John and Tina Turner have both dined here. The atmosphere—gently cooling fans and beautiful Thai art and artifacts—is low-key and not too formal for small diners. Kids might like the mild Indonesian shrimp with peanut sauce, and most will also smile kindly on spring rolls and orange pad Thai noodles. Those with more adventuresome palates should not miss the famous Evil Jungle Prince, a deliciously spicy dish prepared with fresh basil, coconut milk, red chilis, and either meat or vegetables. *Next to the Ambassador Hotel, 2028 Kuhio Ave., Honolulu; (808) 951-9355.*

Oceanarium ★★★★/$$-$$$

It's like eating in an aquarium. There are three restaurants, two of which let you dine beside a three-story, 280,000-gallon saltwater fish tank that holds hundreds of local tropical specimens, including colorful reef fish, manta rays, and sharks. Kids will be fascinated, and the time spent waiting for your meal to arrive will seem to fly (or swim) by. Better still, the prices are reasonable and the food is good. The international menu is eclectic, with salads, sandwiches, burgers, and pastas as well as more substantial surf-and-turf entrées. Kids get a fish mask menu offering spaghetti and a hot dog, and everyone gets their meal on a place mat/chart that identifies the various fish in the tank. *In Pacific Beach Hotel, 2490 Kalakaua Ave., Waikiki; (808) 921-6111.*

Old Spaghetti Factory
★★★/$$

As the name suggests, spaghetti with a variety of sauces rules this chain. You can also get meatballs, spinach tortellini, and baked chicken. Also see Good Eats in Silicon Valley. *In Ward Centre, 1050 Ala Moana, Honolulu; (808) 591-2513; www.osf.com*

Paradise Cove Luau
★★★★/$$$$

The whole family will love this highly commercial, very popular (even with locals) luau extravaganza held at a beautiful oceanfront location west of Honolulu. (Bus transportation is included.) Kids enjoy the show, especially the Polynesian fire dance and the corny parts, and the food is very good. A particularly nice thing about this luau is that it includes activities such as lei-making, and engages guests in demonstrations of Hawaiian activities such as spear-throwing and hukilau fishing. It makes for quite a memorable evening. *Off H-1 West, toward Waianae, next to Koolina Resort; (800) 775-2683; (808) 842-5911.*

Sam Choy's Breakfast, Lunch, Crab & Big Aloha Brewery
★★★★/$$-$$$$

Sam Choy grew up on the North Shore of the island, learning to cook in his father's small café when he was just a *keiki*. Now the author of numerous cookbooks and officially Hawaii's culinary ambassador, he specializes in what could be described as "Hawaiian comfort food." A hearty meal in his spacious, well-priced restaurant is sure to comfort—and satisfy—your family. If you're lucky, you might be seated at one of the tables within a boat hull. Breakfast, lunch, and dinner are served, but whenever you come, arrive hungry—portions are humongous. Breakfast items include omelettes, French toast, and a fisherman's platter with the morning's fresh catch—all served with really good hash browns. Lunch is burgers and sandwiches and noodles, while dinner consists of more pricey crab, lobster, and fresh fish entrées. The Keiki menu is interesting, too, giving kids the option of trying Spam with steamed rice and an egg at breakfast; standard kids' menu items are also available. On Tuesday nights from 5 to 8, the Keiki Menu is specially priced; also there are games to play plus a clown to entertain. *580 N. Nimitz Hwy., Honolulu; (808) 545-7979; www.samchoy.com*

Shore Bird Beach Broiler
★★★★/$

Kids love walking here along the beach and entering the dining room with sand still between their toes. For a pittance—half a pittance for kids ages 3 through 11—you can feast on a buffet of family-pleasing breakfast items that appeal to all ages, including everything from fresh fruit to pastries to yogurt to carved ham. The million-dollar view is free. You'll all be kept cool—and intrigued—by the amazing antique ventilating systems: an 85-year-old straight-line fan assemblage that came from an old ship and a fascinating belt-driven flap-fan system

that meanders through the dining room. The hotel grounds feature a koi pond filled with huge specimens of the fish, some as old as 25 years, plus some turtles. **NOTE:** The restaurant is closed at lunchtime; dinner is a broil-it-yourself affair. *In the Outrigger Reef Hotel, 2169 Kalia Rd., Waikiki; (808) 922-2887; www.outrigger.com*

SOUVENIR HUNTING

Ala Moana Shopping Center

Less than two miles from Waikiki by shuttle, #8 bus, or taxi, this is the biggest shopping center in the islands. It's a great place to buy aloha clothing, at either the Macy's department store or Hilo Hattie *(see below)*. Fabulous soft-fabric-strapped sandals for women as well as a large selection of children's sandals are sold at the Slipper House. Stop in at Sanrio for plastic items, including beach toys, emblazoned with Japanese cartoon characters. At Jungle Fun, kids will go ape over the cute stuffed animals in the front and the video-game room in the back. These stores are on Level One; Levels Two and Three are lined with mall chain stores and upscale designer shops. *1450 Ala Moana Blvd., Honolulu; (808) 955-9517.*

Hilo Hattie

Located on the way from Waikiki to the airport, the chain's flagship store is an easy stop for last-minute souvenirs and gifts. You can find matching aloha outfits for the entire family from the vast selection, and you'll even have a chance to see the factory workers in action. Alterations are free and fast. This branch has a particularly good children's clothing section, as well as videotapes and storybooks about Hawaiian subjects. A free shuttle operates from downtown Waikiki. Combine your visit with breakfast or lunch at Sam Choy's, just a few doors away (see Good Eats). *700 N. Nimitz Hwy., Iwilei; (808) 537-2926. Also in the Ala Moana Shopping Center, 1450 Ala Moana Blvd., next to McDonald's, Honolulu; (808) 973-3266.*

International Marketplace

Built around a 100-year-old banyan tree and featuring a waterfall and koi pond, this indoor-outdoor bazaar sells all kinds of bargain-priced souvenirs and also has an inexpensive Asian food court. *2330 Kalakaua Ave., Waikiki. No phone.*

Little People Hawaii

You'll find all the tropical necessities for kids here, including bobbing hula dolls, aloha Barbie outfits, and colorful plastic fish squirters. *In the Outrigger Waikiki Hotel, 2335 Kalakaua Ave., Waikiki; (808) 922-1772. Also in the Outrigger Reef Hotel, 2169 Kalia Rd., Waikiki; (808) 926-1772.*

The Friendly Isle, also known as Molokai, is the place for families who want a laid-back Hawaiian experience. The island is the least developed one in the state.

Maui

THE SECOND-LARGEST OF the Hawaiian Islands and the most popular outer island among travelers, Maui offers more than 40 miles of white-sand beaches and more than 300 days of sunshine each year. It's famous for its resorts, 10,023-foot-high Haleakala volcano, and calm waters perfect for swimming and windsurfing.

Visiting this island lets you introduce your children to some exciting new activities. Your family can snorkel in the submerged bowl of Molokini Crater, where parrotfish and other dazzling tropical sea creatures dart among the cauliflower coral. You can explore the island's coastline together on a sea kayaking tour, ride along lush tropical trails on horseback, and take a helicopter ride above the otherwise inaccessible valleys of the upcountry slopes.

And whale-watching is prime here.

Though most of Hawaii is sunny year-round, Wailea, which stretches across 22 acres of fabulous ocean-

THE **FamilyFun** LIST

MUST-SEE
MUST-SEE

Cheeseburger in Paradise (page 360)

Haleakala National Park (page 351)

Hana Highway (page 352)

**Iao Valley State Park
(page 352)**

Lahaina (page 353)

Maui Ocean Center (page 353)

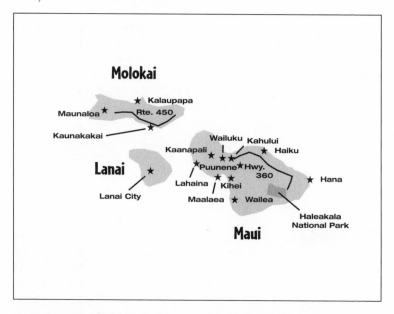

Molokai

★ Kalaupapa
Maunaloa ★ — Rte. 450
Kaunakakai —

Wailuku Kahului
Kaanapali ★ ★★ ★ Haiku
Lanai ★ ★Puunene★Hwy.
Lahaina / Kihei 360
Lanai City Maalaea ★ Wailea Hana

Haleakala
National Park

Maui

front on the southern coast, is Maui's sun belt and home to some of the island's most impressive resorts. Wailea has a chain of five uncrowded beaches and clear waters for snorkeling—and it is a particularly welcoming area for families. A scenic 25 miles from Wailea is the bustling, must-see old whaling town of Lahaina. Other places of particular interest on Maui are the fabulously secluded town of Hana, reached by the spectacular, winding Hana Highway, the chilly upcountry area on the slopes of the Haleakala volcano, and the verdant hills of Iao Valley.

In addition to the island of Maui, the county that is also called Maui includes Molokai and Lanai. For details on these smaller islands, see pages 354 and 361.

CULTURAL ADVENTURES

Alexander & Baldwin Sugar Museum
★/$

In the center of the island across from Hawaii's largest still-operating sugar factory, this award-winning nonprofit museum is housed inside a historic plantation home. Your grade-schoolers will like the photo murals, artifacts dating back to 1878, and a working model of a sugar mill—they provide a look at Hawaiian history. *Off Hwy. 311 at Puunene Ave. and Hansen Rd., half a mile from Dairy Rd., Puunene; (808) 871-8058;* www.sugarmuseum.com

JUST FOR FUN

Haiku ★/Free

This little town on the northeast side of the island, just off the Hana Highway, consists mainly of a tiny old-fashioned plantation store. Though Haiku isn't really a kid-friendly destination, parents and older children find the town's military history interesting. The U.S. Marine base was here during World War II, and the Fourth Marine Division Memorial Park stands just outside of town. After the war, the people of Maui erected a simple memorial in the park in gratitude.

Haleakala National Park
★★★★/$

Like dinosaurs, volcanoes are a natural phenomenon that have long captured kids' imaginations. So visiting this, the world's largest dormant volcano, has got to be at the top of your family's "to do" list. How big is it? Some 10,000 feet high—all of Manhattan would fit inside the 25-square-mile crater. You can reassure fearful young scientists who know all about lava—this volcano last erupted in 1790 and isn't likely to do so again any time soon. Driving to the summit to see the sunrise at Puu Ulaula Overlook is a particularly popular way to experience the volcano. But if getting the crew up and out in the wee hours of

the morning is too daunting, drive up at midmorning or late afternoon, when the views are clearest. It often gets cloudy at noon. Be sure to bring along sweatshirts or jackets—it's usually 30° F cooler on the volcano than at sea level. Kids ages 5 through 12 can participate in the park's Junior Ranger program. Just pick up a free activity booklet at park headquarters, then help them complete the activities required for their age group. The reward is a Junior Ranger button. Three housekeeping cabins on the crater floor are available by lottery; call (808) 572-9306 for details. **NOTE:** Allow three to four hours to drive here from the resort areas on the western side of the island. **ANOTHER NOTE:** Though several outfitters offer popular 38-mile bike rides back down the peak, they are considered pretty danger-

---

Make a Volcano

YOU'LL NEED:

  1 tablespoon of baking soda
  1 or 2 drops of red food coloring
  ¼ cup of vinegar

Build a large, conical mound of packed sand, tunnel out the center, and place a plastic cup inside. To create a whole lotta lava, drop the above ingredients, in order, into the cup, then watch your volcano erupt!

ous and are not recommended for children. *Main entrance is at the end of winding Highway 378; (808) 572-4400;* www.nps.gov/hale

Hana Highway
FamilyFun ★★★★/Free

Also known as Highway 360, this famous one-lane country road stretches 52 scenic and serpentine miles along Maui's northeast Hana Coast from just east of the airport to the small, remote village of Hana. Hacked out by hand with a pick and shovel in 1927, the treacherous byway is reputed to have 54 bridges—each with room for only one car to pass at a time—and more than 600 curves, so you must drive very, very slowly.

Before you set out, stop in the hip town of Paia and drop by Picnics *(30 Baldwin Ave.; 808/579-8021)* to select a delicious takeout lunch from their menu that doubles as a helpful map of the Hana Highway. Then continue on the Hana Highway to Hookipa Beach Park (just before Kokomo Road). There you can enjoy your picnic while you can watch the colorful sails of Windsurfers skimming along the turquoise surf.

Allowing for some stops along the way—you can drive to Hana in about three or four hours. **NOTE:** Recent landslides at Honomanu Bay mean that road repairs will slow traffic even more than usual; contact the Visitor Bureau for the latest information.

After walking around the tiny village of Hana, and perhaps checking out the black sand beach in Wainapanapa State Park, just northwest of Hana, continue on to Oheo Gulch, also known as the Seven Sacred Pools, in Kipahulu Valley. Located almost at the end of the paved part of the road, these pools are spectacularly beautiful and worth the journey to see them. You and your children can take an exhilarating swim in natural pools formed by water cascading down the hill into the ocean.

Allow plenty of time for your return trip because you won't want to drive back in the dark. Or better yet, plan on an overnight excursion and make reservations at one of the area's inns (see Hana Alii Holidays in Bunking Down). Then you can enjoy this fabulous area when almost everyone else has left.

Iao Valley State Park
FamilyFun ★★★★/$

Mark Twain called this beautiful 6.2-acre park the Yosemite of the Pacific. Its centerpiece is the Iao Needle, a natural rock formation that's some 1,200 feet high. At the park's Hawaii Nature Center *(875 Iao Valley Rd.; 808/244-6500)* your kids can try the hands-on exhibits, and check out the glass solarium and touch pools with sea creatures that they can examine and hold. Call ahead to participate in one of the Rainforest Wilderness Walks, which are led by naturalists. On the road in or out of the park, stop at Black Gorge to see if your kids can spot the John F. Kennedy Profile. *On Iao Valley Rd., off Hwy. 32, near Wailuku;* www.hawaiinaturecenter.org

Lahaina
FamilyFun ★★★/Free

Though this town can be miserably overrun with tourists, it is still a must-see. A rowdy whaling village dating back to 1802, it was also once the state capital. Its historic center is a delight, and a stop for a drink or snack at the 1901 Pioneer Inn, the island's oldest lodging place, is highly recommended (see Good Eats). Nearby, the state's largest banyan tree, planted in 1873, offers shady respite. In the late afternoon, countless flocks of birds gather high in the limbs; their stereophonic chittering is delightful. The 1832 Baldwin House *(Front St.; 808/661-3262)* is a small but interesting museum in what was once a missionary's home. Other Lahaina attractions include the *Carthaginian II* Floating Museum, The Hawaii Experience Domed Theater, and the Sugar Cane Train (*see below,* fee for attractions). *On the west side of the island, off Hwy. 30, just south of Kaanapali.*

Carthaginian II Floating Museum ★★/$

Moored at Lahaina Harbor, this restored 19th-century, two-masted square-rigger is a floating whale museum. Kids can also see the museum's videos about whales and listen to recordings of their songs. *In front of Pioneer Inn, Lahaina Harbor; (808) 661-8527.*

The Hawaii Experience Domed Theater ★★/$

The audience is encircled by the movie screen here, which makes the 45-minute movie about the culture and history of Hawaii more exciting than your kids might expect. They'll feel like they're actually biking down Haleakala's slopes, soaring over the Big Island's erupting volcanoes, and scuba diving to see the underwater wonders of the Pacific. (Skip it if anyone is prone to motion sickness, though.) *824 Front St., Lahaina; (808) 661-8314.*

Maui Ocean Center
FamilyFun ★★★/$$

Hawaii's largest aquarium and the largest tropical aquarium in the western hemisphere, this five-acre ocean showcase displays only marine life that is indigenous or endemic to the Hawaiian Islands. Both you and your kids will be

353

MOLOKAI

MOLOKAI IS THE smallest of the Hawaiian Islands, just 10 miles wide and only 36 miles long from its lush eastern end to its flat, arid western end. It is also the least developed, with the fewest facilities for tourists. Now known as the Friendly Isle, in the past Molokai has been called both the Lonely Isle (because of the difficulty in reaching it over the treacherous currents in the Molokai Channel) and the Forgotten Isle. From Maui you can fly to Molokai for just a day trip, although it's nice to stay longer.

The original home of the hula, Molokai has the largest population of native Hawaiians in the islands, which is probably why it retains an authentic Old Hawaii feeling. It also exists in a bit of a time warp: your children may be intrigued to learn that there are no traffic lights (or traffic), no tour buses (or public buses), no shopping centers, no fast-food chains, and no high-rise buildings here. There's also virtually no crime.

Molokai is home to Hawaii's highest waterfall, to its largest reef system, and to its longest beach (three-mile-long Papohaku Beach). The dramatic 3,300-foot-tall sea cliffs on the island's northern coast are the world's highest. You'll want to rent a car to see these sights.

The island is also the site of the isolated community of Kalaupapa, where victims of leprosy were exiled from the mid-1800s to the 1940s. Some sufferers of leprosy (now called Hansen's disease) still choose to live here, although the disease is now curable. Today you can get to Kalaupapa only by small plane or via a strenuous hike or mule ride over a narrow trail down those steep coastal cliffs. It's not really an appropriate destination for families, as the hike is too strenuous for most children, and no one under 16 is permitted on the mule ride.

In addition to seeing the island's major attractions, your family should stop by at least one deserted roadside beach and jump in the water. And don't leave Molokai without buying, and flying, a kite. **Big Wind Kite Factory** *(120 Maunaloa Hwy., in Maunaloa; 808/552-2364)* sells kites from all over the world, including dragon kites, stunt kites, wind socks, and spinners. Free factory tours and flying lessons are available. After making your selections, go have an uplifting experience. The island's trade winds make kite-flying easy.

Molokai has fewer than 700 guest rooms. A modest hotel in central Kaunakakai, the **Hotel Molokai,** *(800/367-5004; 808/553-5347)* is a Polynesian-style structure of brown-shingle, semi-A-frame buildings. Though all the island lodging places accommodate families nicely, the **Paniolo Hale** condo complex *(800/367-2984)*, adjacent to the Kaluakoi Resort, is particularly nice for families and for longer stays. It features screened-in lanais overlooking Kepuhi Beach.

Situated on 54,000 acres, **Sheraton Molokai Lodge & Beach Village** *(8 Maunaloa Hwy.; 877/PANIOLO; 888/729-0059)* is the largest resort on the island. The property offers accommodations in "tentalows" (canvas bungalows), yurts, and cabins that allow guests to combine the comforts of a fine hotel with the excitement of camping out. There are also 22 more luxurious hotel rooms in the lodge, which also houses a swimming pool, fitness center, and spa. It's just a short walk to the beach, and kids love bicycling the dirt roads. Activities, on the Molokai Ranch, of which the hotel is part, include cattle roundups, horseback riding, kayaking, mountain biking, a horse-drawn wagon ride, hiking, outrigger canoeing, archery, snorkeling, and fishing. Most activities cost extra. The Kamali'i EdVenture children's program is for ages 4 through 12. The Keiki Corner also offers supervised activities for ages 4 through 12. Rates include a buffet breakfast; sheratonmolokai.com

wowed by the coral reef displays and the habitat for green sea turtles; especially fun is the walk-through acrylic tunnel that passes through a 750,000-gallon tank filled with the area's ocean life. Indoor and outdoor pools allow you to look at the inhabitants of the undersea world surrounding the islands, including large open-ocean game fish, assorted sharks, sting rays, eels, and sea jellies. Kids especially love the touch pool, where they can hold sea urchins and starfish. *192 Maalaea Rd., off Hoanpiilani Hwy., in Maalaea; (808) 270-7000; www.mauioceancenter.com*

Sugar Cane Train/ Lahaina-Ka'anapali & Pacific Railroad
★★★/$$

Your family will love riding this cute restored antique narrow-gauge steam train as it chugs through the sugarcane fields for a scenic, leisurely six-mile, half-hour trip into or out of Lahaina. En route you'll be entertained by a singing conductor, and from December through April you just might spot some humpback whales as you cross a 415-foot wooden trestle. There's a turn-of-the-century-style depot at both ends of the track. The train departs from the Puukolii Station in the north end and from the main depot in Lahaina by the Honoapiilani Highway, next to Pizza Hut; *(800) 499-2307; (808) 661-0080;* www.sugarcanetrain.com

Cheap Digs

Wailuku
★/Free-$

During World War II, this sleepy town on the northwest side of the island jumped with Marines on their night off. But Wailuku is so untouristy now that it's difficult to even find a promotional T-shirt or a baseball cap in town. Two sites offer glimpses at Hawaiian history. Nearby Kepaniwai Park and Heritage Gardens displays a Hawaiian hut, Portuguese villa, New England saltbox house, and other island homes reflecting Asian and Pacific cultures. The 1833 Bailey House Museum mission home *(2375 Main St.; 808/ 244-3326)*, built of lava rock and native woods, showcases Hawaiian artifacts and crafts and presents a program of crafts and performances (fees). *Off Hwy. 340, about six miles north of the Kahului Airport.*

Whalers Village Museum
★/Free

Hands-on experiences allow the whole family to learn about the life of whales and 19th-century whalers at this museum in Kaanapali Beach, on the northwestern side of the island. A theater screens films on related topics. *In Whalers Village shopping center, 2435 Kaanapali Pkwy., Lahana or Kaanapali Beach, Lahaina; (808) 661-4567;* www. whalersvillage.com

BUNKING DOWN

Embassy Vacation Resort
★★★/$$$$

Located on the sandy shores of Kaanapali Beach on the northwestern side of the island, this 413-suite hotel has a one-acre swimming pool and a 40-foot-long water slide erupting from a volcano. Needless to say, the kids will be happy here. Parents will be pleased with the one- and two-bedroom suites, each equipped with a kitchenette, 35-inch TV set, VCR, stereo and cassette player, and two phone lines. A complimentary breakfast buffet is another nice perk. The daily Beach Buddies program for kids ages 5 through 10 features

Hawaiian-themed arts-and-crafts projects, including decorating coconuts, beach-sand art, and leaf painting. *104 Kaanapali Shores Pl., Kaanapali; (800) 535-0085; (800) EMBASSY; (808) 661-2000.*

Grand Wailea Resort Hotel & Spa ★★★★/$$$$

Among the amazing facilities at this 780-room resort are the world's only water elevator, a rope swing, and rivers that carry swimmers along at varying speeds—from easy currents to white-water rapids. The pool area consists of nine (!) separate pools, including a baby beach and an adults-only pool; seven water slides; waterfalls; caves; grottoes; a hot tub; and a sauna. Rooms and suites are equipped with coffeemakers, and you can rent refrigerators, microwaves, and VCRs. The year-round Camp Grande for kids ages 5 through 12 operates in a facility equipped with a soda fountain, crafts room, movie theater, video arcade, and computer center; it also has its own outside pool and play area. Named after Hawaii's state fish, the Humuhumunukunukuapua'a Restaurant (affectionately known as Humuhumu) floats on a 700,000-gallon saltwater lagoon filled with colorful tropical fish. Guests can select their own Hawaiian spiny lobster from the lagoon for steaming, grilling, or wok-frying. Kids will probably think this is quite yucky, but they can order more

familiar items from the children's menu. *3850 Wailea Alanui, Wailea; (800) 888-6100; (808) 875-1234; www.grandwailea.com*

Hana Alii Holidays ★★★/$-$$$$

This company arranges rentals in detached homes and condos in the Hana area, on the eastern side of the island. With kitchens and other just-like-home amenities, the properties are great for families and are all available by the night. One property, Hale Hana Bay, has an unobstructed ocean view from its front room, making temporary residents think they've died and gone to heaven. You can hear the pounding surf in the front yard and take a five-minute walk to a nearby black-sand beach. During your stay in Hana, you'll most likely experience stormy nights, wet mornings, and glorious sunny days. *(800) 548-0478; (808) 248-7742.*

Hyatt Regency Maui ★★★★/$$$$

Kids love the swinging rope bridge suspended over one of this hotel's two free-form pools, as well as the two swim-through waterfalls and 150-foot lava tube water slide; parents like to get tropical cocktails at the swim-up Grotto Bar. But those are just a few of the fun features of this extensively landscaped 40-acre, 806-room beachfront resort extravaganza. The rooms and suites have refrigerators and coffeemakers, and you can rent VCRs. Daily Camp Hyatt activities for kids ages 5 to 12 include hula dancing, sand-castle building, snorkeling, and more; day camp participants receive a souvenir travel journal filled with suggested activities plus space for recording memories. There's also a night camp that includes dinner and themed evening activities. Free one-hour wildlife tours are held three times a week, introducing kids to the resort's large bird collection, which includes penguins, swans, ducks, and flamingos. The resort's luau and the *Drums of the Pacific* outdoor dinner show are fun for families and open to nonguests. *200 Nohea Kai Dr., on Kaanapali Beach, Lahaina; (800) 55-HYATT; (808) 661-1234; www. hyatt.com*

Kaanapali Beach Hotel
★★★/$$$-$$$$

The luxury resorts along popular Kaanapali Beach are many. This simpler, "Very Hawaiian Hotel" (it is recognized as Hawaii's most Hawaiian hotel) exudes low-key aloha and is a great place for your kids to learn a bit about island culture. Its 430 rooms are in four wings surrounding a lush tropical courtyard holding a child-pleasing, whale-shaped pool. An outdoor bar and grill serves an eclectic island menu that includes authentic native Hawaiian cuisine; Hawaiian music and hula are performed nightly from 6 to 9:30 P.M. Hawaiian crafts

classes are scheduled daily, and complimentary sunset hula shows are presented each evening. The Aloha Passport for Kids program encourages kids to get their "passports" stamped at various activity destinations, the prize being a gift they can play with while staying at the hotel and then keep as a memento of their visit. Under the passport program, kids 5 and under eat free and those 6 to 12 get discounted meals at the hotel restaurants. *2525 Ka'anapali Parkway, on Kaanapali Beach, Lahaina; (800) 262-8450; (808) 661-0011; www.kbhmaui.com*

Outrigger Wailea Resort ★★★/$$$$

What fun! Among the five pools here are ones with a 32-foot-long "drop out" slide, a spiral flume slide, and a water-play station. Your younger kids will like the kiddie pool with a sandy beach and an "infinity" pool, designed to appear as if it extends right into the ocean. Each of the 516 rooms has a private lanai and is equipped with a handy refrigerator and coffeemaker. Kids ages 5 through 12 can participate in the Cowabunga Kids Club Gecko, which offers activities Monday through Saturday, and the whole family will enjoy the evening luau and Polynesian show held on the beachfront grounds four times a week. Also on the premises is Hula Moons restaurant, which serves innovative local cuisine, plus the usual kid-

friendly food. *3700 Wailea Alanui, in Wailea; (800) 367-2960; (808) 874-7800;* www.outriggerwailea.com

Sheraton Maui ★★★★/$$$$

Built on a natural promontory known as Black Rock, this resort sprawls over 23 tropically landscaped acres. Your kids are sure to be enthralled by the nightly sunset cliff-diving ceremony off Black Rock, which starts with the blowing of a conch shell and the lighting of torches. Among the 510 rooms are 31 family suites, each conveniently equipped with a microwave and mini refrigerator as well as two double beds, one pull-down, double wall bed, and a sitting room. A freshwater swimming lagoon meanders through tropical gardens, and the little ones can splash in a one-foot-deep kiddie pool. The Keiki Aloha and Keiki Kamp programs for children ages 5 through 12 operates daily in summer; participants make leis and Hawaiian kites, build sand castles, and learn to hula. Kekaa Terrace has ocean views and a children's menu offering items like pancakes decorated with a chocolate-chip smiley face, pizza, and hot dogs. Better still, kids under 12 eat free when accompanied by a paying adult. *2605 Kaanapali Pkwy., on Kaanapali Beach, Lahaina; (800) 782-9488; (808) 661-0031;* www.sheratonmaui.com

Westin Maui ★★★/$$$$

In a superb location, this 756-room hotel boasts a water wonderland. Its aquatic playground has five small free-form pools featuring a swim-through grotto, a hidden hot tub, and two water slides, one of which is a fabulous 128 feet long with two 270-degree turns and a 23-foot drop. Whee! Two Keiki Kamps for children ages 5 through 12 operate daily, with a special Aloha Program offering lei-making and hula lessons on Friday. The Day Kamp program includes activities, lunch, and a T-shirt; the Nite Kamp program includes snacks, games, and activities such as movies and crafts. All the hotel restaurants are family-friendly and offer kids' menus, but the Colonnade Cafe, which overlooks a lagoon filled with koi, tropical birds, and waterfalls, is particularly nice. *2365 Kaanapali Pkwy., on Kaanapali Beach, Lahaina; (888) 625-4949; (808) 667-2525;* www.westin.com

Good Eats

Bubba Gump Shrimp Co. ★★★★/$$

This link in the *Forrest Gump*-themed chain of casual seafood eateries has a great oceanfront location. Also see Good Eats in San Francisco. *889 Front St., Lahaina; (808) 661-3111;* www.bubbagump.com

Cheeseburger in
FamilyFun Paradise ★★★★/$

Located upstairs on a comfortable open-air lanai, this is the original restaurant in the popular chain. It's casual and noisy, and you'll get the best burger in town, with garnishes of Thousand Island dressing and sautéed onions. Great seasoned fries, big onion rings, and vegetarian burgers, soups, and salads are also available. There's no special children's menu, but the regular menu is filled with things kids like. The attractive logo clothing items are almost as popular as the food. There's live island music from 4:30 to 10:30 P.M. daily. *811 Front St., Lahaina; (808) 661-4855.*

> Only four U.S. states produce **sugar cane**: Hawaii, Florida, Texas, and Louisiana.

Hard Rock Cafe
★★★★/$$

Another hamburger heaven, this one also offers rock 'n' roll memorabilia and T-shirts that are popular with teens and preteens. Also see Good Eats in San Francisco. *Lahaina Center, 900 Front St., Lahaina; (808) 667-7400; www.hardrockcafe.com*

Kimo's
★★★★/$$-$$$

Situated waterfront in the heart of town, this area institution is known for its fresh fish, prime rib, and Hula Pie, made with vanilla ice cream, macadamia nuts, and chocolate

syrup. At night, the torchlit oceanside lanai is primo. This is part of the Duke's Canoe Club chain, which has branches on Oahu and Kauai. *845 Front St., Lahaina; (808) 661-4811.*

Leilani's on the Beach
★★★★/$$-$$$

With a delicious surf-and-turf menu that sometimes includes fresh local rock lobster, this posh (but still okay for kids) spot serves dinner nightly. For more casual lunch and dinner fare, try the Beachside Grill, downstairs, with live music every day from 3 to 6 P.M. This is another link in the Duke's Canoe Club chain. *Whalers Village, 2435 Kaanapali Pkwy., Kaanapali; (808) 661-4495.*

Old Lahaina Luau
★★★★/$$$$

The island's most authentic luau is held oceanside and features traditional hula and a fabulous feast. Reservations are necessary. *On Front St., by Lahaina Cannery Mall, Lahaina; (808) 661-5705.*

Pioneer Inn
★★★/$$-$$$

Built in 1901, this historic building evokes the ambience of turn-of-the-century Maui. The hotel has 50 comfortable guest rooms. Try to plan a late-afternoon snack on the lanai of the Pioneer Inn Grill and Bar so your kids can thrill to the cacophony created by birds gathering in the huge banyan tree across the street. *658 Wharf St., Lahaina; (800) 457-5457; (808) 661-3636; www.pioneerinnmaui.com*

Tobi's Ice Cream and Shave Ice
★★★★/$

Experience the difference between shave ice and a snow cone at this snack stand in Kihei, on the southwestern side of the island. If you want to make a meal of it, the kids won't mind feasting on inexpensive hot dogs, frozen bananas, and ice cream. A few tables and chairs are set out on the porch. *1913 S. Kihei Rd., Kihei; (808) 891-2440.*

SOUVENIR HUNTING

Hilo Hattie

This is *the* place to shop for aloha wear. *900 Front St., Lahaina; (808) 661-8457.*

Maui Swap Meet

At this fun twice-weekly event in Kahului, kids can slurp a shave ice or sip milk from a freshly opened coconut while their Moms and Dads shop for fresh upcountry produce, hand-painted clothing, and beautiful jewelry at a fraction of resort prices. Held on Wednesdays from 8 A.M. to 1 P.M. and on Saturdays from 7 P.M. to noon. *Puunene Ave., next to the post office, Kahului.*

Lanai

Until recently, Lanai was the largest pineapple plantation in the world. Now it no longer exports pineapples, having traded agriculture for tourism by opening two superluxurious resorts, but it is still remote enough to be one of the quietest of the Hawaiian islands.

It has only three paved roads outside of the plantation town of Lanai City, the island's only town and a good place to rent bikes, fish, hike, or go horseback riding.

Both of the island's resorts have all the expected facilities—swimming pools, elegant restaurants—and each has its own championship golf course. The **Manele Bay Hotel** *(800/321-4666)* is perched on a cliff overlooking a white-sand beach and landscaped with formal gardens and waterfalls. The refined, Mediterranean-style, 250-room hotel has traditional early 20th-century island architecture and an Old Hawaii atmosphere. The daily Pilialoha Keiki program for ages 5 through 12 takes kids on field trips to see tide pools and petroglyphs. They'll also fly kites and learn croquet, lawn-bowling, horseback riding, and golf. There's an evening children's program as well.

Situated in the center of the island, **The Lodge at Koele** *(800/321-4666)* is a stunning 102-room hotel featuring lush gardens and croquet and lawn-bowling courts outside, and stone fireplaces, high ceilings, and antiques inside. Young guests may participate in the Manele Bay Hotel's children's programs.

The Big Island's Kona Coast boasts some of the
best scuba diving and snorkeling in the world.

Hawaii

The Big Island (Hawaii)

OKAY, KIDS, HERE'S THE deal: this island's official name is Hawaii, but it is called "the Big Island" so as to avoid confusion with the name of the state. It is twice the size of all the other Hawaiian Islands combined and is as far south as you can get in the United States. But what makes the Big Island really interesting to young visitors is that it is the site of Kilauea, the world's largest and most active volcano.

Formed by lava flows that haven't yet been softened by erosion, the Big Island features varied terrain. You see a forlorn, naked, pock-marked moonscape of volcanic rock on the sunny, nine-mile Kona–Kohala Coast, then move to the windward side of the island, home to the lush, wet, green rain forest of Akaka Falls State Park. And

THE **FamilyFun** LIST

MUST-SEE
MUST-SEE

Hawaii Volcanoes National Park
(page 368)

Mauna Kea's Onizuka Center for International Astronomy
(page 365)

Puuhonua o Honaunau National Historic Park/City of Refuge
(page 366)

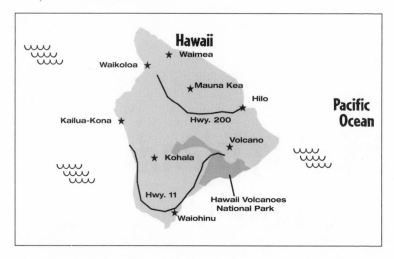

the northern interior of the island is dominated by the vast grassy expanses of the famous Parker ranch, which is the second-largest cattle ranch in the United States.

A rich repository of Hawaiian history, the Big Island is a great place for your family to learn more about the islands. You can show the kids the early Hawaiian petroglyphs and tell them about King Kamehameha, born here, who first united the Hawaiian Islands as one kingdom in 1810. The Big Island is the site of Mauna Kea, a dormant volcano where you can visit the biggest and one of the best observatories in the world. It's the perfect place for stargazing.

The island's main tourist towns are the very popular Kailua-Kona on the barren western side of the island, and the less visited, less accessible Hilo on the lusher eastern side of the island. The island has many

extraordinary, luxurious destination resorts on its western Kona Coast, which is also known for the best snorkeling and scuba diving in the world.

While you're here, take the kids to one (or more) of the island's commercial growers of nuts, tropical flowers, and coffee. The world's largest producers of macadamia nuts, anthuriums, and orchids (you'll see them growing wild on the side of the road!), and the world's only producers of the prized Kona coffee are here. Should you pass one of the area's rustic country stores, stop in and buy the kids some raw sugarcane to chew on (no, the dentist might not approve, but it's fun and you're on vacation). Your family might enjoy some of the many adventure activities here—perhaps a ride in the Atlantis submarine or on a glass-bottom boat.

CULTURAL ADVENTURES

Hulihee Palace and Museum
★★/$

Built in 1838 of coral and lava, this was once a summer palace for Hawaiian royalty. It is furnished in Victorian style and has a lovely view of the harbor. The kids will be most interested in the display of King Kamehameha's war spears. Take the guided tour, and call for the schedule of demonstrations and performances that make a visit even more fun for children. *75-5718 Alii Dr., Kailua-Kona; (808) 329-1877.*

Mauna Kea
FamilyFun ★★★/Free

NOTE: Though we've listed this as one of our must-sees, not all of Mauna Kea is appropriate for families (in fact, in many areas, no one under 16 is permitted). That said, read on. The summit of the dormant volcano Mauna Kea ("White Mountain") is the site of the world's largest astronomical observatory, with 13 telescopes operated by astronomers from 11 countries. A better choice for families is Mauna Kea's Onizuka Center for International Astronomy Visitor Information Station, still high at 9,300 feet and accessible by car. At the station's nightly stargazing program, your kids can view the skies

through telescopes. The program runs 6 to 10 P.M. each night, weather permitting. Children are encouraged to participate in the activities; don't forget warm clothing. The visitor station is about a one-hour drive from Hilo, Waimea, and Waikoloa, and about a two-hour drive from Kailua-Kona. *It's on the access road to Mauna Kea, off Saddle Road; (808) 961-2180; www.ifa.hawaii.edu/vis*

Onizuka Space Center
★★/$

Of particular interest to wanna-be astronauts, this center at Keahole International Airport honors Kona-born astronaut Ellison S. Onizuka and the six others who were aboard the doomed 1986 *Challenger* space shuttle. It's an interesting place to spend some time if your plane is delayed. *Kailua-Kona; (808) 329-3441.*

Parker Ranch Visitor Center and Museum
★★★/$-$$

In the northern interior of the island in Waimea, this 250,000-acre ranch is one of the largest working ranches in the United States. The kids can learn about Hawaiian cowboys at the museum on the premises, where

the *paniolos'* memorabilia is displayed; there's also a slide show and a store. Older kids will enjoy a tour of the historic ranch houses, while their younger siblings will love the nearby Anuenue Playground. *Near the junction of Hwy. 19 east and Hwy. 190 south, Waimea; (808) 885-7655; www.parkerranch.com*

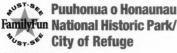

Puuhonua o Honaunau National Historic Park/ City of Refuge
★★★★/$

Centuries ago this desolate, exquisitely beautiful spot was the place where criminals and outcasts escaping punishment or persecution took refuge. Now your family can learn a little Hawaiian history as you check out the exhibits, which include a fishpond, several *hale* (houses), examples of traditional Hawaiian crafts, and an unmortared stone wall that is 1,000 feet long, 10 feet high, and 17 feet wide. You might also see a Hawaiian canoe builder in action. Do allow time for the kids to try playing a game of *konane*—a check-

erslike game played on a stone table. Outrigger canoe rides are sometimes available during special events and celebrations. *One hour south of Kailua-Kona, near Captain Cook; (808) 328-2288.*

JUST FOR FUN

Flumin' Da Ditch Tour
★★★/$$$$

Once an illicit thrill enjoyed only by local children who climbed over barbed-wire fences to indulge, this low-key adventure involves drifting in a five-person kayak down part of the 22 miles of flumes built to carry water from the rain forests to the sugarcane fields. The easy, gentle three-hour tour is led by grown-ups who "flumed da ditch" as kids—and who now do so on inflatable kayaks instead of inner tubes or boogie boards. The excursion is safe for kids ages 5 and older, with the biggest thrills consisting of a ride through a leaking flume's "waterfall" and a float through several dark, enclosed tun-

The Earache Solution

You can often lessen ear discomfort on airplanes by nursing infants, giving tots bottles or pacifiers, and letting older kids chew gum (buy it on your way to the airport because many terminals do not sell chewing gum—workers are tired of cleaning it off floors and chairs). But if your child experiences real ear pain, you can try this funny-looking but often effective trick. Ask the attendant for two plastic cups. Fold a napkin into the bottom of each cup and pour in just enough hot water to moisten the napkins. Then, place the cups over your child's ears, making sure you hold them tightly against his head.

LEARN A LITTLE HAWAIIAN

In ADDITION TO speaking English, Hawaiians sometimes speak their own native Hawaiian language. In fact, there is a movement in the Hawaiian community to perpetuate this ancient language through preschool immersion programs and classes in grade school, high school, and college. The Hawaiian language has five vowels and seven consonants. The melodic words are really quite easy to speak. Here are a few that you and your children can learn and use while visiting the islands.

Aikane (eye-kah-nay) friend
aloha (ah-low-ha) hello, good-bye, love
anu (ah-noo) cold
hahana (hah-hah-nah) hot, warm
hale (hah-lei) house
hana (hah-na) work
haole (how-lee) a Caucasian
heiau (hey-ow) temple
imu (ee-moo) underground oven
kahuna (ka-hoo-nah) priest, teacher, or expert
kai (kah-eye) ocean
kamaaina (kah-mah-eye-nah) native-born local resident
kane (kah-neh) man
kapu (kah-poo) forbidden

keiki (kay-key) child or children
lanai (lah-nigh) porch
lomi lomi (low-me low-me) massage
luau (lew-ow) feast
mahalo (mah-hah-low) thank you
mahimahi (mah-hee-mah-hee) dolphin fish
makai (moo-kigh) toward the ocean
malihini (mah-lee-hee-nee) newcomer, visitor
manuahi (mah-noo-ah-hee) free, no cost
mauka (mau-kah) toward the mountains
menehune (may-nay-hoo-nee) mischievous Hawaiian elf of legend
moana (moh-ah-nah) ocean
nani (nah-nee) pretty
ohana (oh-hah-nah) family
ono (oh-no) delicious, the best
palaoa (pah-lah-oh-ah) whale
pali (pah-lee) cliff
paniolo (pah-nee-oh-loh) Hawaiian cowboy
pau (pow) finished
pupu (poo-poo) appetizer, finger food
wahine (wah-hee-nay) woman
wikiwiki (wee-kee-wee-kee) hurry up, fast

nels. Reservations required. *On the very northwestern tip of the island, off Hwy. 250, Kohala; (808) 889-6922; www.flumindaditch.com*

Hawaii Tropical Botanical Garden
★★★/$$

This spectacular garden grows in a natural tropical rain forest and includes more than 2,000 species of tropical flowers and plants. Your kids will probably be more excited about the koi and the exotic birds, including macaws, that live here, and can expend some energy skipping along paths through the lush

jungle filled with palms, streams, and waterfalls. *At Onomea Bay, eight miles north of Hilo; (808) 964-5233; www.htbg.com; www.hawaiigarden.com*

 ## Hawaii Volcanoes National Park
★★★★/$

Don't even think about leaving the island without bringing the family here to Kilauea, the world's largest and most active volcano. The volcano has been erupting intermittently since 1983, and your kids can look for the lava that's sometimes visible flowing down into the sea. It's

Family-Friendly Lodging Chains and Tour Companies

Several Hawaiian hotel chains and tour companies make traveling easier for families.

Aston Hotels At check-in, guests receive a coupon book for discounts and freebies on dining and shopping. Families that stay at Aston properties on more than one island get "Island Hopper" discounts, and kids under 18 stay free in their parents' room (as long as they don't require additional beds). A new Kid's Connection program for children ages 5 through 12 operates year-round at all Aston condominium

resorts and hotels on Oahu. It teaches kids about Hawaii's culture through activities such as lei-making and tide-pool exploration. Several Aston resorts on other islands also have inexpensive year-round kids' programs. For example, Camp Kaanapali for kids ages 5 through 10 is offered on weekdays at the Aston Kaanapali Shores on Maui. *(800) 92-ASTON;* www.astonhotels.com

Castle Resorts & Hotels Promising kid-friendly accommodations that combine value, convenience, and genuine Hawaiian hospitality, this group of condominium properties is located in key resort areas on four of the islands. Some of the properties feature full kitchens, pools, bar-an amazing but potentially danger-ous phenomenon—be sure to follow the safety precautions explained at the park visitors' center, located across from Volcano House hotel.

While you're at the center, your family can also join an informative ranger-led nature walk, and your kids can learn the legend of Pele, the beautiful fire goddess whose anger is said to cause volcanoes to erupt. Children ages 5 through 12 can participate in the Junior Ranger program, earning a logo patch while learning about the park's resources and how to protect them. Also avail-able at the center is a map of the 11.3-mile Loop Drive around the huge, otherworldly Kilauea Caldera, a crater formed by an eruption of the volcano. Several stops along the drive are particularly worthwhile and fun with kids. The Kipuka Puaulu Bird Park has a pleasant one-mile nature trail that leads past an extensive col-lection of labeled native plants, and Devastation Trail offers a half-mile boardwalk path through a skeleton forest created by a prior volcano eruption. Kids are especially in-trigued by the Thurston Lava Tube, a naturally formed tunnel made of hardened lava. Measuring an extraordinary 450 feet long, it is in

becue areas, and on-site activities. Most also have washers and dryers in each unit. *(800) 367-5004*; www.castleresorts.com

Outrigger Hotels & Resorts These upscale, full-service hotels and con-dominiums are found on Oahu, Maui, Kauai, and the Big Island. Kids 5 through 13 receive a free Island Explorer Kit backpack—filled with goodies like sunglasses and binocu-lars—when staying a minimum of three nights at a participating prop-erty. Waikiki Outrigger Hotels offer a number of programs for families; for example, the year-round Cowabunga Kids Club, based at the Outrigger Reef on the Beach hotel, also runs a "night camp" offering activities on some summer evenings.

Ohana Hotels (*ohana* means family in Hawaiian), a subdivision of the Outrigger chain, offers bargain-priced rooms in 14 off-beach prop-erties in Waikiki. *(800) OUTRIGGER*; www.outrigger.com

Pleasant Hawaiian Holidays This tour packager offers one-stop shop-ping for packages that include a lei greeting, air, car, and hotel. Many family-friendly condominiums are among the lodging choices. *(888) 434-3232*; www.pleasant.net

Premier Resorts Your family can arrange to stay in well-situated, prime condominium properties on Maui and Kauai through this company. *(800) 367-7052*; www.pre mier-resorts.com

a lush tropical rain forest known as the Fern Jungle. Also within the park is the 13,680-foot-high Mauna Loa volcano (it last erupted in 1984); measuring 75 miles by 64 miles, it is the largest mountain on earth in total mass. Awesome! It's possible to hike to the top, but the trek takes three to four days. **NOTE:** Whatever you do, don't collect any volcanic rocks to take home—they're believed to bring *very bad luck*; it's also illegal! (If you'd rather not invoke that superstition, just tell the kids it's nicer to leave them for future visitors to enjoy.) *Along Hwy. 11, on the southeastern side of the island; (808) 985-6000;* www.nps.gov/havo

Mark Twain's Monkeypod Tree
★/Free

On your way to Hawaii Volcanoes National Park, this is a good stop for your Huck Finn fans. The original monkeypod tree on this site was planted in 1866 by Twain himself, but was blown over in 1957. The current tree is growing from the

---

FamilyFun GAME

Race to 20

Two players take turns counting to twenty. On each turn, a player can say one or two numbers. (If the first says "One," the second might say "Two, three.") Try to force your opponent to reach twenty first.

---

roots of the original. On Hwy. 11, in Waiohinu, near the southern tip of the island on the way to Hawaii Volcanoes National Park.

Mauna Loa Macademia Nut Plantation
★/Free

It's not Willy Wonka's Chocolate Factory, but it's as close as you'll get to it in Hawaii. The tour of the world's largest macadamia nut plantation includes both the orchards and the processing plant/candy factory. You'll even get to sample some of the wares. *On Macadamia Rd., off Hwy. 11, five miles south of Hilo; (808) 966-8612;* www.maunaloa.com

BUNKING DOWN

Hilton Waikoloa Village ★★★★/$$$$

With 1,242 guest rooms, this 62-acre oceanfront resort hotel is the largest on the island. The rooms and suites are equipped with coffeemakers and adorned with plenty of fresh orchids; children under 19 stay free in their parents' room. Your kids will love the air-conditioned Swiss trams and the fleet of mahogany boats (both run on tracks) that transport you around the property. The resort has one of the largest petroglyph fields in the world; an interesting collection of birds lives here, too. A swimming and snorkeling lagoon with a sandy bottom and beach holds colorful tropical reef fish and rare green sea turtles, and you and the kids can rent kayaks and paddleboats to take a closer look. Another lagoon is home to the fabulous Dolphin Quest program, which allows guests to get right in the water and mingle with Atlantic bottle-nosed dolphins. Spaces for children and teenagers can be reserved 60 days in advance, while adults are selected on site by a daily lottery. Kids ages 5 through 12 can escape their parents at Camp Menehune, which offers activities daily from 9 A.M. to 4 P.M.; half-day and evening programs are also available, and free drop-in activities are scheduled every day at 3:30 P.M. There's a separate program for teens. Special activities for both adults and kids, such as fish feeding and stargazing, are scheduled regularly. The resort has nine distinctive restaurants. *The Legends of the Pacific* dinner show—staged every Friday evening—features exotic dances and music from the Pacific Rim and a bountiful buffet dinner that includes fresh island fish and whole roasted suckling pig. Kids ages 5 through 12 eat for less than half price and get a special kiddie cocktail. *425 Waikoloa Beach Dr., Waikoloa; (800) HILTONS; (808) 886-1234; www. hilton.com; www. hiltonwaikoloavillage.com*

The **Macadamia** is thought to be the most difficult nut to break open. It takes 300 pounds per square inch of pressure to crack the shell.

Holo Holo In Hostel ★/$

This very small hostel, just one mile from Volcanoes National Park, has one private room that can accommodate a family with one double bed and two single beds; reservations are accepted. There's also a sauna. For more details on hostels, see "Hosteling for Families" on page 215. *19–4036 Kalani Honua Rd., Volcano; (808) 967-7950.*

King Kamehameha's Kona Beach Hotel ★★/$$-$$$

Situated on the king's former estate, this oceanfront hotel is at the north end of the seaside town of Kailua-Kona. A visit here includes some interesting history lessons: a replica of a historical sacred site is on the premises (take the guided tour), and the property displays numerous historical Hawaiian artifacts. The 451 spacious rooms and suites have coffeemakers and refrigerators. Two family-friendly restaurants serve local Hawaiian and American food, and a beachfront luau is held on Sunday, Tuesday, Wednesday, and Thursday. *75–5660 Palani Rd., Kailua-Kona; 800/367-6060; 808/ 329-2911; www.konabeachhotel.com*

Kona Village Resort ★★★★/$$$$

Truly a paradise within paradise,

isolated by ancient lava fields, this remote, plush-yet-primitive resort offers all-inclusive rates and lodging in 125 *hales* (thatch-roofed bungalows). Your family can fulfill the fantasy of being stranded on an island, albeit with every amenity you could want, except clocks, telephones, and TVs. Never fear—even if your kids are TV and video-game fanatics, they'll hardly miss their electronic entertainment here. They (and you) will be having too much fun frolicking at the small, almost-black-sand beach; swimming in pools created from fishponds; playing tennis; sailing on sailboats or outrigger canoes; snorkeling; enjoying excursions on the resort's own boat; taking lessons in island crafts; and participating in guided tours of the large petroglyph field. The complimentary Na Keikis in Paradise program for children ages 6 through 12 includes hula lessons, fishing contests, and coconut painting (it doesn't operate in September or May). Special youth dinners are held each evening for kids ages 6 and older, followed by storytelling, stargazing, and marshmallow-roasting around a bonfire. The casual restaurants all welcome children. Often during dinner, breathtakingly large, winged manta rays appear at the ocean's edge, looking for handouts. The elaborate Friday night luau is considered one of the best in the islands. *(800) 367-5290; (808) 325-5555;* www.konavillage.com

Mauna Kea Resort
★★★/$$$$

All rooms have ocean views at this unique, ultraluxe property composed of two distinct resorts. You can get special family packages at both, and children are presented with an age-appropriate amenities kit upon check-in. A Star Gazing program provides telescopes for viewing the heavenly bodies in the island's clear night sky. Every guest, even the littlest, is loaned a blue-and-white-printed yukata (Japanese cotton kimono) to lounge in and use as a beach cover-up. Guests at each hotel can use the facilities at both; a hotel shuttle transports you between the two properties. Both resorts also share riding stables in Waimea, 12 miles from the hotel.

Mauna Kea Beach Hotel

This classically elegant 310-room property displays founder Laurance S. Rockefeller's extensive Asian and Pacific art collection. Rooms are each uniquely decorated in Hawaiian style with wicker furniture, and each is equipped with a refrigerator. Fac-

ilities include the best resort beach on the island, a palm-shaded pool and hot tub, 13 tennis courts, a fitness center, and three ocean-view restaurants (The Terrace is famous for its Sunday brunch extravaganza). Every Tuesday a traditional luau is held oceanside under a sprawling kiawe tree; you can reserve even if you're not staying there *(808/882-7222)*. A casual clambake under the stars featuring Hawaiian music is held on Saturday. *62–100 Mauna Kea Beach Dr., Kohala Coast; (808) 228-3000;* www.maunakeabeachhotel.com

Hapuna Beach Prince Hotel
The newer of the resort's two hotels has a pool and hot tub, two 18-hole golf courses, and a fitness center. Each of the 350 rooms has an ocean view and spacious lanai and is equipped with a refrigerator and coffeemaker. All the resort restaurants welcome families, and the casual, open-air Ocean Terrace is especially popular for its breakfast buffet. *62–100 Kaunaoa Dr., Kohala Coast; (800) 882-6060; (808) 880-1111;* www.hapunabeachprince hotel.com

The Mauna Lani Bay Hotel and Bungalows
★★★★/$$$$
Set atop a dry 16th-century lava flow dotted with ancient petroglyphs and spring-fed fishponds, this low-key, 350-room, oceanfront resort fulfills the dreams of adults and

children alike. Child-pleasing ponds populated with colorful fish flow right through the vast open-air atrium lobby. Almost all of the guest rooms have ocean views and all are equipped with minibars and VCRs. Your family could spend an entire vacation just relaxing on the perfect white-sand beach, playing at the pool, and lobbing balls on the clay tennis courts, but there are plenty of other activities as well. Take the whole family on both the resort's sunset catamaran cruise and the complimentary tour of the property's ancient petroglyphs. Visiting the royal fishponds, where fish and sea turtles are still raised, is another "must." Kids ages 5 through 12 can participate in Camp Mauna Lani, which operates daily year round from 9 A.M. to 3 P.M. There are several casual restaurants, and the buffet breakfast at the open-air Bay Terrace is famous; it is also open for dinner and has a kids' menu. An optional package includes two daily meals. Note that this property is said to have the most expensive rates in all the islands (for the ultraluxurious bungalows, where Steven Spielberg and Danny DeVito have vacationed). *68–1400 Mauna Lani Dr., Kohala Coast; (800) 367-2323; (800) 327-8585; (808) 885-6622;* www.maunalaui.com

Motel Row
Reasonably priced hotels, many of them beachfront, are clustered in

HAWAIIAN FOODS KIDS LIKE

It's fun to go to a Hawaiian grocery store and fill your cart with food you can rarely find anywhere else. Some of the following items can be found on the menu at Hawaiian restaurants, too.

BAKERY GOODS Look for macadamia nut and coconut cookies, pink guava cakes, and malasadas (Portuguese doughnuts dipped in sugar).

DIAMOND GRAHAM crackers and soda crackers

DIAMOND ROYAL CREEMS, made in Honolulu since 1921.

HAUPIA, a cross between gelatin and custard, that is made from coconut milk.

HAWAIIAN SUN fruit juices

KAUAI KOOKIES

LAPPERT'S ICE CREAM is found throughout the islands.

MACADAMIA NUTS, plain, salted, in brittle, with caramels, chocolate-covered, in cookies, and in pancakes with coconut syrup.

MANAPUA STEAMED BUNS filled with minced pork mixture; also called *char siu bau.*

MAUI ONION RINGS

PINK SHRIMP CHIPS

POHA BERRY JAM

SAIMIN Japanese-style noodles can be found in many restaurants, including McDonald's.

SHAVE ICE is similar to, but better than, a snow cone. It comes in a rainbow of colors and flavors, including versions with vanilla ice cream in the middle, and Japanese-style, with ice cream and small red azuki beans. You'll all love "sucking 'em up." Be sure to buy the biggest shave ice for your little ones—it could be almost as big as a toddler! And don't forget your camera.

TARO AND WONTON CHIPS

TERIYAKI BEEF—it's sweet.

TROPICAL FRUITS, such as apple, banana, guava, mango, passion fruit, papaya, and pineapple.

More daring foods

More adventuresome eaters may want to try these island treats:

CRACKSEED, an island treat that includes preserved sweet and salty fruits. It is an acquired taste, but most first-timers like the pineapple and plum versions.

LOCO MOCO, a rice–ground beef mixture topped with a fried egg and gravy.

MAUI ONIONS are said to be so mild, that they can be eaten like apples.

PLATE LUNCH usually consists of one or two scoops of rice topped with a stir-fry or gravy dish. The best are found at the 22 Zippy's locations in the Islands.

POHOLE fresh fern shoots.

POI, cooked taro root, which resembles glue.

SPAM—the canned meat. More of it is eaten in Hawaii than anywhere else in the world!

Drinks for Adults:

DRY TEDESCHI, pineapple wine

HAWAII-BREWED BEER

KONA COFFEE—don't miss the chocolate–macadamia nut flavor. (Hawaii is the only state in the United States that grows coffee beans.)

the picturesque old town of Kailua-Kona and along the road going south out of town.

Ohana Keauhou Beach Resort
★★★/$$$-$$$$

The hotel is on the edge of Kahaluu Beach Park, which features one of the area's rare sandy beaches (it's also considered the best free snorkeling beach in the state). Some of the 311 spacious rooms are situated right over the lagoon, and almost all have ocean views. Rooms are equipped with coffeemakers, and you can rent refrigerators. Kids will appreciate the swimming pool (there's a wading pool for your younger "fish") and a shallow lagoon with tidal pools where they can usually see endangered green sea turtles. Cultural activities, including lei-making and hula lessons, are often scheduled. Take the kids to the nightly torch-lighting ceremony with chanting and dancing at sunset. Dining is available in several restaurants. *78-6740 Alii Dr., Kailua-Kona; (808) 322-3441.*

Uncle Billy's Hawaiian Family Resorts
★★/$$$-$$$$

This company offers well-priced vacation packages that include hotel room or condominium lodging in either Hilo or Kailua-Kona, plus a car or a neighbor island getaway. There's no additional charge for kids

One Minute of Words

Everybody gets a pencil and paper. Someone has to be the timekeeper (a good job for a grown-up). The time-keeper picks a letter, tells it to everyone else, and shouts "Go!" Players write as many words as possible that start with that letter. When a minute is up, the timekeeper says "Stop!" and all the players put down their pencils. Whoever has the most legitimate words wins. Decide in advance whether you can finish writing a word you've already started when the game ends. Now, give yourself one more minute to write a sentence with as many of the words as you can.

18 and under. *(800) 367-5102;* www.unclebillys.com

Volcano House
★★★/$$

On the eastern side of the island at 4,200 feet above sea level, this modest 42-room lodging on the rim of Kilauea Crater is Hawaii's oldest continuously operating hotel. Although it has been rebuilt several times since it opened with a grass-thatch roof and only four guest rooms, the 42-room hotel retains the charm typical of the great lodges found in many national parks. Note the oversize lava-rock fireplace and lovely wooden tables of native koa and monkeypod in the lobby. Craterside rooms in the main building are choice, permitting you to watch the sun set and rise (when your kids wake you up early) over the volcano. If your family likes roughing it, you can opt to stay in one of the 10 inexpensive rustic cabins located three miles from the main lodge. Each has one double bed and two single bunk beds; linens are provided, but you have to take a short hike to the bathroom. The lodge's Ka Ohelo Dining Room, with its extraordinary views of the volcano, is a great place to relax over a cup of this island's famous Kona coffee (milk for the kids). Kids' portions are available. Plan a breakfast or dinner here, but avoid the buffet lunch, when busloads of tour groups arrive. Because the temperature at this altitude is cooler than at sea level (it averages a crisp 40° F at night), there is always a fragrant fire of ohia logs in the lobby fireplace. In fact, it is claimed that the fire here has never gone out. Staying two nights at the Volcano House allows your family to spend one entire day touring Hawaii Volcanoes National Park, with the tantalizing promise of returning to your cozy room. Kids really enjoy the ranger-led tours beginning on trails that start right outside the hotel. *On Crater Rim Dr., Hawaii Volcanoes National Park; (808) 967-7321.*

Good Eats

Bubba Gump's Shrimp Co. *(808/331-8442)* and **Hard Rock Cafe** *(808/329-8866)* both branches of the national chains can be found on Alii Drive in Kailua-Kona. Here are some more of our favorites.

Oceanview Inn
★★★/$-$$
In the center of things and with an ocean view (as advertised), this simple Kona eatery attracts a loyal local clientele. The extensive and inexpensive family-friendly menu includes Hawaiian, Chinese, and American dishes and sandwiches. Closed Monday year-round plus all of April and September. *75–5683 Alii Dr., Kailua-Kona; (808) 329-9998.*

Sam Choy's Kaloko Restaurant
★★★★/$$-$$$$
This is the original location of this popular chain, which specializes in Hawaiian comfort food as well as more familiar burgers and seafood dishes. Also see Good Eats in Oahu. *73-5576 Kauhola St., Kailua-Kona; (808) 326-1545.*

Taeng-On Thai
★★/$$
Choose from a selection of inexpensive Thai dishes in a pleasant open-air, second-floor dining room. Kids usually like spring rolls and noodle dishes (try pad Thai or chow mein), and there are plenty of mild to hot dishes (you say when) for more mature palates. *Kona Inn shopping center, 75–5744 Alii Dr., Kailua-Kona; (808) 329-1994.*

Souvenir Hunting

Giggles
This happy spot has an exclusive on teddy bears made with colorful island-print fabrics. They also carry aloha wear for kids, island storybooks, kites, puppets, and more. *Coconut Marketplace, 75–5803 Alii Dr. #5, Kailua-Kona; (808) 329-7763.*

Hilo Hattie
It's the best place to buy aloha wear and other Hawaiian souvenirs. Two Big Island locations: *Prince Kuhio Plaza, 111 E. Puainako St., Hilo (808/961-3077); and 75–5597 Palani Rd., Kailua-Kona (808/329-7200).*

Surf or swim the beautiful waters of Hanapepe.
Once Kauai's largest town, the west side hamlet
now has a quiet, Old Hawaiian atmosphere.

Kauai

KAUAI IS THE OLDEST OF the Hawaiian islands and well known for dramatic, lush scenery starring jagged green mountains and steep valleys. Vacationing families also appreciate its uncrowded beaches, numerous waterfalls and rainbows, and rain forests populated with rare native species. Approximately 500 inches of rain each year make this the wettest spot on earth.

This is also one of the quieter, less crowded Hawaiian islands. A local building code requires that no new building on Kauai be higher than a coconut palm (four stories). There isn't much nightlife—and you'll be glad of it if you're awakened at dawn by one of the island's many free-roaming roosters. (Luckily, children seem able to sleep through even vigorous crowing, and you'll prob-ably be able to go back to sleep.) Wild chickens also run loose, to the delight of little kids, who love to chase and feed them.

The most concentrated resort area on Kauai is around the southern tip of the island at Poipu Beach, with

THE **FamilyFun** LIST

MUST-SEE ★ MUST-SEE

Na Pali Coast (page 381)

Poipu Beach Park (page 382)

Spouting Horn Beach Park Blow Hole (page 382)

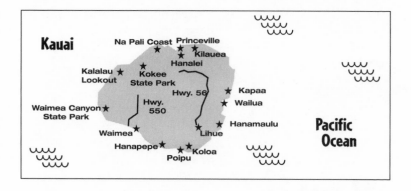

another bunch of resorts on the northern side of the island at Princeville. The most popular tourist towns include Lihue, on the southeast side of the island; Kapaa, on the east side; and Hanalei, on the north side. But the big attraction here is the beach. Find one you like and return again and again, or experiment and try a new one each day.

Kauai has been the setting for many Hollywood movies, including Elvis's *Blue Hawaii* and Spielberg's *Raiders of the Lost Ark* and *Jurassic Park*. You'll probably recognize some of the settings during your family sight-seeing excursions. If your kids like tracking down spots they've seen on the big or little screen, pick up the *Kauai Movie Book* (by Chris Cook/Mutual Publishing Co., 1996).

Another helpful publication is the free *Five Days of Family Fun* brochure distributed by the Hyatt Regency Kauai. Assembled by the staff at Camp Hyatt, the hotel's children's program, it outlines self-guided tours that include a variety of the island's best cultural and outdoor activities; call the hotel concierge desk for a copy *(808/742-1234)*; www.kauai-hyatt.com

CULTURAL ADVENTURES

Grove Farm Homestead
★★/$

This living history museum in Lihue lets your family experience life on a sugarcane plantation circa 1864. On the two-hour guided walking tour you'll see the main house, furnished with koa-wood antiques; the cottages the plantation workers lived in; and some outbuildings and gardens. Most kids like the kitchen best—the tour stops there for cookies just out of the wood-fired oven. You do a lot of walking, so this is not a good choice for children 5 and younger. Reservations are required. *On Nawiliwili Rd., in Lihue; (808) 245-3202.*

Just for Fun

Fern Grotto and Wailua River Cruise ★★/$$

Located in Wailua Marina State Park, on the eastern side of the island near Kapaa, the Fern Grotto is a beautiful lava grotto and waterfall accessible only by boat. For most kids, getting to the grotto is half the fun. As the large flat-bottomed, open-air, canopy-covered cruise boats make their way up the narrow, calm Wailua River, passengers are entertained with historical stories, singing, and hula lessons. Kids also love walking through the tropical rain forest up to the grotto and waterfall. Boats leave every half hour; the round-trip excursion takes about an hour and a half. *174 Wailua Rd., Wailua; (808) 821-6892.*

Lydgate Beach Park ★★★★/Free

This popular spot has one of the island's most kid-friendly beaches, with a calm, ocean-filled pool defined by boulders. Across from the beach in a grassy park area is Kamalani Playground. Designed especially for kids ages 6 through 10, it has a volcano slide, a spider-web rope ladder, a tree house, tire swings, and even caves. Cool! *Off Hwy. 56, just south of Kapaa.*

Na Pali Coast
FamilyFun ★★★★/Free

This gives new meaning to the term "scenic drive." See "A West Side excursion," pages 382-383.

National Tropical Botanical Garden ★★/$$$

Sort of a Noah's Ark for tropical plants, Allerton Garden is just across the road from Spouting Horn Beach (see page 382). It harbors more than a thousand categories of endangered plants from Hawaii and other Pacific islands. Kids will be excited to learn that parts of *Jurassic Park* were filmed here. A 2½-hour tour starts with a ride on an open-air tram that follows the railbed of an old sugarcane train. The docent guides take special pains to interest kids, so it's fun for all ages. Reservations are required. *In Poipu, 12 miles southwest of Lihue; (808) 742-2623; www.ntbg.org*

Old Koloa Town ★★★/Free

It's fun to visit this once-prosperous sugar mill town to browse in the shops and get a cone of terrific Lappert's island ice cream or some

THE FAMOUS "BLACK SAND" beaches of Hawaii were created virtually instantaneously by the violent interaction between hot lava and sea water.

shave ice. Interesting false-front buildings and an old stone sugar mill smokestack are all that remain from the past. *Take Maluhia Rd. exit off Hwy. 50, south of Lihue.*

★ Poipu Beach Park
FamilyFun ★★★/Free

One of the best beaches in the state for kids, Poipu is reputed to be the sunniest on the island. The natural wading pool here is perfect for toddlers and preschoolers, and rest rooms are nearby. A protected cove known as Baby Beach is just to the west. A new playground has an area for children ages 2 to 5 and another for those ages 5 to 12. *On Hoone Rd., off Hoowilili Rd., in Poipu.*

★ Spouting Horn
FamilyFun Beach Park Blow Hole
★★★★/Free

Splash! The ocean sprays up through a hole in the shore lava, creating a natural fountain that's fun to watch. Listen for a groan, which legend says is made by a lizard trapped in the lava tube. **NOTE:** Vendors here sell their shell novelties—but prices can be steep. *On Lawai Rd., across from Allerton Garden.*

BUNKING DOWN

Embassy Vacation Resort
Poipu Point ★★★/$$$$

It's easy for families to make themselves at home here. Located in Koloa near Poipu Beach on the southern side of the island, the luxury property has 210 one- and two-bedroom oceanfront suites with spacious bathrooms with deep tubs and full kitchens complete with washer/dryers. Each of the units is also equipped with a 35-inch TV set, a VCR, a stereo and cassette

---

DAY TRIP

A West Side Excursion

9:30 A.M. Depart from **Poipu Beach** area, following *Highway 530 north to Highway 50 west* into Hanapepe.

10 A.M. Arrive in scenic **Hanapepe**. Once the island's largest town, and alive with GIs on R&R from the Pacific theater during World War II, this is now a tiny, very quiet, uncommercialized old Hawaiian town. Kids can have a bouncing good time on the swinging bridge. While here, check out **Salt Pond Beach**, which still processes salt. It is also popular for surfing and windsurfing and has a protected swimming area that is a favorite with families. Lifeguards are often on duty, and picnic areas, rest rooms, and rinse-off showers are available. Spend some time enjoying the beach and then stop in at the **Kauai Kookie Factory Outlet** to stock up.

player, and two phone lines. Other nice perks: rental cars at a discounted rate and a complimentary breakfast buffet the first morning. The daily Beach Buddies program for kids ages 4 through 10 features Hawaiian-themed arts-and-crafts projects. There is a large swimming pool and a separate children's pool, both unheated. *1613 Pe'e Rd., Poipu Point, in Koloa; (877) 627-2242; (808) 742-1888;* www.point@aloha.net

Holiday Inn SunSpree Resort
★★/$$$

Some ocean-view rooms and cottages are available among the 216 units at this chain, that's within walking distance of popular Lydgate Beach Park and Kamalani Playground. The property features two pools, a hot tub, a fitness center, tennis courts, volleyball and shuffleboard courts, and a restaurant and deli. As you explore the ten acres of grounds, you'll discover both Japanese and Hawaiian gardens and a koi pool. The Kid Spree Vacation Club operates during peak vacation times, offering kids informal instruction in a variety of Hawaiian activities and crafts (fee). *3–5920 Kuhio Hwy., in Kapaa; (800) HOLIDAY; (888) 823-5111; (808) 823-6000;* www.basshotels.com/holiday-inn

Hyatt Regency Kauai Resort & Spa
★★★★/$$$$

Featuring lush gardens, colorful squawking parrots, and Hawaiian artwork, this luxurious 602-room oceanfront resort in Koloa, on the southern side of Kauai, may be the most spectacular on the island. Rooms are decorated with plantation-style furnishings and orchids and are equipped with coffeemakers. You can request a refrigerator at no charge and rent VCRs. The resort's

Noon Lunch at the **Green Garden Restaurant** in Hanapepe. After lunch, *continue north on Highway 50 to Waimea, then take Highway 550 north to* Waimea Canyon State Park.

1:30 P.M. Arrive at the lookout in **Waimea Canyon State Park**, The family will agree that it's Hawaii's answer to the Grand Canyon. Enjoy the view, then *continue north on Highway 550.*

2 P.M. Arrive in **Kokee State Park**. Browse the tiny museum and feed the wild chickens. *Proceed north on Highway 550.*

2:30 P.M. Stop at the **Kalalau Lookout** to view the beginning of the spectacular, lush **Na Pali Coast**. *Keep heading north along the coast.*

3 P.M. Arrive at the road's end, stopping at the **Puu O Kila Lookout** to view the wettest spot on earth.

Window Box Organizer

In the past on family road trips, I've found that keeping books and games organized and within reach (instead of under the seats) was a challenge for my boys, Joshua, 6, and Brooks, 4. I finally figured out the perfect solution: I purchased a plastic window planter and cut two parallel slits through the bottom of one end. I threaded the middle seat belt through the slits, so the box stays safely attached to the backseat. I even attached battery-operated lights (the kind you clip to books) on both sides of the box so the boys each have a lamp for reading. Best of all, the box keeps them on their own sides of the car, reducing the fight factor tremendously.

Angela Ruder, San Antonio, Texas

beach generally has rough surf, but the surfers it attracts are fun to watch. When they want to get wet, kids (and adults) can head for the 5-acre water playground, with its fabulous 150-foot twisting water slide that lands in a pool landscaped to resemble a rustic lagoon. Three hot tubs, four tennis courts, a spa, and an exercise room are also on the premises. Camp Hyatt offers a variety of activities for kids ages 3 through 12. A night camp is also available, as is a complimentary program for teens during the summer. The whole family will enjoy the torchlighting ceremony that takes place nightly at sunset, with chanting and traditional hula, and you can all join in the regularly scheduled workshops in native crafts, including lei-making and poi-pounding. A luau is held under the stars on Thursday and Sunday evenings. You'll also have a choice of six on-site restaurants of varying styles and

cuisines. The hotel offers a free brochure suggesting five perfect family days on the island; it's available from the concierge. *1571 Poipu Rd., Koloa; (800) 55-HYATT; (808) 742-1234;* www.kauaihyatt.com

Kauai Marriott Resort & Beach Club
★★★★/$$$$

An exception to that "no hotel taller than a palm tree" rule (it was built before the law went into effect), this oceanfront 356-room hotel in Lihue is 10 stories tall. About 80 percent of the rooms have an ocean and pool view, and all have refrigerators and coffeemakers. The complex also has 232 one- and two-bedroom condominium units with mini kitchens (a microwave, but no stove) and shared laundry facilities. The 51-acre property also boasts the biggest swimming pool in the islands, five hot tubs, a fitness center, and a lovely white sand beach. Kalapaki Kids Club for guests ages 5 through 12 operates year-round—most days from 9 A.M. to 3 P.M., and some evenings from 6 to 10. Activities center around island culture—including Hawaiian quilt displays, coconut frond-weaving, and hula dancing (call for schedule). *3610 Rice St., at Kalapaki Beach, Lihue; (800) 220-2925; (800) 228-9290; (808) 245-5050;* www.marriott.com

Kiahuna Plantation
★★★★/$$$-$$$$

Situated on 35 acres of beautifully maintained gardens right on Poipu Beach, this 333-unit condominium complex is spread over what was once part of Hawaii's oldest sugar plantation. The two- and three-story units have full kitchens and VCRs. This resort is a good choice for families with young children, especially if you stay in a room set back from the beach and opening onto an expanse of grass that attracts an assortment of birds. The beach itself is reputedly one of Hawaii's best, with a gentle surf that is welcoming of children; great snorkeling is within easy walking distance. You can rent boogie boards and scuba and snorkeling gear and take surfing lessons. The Kiahuna Keiki Klub for kids ages 5 through 12 operates Monday through Friday from 9 A.M. to 3 P.M. You can also take a self-guided tour of the resort's unusual, and very old, Moir Cacti Gardens.

2253 Poipu Rd., Poipu; (800) 367-5004; (808) 742-2200; www.castleresorts.com

Princeville Resort
★★★★/$$$$

This luxurious 252-room resort overlooks extraordinarily beautiful Hanalei Bay and the beginning of the Na Pali cliffs. Because the buildings are built in tiers down the mountain, with the lobby on the top floor and the pool and beach off the first floor, most rooms have great ocean views. Resort highlights include a beautiful white-sand beach, separate adults' and childrens' pools (the grown-ups' one has a swim-up lunch counter), three hot tubs, eight tennis courts, two golf courses, and a spa. Children 5 to 12 can participate in the Keiki Aloha kids program, which includes lei-making, sand-castle building, and a variety of Hawaiian games (fee). There is also baby-sitting service provided for a fee. At sunset several evenings each week you'll be entertained by native Hawaiian dancing and chanting; there's also a luau on Friday night. There are three restaurants—all kid-friendly. *5520 Ka Haku Rd., Princeville; (800) 826-4400; (808) 826-9644;* www.princeville.com

Waimea Plantation Cottages ★★/$$$-$$$$

Once a sugar plantation in Waimea (north of Poipu on the southwest side of the island), the 47 private oceanfront cottages here are all original plantation buildings that have been restored and updated. Great for families—or even two families vacationing together—they offer from one to five bedrooms; the largest can accommodate up to nine people. All have full kitchens and private lanais. The property, set among a 27-acre mature coconut grove, is part of the family-friendly Aston Hotels chain. It offers a pool and volleyball court, and you have access to a palm-dappled black-sand beach. You can take a walking tour of the plantation and the Waimea Sugar Mill Camp Museum—reservations required. *In Waimea; (800) 92-ASTON; (808) 338-1625;* www.waimea-plantation.com

GOOD EATS

Beezers Old-Fashioned Ice Cream ★★★/$
This self-proclaimed "joint," a 1950s-style diner with black-and-white checkered floor and red vinyl booths and counter stools, has a kid-friendly menu of ice-cream goodies: shakes, egg creams, black cows, and more.

FamilyFun SNACK

Pretzel Twist
Give your kids a bag of traditional pretzels and challenge them to bite out every letter of the alphabet.

Breakfast, lunch, and dinner items are served as well, including sloppy joes and burgers. *1378 Kuhio Hwy., Kapaa; (808) 822-4411.*

Brennecke's
★★★★/$$-$$$
Across the street from Poipu Beach County Park, this popular, casual spot has tables overlooking the ocean. You can feast on fresh island fish and hamburgers broiled over kiawe wood (which is the same as mesquite wood except it grows in Hawaii instead of Texas). There is a great kids' menu available at this very kid-friendly eatery. Reservations advised. *On Hoowili Rd., near Poipu Beach; (808) 742-7588;* www. brenneckes.com

Bubba's ★★/$
You'll find *ono* (the best) burgers here (can anyone resist the "slopper"?), not to mention hot dogs, corn dogs, chili, fish, chicken, and Italian sausage. Seating is at a long counter with stools or on a veranda with an ocean view. The kids will want to buy some of the souvenir logo items. *1421 Kuhio Hwy., Kapaa; (808) 823-0069. Also in Hanalei Center, Kuhio Hwy., Hanalei; (808) 826-7839.*

Eggbert's ★★★★/$
This casual, family-friendly spot features a large menu of breakfast specialties, including banana pancakes and more than 150 kinds of omelettes, which are served until 3 P.M.

At lunch, salads and sandwiches are added to the bill of fare, and dinner offers entrées such as meat loaf, roasted pork, fresh fish, and assorted stir-fries. *In Coconut Marketplace, Kapaa, 15 minutes north of Lihue; (808) 822-3787.*

Green Garden ★★★/$-$$

In operation here since 1948, this family-run spot is popular with locals. Gorgeous orchids for sale at great prices decorate the entry, along with a mishmash of souvenirs and hanging plants. Cross ventilation from screened wall openings makes for refreshing breezes and a comfortable meal. The inexpensive, expansive, and eclectic menu offers fresh local items such as ahi (yellowfin tuna) tempura, chicken chow mein, and fruit salad. Dinner items include a Hawaiian luau-style platter, a Japanese-style plate, and a steamed vegetable/grilled tofu entrée for vegetarians. The kids' menu includes a choice of hamburger steak, breaded mahimahi, fried chicken, sweet-and-sour ribs, and shrimp tempura. Portions are big, and most items include side dishes and a drink. For dessert, the whole family might be satisfied with sharing just a slice of the "mile high" homemade pies— perhaps macadamia nut cream or chocolate cream pie. *On Kaumalii Hwy., in Hanapepe; (808) 335-5422.*

Hamura Saimin ★★/$

This is as simple as dining out gets. Just sit down on a squat stool at the serpentine counter of this popular place and soak up the local ambience while downing a bowl of delicious saiman (noodle soup). Kids love it. Slurping is okay, but you might want to observe how the locals twist the noodles in the bowl of their spoon. Save room for a slice of lilikoi pie. You can also order your meal to go. In one corner of the restaurant, Halo Halo Shave Ice serves up that refreshing treat. **NOTE:** Cash only. *2956 Kress St., Lihue; (808) 245-3271.*

Keoki's Paradise ★★★★/$$-$$$

The kids will love eating in this open-air, multilevel restaurant landscaped with cascading waterfalls, koi-filled lagoons, and lush greenery. Antique Hawaiian posters and vintage surfboards line the koa-paneled walls, and a koa bar with a palapa roof rounds out the tropical decor. Open only for dinner, the eatery specializes in fresh island fish, Koloa pork ribs glazed in plum sauce, and a full bone cut of prime rib. Kids can share with their parents or choose from a keiki menu offering pastas and burgers. Live local entertainment is featured on Friday and Saturday nights. Reservations are advised. This is part of the Duke's Canoe Club chain, which also has branches on Oahu and Maui. *Poipu Shopping Village, across from Kiahuna Plantation, Poipu; (808) 742-7534;* www.hula pie.com

Smith's Tropical Paradise Garden
★★★★/$$$$

What is reputedly the island's best luau is preceded at 5 P.M. with an informative tram ride through lush tropical gardens. An hour later, there's a traditional imu ceremony, in which a roasted pig is removed from its underground lava rock oven (keep sensitive youngsters away from this). Then the all-you-can-eat buffet dinner, with the traditional goodies, begins. What's not to like here? Salads, that infamous poi, Jell-O, fried rice, lomi salmon, fresh fruits, kalua pig, teriyaki beef, adobo chicken, sweet-and-sour mahimahi, snowflake and sweet potatoes, hot vegetables, haupia, coconut cake, and rice pudding are included in the basically kid-friendly selections. On Mondays, Wednesdays, and Fridays year-round, dinner is accompanied by singing and dancing, with the pageant show starting in a separate arena at 8. After the torches are lit, your kids' mouths will drop open when Madame Pele makes her fiery entrance, followed by colorful dances and songs from the South Pacific and Hawaii. Reservations are required. *Wailua Marina State Park, Kapaa; (808) 821-6895. www.smithskauai.com*

Tomkats Grille ★★★/$-$$

You can get a burger here that's the cat's meow, and sandwiches and salads, too. Seating is in one of several fan-cooled rooms surrounding a cen-

---

DAY TRIP
A Day on Kauai's East Side

8 A.M. To see the scenic east side of the island, and get some beach time in before the sun is at its zenith, start out early. From the **Poipu Beach** area, *follow Highway 50 north or Highway 56 north.*

8:30 A.M. Watch for the turnoffs to scenic sights. **Wailua Falls**—made famous on TV's *Fantasy Island*—is about four miles east of Hanamalulu via Highway 583. Opaekaa Falls—where scenes from Elvis's *Blue Hawaii* were filmed—is about two miles east of Wailua Bay via Highway 580.

9:15 A.M. Stop for breakfast at **Eggbert's** (see page 386) in Kapaa.

10:30 A.M. After passing through Hanalei town, stop at the scenic overlook to the lushly pastoral landscape of the **Hanalei Valley**— Puff the magic dragon's legendary home. Continue on, driving the winding road that is very much like the famous Hana Highway on Maui, with many one-lane bridges. Have the kids look for houses on stilts. Just before the end of the road you'll see the Dry Cave (described

tral courtyard planted with tropical foliage, including vibrantly colorful ginger. Kids love the small pond filled with koi, and they also like the "kitten" menu offering a grilled cheese sandwich and a corn dog. *5404 Koloa Rd., Old Koloa Town; (808) 742-8887.*

Souvenir Hunting

Coconut MarketPlace

This mall of small shops holds something for everyone. Kids will gravitate to the Gecko Store and Whalers General Store. At lunchtime, choose from among a variety of fast-food spots dispensing pizza, tacos, and fish. Free hula and Polynesian shows are scheduled. *Located 15 minutes*

north of Lihue, between the Wailua River and Kapaa; (808) 822-3641.

Hilo Hattie

You'll find aloha wear for the whole family here. *3252 Kuhio Hwy., Lihue; (808) 245-3404.*

Rainbow Ducks

Toys and swimwear for children, plus everything from a zippered coconut purse to a rubber gecko are on sale here. *Behind the Hanalei School shopping center, in Halalei; (808) 826-4741.*

by one unimpressed kid as "just a big dry cave") and the Wet Cave (which contains a lake) almost at the end of the road. Park at the end of the road at Kee Beach, which was "Bali Hai" in the movie *South Pacific*, and where scenes from the TV miniseries *The Thorn Birds* were filmed. This is the beginning of the spectacularly scenic and green **Na Pali Coast**. Spend several hours on this perfect beach, picnicking on the box lunches you ordered up the night before at your hotel (or picked up somewhere before you arrived).

12:30 P.M. Pack up and head back

to Hanalei. Look around in the old 1926 **Hanalei School** that has been converted into a small shopping center. Indulge in a shave ice.

1:30 P.M. Stop at **Banana Joe's Fruitstand**, just before the Kilauea Lighthouse.

1:45 P.M. Drive in to the **Kilauea Lighthouse** and **National Wildlife Refuge**, where you'll see hundreds of seabirds, including boobies and Laysan albatrosses.

3 P.M. Head back to your resort and spend the rest of the day relaxing by the pool or beach.

Index

A

accommodations (bunking
down), 24–29
B&Bs (bed-and-breakfasts),
25
California
Berkeley, 94–95
Beverly Hills and Century
City, 225–228
Big Sur, 173
Carmel, 168–171
in Disneyland, 257–259
near Disneyland, 259–261
family hostels, 215
Gold Rush Country,
134–136
Hermosa Beach, 275–276
Hollywood, 237–238
Huntington Beach, 281
Knott's Berry Farm,
261–262
Laguna Beach, 287–289
Lassen Volcanic National
Park, 154–155
Long Beach, 278–279
Los Angeles, 222–223
Malibu, 270
Marina del Rey, 273–274
Mendocino/Fort Bragg,
120–122
Monterey, 161–163
Newport Beach, 284–285
Pacific Grove, 166
Palm Springs and
environs, 322–325
Redwood National Park,
153
San Diego, 303–309
San Francisco, 61–70
San Simeon and Cambria,
175–176
Santa Barbara, 193–198
Santa Cruz, 179
Santa Monica, 208–210
Sequoia and Kings Canyon
National Parks, 150–151
Silicon Valley and San Jose,
111–112
Solvang, 184–186
Westwood, 245–246
Yosemite National Park,
144–147

condos, 25–26
cottages, 25–26
farm stays, 25
Hawaiian Islands
family-friendly lodging
chains, 370–371
Hawaii (the Big Island),
365–379
Kauai, 384–388
Maui, 358–361
Oahu, 339–344
hostels (for the family),
26, 215
hotels, 24
inns, 25
lodges, 24
motels, 24
prebooking information, 23,
25, 27, 35
price guide for, 7
resorts, 27
using the Web for, 35, 37
See also camping/
campgrounds
Adventure Playground
(Berkeley, Calif.), 92–93
Ahwahnee, The (Yosemite
National Park, Calif.),
144–145
air travel, 16, 17
with children
car seats for safety, 260
checklist, 17
games/special activities,
239, 335
layover plans, 297
solving the earache
problem, 368
making reservations on the
Web, 35–36
tips for, 206
Alameda Park, Kids World
playground in (Santa
Barbara, Calif.), 194
Alcatraz Island (San
Francisco), 45
Alexander & Baldwin Sugar
Museum (Maui, Hawaii), 352
American Youth Hostels (AYH)
Organization, 215
Anaheim, Calif., 250–265
accommodations, 257–262
in Disneyland, 257–259

near Disneyland, 259–261
at Knott's Berry Farm,
261–262
background information, 251
cultural adventures, 252–253
"just for fun" attractions,
253–257
map, 252
"must-see" list, 251
restaurants, 262–264
in Anaheim area, 263–264
at Disneyland, 262–263
at Knott's Berry Farm, 263
souvenir hunting, 264
Anza Borrego Desert State Park
(near San Diego), 293
Aquarium of the Pacific
(Long Beach, Calif.), 277
audio books (aid to travel),
18, 21

B

B&Bs (bed-and-breakfasts), 25
Balboa Island, Calif., 288
Balboa Park (San Diego),
292–293
Beach towns (Calif.), 266–267
background information,
267–268
Balboa Island, 288
Catalina Island, 278–279
map, 268
"must-see" list, 267
See also Huntington Beach;
Laguna Beach; Long
Beach; Malibu; Marina del
Rey; Newport Beach
Bel Air, Calif. see Westside:
Westwood/Brentwood/Bel
Air area
Berkeley, Calif., 88–101
accommodations, 94–96
background information,
89–90
cultural adventures, 91–92
day trip:
exploring the city, 94–95
"just for fun" attractions,
92–94
map, 90
"must-see" list, 89
restaurants, 96–101
souvenir hunting, 101

Beverly Hills and Century City, Calif., 224–229
accommodations, 225–228
guide to movie-star gazing, 248
"just for fun" attractions, 225
restaurants, 228–229
souvenir hunting, 229
Big Island. *See* Hawaii (the Big Island)
Big Sur, Calif., 172–173
accommodations, 173
"just for fun" attractions, 172
restaurants, 173
Bishop Museum (Oahu, Hawaii), 335–336
Bommers Park (Cathedral City, Calif.), 319
Brentwood, Calif. *See* Westside: Westood/Brentwood/Bel Air area
bus travel, 21–22
Bumpass Hell (Lassen Volcanic National Park, Calif.), 154

C

cable cars (San Francisco), 53
Cable Car Museum (San Francisco), 45–46
Calaveras Big Trees State Park (Murphys, Calif.), 130–131
California
background information, 40–41
KOA kampgrounds, 306
price guide for attractions, accommodations, and restaurants, 41
ratings guide for attractions, 41
California Academy of Sciences (San Francisco), 46–47
Cambria, Calif. *See* San Simeon and Cambria
camping/campgrounds, 26–27
California KOA kampgrounds, 306
Lassen Volcanic National Park, 155
Redwood National Park, 153
resources for tent and RV camping, 38–39
Santa Barbara, 193–195
Santa Cruz, 179
Sequoia National Park, 150
Yosemite National Park, 145
Cannery Row (Monterey, Calif.), 158–159
car travel, 16–19
with children

audio books, 18, 21
games/special activities, 54, 73, 105, 110, 118, 154, 221, 282, 286, 386
preventing motion sickness, 18
road maps/road atlases, 16, 39
road trip survival kit, 19
travel insurance, 28
See also rental car; RVs
Carmel, Calif., 166–172
accommodations, 168–171
cultural adventures, 166–167
"just for fun" attractions, 167–168
restaurants, 171
souvenir hunting, 171–172
Carmel Beach (Carmel, Calif.), 167
Carole and Barry Kaye Museum of Miniatures (Los Angeles), 219–220
cars, renting classic cars in Beverly Hills, Calif., 226
Catalina Island, Calif., 278–279
caverns in Gold Rush Country, 137
Century City, Calif. *See* Beverly Hills and Century City
Cheeseburger in Paradise (Maui, Hawaii), 362
children
air travel with
carry-on car seats, 260
checklist, 17
layover plans, 297
solving the earache problem, 368
tips for, 206
audio books, 18, 21
books featuring Yosemite National Park, 146
dining with
games to play while waiting to be served, 164, 236, 241
solving the "picky eater" problem, 24
film festival for (Santa Barbara, Calif.), 191
games/special activities for children, 100, 146, 183, 212, 214, 226, 257, 336, 346, 353, 372, 378
for air travel, 239, 335
for beach vacations, 162, 169
for car travel, 54, 73, 105, 110, 118, 154, 221, 282, 286, 386

for preserving vacation memories, 45, 128, 212
in restaurants, while waiting to be served, 164, 236, 241
Hawaiian foods that kids like, 376–377
healthy snacks for the road, 58, 93, 109, 135, 174, 280, 388
keeping a trip journal, 45
learning Hawaiian words, 369
packing for the trip (checklist), 32, 81
planning the trip with, 12–13, 14, 15, 165, 227
preventing motion sickness, 18
tour guides on tape for, 318
travel kit for, 19, 27
Children's Discovery Museum (Rancho Mirage, Calif.), 318
Children's Discovery Museum of San Jose (San Jose, Calif.), 105
Chinatown (San Francisco), 85–87
dim sum in, 74–75
classic cars in Beverly Hills, Calif., renting, 226
clothing, packing (checklist), 32
Columbia State Historic Park (Columbia, Calif.), 129
condos, 25–26
cottages, 25–26
Covered Wagon Tours (La Quinta, Calif.), 319
Crookedest Street in the World (San Francisco), 53–54

D

Dennis the Menace Playground at El Estero Park (Monterey, Calif.), 160
Disneyland Resort, The (Anaheim, Calif.), 253–255
parents' guide to, 265

E

earache problem, solving, 368
East Beach (Santa Barbara, Calif.), 193
El Estero Park (Monterey, Calif.), 160
Exploratorium (San Francisco), 47–48

F

family-friendly lodging chains and tour companies (Hawaiian Islands), 370–371

family hostels, 26
in Northern and Southern California, 215
family travel Website, 34
farm stays, 25
film festival for children (Santa Barbara, Calif.), 191
first-aid kit, 33
food
Danish sandwiches in Solvang, 186
dim sum in San Francisco's Chinatown, 74–75
eco-etiquette when eating on the beach, 199
Hawaiian foods that kids like, 376–377
healthy snacks for the road, 58, 93, 109, 135, 174, 280, 388
ice cream parlors in Gold Rush Country, 130–131
Mexican food in Old Town, San Diego, 311
picnic provisions, where to buy
in Berkeley, 94–95
in Sonoma Wine Country, 57
See also restaurants
Fort Bragg. *See* ` Mendocino/Fort Bragg

G

games/special activities for children, 100, 146, 183, 212, 214, 226, 257, 336, 346, 353, 372, 378
for air travel, 239, 335
for beach vacations, 162, 169
for car travel, 54, 73, 105, 110, 118, 154, 221, 282, 286, 386
for preserving vacation memories, 45, 128, 212
in restaurants, while waiting to be served, 164, 236, 241
Gaslamp Quarter (San Diego), 399
General's Highway (between Sequoia and Kings Canyon National Parks, Calif.), 149
George C. Page Museum/Hancock Park (West Los Angeles), 233
Ghirardelli Chocolate Manufactory (San Francisco), 76–77
Giant Forests (Sequoia and Kings Canyon National Parks, Calif.), 149

Golden Gate Bridge (San Francisco), 58
Golden Gate Park (San Francisco), 58–59
Gold Rush Country, 124–137
accommodations, 134–136
background information, 125–128
cultural adventures, 125–129
"just for fun" attractions, 129–134
map, 126
"must-see" list, 125
restaurants, 136
souvenir hunting, 137
Grauman's Chinese Theatre (Hollywood), 235
guided tours, 29

H

Hajeakalia National Park (Maui, Hawaii), 353–354
Hana Highway (Maui, Hawaii), 354
Hans Christian Andersen Museum (Solvang, Calif.), 182–183
Hawaii (the big island), 364–379
accommodations, 372–378
background information, 365–366
cultural adventures, 367–368
"just for fun" attractions, 368–372
map, 366
"must-see" list, 365
restaurants, 379
souvenir hunting, 377
Hawaiian Islands
background information, 328–331
family-friendly lodging chains and tour companies in, 370–371
learning the Hawaiian language, 369
price guide to attractions, accommodations, and restaurants, 329
rating guide to attractions, 329
state symbols, 341
See also Hawaii (the Big Island); Kauai; Maui; Oahu
Hawaii Volcanoes National Park (Hawaii, Hawaii), 370–372
Hearst Castle (San Simeon, Calif.), 174–175, 176

Hermosa Beach, Calif., 275–276
accommodations, 275–276
restaurants, 276
Hershey's Visitors Center (Oakdale, Calif.), 145
Highway 1 South: Monterey Peninsula (and beyond), 156–179
map, 158
"must-see" list, 157
See also Big Sur; Carmel; Monterey; Pacific Grove; San Simeon and Cambria
Hollywood and West Los Angeles, 230–244
accommodations, 237–238
cultural adventures, 231–234
guide to movie-star gazing, 248
"just for fun" attractions, 234–236
restaurants, 238–242
souvenir hunting, 242–244
Honolulu Zoo (Oahu, Hawaii) 338
hostels for the family, 26
in Northern and Southern California, 215
hotels, 24, 25
prebooking information, 23, 25, 27, 35
working with consolidators, 35
See also accommodations
Huntington Beach, Calif., 280–282
accommodations, 281
"just for fun" attractions, 280–282
restaurants, 281–282

I

ice-cream parlors in Gold Rush Country, 130–131
Indian Grinding Rock State Historic Park (Pine Grove, Calif.), 129
inns, 25
insurance, travel, 28
Intel Museum (Santa Clara, Calif.), 106

K

Kampgrounds of America (KOA), 306
Kauai, Hawaii, 380–391
accommodations, 384–388
background information, 381–382

cultural adventures, 382
day trips: east side of the
   island tour, 390–391; west
   side of the island tour,
   384–385
"just for fun" attractions,
   383–384
map, 383
"must-see" list, 381
restaurants, 388–391
souvenir hunting, 391
Kelley Park (San Jose, Calif.),
   108
Kids World playground at
   Alameda Park (Santa
   Barbara, Calif.), 194
Kings Canyon National Park.
   See Sequoia and Kings
   Canyon National Parks
Knott's Berry Farm (Anaheim,
   Calif.), 255–256
Kodak Hula Show (Oahu,
   Hawaii), 336–337

L

La Brea Tar Pits (West Los
   Angeles), 230, 233
Laguna Beach, Calif., 287–289
accommodations, 287–289
cultural adventures, 287
restaurants, 289
Lahaina (Maui, Hawaii), 355
Lanai, 361
Lassen Volcanic National Park,
   153–155
accommodations, 154–155
"just for fun" attractions, 154
map, 154
Lawrence Hall of Science
   (Berkeley, Calif.), 91
Legoland (near San Diego), 295
Living Desert Wildlife &
   Botanical Park (Palm
   Desert, Calif.), 320–321
lodges, 24
Long Beach, Calif., 276–279
accommodations, 278–279
cultural adventures, 276–277
"just for fun" attractions, 277
restaurants, 279
Los Angeles, 216–249
background information,
   217–219
day trips:
   La Brea Tar Pits/George C.
      Page Museum/Universal
      Studios, 230–231;
      Malibu, 269
downtown, 219–224
   accommodations, 222–223

cultural adventures, 219–222
"just for fun" attractions, 222
restaurants, 223–224
map, 218
"must-see" list, 217
See also Beverly Hills and
   Century City; Hollywood
   and West Los Angeles;
   Westside: Westwood/
   Brentwood/Bel Air area

M

Magellan's Catalog (essentials
   for the trip), 275
Magicopolis (Santa Monica,
   Calif.), 205
Malibu, Calif., 268–272
accommodations, 270
"just for fun" attractions, 269
restaurants, 270–272
souvenir hunting, 272
map(s)
   California
      Anaheim, 252
      Beach towns, 268
      Berkeley, 90
      Gold Rush Country, 126
      Highway 1 South, 158
      Los Angeles area, 218
      Mendocino/Fort Bragg, 116
      Northern California's
         National Parks, 140
      Palm Springs and environs,
         316
      San Diego, 292
      San Francisco, 44
      Santa Barbara, 189
      Santa Monica, 204
      Silicon Valley and San Jose,
         104
      Solvang, 182
   Hawaiian Islands
      Hawaii (the Big Island), 366
      Kauai, 382
      Maui, 352
      Oahu, 334
Marin Headlands (San
   Francisco), 46
Marina del Rey, Calif., 272–275
accommodations, 273–274
restaurants, 274–275
Tournament of Lights
   Holiday Boat Parade, 273
Mariposa Grove of Giant
   Sequoias (Yosemite
   National Park, Calif.), 143
Maritime National Historical
   Park Maritime Museum
   (San Francisco), 46–47

Marshall Gold Discovery State
   Historic Park (Coloma,
   Calif.), 133
Maui, Hawaii, 350–363
accommodations, 360–361
background information,
   351–352
cultural adventures, 352
"just for fun" attractions,
   353–354
map, 352
"must-see" list, 351
restaurants, 360–363
souvenir hunting, 363
Maui Ocean Center (Maui,
   Hawaii), 357
Mauna Kea's Onizuka Center
   for International Astronomy
   (Hawaii, Hawaii), 367
medical matters
first-aid kit, 33
preventing motion sickness, 18
solving the earache problem,
   368
Mendocino/Fort Bragg,
   114–123
accommodations, 120–122
background information,
   115–116
cultural adventures, 117
"just for fun" attractions,
   117–119
map, 116
"must-see" list, 115
restaurants, 122–123
souvenir hunting, 123
Mendocino Coast Botanical
   Gardens (south of Fort
   Bragg, Calif.), 118
Metreon (San Francisco), 59
Mexican restaurants in Old
   Town, San Diego, 311
Mission San Juan Capistrano
   (Laguna Beach, Calif.), 287
Mission Santa Barbara (Santa
   Barbara, Calif.), 190
Molokai, Hawaii, 354
Monterey, Calif., 157–164
accommodations, 161–163
cultural adventures, 158–160
"just for fun" attractions,
   160–161
restaurants, 163–164
Monterey Bay Aquarium
   (Monterey, Calif.), 159
motels, 24, 25
motion sickness, preventing, 18
movie-star gazing guide to
   Hollywood and Beverly
   Hills, 248

Muir Woods National
Monument (San
Francisco), 46–47

N

Na Pali Coast (Kauai, Hawaii),
391
National Parks Pass, 143
Newport Beach, Calif., 282–286
accommodations, 284–285
"just for fun" attractions, 283
restaurants, 285–286
souvenir hunting, 286
**Northern California's National
Parks,** 138–155
background information,
139–140
"must-see" list, 139
National Parks Pass, 143
See also Lassen Volcanic
National Park; Redwood
National Park and
Redwood Country;
Sequoia and Kings Canyon
National Parks; Yosemite
National Park

O

Oahu, Hawaii, 332–349
accommodations, 339–344
background information,
333–334
cultural adventures, 335–338
day trip:
a drive around the island,
342–343
"just for fun" attractions,
338–339
map, 334
"must-see" list, 333
restaurants, 344–348
souvenir hunting, 348–349
Oakland, Calif., 99
"off-season" travel, 28–29
Ojai Valley, Calif., 201
Old Town (San Diego), 311
Online Travel (Perkins), 34

P

Pacific Grove, Calif., 164–166
accommodations, 166
cultural adventures, 165
"just for fun" attractions, 166
Pacific Grove Museum of
Natural History (Pacific
Grove, Calif.), 165
packing
checklist, 32
helping the children with, 358

**Palm Springs and environs,
Calif.,** 314–327
accommodations, 322–325
background information,
315–317
cultural adventures, 318–319
"just for fun" attractions,
319–322
map, 316
"must-see" list, 315
restaurants, 325–327
souvenir hunting, 327
Paramount's Great America
(Santa Clara, Calif.), 109–110
parents' guide to Disneyland,
265
pets, traveling with, 321
picnic provisions, where to buy
Berkeley, Calif., 94–95
Sonoma Wine Country,
Calif., 55–57
planning the trip
getting there
air travel, 16, 17
by bus, 21–22
by car, 16–19
by rental car, 22–23
by RV, 20–21
by train, 19–20
involving the children in,
12–13, 14, 15, 165
Magellan's Catalog, 275
money-saving tips, 12, 19,
28–31
budgeting for souvenirs, 196
family-friendly lodging
chains and tour compa-
nies (Hawaii), 370–371
family hostels, 215
National Parks Pass, 143
"off-season" travel, 28–29
package deals, 29–30
Online Travel (Perkins), 34
packing
checklist, 32
helping the children with,
81
parents' guide to Disneyland,
265
pets, traveling with, 321
preparing the itinerary, 13–15
price guide for attrac-
tions, accommodations,
and restaurants, 7
rating guide for attractions, 7
researching your destination,
14
tour guides on tape, 318
using the Web, 12, 31–37
weather, 13, 18

Poipu Beach Park (Kauai,
Hawaii), 384
Puppet & Magic Center (Santa
Monica, Calif.), 205
Puuhonua o Honaunau
National Historic
Park/City of Refuge
(Hawaii, Hawaii), 368

Q

Queen Mary (Long Beach,
Calif.), 276–277
Quicksilver Ranch (Solvang,
Calif.), 183–184

R

Railtown 1887 State Historic
Park (Jamestown, Calif.), 130
**Redwood National Park and
Redwood Country, Calif.,**
151–153
accommodations, 153
"just for fun" attractions,
152–153
map, 151
rental car, travel by, 22–23
resorts, 27–28
restaurants ("good eats")
California
Anaheim area, 263–264
Balboa Island, 288
Berkeley, 96–101
Beverly Hills and Century
City, 228–229
Big Sur, 173
Carmel, 171
Disneyland, 262–263
Gold Rush Country, 136
Hermosa Beach, 276
Hollywood and West Los
Angeles, 238–242
Huntington Beach, 281–282
Knott's Berry Farm, 263
Laguna Beach, 289
Long Beach, 279
Los Angeles, 223–224
Malibu, 270–272
Marina del Rey, 274–275
Mendocino/Fort Bragg,
122–123
Monterey, 163–164
Newport Beach, 285–286
Palm Springs and
environs, 325–327
San Diego, 309–312
San Francisco, 70–83
Chinatown, 87
dim sum in Chinatown,
74–75

San Simeon and Cambria, 165–177
Santa Barbara, 198–200
Santa Cruz, 179
Santa Monica, 210–214
Silicon Valley and San Jose, 112–113
Solvang, 186–187
Westwood, Brentwood, and Bel Air, 246–249
dining with children
games to play while waiting, 164, 236, 241
solving the "picky eater" problem, 24
Hawaiian Islands
Hawaii (the Big Island), 379
Hawaiian foods that kids like, 376–377
Kauai, 388–391
Maui, 361–363
Oahu, 344–348
money-saving tips, 31
price guide for, 7
Ride With Me tapes (tour guides on tape), 318
road maps/road atlases, 16, 39
road trip survival kit, 19
Rockefeller Forest (Humboldt Redwood State Park, Calif.), 152
Rosicrucian Egyptian Museum (San Jose, Calif.), 106–107
RVs, travel by, 20–21
camping/campground information for, 38–39

S

Sacramento, Calif. (day trip from San Francisco), 66–67
San Diego, 290–313
accommodations, 303–307
background information, 291–292
cultural adventures, 292–299
day trips:
San Diego Wild Animal Park, 298–299, 302
Tijuana, Mexico, 304
"just for fun" attractions, 299–303
map, 292
"must-see" list, 291
restaurants, 309–312
Old Town Mexican restaurants, 311
souvenir hunting, 312–313
San Diego Aerospace Museum (San Diego), 296

San Diego Model Railroad Museum (San Diego), 297
San Diego Wild Animal Park (Escondido, Calif.), 298–299, 300
San Diego Zoo (San Diego), 301–302, 312
San Francisco, 42–87
accommodations, 61–70
background information, 43–44
Chinatown, 85–87
cultural adventures, 45–51
day trips:
Marin County, 46–47
Sacramento, 66–67
seals and sea lions, 62–63
Six Flags Marine World, 78–79
Sonoma Wine Country, 55–57
"just for fun" attractions, 52–61
map, 44
"must-see" list, 43
restaurants, 70–83
souvenir hunting, 83–84
San Jose, Calif., *see* Silicon Valley and San Jose
San Simeon and Cambria, Calif., 174–177
accommodations, 176–177
cultural adventures, 174–175
"just for fun" attractions, 175
restaurants, 176–177
souvenir hunting, 177
Santa Barbara, Calif., 188–201
accommodations, 193–198
background information, 189–190
cultural adventures, 190–192
day trips:
Ojai Valley, 201
public parks and gardens, 194–195
"just for fun" attractions, 192–193
map, 190
"must-see" list, 189
restaurants, 198–200
souvenir hunting, 200
Santa Cruz, Calif., 178–179
accommodations, 179
restaurants, 179
Santa Monica, Calif., 202–215
accommodations, 208–210
background information, 203–204
cultural adventures, 204–205

"just for fun" attractions, 205–207
map, 204
"must-see" list, 203
restaurants, 210–214
souvenir hunting, 214–215
Santa Monica Pier (Santa Monica, Calif.), 206–207, 209
Sea Life Park (Oahu, Hawaii), 338–339
seals and sea lions, observing (San Francisco), 62–63
SeaWorld Adventure Park (San Diego), 302–303
Sequoia and Kings Canyon National Parks, Calif., 147–151
accommodations, 150–151
"just for fun" attractions, 148–149
map, 148
shopping. *See* souvenir hunting
Silicon Valley and San Jose, Calif., 102–113
accommodations, 111–112
background information, 103–104
cultural adventures, 105–107
"just for fun" attractions, 107–111
map, 104
"must-see" list, 103
restaurants, 112–113
souvenir hunting, 113
Six Flags Marine World (San Francisco), 78–79
Skunk Train/California Western Railroad (Fort Bragg, Calif.), 119
Solvang, Calif., 180–187
accommodations, 184–186
background information, 181–182
cultural adventures, 182–183
"just for fun" attractions, 183–184
map, 182
"must-see" list, 181
restaurants, 186–187
souvenir hunting, 187
Sonoma Wine Country (day trip from San Francisco), 55–57
picnic provisions, where to buy, 57
Southern California desert
Anza Borrego Desert State Park, 293
Palm Springs and environs, 314–327

souvenir hunting
budgeting for, 196
California
Anaheim, 264
Berkeley, 101
Beverly Hills, 229
Cambria, 177
Carmel, 171–172
Hollywood and West Los
Angeles, 243–244
Malibu, 272
Mendocino/Fort Bragg, 123
Newport Beach, 286
Palm Springs, 327
San Diego, 312–313
San Francisco, 83–84
Santa Barbara, 200
Santa Monica, 214–215
Silicon Valley and San Jose,
113
Solvang, 187
Westwood, Brentwood,
and Bel Air, 249
Hawaiian Islands
Hawaii (the Big Island), 379
Kauai, 391
Maui, 363
Oahu, 348–349
Spouting Horn Beach Park
Blow Hole (Kauai,
Hawaii), 384
Sutter Gold Mine (between
Amador City and Sutter
Creek, Calif.), 132

T

Tech Museum of Innovation,
The (San Jose, Calif.), 107

Tijuana, Mexico (day trip from
San Diego), 304
Tilden Regional Park (Berkeley,
Calif.), 93–94
toiletries, packing checklist, 32
tour guides on tape (Ride With
Me tapes), 318
tour packages, family-friendly
(Hawaiian Islands), 371
Tournament of Lights Holiday
Boat Parade (Marina del
Rey, Calif.), 273
train travel, 19–20
travel
creating a travel scrapbook, 64
journal of your trip, 45
See also air travel; bus, travel
by; car travel; train travel
travel agents, using, 16
travel insurance, 28
Tunnel View (Yosemite
National Park, Calif.), 143

U

Universal Studios (Hollywood,
Calif.), 235–236
University of California
(Berkeley, Calif.), 91–92

V

Van Damme State Park (Little
River, Calif.), 119

W

weather, 13, 18
Web, the
accommodation bookings
on, 35, 37

family travel Website, 34
planning the trip and, 12,
31–37
using, pros and cons, 31–34
**Westside: Westwood/
Brentwood/Bel Air, Calif.,**
244–249
accommodations, 245–246
cultural adventures, 244–245
restaurants, 246–249
souvenir hunting, 249
Will Rogers Beach State Park
(Santa Monica, Calif.), 207
Winchester Mystery House
(San Jose, Calif.), 110–111

Y

Yosemite National Park, Calif.,
140–147
accommodations, 144–147
outside the park, 146–147
cultural adventures, 142
"just for fun" attractions,
142–143
map, 140

Z

Zoological Gardens (Santa
Barbara, Calif.), 193

PHONE NUMBERS/WEBSITES

OUR ITINERARY

TRAVEL BUDGET

TRAVEL JOURNAL

TRAVEL JOURNAL

Also from FamilyFun

Winnie the Pooh characters based on the "Winnie the Pooh" works by A. A. Milne and E. H. Shepard

A Bug's Life, and *Toy Story* © Disney Enterprises, Inc./Pixar Animation Studios

Star Tours and Indiana Jones™ Epic Stunt Spectacular! © Disney/Lucasfilm Ltd.

Jim Henson's Muppet*Vision 3-D © 2001 The Jim Henson Company

IMAX ® IMAX Corporation

NASCAR is a trademark of the National Association for Stock Car Auto Racing, Inc. All rights reserved.

LEGO ® is the registered trademark of the LEGO Group.

Sea World Adventure Park is a registered trademark of the Busch Entertainment Corporation, a division of Anheuser-Busch Companies, Inc.

Universal Studios Hollywood™ © 2002 Universal City Studios.

Marvel Super Hero character names and likenesses ™ & © 2001 Marvel © 2002 Universal Studios.

Jurassic Park—The Ride, ® Universal Studios/Amblin.

Dudley Do-Right's Ripsaw Falls, WossaMotta U. Store: Rocky and Bullwinkle and Friends ™ & © Ward Prods.

Terminator 2: 3-D™ & © Canal+ D.A. All rights reserved.

NickelodeonBlast Zone: © 2002 Viacom International Inc. All rights reserved.

E.T. Adventure, JAWS: ® Universal Studios/Amblin.

PHOTO CREDITS

Cover *(from top to bottom)*:
Team Russell
John Lamb/ Getty Images,
Team Russell
Michael Carroll

Inside:
Ryan McVay/ Getty Images, page 4
Ann Menke/ Getty Images, page 10
Courtesy of San Francisco
    Convention and Visitors Bureau,
    page 42
Stewart Cohen/ Getty Images,
    page 88
Courtesy of Children's Discovery
    Museum of San Jose, page 102
Courtesy of Western California
    Skunk Train, page 114
Wendy Ashton/ Getty Images,
    page 124
Adam Smith/ Getty Images,
    page 138
Digital Vision/ Getty Images,
    page 156
Wendy Ashton/ Getty Images,
    page 180
Digital Vision/Getty Images ,
    page 188
Ty Allison/ Getty Images, page 202
Courtesy of Page Museum, page 216
Courtesy of © Disney, page 250
Peter Cade/ Getty Images, page 266
C. Wolcott III Henry/Getty Images,
    page 290
Courtesy of Palm Springs Ariel
    Tram, page 314
Donna Day/ Getty Images, page 330
Bernard Roussel/Getty Images,
    page 348
Jeff Maloney/Getty Images, page 362
Lori Adamski Peek/ Getty Images,
    page 378